Radical Political Economy

OTHER BOOKS BY HOWARD SHERMAN

Macrodynamic Economics:
Growth, Employment, and Prices

Introduction to the Economics of Growth,
Unemployment and Inflation

Elementary Aggregate Economics

Profits in the United States:
An Introduction to the Study of
Economic Concentration and Business Cycles

The Soviet Economy

RADICAL POLITICAL ECONOMY

Capitalism and Socialism from a Marxist-Humanist Perspective

HOWARD SHERMAN

Basic Books, Inc., Publishers

NEW YORK   LONDON

TO

The people of Czechoslovakia
January to August 1968
when they tried to build
"socialism with a human face"

Ho Chi Minh
and the people of Vietnam

The radical left movement
of the United States

PREFACE

I am a Marxist. Hopefully, however, the reader will discover that I am an independent and nondogmatic Marxist—that is, I follow the method of Marx, but not necessarily any specific analysis by Marx. It is a Marxism indistinguishable from the mainstream of radical Left thought in the United States. It is a Marxism which tries to incorporate the best tools and findings of non-Marxist social science.

I am not only a Marxist, but a Professor of Economics at the University of California. Perhaps this is a sign that "the times they are a changin." It is a reflection of the radicalization of a significant number of American students and faculty by the Indochina war and by the militant black struggles here.

My viewpoint, of course, derives from my own experience. I was born into a white, middle-class, Jewish, American family in the midst of the Great Depression. My formal education was in American schools and universities.[1] My initial political outlook was shaped by the very favorable American attitude to the Soviet Union during the Second World War. Then, for more than ten years at the peak of the cold war (1946 to 1956) I was a radical student activist. Forced, I thought, to choose between Joe McCarthy and Joe Stalin, I chose to believe in the Stalinist brand of Marxism. With the denunciation of Stalin and the Polish and Hungarian revolutions, my theological faith was shaken, so I was ready to participate in the renaissance of Marxist thought that has taken place since that time.

On the basis of overwhelming evidence, I believe as strongly as before in the need to fight against the evils of capitalism in America, including discrimination, imperialism, and repression. It seems that only a socialist revolution can lay the foundations for a society where there is equal opportunity for all people, continuing economic prosperity, freedom of expression in culture, politics and science, and peace. I have, however, come to realize that socialism is no immediate and automatic panacea. Although it offers the institutional basis for coping with all problems, most political-social problems will persist, though in lessened degree. Therefore, long after the socialist revolution has been consolidated in a world free of war, we must have a continuing fight by every alert individual for more political democracy, less bureaucracy and alienation, elimination of racism and male supremacy, and further reduction of economic inequality.

Politically, this has caused me to affiliate with the worldwide Democratic

Communist party. Unfortunately, I am its only member at the moment. Still, I can imagine its manifesto: A specter is haunting the Communist parties—the specter of Democratic Communism. Our ideology is one of democracy and socialism, of nondogmatic Marxist humanism. Poland and Hungary in 1956 and Czechoslovakia in 1968 revolted under this banner. The independent policies of Tito's Yugoslavia, Castro's Cuba, and Mao's China each reflect some progress in this direction. Some of the socialist countries have moved, however slowly and hesitantly, toward real democracy; while much of the rest of the world has movements trying to end imperialism and move toward socialism. The ideology of Democratic Communism is thus not mere wishful thinking, but is already a power moving with the historical tide.

Acknowledgments

Little or nothing in this book is a unique discovery of mine, but this book does attempt to gather together in a unified whole all the contributions to political economy of the recent outpouring of New Left, radical, and nondogmatic Marxist thought. All my own previous works have been meant as initial studies building toward this volume, and I am indebted to the very many people who have read and criticized them. I have endeavored to rewrite in that light all my relevant published works that are included herein, and have attempted to correct some of the grievous errors revealed by time and by many critics. "The days are past when an economist was wont to write a big book from scratch and then present it for his readers to judge. A more fruitful approach would seem to be the method . . . whereby the more bulky volumes are not published until the results of partial studies have stood the test of constructive criticism that is bound to enrich every such work."[2]

I especially want to thank the following individuals for reading and criticizing an earlier draft of the whole manuscript: Martin Bronfenbrenner, Richard Edwards, Joe Harris, Oldrich Kyn, and Paul Sweezy. Important improvements to particular chapters were suggested by Eugene Anderson, Ramesh Bhardwaj, Peter Clecak, Ronald Chilcote, Bernard Corry, Peter Diamond, William Domhoff, Mathew Edel, Gregory Grossman, Franklyn Holzman, E. K. Hunt, Victor Lippit, Bernd Magnus, William Mandel, Stanley Moore, Martin Orans, Bernard Saffran, Lynn Turgeon, Benjamin Ward, Ronald Weil, and Michael Zweig. These criticisms and suggestions led to immeasurable improvements in this book, but I fear that the author has sole responsibility for the final draft. I am also grateful for the research done by Kathy Pulling. Finally, I am most grateful to Barbara Deckard for inspiration and moral support.

I also want to thank the following publishers for permission to use parts (always in revised form) of my own published articles and books: *Profits in the United States* (Ithaca: Cornell University Press, 1968); *The Soviet Economy* (Boston: Little, Brown and Company, 1969); "Pirenne versus Marx," *Spoudai* (March–April 1965); "Marxist Economics and Soviet Planning," *Soviet Studies* (October 1966); "Marx and the Business Cycle," *Science and Society* (Fall 1967); "Material Incentives in Socialism," *Monthly Review* (January 1968); "The Revolution in Soviet Economics," in Alex Simirenko, ed., *Social Thought in the Soviet Union* (Chicago: Quadrangle Books, 1969); "Economics of Pure Communism," *Soviet Studies* (July 1970); "Marxist Theory of Value Revisited," *Science and Society* (Fall 1970); "Socialism and Democracy in Czechoslovakia," *Monthly Review* (May 1971); "Marxist Models of Cyclical Growth," *History of Political Economy* (Spring 1971); and "Reform or Revolution," in Raymond Franklin, ed., *Party and Class* (New York: New Critics Press, 1971). Even where the present book covers some of the same ground (a few chapters in the case of *The Soviet Economy*) that material has been completely rewritten in the context of the broader political-economic framework used here.

A Note on Style and Exposition

Every effort has been made to make this book readable rather than esoteric. For example, no foreign words are used (contrary to the practice of many "erudite" authors), and even in the footnotes the attempt has been made to cite works in translation rather than in foreign languages. Some purely historical material, such as how to interpret Marx on some subject, has been left to Appendices (1 and 2). All the technical and mathematical material has been relegated to Appendices (3, 4, and 5) where economists may enjoy it to their heart's content. Finally, the interested reader will find lengthy suggestions for further reading, arranged by chapter, at the end of the book.

NOTES

1. The terms "America" and "American" are used throughout this book to refer only to the United States and its people. This is purely for convenience and ease of writing. The terms rightfully should be applied to all of the Western Hemisphere and its peoples. There is, however, no term in English to describe the United States or its people in one word—and even the awkward phrase "North American" should include Canadians.

2. Joseph Goldman and Karel Kouba, *Economic Growth in Czechoslovakia* (Prague: Academia, 1969), p. 7.

CONTENTS

PART III

THE POLITICAL ECONOMY OF SOCIALISM

PART IV

THE POLITICAL ECONOMY OF COMMUNISM

APPENDICES

PART I

INTRODUCTION

CHAPTER

1

Methods of Social Analysis

Like ancient Gaul all social science can be divided into three parts, having three strikingly different viewpoints. One view is conventional (conservative or liberal) non-Marxist social science, the second is dogmatic Marxism, the third is radical or nondogmatic Marxism. The usual non-Marxist view is sometimes labelled "Western," but this is misleading. "Western" social science does not really refer to a geographical area, but includes all those social scientists who tend to defend the established system of Western Europe, Japan, and America. On the other hand, dogmatic Marxism puts Marx (who would turn in his grave if he knew it) into an official, institutionalized mold, which is used by all those who tend to defend the established system of various Communist-led countries.

The third contemporary view of the social sciences is the radical Left or nondogmatic Marxist view, which is critical of all existing establishments and regimes. It is a humanist critique in that it always attempts to see from the viewpoint of the oppressed and wretched of the earth. "Marx's aim was that of the spiritual emancipation of man, of his liberation from the chains of economic determination, of enabling him to find unity and harmony with his fellow man and with nature."[1] Within the humanist framework, this book attempts a comparative analysis of "capitalism" (the theoretical system and the impure examples, mainly America) and "socialism" (the theoretical system and the impure examples, mainly the Soviet Union).[2]

Conservatives have even denied the existence of radical political economy (or nondogmatic Marxism) as a unified body of thought. The conventional economist, Robert Solow, at the meetings of the American Economic Association in December 1970, declared: "neoclassical economics is pretty clearly a scientific paradigm. . . . Radical political economics is no such thing." This book is devoted to showing that Solow is wrong. It shows that radical political economy *is* a scientific paradigm, that is, that it provides a systematic and complete framework of analysis.

The Plan of Attack

We begin with the historical genesis of capitalism. Next, a simple economic model is used to explore poverty and exploitation. It is expanded by stages to consider waste, unemployment and monopoly. On this foundation of economic and class interest, the model is further complicated by consideration of the politics of the capitalist state and international relationships. Finally, other social cleavages, such as racial and sexual, are added to complete the description, and lead to the issue of reform or revolutionary solutions.

American radicals must also face the problems of the "socialist" countries in order to gain a better perspective on international issues and future alternative systems (but not to give advice to those countries, since that is the task of their own radical movements). Therefore, in Part III there are ten chapters on socialism paralleling each of the earlier ten chapters on the same problems under capitalism, though the content differs in various degrees. The fourth and last part of the book explores the feasibility of a communist society operating on the principle "from each according to his ability, to each according to his need."

Comparative and Historical Analysis

Most non-Marxist social scientists use "comparative analysis" as if they were comparing randomly different social-economic systems. They abstract from time and history, so they speak as if we are free to choose any system at any time. They also tend to see all problems as eternal, so they see no difficulty in using the same categories to analyze different societies.

Dogmatic Marxists condemn non-Marxist social science (or "bourgeois" social science, as they call it) for this practice. Dogmatic or vulgar Marxists use an "historical" analysis, which assumes that one system "inevitably" changes to another through revolution. No choice can be made; we can only slow down or speed up history. Moreover, two successive systems— such as capitalism and socialism—are so different that they cannot be compared in the same categories.

Nondogmatic or progressive Marxists (called "revisionists" by their op-

4

ponents) agree that in the very long run we can speak of a "stage" of history more or less dominated by capitalism, though with many remnants of earlier systems in some areas of the globe. We note that there have been some major socialist revolutions, and we do everything possible to encourage more. Nevertheless, we recognize that the main characteristic of our present era is the simultaneous existence of at least two major competing systems. Faced with the existing situation, radicals cannot refuse to make a detailed comparison of the two systems.

Dogmatic and Nondogmatic Marxists

The post World War II era has witnessed the wreckage of dogmatic Marxism and its split into several warring factions, each claiming to be the only genuine Marxism: Soviet, Chinese, Yugoslav, Cuban, Trotskyite, socialist, syndicalist, and other versions. Amid this chaos have arisen many independent Marxists who attempt to follow the method and spirit of Marx, rather than his exact words in the new and different situations of today. Nobody, not Marx or Lenin, Mao or Trotsky, has a monopoly on the perfect truth. Although aided by previous theory, every individual radical, nondogmatic Marxist must consider anew the particulars of each new situation.

In this respect, progressive Marxists may rely on Marx's own attitude. When Marx once heard of a particulary dogmatic and mechanical application of his theories, he was heard to exclaim, "I am not a Marxist." So today the progressive Marxists take Marxism primarily as a method of approach to problems, which must be tested in practice, some of it rejected, and always new additions made to it. For the Stalinists, however, dogmatic Marxism was more than a scientific belief; it was a religious faith and a way of life. The believer accepted the TRUTH as given from the mountain by Stalin. And when one believes, it is possible to accept any theological twist as truth, even when the exact opposite was accepted the previous day.

It should be noted that in most countries the new wave of Marxism, or neo-Marxism or post-Marxism, has come from former dogmatic Marxists. In the United States, where Marxism has never been recognized or respectable in the social sciences, the same positions have been slowly approached by radical, Left dissenters from the usual non-Marxist social sciences. For example, C. Wright Mills can be considered either a radical non-Marxist sociologist or a nondogmatic Marxist. Similarly, there are now radical, Left, opposition organizations in each of the social sciences. This book might be taken as a manifesto of the radicals in economics, the Union for Radical Political Economics, except that no one invited it, and that each member has fiercely differing views on every specific topic—though most seem to share the general methodology of nondogmatic Marxism.

The Method of Marxism

"Marxism is not a dogma, but a guide to action."[3] In the radical view the main contribution of Marx is not any divine wisdom about the world, but rather a method of approaching theoretical problems and of applying theory to practice. "Orthodox Marxism is not an uncritical recognition of the results of Marxist investigations, it does not mean a 'faith' in this or that thesis, nor is it the interpretation of a 'sacred' text. Orthodoxy in questions of Marxism refers exclusively to method."[4]

It follows that there is no such thing as a single, definitive, correct interpretation of Marx; there is only the Marxist way of doing things. ". . . Disputes in which scholars try to snatch from each other the exclusive privilege of using 'genuine Marxism' . . . are sterile verbalism. One can [only] argue whether a given theory fulfills more or less well the requirements of scientific thinking, which include the essential rules of the method worked out by Marx."[5]

Full discussion of Marx's method would require a volume by itself, so we can only outline its main characteristics here. First, the goal is not just an "objective" understanding of the world, but the production of tools to change the world. No social scientist is unbiased; all come from a particular social environment, and all have tentative conclusions (conscious or unconscious) on any issue they are investigating. When the alternatives are destruction—by nuclear or ecological means—or building a better, rational society quickly enough to prevent catastrophe, how can anyone remain detached? Moreover, a social science that presented no conclusions would be useless. Imagine an engineer who tells us there are ten different ways to build the bridge we are considering, but refuses to tell us which he believes best under the circumstances (admitting that further knowledge may change his judgment in the future).

The point is not to find a disinterested man, because there are none such, but to find a man interested in change from the viewpoint of humanity. Marxist humanism is the radical critique of all existing institutions from the viewpoint of the oppressed, feeling with them the most violent indignation and hatred against any discrimination, exploitation, or political repression.

This book is as true and honest as the author can make it, but it certainly does reach policy conclusions, which are meant to be partisan in favor of the interests of the wretched of the earth.

Interconnection

A second feature of Marxist method is its emphasis on interconnections. All events and institutions must be taken in their connections with the rest of society to be fully understood. Moreover, all society must be understood in its relation to the natural environment, which itself is an interconnected ecological web of flora, fauna, and physical environment. In the broadest sense, man's economic activity is the productive interaction with nature *and* the human relationships among the producers and consumers.

Economic activity must always be seen in its two aspects: (1) the interaction of nature and man, and (2) the interaction among humans. The first aspect centers on the "forces of production," by which we may include the machinery and factories, the land and resources, the number and skill of the labor force, and the level of technology; these factors determine how much can be produced. Only in a one-man Robinson Crusoe society, however, are we solely concerned with the relation of man to things. In all social situations, our political-economic investigations must begin with the relations between human beings in production.

Who does the actual work? Who gives orders? In what hierarchy are the order-givers arranged? Who has a right to possession, ownership, or consumption of the product?

Once we have ascertained these relations, we may look at the whole superstructure of society built upon this economic base. In the superstructure we include institutions such as the family, school system, and political system, as well as art and culture and all systems of ideas, philosophy, religion, and the social sciences. A philosophy does not emerge from the mind of a great man at random in a social vacuum; rather, it is a function of a given social environment with given social problems. Thus one would not look for a hippie outlook in ancient Egypt or a pantheon of gods in modern America. Each of these is explicable by particular social needs on a given socioeconomic base. Of course, most of these relationships between ideas and social environment are quite subtle and indirect. Some are obvious, though, such as the fact that almost all Southern preachers before the U.S. Civil War taught that slavery was divinely ordained.

Naturally, *once an idea has arisen*, it is part of the whole social equation. These ideas influence political decisions, and political decisions have immense effects on the socioeconomic base. For example, most laws merely reflect the relationships of production, whether they are laws on the holding of slaves or laws on the holding of private property.[6] Yet these laws are then backed by the full force of the state, so they regulate our

7

economic activity. Laws—and the armed force to apply them—upheld in the Roman Empire human relationships that led to technological stagnation and exhaustion of the land (see Chapter 2). Thus, once ideas have arisen from the socioeconomic base, they react back on the base. Ideas influence politics, which determines laws, which regulate human relations of production, which may speed up or hold back the development of the forces of production. We do not deny the influence of systems of ideas, only we emphasize that the ideas themselves emerge from a given set of sociopolitical institutions which are founded on a given economic base.

The Marxist method studies a given social process in terms of its own internal development as well as the social environment in which it exists. For example, the work of a particular artist reflects previous trends in art, but also reflects—and affects—a given social environment. For example, the art of Diego Rivera is much influenced in its technical forms by the French and Italian art at the time he studied in Europe. His art also reflects his own family background and his personality, but is most strongly a reflection of the Mexican revolution in which he participated. On the other side, his artistic representation of Indian and Mexican culture undoubtedly touched emotional chords in many Mexicans, propelling them to push the revolution still further.

Similarly, in child psychology a child must be understood in terms of his own physical and psychological development within a particular family environment, which is located within a particular social environment, which is located within a particular natural environment. Or, for example, if we are considering the effects of the possible extinction of some animal, we must recognize that it is interconnected with all the other flora and fauna of that environment—the wolf may need deer on which to feed, but the deer may need wolves to keep their population down to the limits of the available sustenance.

Some of these methodological principles may seem simple platitudes, yet they are frequently violated by both non-Marxist and dogmatic Marxist writers. Non-Marxist social science, for example, often considers economic production in complete isolation of social relations, such as the many discussions of Robinson Crusoe's problems. Moreover, academic non-Marxist social science rigidly divides the area into "pure" fields of economics, politics, sociology, and psychology. In this way, the economist may consider what government economic policy "should be" in a given situation; the political "scientist" asks how it "should be" administered, whereas few social scientists ask about the relationship of economic interests to particular political policies, or whether class interests may prevent or emasculate a given policy (such as all the loopholes in our supposedly progressive tax rates).

On the other side, dogmatic Marxists tend to see the relation of the economic base to the political superstructure as one-sided and absolute, that is, a vulgar economic determinism. For example, if a person earns much more than the average wage, then he is automatically assumed to be corrupted by the system and a supporter of the status quo. Similarly, it is assumed that the capitalist state is so absolutely dominated by the capitalist class, even when it is democratic in form, that no real reforms are possible, and all reforms are a deception rather than any aid to the working class.

Some dogmatic Marxists support the strange notion that radicals should support the most reactionary candidate so that the revolution will come sooner. This is related to their view of working class psychology, which is that bad enough conditions will automatically lead workers to attack capitalism and support a socialist revolution. If one follows such a view, it is naturally not too important whether one takes time to find out what issues really worry workers, or to fight on those issues, but only to keep repeating the need for a socialist revolution. Finally, under socialism this vulgar view promotes the dangerous notion that since the capitalist class is gone, it is only necessary to have one political party, whose leadership will automatically know and follow the true best interests of the working class.

Conflict

The third aspect of Marxist method most clearly distinguishes it from the method of conventional non-Marxist social science. Whereas much of non-Marxist social science is devoted to the study of harmony and equilibrium, Marxism explores the tensions and conflicts within each process, and expects to find these disharmonies or "contradictions" at the heart of each social problem. The Marxist emphasis on interconnection might be mistaken for the fashionable functionalist view in academic non-Marxist social science, that is, the view that each institution in society serves a function as part of one interconnected organism. But the functionalists, such as Talcott Parsons, sneak in the judgment that those institutions are "good" which function as stabilizers and upholders of the status quo.[7] Parsons assumes that there are no class divisions in American society, but a basic harmony; so any institution that functions to preserve this society is good for everyone. Marxism, on the contrary, looks at most institutions in a given society as functioning to serve the interests of the ruling class of that society; they are not "good" from the viewpoint of the great mass of the oppressed.

In each social process we try to examine both the unity of interests and the conflict of interests that exist in human relationships. For example, there are certain harmonious as well as conflicting interests between workers and capitalists, husbands and wives, parents and children, or tenants and landlords. In the case of workers and capitalists, capitalists cannot survive without workers from whom to extract profits, yet under capitalism workers cannot survive either without capitalists to hire them. The conflict comes when we look further than survival to the division of the product, and to their conflicting interests on the entire spectrum of political issues from taxation to militarism.

Change

The last major characteristic of the Marxist method to be considered here is the recognition and emphasis on change, evolution, and development. This is one reason for suspicion of all rigid, static definitions. For example, the modern horse is defined by its characteristic hooves, but then can we call the three-toed horse a "horse"? Similarly, at what point in evolution does the anthropoid become a "man"? Human history is full of these changes. For example, there was a mighty and apparently stable structure called the Roman Empire. But in reality it was not a fixed structure, but a changing process, subject to a slow decline and fall, after which it became something else.

On the one hand, we emphasize that present change is based on past evolution. To understand the French Revolution it is necessary to examine minutely the economic, political, social and ideological trends of the previous centuries. Thus we may subject to deserved ridicule those "explanations" for social phenomena, say the recent trends in student protest, as a mere sudden and random thing—or, at best, caused by a change in psychology due to parental permissiveness.

On the other hand, we urge that social scientists keep in mind that real change does occur. In some ways, the French Revolution was like a volcano, with a slow accumulation of disrupting forces, and a final explosion. What follows the explosion is really new, even though it is related to and based upon social environment and forces present before the explosion. One often finds superficial forms continuing or repeating in spite of a profound change in content. Thus we also subject to criticism those views, such as Spengler's, which see nothing but eternal repetition and no real change.

These views did not disappear entirely with the demise of the grand metaphysical systems of the early nineteenth century. In the 1890s Alfred Marshall took as his motto: "Nature [including society] does not make leaps." Even in 1969 a non-Marxist social scientist said: "Change is . . . *not* natural, *not* normal. . . . Fixity is."[8] By contrast, nondogmatic Marxists investigate society in terms of its major changes, sometimes slow, sometimes in sudden leaps.

While some "explanations" see student protests coming out of nowhere, there are the equally erroneous explanations of recent student protest movements that see them as no more than repetitions of their parents' protests at the same age—a mere continuation of the eternal gap between generations. To really understand the new trends among students and youth, it would seem necessary to examine both their continuity with earlier generations of protesters, and with the quite unique characteristics of the present generation of youth and their environment (for example, the present possibility of destroying all life in the world by nuclear bombs or other means). In traditional Marxist language, one could say that it is necessary to study both revolutionary jumps from one quality to another in each social process, and the long quantitative evolution that leads to those jumps.

Changes that occur must be analyzed in terms of the conflicting forces that are the content of each social interconnection. For example, an analysis of the great financial crash of 1929 must examine the previous years of apparently stable prosperity. Within that process of prosperous expansion, one must locate the tensions that grew and grew up to the explosion of 1929. At any given time before the peak of expansion and the beginning of the crisis, one would have found the forces of harmony and equilibrium dominant. Our understanding of the final crash, however, is dependent on accurate examination of the growing economic disproportions, even though they may have been very minor at earlier stages. For example, throughout the 1920's as income grew, the rich, the capitalist class, took a larger and larger proportion of it for themselves.

Thus one growing disproportion in the 1920's lay in the rapid increase of output while the consumption of workers was restricted by their receipt of a declining portion of national income. It is interesting that Marx was able to see some of these conflicts in the economy as early as the mid-nineteenth century, while most other economists were still talking about depressions as the result of external factors, such as sun spots, or random factors, such as inexplicable panic psychologies (there are even explanations of the 1929 crisis in terms of an unexplained panic or pessimism).

Our view sees social change occurring as the result of conflicts within each process and the processes as interconnected. Thus, the forces of production—the machinery and factories, the numbers and skills of labor, the knowledge of natural resources, and the level of technology—have usually been expanding, and at an accelerating rate in recent centuries. On the other hand, given productive relations, such as slave and slaveowner,

11

or propertyless worker and property-owning capitalist, are rigidly fixed in a given legal system and defended to the death against radical change. Eventually, these fixed human relations and institutions conflict with the expansion of the productive forces, as, for example, in the stagnation of technology in the later stages of the Egyptian or Roman empires.

This tension within the economic base of society is reflected in the political superstructure in the conflict of interests between the ruling class that would preserve the status quo at all costs, and classes of oppressed or new incipient ruling classes that would change it. The social conflicts are further reflected in differing ideologies, such as the views of Rousseau or Voltaire criticizing the old regime before the French Revolution. But, of course, ideas are not mere reflections of social-political conflicts. Once the ideas become widely disseminated, they are the most important weapon for a change (or else may be a defensive weapon for the status quo). When the ideas have penetrated far enough, a decisive change or revolution may occur in the political superstructure of society. Then in turn, the new superstructure is the most decisive instrument for carrying through a change in the productive relations among people. Finally, then, the new productive relations allow an harmonious and rapid expansion of the productive forces of society, as when the abolition of feudal restrictions in England led to a flowering of capitalist industry. The new expansion will lead to new tensions and conflicts, and further development through that process.

NOTES

1. Erich Fromm, *Marx's Concept of Man* (New York: Frederick Ungar, 1961), p. 3.
2. The terms "capitalism" and "socialism" are defined in later chapters.
3. V. I. Lenin, *The Teachings of Karl Marx* (New York: International Publishers, 1964), p. 53.
4. George Lukacs, quoted in Peter Gay, *The Dilemma of Democratic Socialism* (New York: Collier, 1952), p. 144.
5. Leszek Kolakowski, *Toward a Marxist Humanism* (New York: Grove Press, 1969), p. 183.
6. ". . . Legal relations and also forms of the state are to be explained neither by themselves nor by the so-called universal development of the human mind, but on the contrary have their roots in the material conditions of life." Marx, cited in Stanley Moore, *Critique of Capitalist Democracy* (New York: Paine-Whitman, 1957), p. 58.
7. See the full explanation of Parsons' approach in Don Martindale, ed., *Functionalism in the Social Sciences* (Philadelphia: American Academy of Political and Social Sciences, 1965).
8. Robert A. Nisbet, *Social Change and History: Aspects of the Western Theory of Development* (New York: Oxford University Press, 1969), p. 270.

CHAPTER
2

Precapitalist Societies

Chapter 1 discussed the Marxist (or radical Left) approach to the historical process. Now we must begin to look at the actual historical record. Although most of this book is devoted to capitalism and socialism, the present chapter tries to provide a historical perspective by looking briefly at earlier types of societies. Before we can examine specific societies, however, we must spend a little time on a general overview of social evolution. Can we talk about social evolution at all? Is the progression purely random? Or is the evolution of society rigidly programmed?

Social Evolution

The vulgar or dogmatic view interprets Marx to mean that human society must "inevitably" pass through certain preordained stages: primitive communism, slavery, feudalism, capitalism, socialism, and communism. Thus, the Soviet "Marxism" of Stalin insisted on a simple unilinear view of rigidly similar evolution in all societies: "All peoples travel what is basically the same path. . . . The development of society proceeds through the consecutive replacement, according to definite laws, of one socioeconomic formation by another."[1]

Strict economic definitions are given of the various stages of society. "Primitive communism" means collective ownership and use of all goods at a very low technological level. "Slavery" means private ownership by individuals of land and human beings. "Feudalism" means control, but not ownership, of land and workers, so the serfs are bound to the land and the king may transfer control of the land from one landlord to another, but the feudal landlord does not own the serf and may not sell him (nor can he sell the land). Under "capitalism" capitalists buy and sell land, buy and sell factories and equipment (which become much more important than land), and buy workers' power to labor (but may not buy and sell workers, as was the case in slavery). Of course, slave-owners and capitalists own all the products produced under their direction, and may sell them for a profit in the market; feudal lords owned the product produced on their own land, but not that produced on the serf's land (though much of it might be owed to the landlord as rent).

"Socialism" is defined by the Soviets to mean social ownership of the means of production, with continued differences in wages according to work done, and purchase of consumer goods for private use. "Communism" is said to mean social ownership plus sharing of goods according to "need" (no wages or prices).

Many areas of the world, however, have not followed this exact progression. Moreover, the models are never met in pure form, and real societies always contain elements of other systems. The narrow or dogmatic version of Marxism not only turns out to be wrong on methodological and factual grounds, but more recently published manuscripts of Marx show that his view was quite opposite and was at an entirely different level of sophistication.[2] A very careful summary of Marx's manuscripts finds that "the general theory of historical materialism requires only that there should be a succession of modes of production, though not necessarily any particular modes, and perhaps not in any particular predetermined order."[3]

The fullest, concrete Marxist study of the socioeconomic stages in man's early history concludes from a lengthy study of the archaeological and anthropological facts that "it is not in the least surprising that the development of societies observed in different parts of the Old World, to say nothing of the New, should exhibit divergence rather than parallelism. This conclusion does not invalidate the use of the term 'evolution' to describe social development."[4] In fact, one can still use the analogy between social and organic evolution because "organic evolution is never represented pictorially by a bundle of parallel lines, but by a tree with branches all up the trunk and each branch bristling with twigs."[5] The evidence shows not only divergence and differences, but also convergence and broad similarities. Of course, there are a great many differences in detail between the processes of cultural evolution and organic evolution. "But to admit this is not to deny cultural evolution, to deny that cultural change is an orderly and rational process that can be understood by the human intellect without invoking any necessarily incalculable factors and miracles. On the contrary, it can be described in general intelligible formulae . . . there is no need to assume supernatural interpositions."[6]

Nondogmatic Marxists emphasize that there are many alternative evolutionary roads followed by human societies. Some very specific qualifications to any general schema must be stressed. First, even similar stages of evolution will be found at very different times in different places. Second, there are cases of regression from a "later" to an earlier stage. Third, older

modes of production may persist for centuries next to newer, "more advanced" modes both within the same society and in neighboring societies.
Thus, although large slave plantations came to dominate ancient Roman
agriculture, large numbers of small peasant farms continued to fight for
existence.

Fourth, many of the political-economic transformations in man's history did not take place through the internal evolution of one society,
but through diffusion from a more advanced society. Diffusion has come
in many guises, including conquest, colonialism, trade, and religious and
political missionary work. Obviously, diffusion opens the possibility for
jumps over the stages of history. Thus, primitive as well as slave and
Asiatic societies have been brought straight to capitalism; primitive as
well as feudal societies have jumped to socialism. Perhaps even the
recorded jumps from primitive to feudal societies (as in the case of the
German barbarian tribes) were all caused by diffusion. Moreover, diffusion may be "regressive" as well as "progressive." In later chapters
it will be seen that the diffusion of capitalism by conquest in the last
four centuries has not resulted in advance, but in deformed socioeconomic
structures and stagnation in the conquered areas (such as India, Ghana,
Cuba to 1959, Vietnam, and so forth).

With all these qualifications, one can still speak of an evolutionary
social process. The analogy of Marx with Darwin might even be extended
to speak of the survival of the fittest society. That society will survive
whose socioeconomic institutions (or class "relations of production") are
best adapted to the fullest development of the means of production and
the fullest development of human potential. It might be said that such
a framework, with all of its qualifications, is a truism to any rational social
scientist. Yet one set of institutional pressures and ideological commitments has led dogmatic Marxists to speak of universal, unilinear evolution. A different set of institutional pressures and ideological commitments
has led some conservative Western social scientists to deny any validity
to the concept of social evolution.[7]

Primitive Societies

Engels did the earliest systematic Marxist work on primitive societies.[8]
Naturally he built his general analysis on the known anthropology of his
day, mostly Morgan's work, now completely outdated. In Stalin's era
Soviet Marxists raised the detailed structure of Engels' classifications to
a divinely given "truth." They held that *every* society begins with the
stage of primitive communism, which is *always* subdivided into the

stages of (1) the primitive herd, (2) the primitive community, (3) matriarchal clan society, (4) patriarchal clan society, and (5) break-up of tribal society.[9] Now even Soviet Marxists have recognized that no such detailed universal stages can be read into the evidence.[10] They have reverted to the more neutral, open-ended non-Marxist classifications such as Old Stone Age and New Stone Age.[11]

What is important in Engels is not his now obsolete classifications of primitive societies, but his fundamental point that such societies were very different from ours in basic ways. Not only were family structures different (discussed in a later chapter), but in the most primitive societies there is little or no evidence of class division and class repression. One British archaeologist with a Marxist approach lists the characteristics of most areas of man's settlement in our first half million years or so as follows: (1) very small communities; (2) communities that are quite isolated, self-sufficient, with little or no trade; (3) no writing; (4) a homogeneous group of people; (5) no full-time specialists; (6) the economic unit is the family or extended family of kinsmen; (7) relationships are personal and status hereditary, rather than economic; and (8) little or no political institutions.[12]

Many non-Marxist anthropologists have given us detailed studies showing the validity of this view in at least some areas. Even Nash, who criticizes Engels' detailed stages of evolution, reports one contemporary primitive community where even today "there is no private property in productive goods, and whatever the hunting band manages to kill is shared out among the members of the group."[13] In general, the most primitive societies have no market exchange, no money, and no economic competition in the modern sense.[14] It is true that even the most primitive peoples known to anthropologists usually own their weapons, tools, and ornaments as individual private property; but the basic "means of production" at this stage are the hunting grounds, and these are owned collectively.[15]

The point cannot be overstressed that in primitive societies men are not hired for jobs, they are not paid money, and purely economic relations do not prevail in any area (nor is force used in most cases). Rather, "men work together because they are related to each other, or have social obligations to one another."[16] Furthermore, work is done collectively and the results shared collectively. Or as another non-Marxist anthropologist writes, "with qualifications such as the special shares locally awarded for special contributions to the group endeavor—the principle remains . . . 'goods collectively produced are distributed through the collectivity.' "[17]

Dogmatic Marxists have referred to societies with these characteristics as "primitive communism." This term is quite misleading, however, partly because primitive societies reveal such a wide range of structures that it is wrong to force them all into any one box. More important, the term implies that this was a golden age of innocence with a consciously chosen collective ideology. On the contrary, the "communist" features observed in some primitive societies are imposed by dire necessity for bare survival (and it is hardly much "communism" to find cooperation within a family group of perhaps ten to fifteen members). Collective activity is necessary because life is very insecure and on the margin of subsistence, so each person knows that his own life depends on his neighbors' cooperation and "generosity." Moreover, the results of a hunt may come in all at once, and there is no way to preserve perishable goods in the primitive situation. Furthermore, any man who is not "generous" and who does not fulfill his traditional "voluntary" social obligations would eventually be left out of the tribe, to face almost certain death through inability to cope with the world alone.[18]

Slave, Asiatic, and Alternative Modes of Production

Evidence on transformation from "primitive communism" to the classic type of slavery is mostly limited to Egypt; elsewhere evolution took different paths. Even Greek and Roman slavery seems obviously to be explained in part by diffusion from the former areas. Going further afield, an independent evolution may be assumed for the Inca, Mayan, and Aztec areas of America. Information on these areas, however, is very limited; and even that limited information shows great differences from the Middle Eastern pattern, both in the institutional and the technological developments.

Furthermore, in India and China and in Mesopotamia itself, although slavery does appear at some time after the agricultural revolution, it is *not* the predominant system in most of these areas. In Mesopotamia, it is true that "at the bottom of the social hierarchy were slaves, individuals who could be bought and sold. . . ."[19] Still, the rest of the social hierarchy was very complex, including free craftsmen as well as priests, warriors, and several ranks of a nobility that might well be called feudal. To complicate matters, it was the priesthood that was mainly in control in early times, only later giving way to a degree to the warriors. The complex interaction of church and government in most or all of these early societies is another feature usually overlooked in the dogmatic Marxist model.

In India, a sophisticated Marxist analysis by Kosambi still seems to find primitive communist hunters and gatherers in the earliest remains.[20] In the period following the agricultural revolution, however, he discovers only a small amount of slavery. Not only is the percentage in the total population very low, but almost all the slaves are either domestic servants or held by the royal family.[21] India from that time until well into the twentieth century was mainly characterized by the caste system. In this system each person's rank and occupation in society was fixed by birth to be the same as that of the parents. Yet there was no slave caste; even the lowest caste was theoretically free (though with many restrictions) and was paid some pittance for its product or services. In the countryside during most of Indian history, farmers were "free" men owning their own product *except* for taxes, rents, and tributes, which left very little. Actually, it was usually the village commune that owned or possessed the land rather than the individual farmer. Finally, above the village commune there was imposed by a conquest a ruling hierarchy, which extracted tribute from the village.

In China, even an official Chinese Communist history states that slavery existed only as a small part of the whole economy, and only from the Shang to the Ch'in dynasties.[22] The main economic basis for society in these dynasties was the peasant commune, which possessed its land in return for the payment of a tribute to the noble landowners. After the Ch'in dynasty, a very small amount of slavery continues up to the Yuan dynasty. The official history terms the dominant system after the Ch'in dynasty "feudalism" in view of the decentralized power of many provincial warlords (most Marxists place the beginning of "feudalism" in the Chou dynasty, just before the Ch'in). Nevertheless, the peasant commune and its tribute remain the economic base for a very long time. Even through the nineteenth century the important role of the Chinese extended family is reported by all observers.

In the light of the new facts on precapitalist societies revealed by archaeologists, anthropologists, and economic historians—and because of the mind-freeing renaissance of Marxist thought in recent years—a very heated debate has taken place concerning the classification of societies into the Marxist stages of history.[23] Although the discussion continues, some new and less dogmatic views have already been accepted, even in the Soviet Union.

One of the new trends is the revival of interest in what Marx called the Asiatic mode of production (sometimes referring to its Oriental form and sometimes to its Slavonic form). Marx defined it as based in large part on the continued existence of communal property, with the entire tribe (or kin group) owing tribute in the form of goods or services to various ruling classes. Logically, it might be viewed "merely" as a transitional form from primitive communism to slavery (or, at least to feudalism). Yet the facts show, as Marx argued, that this is a surprisingly stable economic mode, lasting in some areas for thousands of years.

Stalin, however, did not like the concept of the Asiatic stage because it complicated his simple unilinear picture and because it implied no compulsion to "progress" (toward Stalinist socialism) in some societies. For propaganda and diplomatic reasons, these features were unattractive to Stalin. Therefore, he prohibited all Soviet Marxists from making use of the concept of the Asiatic mode of production. It is only recently that many Marxist writers have come to use this term as the best description of ancient India, China, and Mesopotamia, perhaps the Inca Empire of Peru, and much of Oceania and Africa at times, though with many unique features in each case. They argue that the institution of the Asiatic mode may have been a major reason for the comparative stagnation of many of these economies for many centuries.

In a striking turn away from dogmatism, several Marxist scholars have emphasized that many economies *never* went through a slave phase. Soviet theory has specifically rejected the dogma of a universal stage of slavery.[24] Moreover, in addition to the "Asiatic" alternative, the more recent of Marx's writings brought to light indicate that for Marx himself, "feudalism seems to be an *alternative* evolution out of primitive communalism. . . ."[25]

The Transition to Class Society

When "civilization" became established in the Middle East in the Bronze and Iron Ages, it was marked by (1) large-size communities, (2) taxes, (3) public works, (4) writing, (5) use of mathematics and astronomy, (6) internal and foreign trade, (7) full-time specialists such as farmers and metallurgists, (8) political organization beyond family or kinship, (9) a privileged ruling class, and (10) an exploited class of workers (whether slaves or feudal serfs or peasants paying tribute).[26] The key revolution, however, is the earlier transformation from hunting and gathering (in savagery or primitive communism) to animal herding and agriculture.[27] Once this initial agricultural revolution has taken place, it may be argued that the coming of "civilization" (and class rule) depends merely on further quantitative increases in community size and productivity.

How did the agricultural revolution occur, and how did it end the primitive classless societies of these areas (and bring about class rule)? We know there was a slow expansion of knowledge and improvement of tools over hundreds of thousands of years.[28] Then, in a few particularly fertile areas—perhaps more or less independently in China, Mesopotamia, Egypt, Mexico, and Peru—men discovered how to tame and breed animals and how to grow desired plants. This "revolution" did not occur in a momentary flash of insight to some individual. Rather, it seems to have been a very gradual process over thousands of years.

Recent work presents a detailed picture of this process based on the latest available evidence for Mesopotamia and the Aztec areas of Mexico.[29] First, communities became more permanently settled, intensively collected food, and hunted in a given smaller area than previously. Second, the New Stone Age saw better tools being produced, including improved bows, drills, digging tools, and even boats and nets. Third, some crop, wheat for example, that was already growing in the area might be (1) moved to different areas as desired, (2) protected by such means as removing any weeds, and (3) eventually selected so as to obtain the desired food characteristics. Similarly, hunters of goats or cows might (1) begin to follow one particular herd, (2) protect it against its other enemies, and finally (3) feed and shelter it at times. All these changes could take thousands of years.

Once the pastoral-agricultural revolution is well under way, several important changes occur as a direct result. Obviously, the level of productivity per worker increases. The first consequence of this fact is a much higher population density; herding and agriculture can support many people per square mile, whereas hunting and gathering require several square miles per person. At the same time, agriculture means that the population must settle in one place rather than move here and there around the country. Such large, settled agglomerations mean the founding of permanent villages and, eventually, towns and cities in the most favored places.

There is enough economic surplus over immediate needs that the economy may support various specialists, such as carpenters, shoemakers, and the like. Specialization, in turn, calls for exchange of products between individuals and between groups. When exchange becomes too complex for barter to be convenient, money, the medium of exchange, rears its ugly head. Moreover, the higher productivity makes available hoards of "money" (whether cattle or gold) as well as consumer durables. Then, the specialization and exchange slowly destroy the collective use and possession of the hoards and the durables, so some individuals come to own more wealth than others.

With this increase of private property and the larger, more permanently located groups of people, there is a need for broader and stronger political structure to replace the family unit.[30] At first, both in possession of private property and in control of political power, the families or clans retain the semblance of unity and direction. But just as individuals slowly accumulate private property, as there is more of it and as specialists demand more, so too do individuals slowly accumulate more political power as politics grows more complex.

A war chief may be elected from time to time in small tribal conflicts; the post is likely to become lifetime or even hereditary as larger armies come into being. The area and intensity of wars are increased at this time because wars for economic motives are used by advanced agricultural societies for the acquisition of cattle or slaves. Most large-scale introductions of slavery seem to follow as the *effect* of a war of conquest. Yet such wars only seem to follow as the *effect* of a new technology, high enough so that it is profitable to keep a slave (because he can produce a surplus). Slavery and wars of conquest are thus interwined as cause and effect at a certain level of economic evolution.

A similar increase of power may accrue to those in charge of public works. A director of irrigation for a small tribe may be appointed for a short time in one season; a director of irrigation for a large agricultural area along the Nile must be given more power for a lengthy period of time. Thus, in Egypt, the government separates from and rises above family or clan for two different kinds of reasons: (1) to carry through public projects, including irrigation and warfare, and (2) to guard private property, including slaves (and to prevent slave revolt).

The main question of this section must still be faced more directly and analytically. How and why were so many primitive economies transformed into slave economies (and other kinds of class societies, feudal or "Asiatic") in the ages following the agricultural revolution? The dogmatic Marxist answer was that better technology led to a higher product per worker. The higher product, in turn, meant that a society could for the first time "afford" to have some nonworking individuals (such as slaveowners, landlords, priests, full-time warriors). Conversely, until product per worker passed the point where one worker could just keep himself alive, there could have been no surplus left for the ruling classes. Before that point, slavery or serfdom could not pay—hence prisoners were simply killed or eaten. Even some otherwise anti-Marxist writers agree that "among hunters and fishers the requirements of a nomadic existence render slavery rather unproductive; out of eighty-three hunting and fishing tribes examined by one student, in sixty-five there were no slaves. On the other hand, among agricultural tribes slavery tends to be productive and therefore more widely used."[31]

Nevertheless, this simplistic argument of direct economic determination, with a one-to-one relation of productivity and institutional change, must be considerably modified. In the first place, there are a few exceptionally well-off societies with some specialists and some slaves even before the agricultural revolution.[32] Moreover, in the period immediately after the agricultural revolution, most of the earliest farming communities were mainly nonstratified, nonclass, nonslave societies. While a surplus product above some very minimum point of subsistence may be a necessary condition, it is clearly not a sufficient condition to ensure the emergence of full-time specialists and a class-divided civilization.

Furthermore, where the earlier Marxists speak of a "surplus" as an easily recognizable phenomenon, its amount rather turns out to be itself conditioned by ideology and sociopolitical institutions. Even in terms of food alone, the number of calories required to sustain life varies not only according to geographical facts, such as temperature, but also according to the type of activity an individual does.[33] The necessary calorie consumption not only depends on the type of economic work done, but also on activities considered necessary for recreation or religion: for example, the great amount of dancing done by primitive men. Finally, while the *potential* surplus over subsistence depends merely on technology and labor available (in a given geographical environment), the *actual* surplus gathered depends on governmental institutions as well.

The appearance of class rule coincides with the beginnings of formal governmental structure in many societies. Both class rule and government, however, usually come with very long and varied lags after the agricultural revolution (and both usually arise with the conquest of one community by another). Nevertheless, it is only these basic institutional changes to class rule and government that provide a stable base for further progress. *After* these changes, there appears a comparatively rapid technological advance (and increased potential surplus) and quite rapid population increase.

Nondogmatic Marxists maintain that in the very long run, the agricultural revolution "leads to" economic surplus which "leads to" the possibility of a profitable slavery, but the process involves long, constant, and complex interactions between economic developments and ideological-social-political changes. The concept of a "surplus" over basic needs is certainly not a figment of imagination. Even a hundred years ago, agriculture still required 60 or 70 per cent of the U.S. population; whereas in the 1970's there is "overproduction" of farm commodities with only 6 or 7 per cent of the population working in agriculture. Yet when the effective surplus in a primitive community can be drastically modified by changes in religion, not to speak of government, it is well to realize that it is anything but a simple technological concept. Moreover, the greater agricultural surplus affects organization (such as class relationships) slowly over a long period, not at a precise point.

Finally, we might note that class rule was a useful or even necessary means to advance the level of technology and general culture far beyond what it had been. Primitive societies create neither pyramids nor vast irrigation projects, neither Plato's philosophy nor Euclid's geometry. It required exploitation of the many to give leisure time to a few individuals. A *much* higher level of technology is required to have leisure time for everyone in a classless society.

Slavery to Feudalism in West Europe

While recent Marxist debates have restricted the use of the classification of "slavery," the term "feudalism" has been expanded to cover a very wide variety of economies. In fact, "feudalism" is much too loosely applied, since it has been used to cover contemporary Northern Nigeria and parts of Latin America as well as Tsarist Russia to 1867 and China to 1911! More interesting is the work that has been done toward subclassifications within feudalism. Feudal societies have been classified into evolutionary or progressive feudal structures and devolutionary, stagnant, or regressive feudal structures.[34] For example, West European feudalism led forward to capitalism, yet Byzantine or Arab feudalism had enough different features to lead to dead ends. In addition, medieval Russia is a case in which stagnant feudalism is similar in many respects, and hard to distinguish, from the Asiatic mode of production.

The discussion of "feudalism" in this chapter is mainly concerned with the unique case of medieval Europe. It is perhaps the best known and best researched case. Yet, there is so little quantitative data or definite knowledge that extremely different views of the period persist. One famous historian, Henri Pirenne, contends that medieval European economic development was determined by the operation of forces external to that society.[35] The most dogmatic Marxists, on the contrary, have tended to see the developments purely in terms of the internal evolution of European society based on conflicts within it. Even the so-called "objective facts" of medieval history have a different appearance when viewed from these opposing positions.

To illustrate the difference that approach makes, did the Roman Empire fall because it rotted away from within, or was it toppled from the outside? How the mighty Roman Empire declined and the medieval world came into being is a question that has been answered in many ways. The prevailing view used to be that the empire was simply inundated in the fourth and fifth centuries by waves of Germanic barbarian invasions.[36]

Pirenne argues that the Germanic invasions did not interrupt the basic socioeconomic continuity; that agriculture in the Merovingian period (fifth to seventh centuries) followed the Roman pattern; and that the Roman peasant, who was already tied to the land, simply became the serf of the medieval period. Pirenne declares that Merovingian commerce continued to thrive, that trade was brisk with the Byzantine Empire across the Mediterranean, and that Merovingian power was built on the taxes from this commerce. Moreover, the Merovingians still had a certain amount of industry, professional merchants still exported their products, and they even continued to issue the Roman *solidus* with the emperor's picture on it.

Pirenne finds that "feudalism," defined as a fragmented political-economy based on the independent manor, did not begin until the end of the eighth century (Carolingian period). At that time the Arabs suddenly burst into the Mediterranean, disrupted its commerce, and limited the Franks to a land empire with a northern center of gravity. Only then, as trade declined, was there a tendency toward economic self-sufficiency on the estate of each feudal lord, followed by political disintegration of the central authority in the face of landlord power.

Most Marxists admit that invasions by the Germans and Arabs, as well as the Slavs, Vikings, and Huns, were the catalyst that finally ended the Roman political-economic entity, but they maintain that the underlying process of disintegration began in noticeable degree by the second century.[37] The latifundia had almost entirely eliminated the independent peasant through competition based on cheap slave labor. The absentee slaveowners let technique stagnate, while the slaves often revolted or destroyed machinery (so that only the crudest implements and simple one-crop systems could be used).[38] The result was the exhaustion of the land, and the disappearance of the military reservoir of peasant soldiers. Similarly, slave labor in industry meant that it was unprofitable to use complicated machinery, so the benefits of large-scale enterprise were largely lost to the Romans. Since there was little use of large, specialized machinery, and since transport costs were very high, a strong tendency developed for industry to decentralize out to the frontiers (where the army constituted the one mass demand for goods). By the fourth century trade had degenerated, except for a few luxury goods, from international to regional and finally to local commerce.[39]

"Feudalism" or serfdom began to evolve through several paths long before the main barbarian invasions.[40] Whereas the slave was owned in body, the serf was merely bound to some estate to which he owed services or a share of his produce. The slave was often "emancipated" into a serf in order to obtain more efficient production and more secure military support. The free peasant was "persuaded" into becoming a serf in order to be protected against imperial taxes as well as against barbarian plunderers. Finally, some of the Germanic tribal members were reduced to serfdom through long reliance on their tribal chiefs for protection and leadership.

While Pirenne dates feudalism from the end of the eighth century, most Marxists place its beginning in approximately the fifth century (the Merovingian reign). The Merovingian period was already characterized by self-sufficient estates run by serf labor, a minimum of industry, a balance of trade unfavorable to Europe, and an absence of the formation of new cities.[41] Furthermore, Pirenne gives heavy weight to his evidence that the Merovingian kings kept issuing coins like those of the Roman Empire, whereas it appears that the new coins were issued mainly for prestige value, and were more often used as jewelry than money.[42]

Contrary to Pirenne, most writers argue that Mediterranean trade was thoroughly disrupted in this period, and that trade in the North had already assumed prominence. The unfavorable balance of trade resulted from the fact that Merovingian commerce in the Mediterranean was mostly limited to the *import* of a few luxury items from the more advanced East.[43] Moreover, it was the strength of local manorial economies and the self-sufficient decentralized production, which, long before the Arab invasions, caused both the decline of international trade and the fall in payment of land taxes to the Merovingian treasury.

In the case of Western Europe we may surely conclude that the transition from slavery to feudalism resulted from internal evolution in that area plus the impact of external events (such as the Germanic and Arabic invasions). How much quantitative importance to ascribe the different factors is under continuing debate. But only a dogmatist or theologian would claim that the evolution was the result *only* of internal or *only* of external changes. It is perfectly consistent with Marx's view to say that both contributed (the only "external" causes that Marx would not admit are supernatural ones).

NOTES

1. Otto Keiusinen, ed., *Fundamentals of Marxism-Leninism* (London: Lawrence and Wishart, 1961), p. 153.
2. Karl Marx, *Pre-Capitalist Economic Formations* (New York: International Publishers, trans. 1964).
3. Eric Hobsbawm, "Introduction" to Marx, *Pre-Capitalist Economic Formations*, *op. cit.*, p. 19.
4. V. Gordon Childe, *Social Evolution* (London: Watts and Co., 1951), p. 166; also see his many other, more detailed, works.
5. *Ibid.*, p. 166.
6. *Ibid.*, pp. 175 and 179.
7. See, e.g., Manning Nash, "The Organization of Economic Life," in George Dalton, ed., *Tribal and Peasant Economics* (Garden City, N.Y.: The Natural History Press, 1967), pp. 3–4.
8. Frederick Engels, *The Origin of the Family, Private Property, and the State* (New York: International Publishers, 1942, first publ. 1884), although Engels' work grew out of Marx's earlier researches; see, e.g., Marx, *Pre-Capitalist Economic Formations*, *op. cit.*
9. See description of stages in M. W. Thompson, "Translator's Foreword," in

A. L. Mongait, *Archaeology in the USSR* (Baltimore: Penguin Books, 1961, first publ. 1955).

10. Mongait, *op. cit., passim.*

11. For an excellent discussion of the technological distinction, see Jacques Bordaz, "First Tools of Mankind," *Natural History Magazine*, 68 (January–February 1959): 36–51 and 92–103.

12. V. Gordon Childe, *Social Evolution* (London: Watts and Co., 1951); also see Grahame Clark, *From Savagery to Civilization* (London: Cobbet Press, 1946).

13. Nash, *op. cit.*, p. 3.

14. See, e.g., George Dalton, "Economic Theory and Primitive Society," in Peter Hammond, ed., *Cultural and Social Anthropology* (New York: Macmillan Co., 1964), pp. 96–115.

15. V. Gordon Childe, *Social Evolution* (London: Watts and Co., 1951), p. 67.

16. Daryll Forde and Mary Douglas, "Primitive Economics," in George Dalton, ed., *Tribal and Peasant Economics, op. cit.*, p. 17.

17. Marshall D. Sahlins, "On the Sociology of Primitive Exchange," in Michael Banton, ed., *The Relevance of Models for Social Anthropology* (New York: Praeger, 1965), p. 142.

18. See, e.g., Stanley H. Udy, Jr., "Preindustrial Forms of Organized Work," in Peter B. Hammond, ed., *Cultural and Social Anthropology, op. cit.*, pp. 115–124.

19. Robert M. Adams, *The Evolution of Urban Society* (Chicago: Aldine Publishing Co., 1965), p. 102.

20. D. D. Kosambi, *Ancient India* (London: Routledge and Kegan Paul, 1965).

21. *Ibid.*, pp. 22–24.

22. Written anonymously, *An Outline History of China* (Peking: Foreign Languages Press, 1958).

23. For some discussion and sources, see Hobsbawm, "Introduction" to Marx, *Pre-Capitalist Economic Formations op. cit.*, pp. 60–65.

24. Hobsbawm, *op. cit.*, p. 62.

25. *Ibid.*, p. 28.

26. V. Gordon Childe, "The Urban Revolution," *Town Planning Review*, 21 (1950): 3–17.

27. See, e.g., Robert Redfield, *The Primitive World and Its Transformations* (Ithaca: Cornell University Press, 1953).

28. Childe, *Social Evolution*, op. cit., p. 161ff.

29. See, e.g., Robert M. Adams, *The Evolution of Urban Society* (Chicago: Aldine Publishing Co., 1965), pp. 39–43.

30. Though Adams, *op. cit.*, p. 42, notes that most of the population increase appears to have come *after* the settled communities and governments were formed.

31. R. A. Dahl and C. E. Lindblom, *Politics, Economics, and Welfare* (New York: Harper & Row, 1953), p. 281.

32. See, e.g., Redfield, *op. cit.*, p. 5.

33. See, e.g., Martin Orans, "Surplus," *Human Organization*, 25 (Spring 1966): 24–32. Also see Harry Pearson, "The Economy Has No Surplus," in H. Pearson, Karl Polanyi, and C. Arensberg, eds., *Trade and Market in the Early Empires* (Glencoe, Ill.: The Free Press, 1957), pp. 320–341.

34. Owen Lattimore, "Feudalism in History," *Past and Present*, 12 (November 1957): 47–57.

35. Henri Pirenne's views of medieval history are to be found mainly in *Mohammed and Charlemagne* (London: Allen and Unwin, 1939); *Medieval Cities* (Princeton: Princeton University Press, 1925); and *Economic and Social History of Medieval Europe* (New York: Harcourt Brace, 1956).

36. See, e.g., the discussion and works cited in R. Koebner, "Settlement and Colonization of Europe," *Cambridge Economic History*, 1 (1942): 1–88.

37. A Marxist view is presented in F. W. Walbank, *The Decline of the Roman Empire in the West* (London: Cobbet Press, 1946). The Marxist explanation as to why the East Roman Empire did not suffer the fate of the West is given in A. Sharf,

Precapitalist Societies

"Heraclius and Mahomet," *Past and Present*, 9 (April 1959): 1–16. The dogmatic Stalinist view of feudal origins was presented in A. M. Pankratova, ed., *History of the USSR*, vol. 1 (Moscow: Foreign Languages Publishing House, 1947), and is criticized in A. Vucinich, "Soviet Theory of Social Development in the Early Middle Ages," *Speculum*, 26 (April 1951): 243–254.

38. F. A. Thompson, "Peasant Revolts in Late Roman Gaul and Spain," *Past and Present*, 2 (November 1952): 11.

39. Similar Marxist analyses of land exhaustion and the relatively low labor productivity of slavery may be found for Ancient Greece in F. W. Walbank, "Causes of Greek Decline," *Journal of Hellenic Studies*, 64 (January, 1944): 10–20; for ancient Egypt and Persia in V. G. Childe, "The Birth of Civilization," *Past and Present*, 2 (November, 1952): 1–11; and for the U.S. South before the Civil War in Eugene D. Genovese, *The Political Economy of Slavery* (New York: Pantheon Books, 1965).

40. M. Gibbs, *Feudal Order* (London: Cobbet Press, 1944).

41. C. M. Cipolla, "Encore Mahomet et Charlemagne," *Annales d'histoire economique et sociale*, 4 (New Series, 1949): 9.

42. C. M. Cipolla, *Money, Prices, and Civilization in the Mediterranean World* (Princeton: Princeton University Press, 1956).

43. D. C. Dennett, "Pirenne and Mohammed," *Speculum*, 23 (April, 1948): 165–190.

PART II

THE POLITICAL ECONOMY OF CAPITALISM

CHAPTER
3

Origins of Capitalism

This chapter summarizes the basic institutions of capitalism, then returns to the historical narrative to relate briefly the rise of capitalism.

The Capitalist Model

Capitalism may be defined as an economic system in which one class of individuals ("capitalists") own the means of production ("capital" goods, such as factories and machinery), hire another class of individuals who own nothing productive but their power to labor ("workers"), and engage in production and sales in order to make private profit.[1] We must now clarify these features and see their immediate implications.

All capitalist effort is directed to selling things in the marketplace. In the conservative view, this is a very favorable feature. As we shall see in the next chapter, the argument is that capitalists must produce what consumers want if they are to sell their goods. Therefore, the market *automatically* means that the mixture of outputs will tend to conform with the preferences of consumers. Furthermore, they argue that such competition will *automatically* tend to lower costs and prices toward the minimum level of cost with efficient output, since the inefficient, high-price producers will be unable to sell their goods in the market.

Radicals, on the other hand, point out that the market responds only to preferences based on wealth, that is, the preference of a poor man without money is unheeded. The rich man may satisfy his preference for a palace, while the poor man's preference for food is unfilled and he suffers malnutrition. Furthermore, we shall see that production for the market means full employment only so long as there is a demand for all the goods in the market. When there is an over-all lack of demand, production and employment decline.

Capitalism characteristically uses "money" as the means of exchange in the market. In the conservative view, the use of gold, tokens, or paper money is a great advance over barter, because the individual can spend a few dollars for one thing and a few dollars for another as he chooses. Under barter, the farmer might bring his cow to market, and have to trade the whole cow to the shoemaker for shoes. Since he could use only one or two pairs of shoes, he then had to trade the other shoes for other goods, a very complex process.

Radicals certainly agree that money is a useful tool, but they also believe that "money is the root of all evil." On the one hand, that saying refers to the fact that the use of money and the competitive market system normally results in a dog-eat-dog kind of psychology, and in robbery, both criminal and "legal" (via exploitation of workers). We shall also see that the use of money opens the door to the possibility of inequality of demand and supply. When one gets money, it may be hoarded, rather than spent. Thus the process of circulation is not always smooth, and the amount of money searching for commodities may be much more or much less than the amount of commodities at present prices.

Another feature of capitalism is the buying and selling in the competitive market of the workers' ability to labor. Conservatives point out that this is a great advance over slavery or serfdom in that the worker is free to go where he likes and get employment in any job. Radicals point out that the worker is also "free" to be fired, and he no longer has even the security of his tiny plot of land on the feudal manor. When millions of people are unemployed, the freedom to switch jobs does not appear to be a very useful freedom; it is rather the freedom of the capitalist to hire and·fire as he pleases. This job insecurity, plus the knowledge that one is producing for someone else's profit, robs work of its pleasurable "creative" possibilities and tends to produce alienation.

Finally, there is the fact that capitalist production is conducted for private profit. Conservatives tout this feature as meaning that each capitalist will strive for the utmost efficiency, thus lowering costs for all consumers. And, as we have noted, the capitalist will try to satisfy the preferences of all consumers, at least those who can pay money for their desires. Radicals argue that the private profit motive often means efficiency, not in reducing costs, but in milking the consumer, especially when monopoly power allows high prices and high profits. Moreover, production for profit means that if the profit perspective is dim, production is cut back, and mass unemployment results. Many other results might be cited. For example, pollution is a cost to society, but not to the individual firm, so it is left out of enterprise planning considerations. But detail on these points must await later chapters.

32

The Rise of Capitalism

Pirenne recognizes a vast increase by the eleventh century in international trade, caused by the Crusades. In the Crusades Western Europe regained that control of the Mediterranean which it had earlier lost to the Moslems. "At the beginning of the twelfth century a new and external impulse affected the economic activity of the Netherlands. Just as the closing of the Mediterranean by Islam had put an end to their relations with the Southern countries, so these were resumed with the revival of navigation there by the Christian countries."[2] The new merchants,—recruited from the mass of vagabonds, small itinerant merchants, and landless younger sons of peasants—needed new trading posts as well as permanent commercial centers. They constructed large new residential areas, usually around old feudal centers, that became the towns of the later Middle Ages.

Pirenne argues that the great increase in international trade, in industry, and in the use of money led to the end of serfdom in Italy and Flanders by the thirteenth century. The towns offer a haven for rebellious serfs, who must now be given better terms in the countryside. Moreover, the use of money and the certainty of markets induce the lords to begin to produce for the market and to collect money rents, in order to buy the manufactured products and luxuries offered by the towns and the trade with the East.

Most Marxists, on the contrary, hold that the upswing in European agriculture and industry beginning in the eleventh century was caused primarily by the cumulative effect of new inventions which made available more animal, water, and wind power. These technological improvements themselves resulted from the insufficient supply of labor, which motivated the landlords to find substitutes for human labor. It also resulted from the fact that West European feudalism gave the serf far more reason for initiative—both in making and in using inventions—than was allowed the peasant by Eastern forms of serfdom and slavery.[3] The remnants of slavery were, in fact, ended about this time because the new methods made it more profitable to use serf or even free labor.

The majority of Marxists argue against Pirenne (and against Paul Sweezy, who took a similar position) that the growth of trade and industry in the cities did not primarily result from the external stimulus of the increased Mediterranean commerce, but rather from the improved agricultural productivity that made available a surplus for the local market of both food and artisan-made goods.[4] It was from this local trade that the cities arose,

33

more money came into use, goods began to be traded at greater distances, and industry started to be concentrated in the towns.

The improvements in power and transportation made it profitable for the first time to concentrate industry and produce on a mass scale for a wide market (as it had *not* been profitable in the Roman Empire).[5] Thus it is industrial innovation that leads to commercial revolution and not vice versa. Marxists like Dobb[6] and Kosminsky[7] admit that Pirenne's concepts of widening market and use of money were important phenomena caused by nascent capitalism. The beginnings of the process, however, they trace to basic agricultural and industrial developments (which even led at an early period to *increased* exploitation of serf labor by the feudal lords).

Serfdom did not disappear in a simple one-to-one proportion with the widening market. In the twelfth century there was indeed increased industrial productivity, which created a larger marketable surplus, and thereby stimulated commercial activity; greater use of money and some switch from services to money rents resulted. There was a tendency throughout the twelfth to fifteenth centuries toward more money rents by the less powerful smaller landlords who could not resist the peasants' demands. But in the thirteenth and early fourteenth centuries there was a "feudal reaction." The increase in profit from marketing in the growing urban areas caused the greater lords to demand *more* demesnial land and *more* services from the serfs. By working the serfs harder, they tried to produce more output in order to make more profits. The peasant revolts were not designed to end some archaic feudal leftovers, but to prevent the reimposition of feudal burdens.

Marxists (and other critics of Pirenne) argue that the eleventh to thirteenth centuries saw a great revival of European international trade. They contend, however, that trade had never ceased entirely either in the Mediterranean[8] or in the North,[9] and that its existence and expansion were due in the main to the innovations mentioned above. Furthermore, the Crusades themselves are not viewed as an accidental "external" factor, but as the result of those same internal economic developments.

The Crusades were not undertaken for religious reasons, nor were they due to Turkish molestation of pilgrims, for the Turks continued the Moslem policy of tolerance.[10] Developments on the Moslem side did lead to increased attacks on Byzantium, but the West would have normally sent only token aid, since it had no great love for Byzantium. In fact, because the Italian merchants already had trade with the Moslems, they remained neutral until the first Crusade was almost won. The basic reasons for the Crusades may be seen in the internal developments of France, where it had the most powerful backing. France had been growing stronger, it had more trade relations and interest in the East, and it needed an outlet for social unrest at home. Additional promotion was given by the Venetian oligarchy, which wanted to expand its own Eastern trade and influence.

H. K. Takahashi, closely following Marx, emphasizes that there are two roads to capitalism: via the master craftsman or via the big merchant.[11] Takahashi argues that only the first way was really revolutionary, because the craftsman represented a new class which made a real break with the feudal rulers, as in England and France In these areas the increase in capitalist production led to a struggle for power between the old and new ruling classes. This struggle was reflected in ideological battles (fought by such writers as Rousseau, Locke, or Voltaire), political clashes, and finally in actual bloody fighting (such as the English revolution of 1648 or the French revolution of 1789).

By contrast, where the big merchants gained control of industry through the putting-out system, they worked hand in glove with the feudal lords to bolster the status quo, as in East Europe or Japan. As soon as the merchant accumulated some wealth, he bought land and intermarried with the landholding class. In fact, most Marxists contend—exactly opposite to Pirenne's viewpoint—that a virile bourgeois capitalism never fully developed in the merchant-dominated areas.[12]

It is not yet possible to give a fully satisfactory description and explanation of the origins and demise of the feudal economy that characterized medieval Europe. The statistics available for most of the medieval period are so poor that any view of its economic development must be purely speculative. Pirenne, for example, points to the continued use of African papyrus in Europe as proof of his thesis that trade continued at a high level in the Merovingian period. His critics, on the other hand, direct attention to the consumption of pepper in the Carolingian period as evidence that only then did medieval trade reach significant proportions. There are no reliable, quantitative data until a much later period. In spite of the arguments over points of fact, however, the principal differences in interpretation are not rooted in differences in empirical knowledge. All recent writers have had access to approximately the same meager evidence; preconceived dogmas have in part determined the interpretation of these few facts. Obviously, the Marxist *method* does not require that facts be one way or the other. For example, it suffices to say that European capitalism was born out of European internal evolution *and* its (mostly exploitative) relations with other continents.

NOTES

1. O. Lange, "Marxian Economics and Modern Economic Theory," *Review of Economic Studies*, 2 (1935): 201: ". . . capitalism means an exchange economy with private ownership of the means of production, to which the further sociological datum

is added that the population is divided into two parts, one of which owns the means of production while the other part, owning no means of production, is compelled to work as wage earners. . . ." Conservative economists neglect the "sociological datum."

2. H. Pirenne, "The Place of the Netherlands in the Economics History of Medieval Europe," *Economic History Review*, 2 (January 1929): 40. Also, for a direct contrast with Marx, see H. Pirenne, "The Stages in the Social History of Capitalism," *American Historical Review*, 19 (April 1914): 494–515.

3. The contrasting developments in China caused by a very different type of "feudal" institution are examined in a Marxist approach by Wu Ta-k'un, "An Interpretation of Chinese Economic History," *Past and Present*, 1 (February 1952): 1–13.

4. Numerous Marxist writers take this position in a symposium on *The Transition from Feudalism to Capitalism* (New York: Science and Society, Inc., 1954).

5. Samuel Lilley, *Men's Machines, and History* (New York: International Publishers, 1966), p. 42.

6. M. Dobb, *Studies in the Development of Capitalism* (London: George Routledge and Sons, 1946), Chapter 2.

7. E. Kosminsky, "Feudal Rent in England," *Past and Present*, 7 (April 1955): 12–36.

8. See R. S. Lopez, "The Trade of Medieval Europe in the South," *Cambridge Economic History*, 2 (1952): 257–354.

9. See H. Postan, "The Trade of Medieval Europe: The North," *Cambridge Economic History*, 2 (1952): 159–163.

10. C. Cahan, "Introduction to the First Crusade," *Past and Present*, 6 (November 1954): 6–30.

11. H. K. Takahashi, in *The Transition from Feudalism to Capitalism*, op. cit., pp. 30–55.

12. *Loc. cit.*; also see R. H. Hilton, "Capitalism—What's in a Name?" *Past and Present*, 1 (February 1952): 32–44; P. Vilar, "Problems of the Formation of Capitalism," *Past and Present*, 10 (November 1956): pp. 15–39; and A. B. Hibbert, "The Origins of the Medieval Town Patricate," *Past and Present*, 3 (February 1953): 15–27.

CHAPTER
4

Value and Market Allocation

Marx began his analysis of capitalism with an exploration of the value of commodities and the reflection of values in prices. Similarly, the "classical" economists of the late eighteenth and early nineteenth centuries (such as Adam Smith and especially David Ricardo) made value a central focus of their whole analysis. Likewise, the "neoclassical" economists (such as Leon Walras and Alfred Marshall), from the 1870's to the present, have concentrated on value and price theory.

Marxists have used the theory of value and individual prices ("micro" economic theory) as an analytic framework on which to build understanding of the distribution of aggregate income among classes and aggregate movements of all prices and outputs in depression and inflation ("macro" economic theory). Neoclassical economists have used the concepts of value and price theory as an analytic framework to study how the capitalist market allocates resources (labor, capital, and raw materials) to different industries, how consumers decide which commodities to buy, and how capitalists decide what commodities to produce and what technologies to use in production.

Much of the effort spent on discovering the "real value" of goods that lies behind prices has been wasted, though it has sometimes led to interesting results (as with Marx). "The concept of *value* seems . . . to be a remarkable example of how a metaphysical notion can inspire original thought, though in itself it is quite devoid of operational meaning."[1] In the case of neoclassical economics (long the core of non-Marxist social science) the main result of value and price theory, the understanding of how the market allocates resources, is useful to managers of capitalist enterprises in calculating how to maximize profits. Neoclassical theory may also be useful to a capitalist government in deciding how to induce (minor) changes in action from private firms. Whether it is also useful to socialist managers and planners will be discussed in detail in a later chapter.

On the whole, however, micro price theory and the role of market allocation are not very helpful to the understanding of the main socially relevant problems of today. Therefore, except for a few useful elementary points, this brief chapter must be considered as a history and critique of largely irrelevant thought. For some readers with previous "training" in economics, it may help to get rid of some useless baggage; other readers may wish to skip it.

The Classical Approach

Adam Smith wrote that "labour . . . is the real measure of the exchangeable value of all commodities. The real price of everything, what everything really costs to the man who wishes to acquire it, is the toil and trouble of acquiring it."[2] Ricardo wrote somewhat differently that "the value of commodity, or the quantity of any other commodity for which it will exchange, depends on the relative quantity of labour which is necessary for its production. . . ."[3] Smith presented several other theories along with the labor theory, and Ricardo never completed a consistent presentation of it. The question of their exact views on the labor theory of value is very complex, and need not detain us here.[4] What is important is only that one strand of classical thought did favor a labor theory of value, and that Marx seized on that strand as the basis for his work.

The Marxist Value Theory: A First Approximation

In a capitalist economy, Marx states that the value of any commodity is determined by the amount of labor embodied in it (including the "congealed" labor embodied in the plant, equipment. and raw materials used up in the process of production).[5] Marx does not "prove" this statement because he assumes agreement with a line of classical thought which, as seen through Marxist glasses,[6] might be stated as follows: Suppose we examine an economy in which each producer is an independent unit, doing his own work, hiring no one, and being hired by no one. He may produce farm goods, or may hunt for animals, or may do handicraft work.

To begin with the simplest case, assume that the producer also makes his own machinery and mines his own raw materials from scratch, à la Robinson Crusoe. In this case, it is almost a platitude that products exchange according to their labor costs. Suppose that some men hunt beaver, while others hunt deer. If it takes on the average twice as long to catch a deer as to catch a beaver, then a deer-catcher will demand two beavers for one deer (or twice as much "money" for a deer than for a beaver).

If the market rate of exchange is only one for one, the hunters will switch over to catching beaver, because it takes only half the time and the reward is equal. As hunters quit catching deer and the supply of deer in the market decreases, competition for the smaller supply must force a rise in the price of deer, till one deer is exchanged for two beavers. Only then will an equilibrium exist, in which it is equally profitable to catch deer as beavers, so that there will be no further switching. Thus, when the system comes to rest, the ratio of prices in exchange will equal the ratio of labor times expended.

If it is necessary to purchase equipment from others, such as a bow and arrows, the answer is still basically the same (although everyone may gain from the greater productivity due to the specialization of labor). If the bow and arrows are offered at a price relatively greater than the labor time bestowed on them, the hunters may go back to making their own bows and arrows. Still, the bow and arrows must be included in the price of deer at the labor cost of making them, regardless of whether the bow and arrows are made by the hunter or someone else.

In the modern case, suppose a society that regularly uses money, is capitalist in the sense that there is private ownership of productive facilities, the goal of production is private profit, and capitalists are free to hire and fire workers. In this case, the "capitalist" supplies capital in the form of factories and equipment, while "workers" supply the labor power needed for production (here we ignore landlords and land). The final product must sell for a price equal to the total labor put into it, including the labor that went into producing the factories, raw materials, and equipment that were used up in the productive process.

The argument is essentially the same as in the simple economy of independent producers. If the capitalist tries to sell (or exchange) the product at a higher relative price than is justified by the labor in it, then other people can produce it for less, either for themselves or to sell in competition with him. In other words, if the price is above the labor value, so that a profit above average is being made, other capital will flow into the industry and increase its supply until by competion the price falls to the level of its total (labor) value. Yet the capitalist can at least obtain that price because no one can produce it for less. If the price should fall below the (labor) value, profit will be below average, capital will flow out, and supply will drop. Eventually, in the long run, competition will force the price back up to its full (labor) value, and only then will equilibrium be reached.

Marx immediately notes several common-sense qualifications to the "law of value." First, it applies only to labor expended under the usual contemporary technological conditions. If a person produces an automobile by hand, the product will still have a value equal only to the labor necessary to produce it in the usual mass production process. Second, the product must have a utility; labor expended on useless objects does not count. Notice, however, that although utility must be present for any value at all, it does not determine the *quantity* of value produced. Utility may be a factor determining demand, but if we assume that supply and demand are now balanced and equal, then the quantity of value must be determined by something else, namely the labor expended. In other words, on these assumptions (and several others discussed below) the demand will determine the distribution of labor among industries or the amount of each product, but it cannot affect the relative price or exchange ratio of products.

Finally, expenditure of more skilled labor will count as some multiple of an hour of average labor expended. The labor expended in "producing" (educating, training) the more skilled worker (for example, an engineer) is greater than that expended in producing an ordinary worker; therefore, he passes on to the product a greater value per hour. Marx does not mention these three qualifications each time he uses the law of value, but they are to be understood. This is a perfectly legitimate procedure of scientific abstraction from those complications which Marx believed to be irrelevant to his main argument.

The Neoclassical Approach

During Ricardo's lifetime, the labor theory of value ruled supreme, but soon after it was challenged by critics and weakened by "supporters." The process continued from the 1820's to the 1870's. John Stuart Mill in the 1840's and 1850's could be considered as a supporter of the labor theory only with a considerable stretch of imagination, for he identified cost of production with labor *plus* abstinence from consumption. Moreover, Mill strengthened the trend toward concentration on micro problems in a static analysis, quite alien to the classic attention to the evolution of the economy as a whole.

The main neoclassical "revolution," however, came in the 1870's with Jevons, Menger, and Walras who emphasized the theory of marginal utility to the exclusion of almost all else. These marginalists saw the problem of economics as the optimizing of production and consumer satisfaction with given amounts of labor, resources, and technology. Hence, they began with the psychological reaction of consumers to commodities, and not with the relations of man to man, as Marx always did. In fact, several of them consciously aimed at replacing Marx's growing influence.[7] The theory of marginal utility argued the influence of consumer demand on prices. It stated that consumers spend money according to the additional satisfaction (or utility) that they obtain from one additional (or marginal) unit of the products. They concluded that, under pure competition, prices would have to be proportional to the marginal utility of the products.

Alfred Marshall was the first great economist to attempt a synthesis of the classical cost of production theory (derived from the labor theory) with the marginal utility theory of the early neoclassical writers.[8] In the English-speaking countries, Marshall's was the definitive work followed in all details for many years, and is still followed by all present-day neoclassical writers in most of the important and relevant points[9] (though he is now disputed in many details, and more sophisticated Western theorists rather trace their origins to Walras[10]).

Marshall evolved the concepts of "long-run" and "short-run" time periods.[11] In the short run, production is limited to present capacity because the time is too short for new investment to result in more available capital or greater capacity to produce. The long run is a long enough time for new investment to put more capital goods in place and expand the capacity to produce.

THE LONG RUN

In the long run, says Marshall, the "price" equals the "cost" of production (including an average profit).[12] If profit is above average in one industry because of high prices, capital moves (assuming pure competition) into this industry so that increased competition in supply lowers prices till they equal costs. If profit is below average in one industry because of low prices, capital moves out of that industry so that restricted competition in supply raises prices till they equal costs.

What is the importance of the demand for goods or their utility to consumers in this case?[13] Suppose that for some reason radios suddenly become twice as desirable to consumers. We would then argue that the demand for radios would double at any given price. If we were selling a million radios for a dollar apiece, we could now sell the million radios for two dollars apiece. In the long run, however, two million radios will be built, and the cost per unit for the second million radios will be the same as for the first million radios (because Marshall assumes, as the simplest case, constant costs at any scale). There is then no reason in a purely competitive system for the price to change in the long run (so long as there is no change in the technology of production). Therefore, in the long run, a change in utility or consumer demand will change the amount of production of a particular commodity, and will thereby change the allocation of resources. *The change in demand, however, will have no effect on the long-run price (or "value") of that commodity.*

THE SHORT RUN

In Marshall's "short run," supply can be expanded or contracted within the limits of existing factories and equipment.[14] The cost may vary as supply varies, but for any given supply, it is fixed. As we approach a "maximum" or very intensive use of capacity, the cost per unit tends to increase. Thus, as output rises in the short run, the additional cost per unit must rise. On the other hand, it is a platitude that to sell the higher output, the industry must lower its prices. Thus, as output rises in the short run, the additional revenue per unit must fall. As a result, a point is reached where rising costs per unit and falling prices per unit mean an end to additional profit from additional output; that is, profit is at its highest point and will fall if more is produced. Therefore, output and prices are set at this point where no additional profit is to be made by producing more output. In the short run, then, price is set by both demand and cost conditions. Nevertheless, in the long run price is set by cost alone (under certain simplifying assumptions).

History of the Debate on Value

Soon after the third volume of Marx's *Capital* was published in 1894, important attacks were made on it by prominent economists. The most famous of all was the criticism by von Bohm-Bawerk.[15] In his attack, von Bohm-Bawerk claims that the marginal utility theory is the only valid theory of value; that the labor theory of value is contradicted by the facts of relative prices; and that Marx's qualifications to the labor theory (especially in the third volume of *Capital*, discussed below) are in complete conflict with his basic theory of value (stated in the first volume of *Capital*).

The fact that one of the first uses of neoclassical theory was in an overall attack on Marxism brought immediate Marxist attacks on it.[16] By the 1900's, when the two sides had crystallized, there was no chance for a fruitful discussion between them nor for any open-minded consideration of one by the other. It was this tradition which helped freeze the dogmatic Soviet position until very recently. The dogmatic Marxist answer admits nothing and challenges each of von Bohm-Bawerk's arguments. On the one side, they argue that Marx's qualifications to the labor theory merely complicate, but do not contradict his basic theory of value; and that this theory is in very good accord with the economic reality.

On the other side, Marxists attack the marginal utility theory on many different grounds.[17] In the first place, they attack the motivations of its founders, claiming that its only reason for being is the refutation of Marx. Second, they criticize its social and ethical connotations and conclusions— that is, the defense of capitalism and private profit. (Though it is true that the early marginalists drew such conclusions, it is not so clear that these conclusions are a *necessary* result of their technical analysis.) Finally, the Marxists criticize the methodology of marginal utility economics. It is a subjective theory, and lacks the objective measure of labor expended. It is very formal and technical, and far from the real problems of political economy. Conceding all these criticisms, it should be noted that they do not amount to a refutation of the early marginal utility theory, much less to the modern formulations of it in conjunction with marginal productivity and long-run cost of production.

CONTEMPORARY VIEWS

Most conservative neoclassical economists continue to argue that Marxism is all wrong and in complete contradiction to neoclassical economics.[18] Similarly, most dogmatic Marxists continue to argue that neoclassical economics is all wrong and in complete contradiction to Marxist economics.[19]

Many liberal neoclassical economists argue that Marxist economics is a very special case within the framework of neoclassical economics, that its price theory agrees with neoclassical theory under very restricted assumptions.[20] On the other hand, most nondogmatic Marxists consider neoclassical economics as a technical adjunct to Marxism, with a very restricted field of vision (tied to a faulty ideology).[21] These two views are not necessarily contradictory. Radicals may consider that neoclassical price and allocation theory is a useful adjunct to the broader Marxist view of the political-economic evolution of capitalism. Yet we may still recognize that Marx's own statements on price theory represent a special and limited case within neoclassical price theory.

Neoclassical theory is best developed in the short-run, static analysis of micro economic problems; it studies the economics of maximization of output from given resources, and may therefore be useful to factory managers in capitalism or socialism (or socialist planners). Marxist theory holds primarily as an analysis of the basic institutions and the dynamics of the economy as a whole; it is therefore most useful in understanding such macro economic problems as the business cycle and the long-run evolution of capitalism.

43

Marxist Price Theory as a Special Case of Neoclassical Price Theory

Marx's labor theory of value states that individual prices are proportionate to the labor expended in the production of the product. This is a special case of neoclassical price theory in which:

1. There is pure and perfect competition
2. Prices are in long-run equilibrium
3. There is a demand for each commodity, specifically, the labor expended in each industry is only that which is "socially necessary" in the sense that it is proportionate to the demand for that product (at its long-run price)
4. The labor expended in each industry is also "socially necessary" in another sense, that the average available technology is employed
5. Labor is homogeneous, or the labor employed in each industry (and firm) is of average quality
6. All industries have a uniform ratio of expenditure for living labor power to expenditure on plant, equipment, and raw materials used up in production per unit of output
7. There is a constant level of cost per unit of output at any level of long-run output

These seven points are discussed in detail in Appendix 1.

We conclude from this analysis that Marxist price theory and neoclassical price theory are perfectly compatible. To analyze one actual set of prices, however, the Marxist would have to go through at least seven highly complicated approximations to take account of each of the qualifications mentioned above. Therefore, as a workable theory of relative individual prices the Marxist theory is practically impossible to use, not because it is wrong, but because it is needlessly complex to a very high degree. The progressive Marxists conclude that the neoclassical price theory may be a more useful analytic tool for understanding the narrow issues of how to set prices and allocate resources.

Recent intensive discussions, however, have shown that the neoclassical theory makes just as many unrealistic qualifications and abstractions. In fact, neoclassical theory is too abstract and complex to be actually used for the practical business of setting socialist prices, as we shall see in a later chapter. Finally, a new version of the labor theory proposed by Sraffa seems more useful than even the neoclassical theory for price analysis![22]

Neoclassical Economics as a Special Case of Marxist Political Economy

One modern American economist, Robert Campbell, contends that Marx made use of the classical theories of value up to the time of Ricardo, but that Marxists have missed the generalization and unification of value theory that came "in the late nineteenth century with the concept of general equilibrium and the reduction of all explanations to the common denominator of utility. . . ."[23] Moreover, he believes, the "new basic insight" of the utility school, that economics is "the theory of allocation of scarce resources among competing ends," was never learned by Marxists.[24] Therefore, he concludes, "the bondage of a Marxist heritage in economic theory is not so much that the Marxist view is simply wrong in one particular (i.e., that it assumes that value is created only by labor) as that it does not comprehend the basic problem of economic theory. . . ."[25]

Marx, of course, does *not* present a systematic theory of the allocation of scarce resources, though one may be *inferred* from his theory of value. He does often refer to the allocation of capital among industries according to the profitability of the different industries, which in turn would be a function of the given distribution of consumer demand.[26] For the most part, though, it is true that Marx did not emphasize demand, let alone changes in demand; nor did he consider in detail the problems of producing proportionate to that demand; nor did he consider at all the related problems of choice among scarce resources and capital. In fact, Marx never did discuss in detail the marginal utility "revolution" of the 1870's, which occurred late in his lifetime. His scathing references to the utility theories of the "vulgar economists" concern the much earlier and superficial versions, and do not relate to marginal utility theory. Engels did mention marginal utility in a critical vein a few times in the voluminous letters of his later years.[27]

Nondogmatic Marxists nowadays admit that, with respect to the allocation of scarce resources, the neoclassical economists "have developed a price theory which is more useful in this sphere than anything to be found in Marx or his followers."[28] Yet the allocation of scarce resources on the basis of micro price theory is not the whole of economics, and certainly far from the whole of political-economy.

Marx would never have agreed that allocation of scarce resources is *the* basic problem of economics (though it is related to the distribution of income and other basic problems). In capitalism this problem appears mainly as a *technical*-economic problem for a single firm, a so-called micro problem. Marx, however, was simply not interested in the technical micro problems of the capitalist firm, such as where to invest, what technology to use, how much to produce, or how many workers to hire. Marx was interested in the *political*-economic problems of the economy as a whole, so-called macro problems of strategy for government or for whole economic classes.

What is it that makes people keep reading Marx while other economists gather dust on the shelves? Even in the abstruse subject of value, Marx sees human relations where other economists see statistics and graphs. Human beings make commodities; commodities do not make human beings (though it often feels that way in our upside-down, commodity-oriented society).

Suppose we ask a neoclassical economist what determines the price of a ton of steel. He will tell us about the demand in the market, derived from the demand of consumers for pots and pans and so forth. He will tell us about the cost of supply in terms of the dollars and cents of each commodity and service going into the steel.

But if we ask Marx, he gives us an agonizingly real picture of the steel worker, stripped to the waist and dripping sweat, working at the furnace. If we ask about the cost of the furnace and other precision machinery, then he paints the picture of the painstakingly careful labor that went into its production. He will also call our attention, as we shall see in the next chapter, to the miserable wages paid the steel worker, and to the immense profits of the capitalist owner (who may be merely clipping coupons a long way from the steel plant). Thus Marx is concerned with the underlying *human* relations in the production process. It is in this sense that he thinks of the expenditure of human labor as underlying the value of goods. The important thing he gives to us is a view of human relationships, not a metaphysical statement about the determination of prices "beyond supply and demand." Unfortunately, many of his followers have lost the human insight, and only retained the absolute, metaphysical statement about value when they try to state Marx in "pure" economic language.

Marxism may use a crude price theory, but the scope of its political economy is unbelievably broader than the abstract and narrow world of neoclassical economics. Leaving aside social and political struggles for the moment, Marxist economics long ago criticized neoclassical and classical economics in the same way that Keynesians do now. Marx pointed out that capitalism faces a strange new problem unheard of in previous societies: not the scarcity of output and resources, but the excess of output and resources relative to the effective money demand for them. This problem opens up a whole new field of economics, the Alice-in-Wonderland economics of business cycles, general unemployment, depression and inflation, and lack of aggregate excess of demand. It is then apparent that the main body of neoclassical analysis is limited to the rare and accidental case of an exact full-employment equilibrium of aggregate supply and demand.

Furthermore, most neoclassical analysis limited itself to the activities of particular enterprises and their interactions. Very little neoclassical analysis is devoted to aggregate economic events, the area which Marx investigated in a very detailed and comprehensive manner. The few neoclassical concepts concerning aggregate economics, such as the celebrated Say's Law (discussed in Chapter 7), have since been shown to be both superficial and inaccurate. These same concepts, as they existed in classical economics, were sarcastically dissected by Marx a hundred years ago.

Moreover, neoclassical price theory usually limits itself to a static picture, disregarding time. At best, it compares two such static pictures. Marx always concentrates on movement, As we shall see, he presents very detailed theories, both of short-run business cycle movements, and of the long-run evolution of capitalism.

Finally, neoclassical theory always remains at the level of *technical* economics, concerned with the price and production relationships between commodities (though it implies, usually in a devious and hidden manner, a very particular political ideology in defense of the status quo). Marx wrote openly on the vast problems of *political*-economy, concerned with the social relationships between men; *for this purpose micro price theory is only a small and not too important tool.* Marx explores the basic institutions of capitalism, asking which class of men own the means of production, and which class of men exert labor power and do the productive work. What are the economic links binding the two classes together? What human relationships are reflected in the value of commodities?

Neoclassical economics has nothing to say about the role of government, except the common belief that the economy will work automatically and well without any government (except to guard private property). Long before Keynes, Marx recognized the immense economic role played by governments in capitalism, in aiding the initial development of many industries as well as in measures to mitigate the business cycle

Of course, modern Keynesian economics has a much more precise knowledge of the technical possibilities open to government intervention in capitalism. But Marx's political economy goes further to discuss an aspect of government in capitalism which Keynes never recognized. Marx discussed the determination of government policy and structure by the nature of the economic relationships (analyzed here in a later chapter). In other words, Marxists emphasize that the technical possibilities apparently open to government are in reality drastically limited by the political and economic self-interest of the ruling capitalist class (both domestically and in the network of imperialist relationships abroad).

NOTES

1. Joan Robinson, *An Essay on Marxian Economics* (New York: St. Martin's Press, 1960, first ed. 1942), p. xi.
2. Adam Smith, *The Wealth of Nations* (New York: Modern Library, 1937, first publ. 1776), p. 30.
3. David Ricardo, *Principles of Political Economy and Taxation*, ed. by P. Sraffa

and M. Dobb (Cambridge: Cambridge University Press, 1953, first publ. 1821), p. 5. Also see George Stigler, "Ricardo and the 93 Percent Labor Theory of Value," *American Economic Review*, 48 (June 1958): 357–367.

4. See, e.g., Eric Roll, *A History of Economic Thought* (New York: Prentice-Hall, 1942); also see Ronald Meek, *Studies in the Labor Theory of Value* (New York: International Publishers, 1956).

5. See Karl Marx, *Capital* (Chicago: Charles H. Kerr and Co., 1906, vol. 1, first publ. in German 1867), vol. 1, part 1. Whenever there is a reference hereafter to *Capital*, vols. 1, 2, or 3, it will be to the Charles H. Kerr edition.

6. See, e.g., Paul Sweezy, *The Theory of Capitalist Development* (New York: Monthly Review Press, first publ. 1942), Chapter 3.

7. R. Meek, *Studies in the Labor Theory of Value, op. cit.*, pp. 250–251. For the contrary view, see Martin Bronfenbrenner, "Marxian Influences in 'Bourgeois' Economics," *American Economic Review*, 57 (May 1967), 624–635.

8. Alfred Marshall, *Principles of Economics* (New York: The Macmillan Co., 1953, first ed. 1890).

9. See any modern text on microeconomics, e.g., Paul Samuelson, *Economics* (New York: McGraw-Hill Book Co., 1970).

10. Leon Walras, *Elements of Pure Theory* (Homewood, Ill.: R. D. Irwin, transl. 1954, first publ. 1874).

11. Marshall, *op. cit.*, p. 330.

12. *Ibid.*, pp. 337–350; 503.

13. *Ibid.*, pp. 348–349.

14. *Ibid.*, pp. 337–350; 363–380.

15. Eugen von Bohm-Bawerk, *Karl Marx and the Close of His System*, ed. by Paul Sweezy (New York: A. M. Kelley, 1949, first publ. 1897).

16. See, e.g., Louis Boudin, *The Theoretical System of Karl Marx* (New York: Monthly Review Press, 1968, first publ. 1907).

17. See, e.g., Meek, *op. cit.*, pp. 243–256.

18. See, e.g., Robert Campbell, "Marx, Kantorovich, and Novozhilov," *Slavic Review*, 20 (October 1961): 403.

19. See, e.g., *Political Economy*, a textbook issued by the Institute of Economics of the Academy of Sciences of the USSR (London: Lawrence and Wishart, 1957), pp. 389–396.

20. See, e.g., the brief but pithy comment by R.D. Dickinson, "Notes to Article by L. Johansen, 'Labour Theory of Value and Marginal Utilities,'" *Economics of Planning*, 3 (December 1963): 239–240.

21. See, e.g., Oskar Lange, "Marxian Economics and Modern Economic Theory," *Review of Economic Studies*, 2 (June 1935): 189–201.

22. Piero Sraffa, *Productions of Commodities by Means of Commodities* (Cambridge: Cambridge University Press, 1960). See other references to Chapter 5.

23. Robert W. Campbell, *loc. cit.*

24. *Ibid.*, p. 404.

25. *Ibid.*, p. 404.

26. Marx did use the concepts of relative prices and general equilibrium in *Value, Price, and Profit*, when it was necessary to refute the wages-fund doctrine.

27. All the scattered references of Marx and Engels to this subject are mentioned in P. J. D. Miles, *The Political Economy of Communism* (Cambridge: Harvard University Press, 1964), pp. 50–51.

28. Sweezy, *op, cit.*, p. 129.

CHAPTER
5

Poverty and Exploitation

The value theories developed in Chapter 3 may have seemed tame and neutral politically. Here, however, we shall see that these have very different implications and ideological positions on some highly controversial issues: how capitalists make profits and whether workers are "exploited." Before probing these problems in theory, it is helpful to state the present factual situation to which they are relevant.

Poverty and Inequality in America

Everyone knows that much of the world lives in poverty, but it is more surprising to learn of the vast amount of poverty in the richest country in the world. In 1966 in absolute figures, 14 per cent of all American families had less than $3,000 income; 46 per cent had less than $7,000 income; and 59 per cent had less than $9,000 income.[1] What do these figures mean in human terms?

According to the definition of the Social Security Administration, an urban family of four persons was below the poverty line if it had an income below $3,150 in 1966. This definition, however, is much too narrow. It is based on an "economy diet . . . meant for emergency or temporary use when funds are low—in other words a diet which over long periods of time does not meet minimum nutritional requirements."[2] Yet more than 24,836,000 Americans were below that poverty line.[3] This means that most of them were undernourished, insufficiently clothed against the weather, and lived in rat-infested slums—and obviously could not support their children through a good higher education.

The Bureau of Labor Statistics calculates a "moderate but adequate city worker's family budget." It is certainly not extravagant: it assumes that clothes are replaced only after three years' time, and that the worker runs a used car or uses public transport. Furthermore, it permits only a movie every two or three weeks, only books and materials as school expenses, allows nothing for college and no saving for emergencies.[4] Because of inflation, even this limited budget was calculated as $9,100 for 1966; which meant that 59.4 per cent of American families fell below that line.

Besides these absolute low income levels, the relative inequality of income distribution is even more striking, as revealed by the official data in Table 5–1.

TABLE 5-1

Inequality of Income Distribution, U.S.A., 1966

	PERCENTAGE OF INCOME RECEIVED BY EACH FIFTH (20%) OF FAMILIES	PERCENTAGE OF INDIVIDUAL INCOME RECEIVED BY EACH FIFTH (20%) OF UNRELATED INDIVIDUALS
lowest	5.4	2.9
second	12.4	7.6
middle	17.7	13.3
fourth	23.8	24.2
highest	40.7	52.0
Total	100.0	100.0
top 5%	14.8	21.8

Source: U.S. Bureau of the Census, *Statistical Abstract of the United States: 1968* (Washington, D.C., 1968), p. 324.

On one side are the very poor, the lowest 20 per cent of families with 5.4 per cent of all family income (and the lowest 20 per cent of unrelated individuals with only 2.9 per cent of all individual income). On the other side are the rich, the top 5 per cent of families with almost 15 per cent of all family income (and the top 5 per cent of unrelated individuals with almost 22 per cent of all individual income). Then there are the "elite," the very rich; these are the top 2 per cent whose incomes are above $25,000 per family. Finally, there are the very, very rich; those were the mere 0.08 per cent of all taxpayers who had over $200,000 income in 1966.

Because income is highly concentrated, so also is saving. A small number of individuals and firms do most of the saving and investment of capital in the United States. In 1965 personal saving by individuals in America was only 25 billion dollars, whereas saving by businesses and corporations was 83 billion dollars. Even within the category of personal savings, households in the lower two-thirds of the income range did no saving at all!

On the contrary, most of these two-thirds consumed more than their total income. More than half of all the personal savings available for investment were supplied by those in the upper 5 per cent income bracket.

Class and Income Distribution

Classes are defined here in terms of their relations to the productive process. "Classes are groups of people such that one group can appropriate the labour of another because of their different positions in a definite structure of social economy."[5] The capitalist class is defined as that group which owns the capital goods: the factories, machines, and raw materials. The working class is that group which sells its ability to labor to the capitalist. In later chapters concerning political analysis, we shall have to examine many social and psychological factors related to class, and shall have to deal with many intermediate groups. Here we wish merely to see the relations between class, as roughly defined in purely economic terms, and income.

Income is not randomly distributed among all individuals. On the contrary, income distribution is closely related to the type of income. Does most of a recipient's income come from labor, such as wage income; or does it come from property, such as rent, interest, or profits? Knowing this fact about a recipient, we can make a good guess about his income bracket.

Almost all the bottom 59.4 per cent of families in 1966, those with less than the "moderate but adequate" budget, were working class families. Most of their income came from wages and salaries earned by their labor. On the other hand, most of the income of the top 2 per cent came from ownership of property in the form of rent, interest, or profit—in short, the income of the capital class. Moreover, the very, very rich elite in 1966—those less than one-tenth (0.08 per cent) of all the taxpayers who had over $200,000 income—collected 23 per cent of all dividends and 37 per cent of all capital gains. Fully, 90 per cent of the income in that tax bracket was from property, and only 10 per cent of their income was from wages and salaries.[6]

Privately held wealth is even more concentrated than current income. Three American academic economists estimated in 1953 that only 0.2 per cent of "spending units" (that is, one in 500 individuals or families reporting to the Internal Revenue Service) own 65 to 71 per cent of all publicly held stock.[7] Another conservatively calculated estimate finds that in 1956 some one-fourth of all American privately owned wealth was

51

owned by only ½ of 1 per cent of all Americans.[8] The same study found that just 1.6 per cent of the people held 32 per cent of the wealth, including 82 per cent of all stock.

Notice the cumulative and self-reinforcing nature of the concentration of wealth and income. The high concentration of stock ownership leads to a high concentration of income from profits. This income is so concentrated that its recipients are in the highest income brackets. But it is only these higher income brackets that are able to save significant amounts. Therefore, they are the ones who make large investments, thus increasing their stock ownership. In other words, large ownership of stock leads to high income in the form of profits; but high income leads to more stock ownership.

The process of wealth and income concentration is self-reinforcing in other ways. For example, one vital prerequisite of upward mobility is education. But many careful studies have revealed that in a large percentage of cases "the father's income rather than the boy's brains determines who shall be college trained."[9] If you are poor, it is hard to support yourself through college even with average intelligence. If you are rich but not bright enough to get into top universities, you can always find some private university willing to accept you for enough money.

Even with an education, though, the poor man can only attempt to work his way up in business from the point at which he is hired. The rich heir to a business may have little education and less intelligence, but may still step into his father's shoes if he controls enough stock in the corporation. "It is very difficult to climb to the top. . . . It is easier and much safer to be born there."[10] In fact, many of the wealthy today merely inherited a great deal of stock. From 1900 to 1950 some 70 per cent of the fathers of the very rich were big businessmen.[11] It is true that most of the very rich have "worked" as big businessmen; nevertheless, completely leisured coupon-clippers increased from 14 per cent of the very rich in 1900 to 26 per cent by 1950.[12]

There has also been a long-run trend toward less self-employment, with more people simply employees of businesses. In 1800, perhaps 80 per cent of the occupied population were self-employed entrepreneurs.[13] By 1870 only 33 per cent of the occupied population were self-employed entrepreneurs. By 1940 all self-employed entrepreneurs were only 20 per cent of the occupied population. This self-employed category includes all businessmen (big and small), all farmers (big and small), and all independent professionals. The percentage of those whose income came mostly from work for others thus rose from about 20 per cent of the occupied population in 1800 to 67 per cent in 1870 to 80 per cent in 1940. This trend has continued in recent years.

Theories of Income Distribution

Adam Smith talked about *rent* going to the owners of land, *wages* going to labor, and *profits* going to the owners of capital. What determines the share if each of these types of income in the net national income? This fundamental question has received various answers from economists, differing greatly according to their basic world views. In fact, there are really two closely related questions: (1) What determines the share of each type of income? and (2) Is the present distribution of income among different types good or bad?

To simplify the question a bit, we shall ignore in this chapter the rent of land. In the modern United States and most industrialized economies, the rent of land is a very small category, so we can ignore it without leaving out an essential piece of the argument. That leaves Adam Smith's two categories of wages and profits. We define "wages" to mean all labor income, including time and piece wages, monthly salaries, commissions, bonuses, and managerial salaries. We define "profits" to mean all the return on capital. For the purposes of this argument we include as profits both the return on the entrepreneur's own capital (called dividends), and the return on borrowed capital (called interest). For some other purposes in later chapters, it will be necessary to distinguish these two forms of profits. "Capital" is the money used to buy factories, machinery, and raw materials.

Adam Smith seems to have two distinct views of profits and wages mixed together in various places. On the one hand, he speaks of wages as equal to the necessary subsistence of the worker; he viewed the whole product as due to the worker's labor, and thus considered profits as a "residual" surplus after paying wages. On the other hand, he frequently spoke of wages as a cost of procuring labor, and profits as a "cost" of procuring capital.

The notion that profits are a mere residue or deduction from the workers' product led directly to Marx's view of profit as exploitation. This view is the forerunner of the modern radical viewpoint. The other notion, which was emphasized more in Smith's own work and in the other classical economists, was that profit was a just and natural cost of production. It led eventually to the neoclassical idea of profits as equal to the marginal product of capital. This idea of profits as a justified cost is the forerunner of the modern conservative viewpoint.

The concept of profit as a cost of production was developed further in the 1820's by the economists W. Senior and J. B. Say. They each argued that provision of capital for production is a subjective cost to the capitalist.

The capitalist practices abstinence from consumption in order to invest capital; therefore he is morally justified in making a profit from his investment. At the same time they argued that prices are the result of the utility that a product has for consumers, and the payment to capital and labor results from the need to use them to produce the final product—so the demand for capital and labor is a demand that is *derived* from the demand for products to satisfy the consumer. Thus prices result from subjective consumer desires (or utilities), and costs result from subjective unpleasantness (or disutility) in providing labor (hard work) and capital (abstinence).

Surplus Value

Quite different was the view of Karl Marx propounded in the 1850's and 1860's.[14] Marx stated that commodities derived their value solely from the labor put into them. Workers were paid only their necessary value in the marketplace, that is, the value of their means of subsistence. Profit is the "surplus value" or residue of the worker's product that remains after the worker is paid.

Marx finds a confusion in Adam Smith's version of the labor value approach to wages and profits. If all products, including labor, are bought and sold at their labor value, how is it possible to make a profit? If, for example, a chair takes a total of eight labor hours to produce, and if it is exchanged for other products (or money) also produced by eight hours of labor, where is the profit? If a capitalist hires a worker for eight hours, pays him for eight hours, and sells the product for eight hours' value, how can he make a profit? Yet Marx resolutely stands by the labor theory of value and does *not* argue that the capitalist normally makes profit either by cheating the consumer or by cheating the worker (if "cheating" means buying or selling below or above value). On the contrary, Marx argues that the capitalist normally makes his profit by selling the product at *its* value, while buying the worker's power to labor or labor power at *its* value.

Marx's point rests on a very simple distinction, which he claims was overlooked by Adam Smith and most of the classical economists. There is a difference between the value of what the worker produces and the value of the worker's own ability to labor (or his labor power). The wage of the worker, or the value of his labor power, is determined by the labor expended in producing the worker. That labor includes what is necessary for his food, clothing, shelter, and education as well as the food, clothing, shelter, and education of his family (under the conditions and traditions of the given time and place).

The worker's labor embodied in the final product, however, is much greater than the labor that is required to keep the workers functioning. In other words, a worker produces far more in a day than the wages paid to keep him alive and functioning. In Marx's terms, the value produced is much greater than the "necessary value" to pay for the worker's own subsistence. This difference is profit or "surplus value," which reflects the objective fact of excess labor expended by the worker. (Of course, for Marx—and all other economists—what is divided is only the *net* product, after deduction for depreciation of machinery and depletion of raw material inventories.)

Certainly, we may question Marx further. Even if all other products are sold at their cost of production in terms of labor hours, what makes Marx think that the worker's labor power is sold at his own cost of production in labor hours? For other commodities, one can argue that they exchange according to their labor cost on the basis of competitive equalization of prices and profits by supply and demand. Isn't it true, however, that the supply and demand for labor have many unique features? Suppose wages are above or below the long-run labor value of the worker. Will this automatically raise or lower the supply of labor?

Only if we accept Malthus's theory of population will a rise in real wages lead to a population rise (due to our animal instincts to produce more babies), and a fall in real wages lead automatically to a decline in population (due to starvation and plague).[15] Marx called this theory a libel on the human race and certainly did not believe in it.[16] Marx rather argued that wages are kept down by a reserve army of unemployed. This reservoir of workers is kept filled by constant technological innovations, which reduce the demand for workers. This explanation, however, is much looser than the rigid Malthusian statement. In Marx's view, certain counteracting forces may allow some part of increasing productivity to become part of workers' wages. The counteracting forces would include trade union activity, a swift enough rise in demand for products, and government intervention.

Cost of Production Theory

Alfred Marshall in the 1870's combatted Marx's labor theory with a far more sophisticated version of the view first put forth by Say and Senior. Marshall substituted the word "waiting" for "abstinence," but still considered a normal profit (or interest on the entrepreneur's own capital) to be part of the long-run "cost" of production. He admitted that this semantic change was in part a direct result of the ridicule with which Marx treated the concept of the "abstinence" of the rich capitalist as an apologia for profit.[17] But the difference is perhaps more than a word.

Those who speak of "abstinence" think of a real sacrifice of consumption in order to invest. Marshall simply emphasized the time factor involved in "waiting" for the return on the investment, which meant that the availability from profits of more funds for future consumption must be balanced against less funds for present consumption. Marshall criticized Marx's labor theory on this basis, saying:

it is not true that the spinning of yarn in a factory, after allowance has been made for the wear-and-tear of the machinery, is the product of the labour of the operatives. It is the product of their labour, together with that of the employer and subordinate managers, and of the capital employed; and that capital itself is the product of labour and waiting; and therefore the spinning is the product of labour of many kinds, and of waiting.[18]

Furthermore, Marshall himself and his followers up through Keynes gave the story much more of a pragmatic or operational twist. *If* we have the institution of private property, then a profit is a necessary cost to the society of inducing the capitalist to part with his liquidity while waiting for the return of his investment and the interest on it. This view is slightly more neutral (or at least more sophisticated) with respect to class conflict than the earlier dogma of profits as the justifiable reward for abstinence.

Marginal Productivity

We have seen that J. B. Say in a crude form, and Marshall in a more elegant form, argued that profits and wages are both costs of production. These writers discussed most of the elements that appeared as the modern theory of marginal productivity in the writings of John Bates Clark (1847–1938). Clark's most important book, *The Distribution of Wealth* (1899), is dedicated to the proposition that workers and capitalists each receive in income exactly what they contribute as their marginal product. In other words, a worker's wage will just equal the additional (or marginal) product he adds to output. Likewise, the profit of the capitalist will just equal the additional (or marginal) amount of product added by the piece of capital that he adds to the productive process.

The argument is very simple. Suppose there is a fixed amount of capital (a given factory and machinery). Suppose we ask how many workers should be added by the rational capitalist to maximize his profits. Suppose each additional worker adds something to the product, but that each additional worker adds less than the one before him. This is so because there are only so many machines for them to use, so they can add very little beyond the optimum capacity of the given factory. Keeping the same number of machines, as the capitalist adds workers, their additional product will probably decline. In this case, the capitalist should then continue to add workers until he finds the product of the last worker is just equal to his cost or wage. In that case, the last worker makes no additional profit for the capitalist. Therefore, he should hire no more workers. Therefore, the wage will just equal the additional (or marginal) product of the last worker.

Notice that what Clark has arrived at is a rule for the capitalist to follow if he wishes to maximize his profits. If he does act this way (and he usually does), then it is a platitude that the wage is the same as the marginal product—workers are not hired if they produce a lower marginal product. Clark thought that he had thereby proven that this is a just and ethical distribution of income. Clark does the same thing for profits. In Clark's simple example, each additional machine adds less to the product than the previous machine (because workers and perhaps factory space are limited). In that case, the capitalist should only add machines till the additional product of one more machine will just equal its cost. Beyond that point, more machines give no more profit, so no more machines should be bought. Therefore, the cost of providing an additional machine (whether out of the capitalist's own capital or from borrowed capital) will just equal the value of its additional (or marginal) product. He concludes that what is paid to labor is *its* own marginal product. Therefore, there is no such thing as exploitation.

This conservative theory is followed by most of the present textbooks of economics. The most widely used textbook at this time is that written by Paul Samuelson, who says: "After allowing for all depreciation requirements, capital has a *net productivity*."[19] By this, he just means that (1) machines as well as labor must be used to produce anything in modern industry, and (2) the use of more machines will increase the product per worker. In this way, he leads into the theory of marginal productivity, and specifically endorses Clark's theory of income distribution. He states the basic theory just as Clark did, except that he is a little more careful about the political-ethical conclusions. He still leaves the strong impression in the reader that this theory proves that everyone is paid their "just income" according to their contribution.

Radical Critique of Marginal Productivity Theory

It is important to give the devil his due. Samuelson does show that marginal productivity theory does give a general notion of how to allocate resources. It tells the capitalist to keep hiring workers (or adding machines) as long as they produce extra profit. When the additional profit approaches zero (because the additional product drops down to the cost level), then the capitalist should stop adding workers, and the same argument tells him when to stop adding machines.

Samuelson also shows that these are useful rules for socialist managers or socialist planners to follow in allocating resources among different possible investment projects. They must "introduce first those investment projects with the higher net productivity."[20] They must use every additional worker and every additional machine in each project just up to the point where an additional unit would cost more than it adds to the product. In relation to the allocation of capital (factories and machines), this means that socialist planners must use something like a profit or interest rate to calculate which projects will bring the most return to society, and which have returns too low to warrant investment. Finally, Samuelson adds quietly a point about interest or profits under socialist planning which should be loudly and repeatedly stressed: "But, of course, no one necessarily receives interest income from them."[21] In other words, a planned socialist economy would have to calculate rates of return on different uses of capital to decide where to allocate it, *but it would not have to distribute any of these returns as income to any individual.*

We are concerned here, not with the allocation of resources, but with the distribution of income to individuals. What we mean by exploitation is that, under capitalism, capitalists own resources, but put forth no effort, yet receive a large share of national income. In supporting the argument that workers are exploited, radicals have attacked the marginal productivity theory on several levels: (1) that it is a tautology; (2) that the marginal product of capital can't really be measured; and (3) that it confuses the productivity of capital and the productivity of the capitalist.

On the first level, it was indicated earlier that, given its assumptions, the analytic conclusions of marginal productivity follow practically by definition (but not its political-ethical conclusions). If it is assumed that the capitalist always acts to maximize profit, then he will never hire an additional worker who would cost more than he produces. He will only keep hiring workers who produce a surplus above their wages. If the product of the last worker hired is defined to be the marginal product, then it follows that his wage must be equal to that, neither more nor less. Similarly, a unit of capital will be utilized only if the additional product from its use equals the additional cost of its use. Given the assumption of profit maximization, these are tautologies which use an odd terminology to describe a logical result: they are tautologies in the sense that the conclusions are hidden in the definitions. But, of course, such tautologies tell us little or nothing of the real world, and do not automatically lead to *any* policy conclusions.

Second, many recent critics have argued that the theory is unrealistic, since it does not refer to anything measurable .What is meant by a "unit of capital"? If it means a particular machine, how can we talk about moving it to a better use? Particular machines are designed to do particular jobs. If we find that its marginal product is less than its cost in this industry, how can it be moved to another industry, since it is not designed for other work? Furthermore, the theory assumes that you can add or subtract small units of capital at the margin. But most machines are a very considerable investment, so we cannot pretend that they are infinitely divisible.

Third, even admitting that the theory says something about how capitalists should invest, and that it has some roughly definable meaning, still it only tells us about the production contributions of labor and capital; it says *nothing* about the contribution of the capitalist. This is probably the most important point of criticism. Radicals admit that a machine may increase production, that workers need them, and that they increase the productivity of the worker. In that sense Samuelson is right to say that "capital" has a "net productivity." But it is the physical capital that is productive (jointly with the worker), and *not* the capitalist. The capitalist owns the capital, but he is not himself the machine. The machine does the work (with the worker); the capitalist gets the profit.

In any society it is correct to allocate machines so that the rate of return from adding one machine equals its cost. But that does not say that we need to have a society where private capitalists provide the money to buy the machines. It certainly does not say that the rate of profit (of the capitalist) is just because it equals the marginal product of the capital. This theory provides a certain description of the process of allocation of capital, but adds nothing to the older ethical justifications of profit income in terms of the "abstinence" or "waiting" of the capitalist.

It is true, as Marshall said in an attack on Marx, that "if we admit that it [the value of the commodity] is the product of labour alone, and not of labour and waiting, we can no doubt be compelled by inexorable logic to admit that there is no justification for interest, the reward of waiting; for the conclusion is implied in the premise."[22] The implication of the "waiting" theory of interest or profits is that the capitalist has a moral right to a part of the product. On the contrary, that the capitalist takes part of the product produced by the workers is "exploitation" in the radical view (and must lead to poverty, alienation, and eventual workers' revolution).

Radicals agree that the actual machines are a necessary or "productive" part of the physical productive process; they would even agree to the importance of managerial labor. Radicals argue, however, that this productivity of physical capital goods (created by another labor process in the past) is quite different from the ability of capitalist owners to capture a

59

certain portion of the product as interest or profit. "It is, of course, true that materials and machinery can be said to be physically productive in the sense that labor working with them can turn out a larger product than labor working without them, but physical productivity in this sense must under no circumstances be confused with value productivity."[23] In other words, "under capitalism 'the productiveness of labor is made to ripen, as if in a hot-house.' Whether we choose to say that capital is productive, or that capital is necessary to make labor productive, is not a matter of much importance. . . . What is important is to say that owning capital is not a productive activity."[24] This is clear in the case of a mere coupon-clipper (as most stockowners are today). The fact that some of them may otherwise perform productive labor through their own managerial work is not in contradiction to the fact that they also make money by mere ownership of capital.

The Division of Income between Wages and Profits

The radical view of income distribution begins with consideration of the labor of humanity operating on nature as the ultimate source of all production. The radical interpretations of profit and wages emphasize the sociological facts that *the capitalist class has a monopoly of the means of production, whereas the working class owns only its own labor power. Assuming* these institutional conditions, the capitalists *must* be paid a profit or they will not invest their capital (or, if you wish, under these conditions they are able to extract or "exploit" this profit from the social product). This is not a quantitative economic theory of prices and wages, but primarily an historical or political-economic statement of the qualitative relationships of "capitalism."[25] Profit is not traced to a single "cause," but to the functioning of the capitalist economy as a whole within the given class and institutional framework. Profits are viewed as the residual product after wages are paid.

In the theory of wages radical economists do not merely state that the worker is paid the "value" of his labor power, for this is an unproven catechism. The practical problem is to explain why long-run wages remain at a level that does not eat up the profits of capital. In empirical terms there was an amazing degree of agreement concerning the wage level among nineteenth century economists. It is not Marx but Marshall who states: "If the economic conditions of the country remain stationary sufficiently long, . . . human beings would earn generally an amount that corresponded fairly well with their cost of rearing and training, conventional necessaries as well as those things which are strictly necessary being reckoned for."[26] In other words, the long-run price of labor power is the cost of "producing" the worker (under present cultural conditions).

We saw that the United States still has "poverty," one evidence of which is the fact that the one-third of our family units with the lowest incomes goes into debt in an average year. For the wage workers as a whole, it may be claimed that the debts of some just about equal the savings of others. And we saw that most workers' families earn less than the "modest but adequate" Labor Bureau budget. Thus, it is true that consumption spending ordinarily runs 95 to 100 per cent of wages in the long run.[27] To this extent, Marx's theory of wages at "subsistence according to the cultural standard of the country" is proven. Admittedly, however, the "cultural standard" has risen greatly, so that the average American wage is not what the rest of the world would normally call a "subsistence" wage. The modern radical point really has nothing to do with physical subsistence theories. It is rather the point that workers' wages seem to just equal the minimum accepted consumption level of society. Therefore, on the average they spend all their income on consumption, and have no savings available for investment in capital.

Disagreement among economists has centered on the question of *why* the long-run wage level remains this low. Why do wages not rise till workers have the entire net product and there are no profits? As usual, we may think about the factors of supply and demand on either side of the labor market.

On the supply side, the number of workers available at the going wage depends on (1) the amount of population, (2) laws, such as those about child labor and retirement benefits, and (3) sociological attitudes, such as those toward women working. Laws and basic attitudes about work change very slowly, so we may assume they are constant. The classical economists, such as Malthus, put great stress on population in its effect on wages. High wages would lead to more births and more survivals, and the higher population would increase the supply of workers, so this would hold down wages. Radicals have mostly rejected the population factor as being of prime importance because (1) human beings do not react so directly to changes in income (at least, above the starvation level); and (2) population takes a long time to change, while wage rates change fairly often and rapidly.

On the demand side, the marginal productivity theory correctly concludes that demand for labor is much affected by changes in technology, which may substitute machines for workers. This, however, is also a small part of the causes affecting wages, mainly because technology also changes fairly slowly. It may help us to understand long-run changes in wages to some extent, but it is of no help at all in understanding, for example, why wages decline in a depression.

61

Most radical economists believe that it is most important to examine the over-all demand for goods in the economy, since that is the main determinant of the demand for labor.[28] Workers are hired only so long as the capitalist expects to sell the goods they produce. When the over-all or aggregate demand for goods is less than the supply in the market, production declines and workers are unemployed. *Unemployment of workers is the strongest factor holding down wages* (see Chapter 7).

The unemployment may be traced to lack of aggregate demand for goods, though it may be aggravated in the long run by a shift to machinery in the production of the goods. The reasons for the lack of demand are very complex, and will be discussed in later chapters concerning depressions and unemployment. It should be noted here though, that this means both that aggregate factors largely determine wages and that wages help determine the aggregate factors. It is a circular process in which (1) workers are unemployed because there is not enough demand for the goods they produce, but (2) there is not enough demand for goods partly because workers do not have enough wages to spend, and that is partly because many workers are unemployed. In other words, we shall find that demand is partly dependent on total income and partly on the distribution of income (since the poor must spend a much larger percentage of their income than the rich just to stay at minimum consumption levels).

Beyond the aggregate factors which determine the demand for workers, radicals emphasize that this is no longer a world of pure competition, but of monopoly. We shall see that the wage rate represents a bargain, within the broad limits allowed by aggregate supply and demand, between labor and capital, which is directly influenced by their relative power. On the one side stands the enormous power of the largest corporations, both in economic terms and in political influence. On the other side stands the vast numbers of workers, some unorganized and powerless, some organized into unions with a small amount of power. In Chapter 8, there is an analysis of monopoly, including its effect on wages. In addition, a later chapter deals with the immense impact of the government on the struggle over income distribution.

Tentative Conclusions

Of course, many of these factors are recognized to a small extent by neoclassical economists, and many more are recognized by the liberal wing of Keynesian economists. So all economists have some slight measure of agreement on *how* wages are determined, at least in broad analytic outlines, though we disagree violently over the importance of different factors. But when it comes to an interpretation of the facts of wage and profit income distribution, there is no agreement at all.

The political or ethical interpretation of the conservatives is still that profits are justified. They talk about the productivity of capital, and they claim that capitalists must be paid profits or else they will not *abstain* from consumption and *wait* for their returns from investment. This view is, of course, supported by all capitalists and their sympathizers.

The political or ethical view of the radicals is that profits are unjustified. They argue that capitalists merely own capital, but they themselves produce nothing. They use their monopoly of capital to *exploit* the workers by taking some of the workers' product as profits. In this view *any* profits are bad. This view is approved by many workers and by those radicals who sympathize with the workers' view.

It could be said that both sides are "merely" emphasizing different aspects of the same reality. They choose to emphasize those aspects of reality congenial to their own conclusions. Most people also tend to choose theories that are to some degree in accordance with their own interests. Even among economists, those who most loudly claim to be objective usually turn out to be the most partisan advocates when their masks are removed.

At any rate, the system of production for profits influences a great many other political, social, and economic variables in addition to the distribution of income (for example, the alienation of workers). Whether one concludes that profits are justifiable or whether one concludes that profits are the unjustifiable result of exploitation, the question remains as to whether the goodness or badness of the resulting distribution of income may be overbalanced by other aspects of the profit system.

Thus, conservatives tend to apologize for extremely unequal income distribution by saying that it is necessary for efficiency and incentives to work. They argue that the alternative, socialism, would find production inefficiently organized and workers lazy. On the other side, radicals argue that the system of private profit and limited wages is responsible not only for unequal and unjust income distribution, but also for unemployment and depression, for militarism, pollution, intensification of racism, alienation, and many other evils. Each of these issues will be discussed in later chapters.

N O T E S

1. U.S. Bureau of the Census, Dept. of Commerce, *Statistical Abstract of the United States: 1968* (Washington, D. C., 1968), p. 326.
2. Donald Light, "Income Distribution," *Occasional Papers of the Union for Radical Political Economics* (December 1969), p. 2.

3. U.S. Bureau of th Census, *op. cit.*, p. 330.

4. Light, *op. cit.*, p. 3.

5. Lenin, cited in Stanley W. Moore, *The Critique of Capitalist Democracy* (New York: Paine-Whitman Publishers, 1957), p. 24.

6. U.S. Internal Revenue Service, *Statistics of Income, 1966: Individual Income Tax Returns* (Washington, D.C.: U.S. Government Printing Office, 1968).

7. Keith Butters, Lawrence Thompson, and Lynn Bollinger, *Effect of Taxation on Investments by Individuals* (Cambridge: The Riverside Press, 1953), p. 400.

8. Robert Lampman, *The Share of Top Wealth-Holders in National Wealth* (Princeton, N.J.: Princeton University Press, 1962), p. 24.

9. C. Wright Mills, *White Collar* (New York: Oxford University Press, 1956), p. 267.

10. C. Wright Mills, *The Power Elite* (New York: Oxford University Press, 1959), p. 115.

11. *Ibid.*, p. 105.

12. *Ibid*, p. 108.

13. For this estimate and other facts in this paragraph, see Mills, *White Collar, op. cit.*, pp. 63–64.

14. Karl Marx, *Capital* (1867), vol. 1, parts 2 and 3. Marx was influenced by Hegel's concept of the alienation of labor. See Herbert Marcuse, *Reason and Revolution* (Boston: Beacon Press, 1961).

15. Reverend Thomas Malthus, *Essay on Population* (New York: E. P. Dutton & Co., 1958, first publ. 1798).

16. Marx, *Capital*, vol 1, pp. 675–677.

17. Alfred Marshall, *Principles of Economics* (New York: The Macmillan Co., 1953, first ed. 1890), p. 233.

18. Marshall, *op. cit.*, p. 587.

19. Paul Samuelson, *Economics* (New York: McGraw-Hill, 1970, 8th ed.), p. 574.

20. *Ibid.*, p. 580.

21. *Ibid.*

22. Marshall, *op. cit.*, p. 587.

23. Paul Sweezy, *The Theory of Capitalist Development* (New York: Oxford University Press, 1943), p. 61.

24. Joan Robinson, *An Essay on Marxian Economics* (New York: St. Martin's Press, 1960, first ed. 1946), p. 18.

25. See, e.g., Sweezy, *op. cit.*, pp. 23–40.

26. Marshall, *op. cit.*, p. 577.

27. Milton Friedman, *A Theory of the Consumption Function* (Princeton, N.J.: Princeton University Press, 1957), pp. 69–79.

28. See Nicholas Kaldor, "Alternative Theories of Distribution," in his *Essays on Value and Distribution* (Glencoe, Ill.: Free Press, 1960).

CHAPTER
6

Growth, Waste, and Pollution

Most Western economists now concede that Marx was the first to state the basic structure of the industrial capitalist economy as a whole (its macro economic framework).[1] In an otherwise vicious attack on Marx, a leading Western economist admits: "We can make a deposition . . . that Marx did . . . innovate two-sector models of reproduction and growth."[2] For seventy years the dominant neoclassical economists paid very little attention to the macro economic structure, since they assumed that in the economy as a whole demand would automatically equal supply. More strangely, Marxists did little to develop this area, and were mostly content to repeat the master's words or to describe current events. Interest was rekindled in Marx's macro analysis only after Keynes independently rediscovered the same aggregate relationships during the Great Depression of the 1930's[3]; and again after World War II when attention turned to long-run growth.

Static Equilibrium

Static equilibrium of the economy as a whole (or "simple reproduction" in Marx's terms) is the case of a long-run equilibrium, in which there is no change from year to year in the volume of production nor in the capacity to produce.[4] Of course, this case is fanciful, and is examined only as an aid to analysis; no static capitalist economy has ever existed.

The value of the national product from a cost point of view may be divided into spending for materials and machinery (called "constant capital" by Marx); spending for wages and salaries (or "variable capital"); and the amounts paid of profits, rent, and interest (or "surplus value").

(Marx's definitions are explored in detail in Appendix 3 to this book.) All production is also divided into two departments, according to the kind of goods produced. Department one (the investment department) produces means of production for investment in maintenance and expansion of capacity. Department two (the consumption department) produces articles of consumption. Of course, at this point the analysis neglects the consideration of purchases by government and by foreign buyers.

How do we utilize these concepts? First, we may look at the demand and supply for each department's goods under static equilibrium (or simple reproduction). Department one's investment goods are demanded for replacement of used materials and machinery in both departments. Since, by assumption, there is no expansion of either department, there is *no* net investment (that is, investment above replacement). Therefore, equilibrium under these conditions means that the aggregate demand (and the aggregate supply) for investment goods must just equal the total used-up amount of materials and machinery in the period.

Department two's consumer goods are demanded by the workers and capitalists of both departments to the extent of their total incomes. Since there is no net investment, there is no saving of income. All wages and salaries and all profits, rent, and interest are spent for consumer goods. Therefore, equilibrium in this sector means that the aggregate demand (and the aggregate supply) for consumption goods must just equal the total wages and salaries paid to workers plus the total rent, interest, and profit appropriated by capitalists. These conditions for static equilibrium (or simple reproduction) are restated in equations in Appendix 3 to this book.

Dynamic Equilibrium

Dynamic equilibrium (Marx's "expanded reproduction") means the condition of equilibrium of aggregate supply and demand in a growing capitalist economy. In each department value still equals spending for used-up materials and machinery; wages and salaries; and rent, interest, and profits (or constant capital plus variable capital plus surplus value). The movement from static to dynamic equilibrium is achieved solely by a change in the use of the capitalists' profits (assuming no rent or interest for the time being). In other words, the total amount of aggregate supply and demand cannot be changed at will, but capitalists can change the *composition* of their demand. Instead of spending all their profits for consumption, the capitalists cause growth by saving and investing some part of their profits.

In the aggregate all wages and salaries are still spent for consumer goods. What is new is that total consumer demand now includes only part of capitalist profits, so the aggregate supply of consumer goods must be adjusted to that proportionately lower consumer demand. On the other hand, the supply of investment goods must be proportionately increased to equal the replacement demand for used-up materials and depreciated machinery *plus* the new demand from that part of profits reinvested in net investment (or new added materials and machinery). These conditions of dynamic equilibrium (or expanded reproduction) are restated in equations in Appendix 3 to this book.

Economic Growth[5]

So far a simple statement has been made of the conditions of equilibrium of aggregate supply and demand. For now, we assume these conditions exist, and that effective demand rises at just the same rate as aggregate supply. The complex cases of disequilibrium (inflation and depression) are left to the next chapter. Here, the simpler question is asked: How fast is it technically possible for the economy to grow? What is the maximum *potential* rate of growth of output obtainable by the economy? Since all problems of demand are assumed away, the remaining problem may be resolved into two questions. First, how much of each input (land, labor, capital) can be procured under existing circumstances for use in production? Second, how much output can be obtained from these inputs in the production process?

Production Determined by Labor, Capital, Natural Resources, and Technology

Many different physical inputs constitute the production base of an economy. For convenience, these may be grouped into the three categories of capital, labor, and natural resources. *Capital* includes inventories of raw materials and goods in process as well as all plant and equipment. *Labor* means the number of man-hours available as well as the degree of skill of the available labor force. *Natural resources* include all useful materials (including land) known to be in the territory of the economy. Resources may be depleted by use or by natural erosion, but may be increased by new geological discoveries. *Technology* is the knowledge that determines how much output can be produced by a given combination of inputs.

Therefore, the level of potential output is a function of the presently available (1) technology, (2) natural resources, (3) capital, and (4) labor. A thorough analysis of the growth potential of any existing economy should consider each of these inputs in turn as well as the interrelations between them.

Full Capacity Growth

It is more convenient for our purposes, however, to estimate the potential growth of output in relation to the increase of capital and the product per unit of capital (allowing the product per unit of capital to reflect changes in technology, natural resources, and the labor supply). This approach is similar to that developed by the modern non-Marxist economist, Domar.[6] Domar rediscovered this approach by himself, but after arriving at it independently, he later discovered that the same theory had been fully described and mathematically presented two decades earlier by the Soviet economist, Feldman.[7] Feldman in turn shows explicitly how his growth theory evolved from Marx's reproduction schema and other discussions by Marx. Tragically, Stalin disliked Feldman's approach, so the author and his theory disappeared from the Soviet scene in the middle of one night.

It is a truism that the national product or output must equal the output per unit of capital times the amount of capital in use:

$$\text{output} = \left(\frac{\text{output}}{\text{capital}}\right) \quad (\text{capital}).$$

Of course, this formula is always true by definition, and the only question is whether it is fruitful to think in these terms.

In the United States about three dollars of capital goods are in use for every dollar of national product produced each year. So the ratio of output to capital is about one-third. Therefore, if the value of the capital stock, including all machines and factories, is about three trillion dollars, the United States produces annually about one trillion dollars in output.

Now this analysis may be extended to a growing economy. The rate of growth of output is determined by the growth of capital and the changes in output per unit of capital. Thus the equation of growth may be stated:

$$\frac{\text{increase in output}}{\text{output}} = \left(\frac{\text{increase in output}}{\text{increase in capital}}\right)\left(\frac{\text{increase in capital}}{\text{output}}\right).$$

This equation also is true by definition. It becomes a prediction rather than a truism only if we assert that these ratios are particular constants.

Growth, Waste, and Pollution

The increase-in-output/output is, by definition, the "rate of growth." Notice also that the increase-in-capital is, by definition, the amount of new investment, which is here assumed to be all the output that is "saved" (not consumed). So the formula merely affirms that the rate of growth of the economy depends on how much is saved and invested, and how much is produced by the new investment.[8]

Growth and Distribution

We have stated in its simplest form some of the most basic essentials of the theory of growth, derived mainly from Marx, but accepted by almost all economists East or West. Marx's distinctive contribution comes in his division of income into wages and salaries (or variable capital) and profit income (or surplus value, still assuming rent and interest are zero). Marx argues that all or almost all wages are consumed and none are invested. Therefore, all saving and investment must come out of profits, whose recipients do invest a major proportion of their income, since even relatively high consumption leaves them with much saving.

These tendencies described by Marx are supported in empirical studies conducted by quite conservative Western economists. Thus, Milton Friedman finds that from 1890 to 1950 in the United States the average ratio of consumption to income is decidedly higher for wage earners than for entrepreneurial groups.[9] Specifically, in the modern capitalist United States he finds that in 1948–1950 the ratio of consumption to income was only 0.77 for business owners and 0.88 for farmers, but was 0.96 for industrial wage earners.

From these and other facts, Marxists conclude that the amount of investment is constrained by the amount of profit income; and that the higher the proportion of profit income, the higher may be the proportion of investment and saving. More particularly, investment can only be as large as the nonconsumed proportion of profit income; so investment potential is more to the degree that capitalists consume less. Thus, Marx observed that wages in the early British industrialization period were held down to abysmally low levels, so that the profit income was relatively large. At the same time the puritanical (and greedy) outlook of the new industrialist class limited their own consumption, and made accumulation of capital their one and only god and desire. For these reasons, investment was a relatively high proportion of income (while new inventions held up the product per unit of capital), so that a rapid rate of growth resulted.

The simplest Marxist theory of economic growth and distribution is restated in a formal model in Appendix 3 to this book.

69

Increasing Misery (and the Trend in Income Distribution)

Marx discussed the long-run trend in income distribution in his famous doctrine of increasing misery.

The same causes which develop the expansive power of capital, develop also the labour-power at its disposal. The relative mass of the industrial reserve-army increases therefore with the potential energy of wealth. But the greater this reserve-army in proportion to the active labour-army, the greater is the mass of a consolidated surplus-population, whose misery is in inverse ratio to its torment of labour. The more extensive, finally, the lazurus-layers of the working-class, and the industrial reserve-army, the greater is official pauperism. *This is the absolute general law of capitalist accumulation.* . . . Accumulation of wealth at one pole is, therefore, at the same time accumulation of misery, agony of toil, slavery, ignorance, brutality, mental degradation, at the opposite pole. . . .[10]

The question of exactly what Marx predicted—for example, an absolute decline in wages or merely a decline in the wage share of income—need not detain us (the interpretation of Marx on this point and the related falling rate of profit theory is discussed in Appendix 2 to this book). What is important is what has happened in reality, and why.

It is clear that the *absolute* level of real wages in the advanced capitalist countries has risen very significantly at a fair pace over the last century (as even most Soviet economists now admit). What is highly controversial is *relative* share of labor, that is, the trend in the distribution of income between capitalists and workers. There are three points of view on the data, each buttressed by mounds of statistics, corresponding to three political points of view: reactionary, liberal, and radical or Marxist.

The reactionary view of this "best of all possible worlds" is that labor's share of income in the advanced capitalist countries has risen in the long run, and that an equalitarian capitalism is just around the corner. They reach this conclusion by choosing to examine the best periods of wage advance in the most favored capitalist countries. They also sometimes use the device of including in the workers' share most government expenditures, from unemployment and welfare payments to military expenditures.

By "liberal" is meant those who see problems in capitalism, but believe it can and should be rescued by reforms. The liberals have mostly favored greater equality by taxes and welfare payments, while remaining within capitalism. They claim that as a result of those reform measures already enacted, and other forces, there has been no long-run trend in either direction. The longest series of official statistics does seem to show that the percentage of wages and salaries in national income in the mature capitalist countries has remained roughly constant over the long run since Marx wrote.[11]

The radical or Marxist position is that the share of labor—*relative* to profits—in the advanced capitalist countries has significantly declined over the past century.[12] The official data must be carefully reexamined to reveal the real situation. In the first place, an increasing part of what capitalism calls "cost" rather than profit is wasteful or harmful expenditure from the worker's view. This includes most advertising and selling expenses, as well as other wastes described in the next section.

In the second place, there has been an immense increase in the revenue going to government, officially classified as neither wages nor profits. Since such a large part of this government income is used to finance wars, some Marxists consider *all* the government product as surplus rather than necessary labor. That is not correct since some government expenditures, such as for health and education, do benefit the working class, and must be included in their necessary subsistence so as to constitute part of real wages. Nevertheless, we may tentatively conclude that the increase of government expenditure does lower labor's share of national income—but leave further discussion of this point for the next section.

Leaving government aside for the moment, the share that workers obtain from their increasing productivity depends on their bargaining power. In the modern context, the combatants in the negotiating struggle over wages are the trade unions on one side and the giant corporations on the other (monopoly power is considered in detail in Chapter 8). Their bargaining power depends in turn on the demand for labor, based on capitalist investment, and the supply of labor, shown in the unemployment rate.

Unemployment of a significant number of workers both holds down wages *and* is itself another source of misery. The misery of unemployment comes not only from lower income, but also from insecurity and involuntary idleness. Capitalism has shown a tendency toward considerable long-run unemployment in all peacetime years. Some 5 per cent or more is "normal" for peak "prosperity" years (and official U.S. statistics vastly understate unemployment). Even in the economic prosperity of the Vietnam war, unemployment in 1970 rose to 5 or 6 per cent. On the one hand, demand for consumer goods is always limited under capitalism by the limited income going to the working class (and the large income of the rich, who save a high proportion of it). On the other hand, the potential supply of goods is increased by technology without increasing employment, through the substitution of machines (and whole automated factories) for workers. In addition to technological long-run unemployment, unemployment increases to large numbers periodically as business goes through the cycle of "prosperity" and depression (explored in Chapter 7).

As a result of unemployment pressures (and military expenditures, and

71

other forces—especially monopoly power), the share of labor in the national product has declined, but perhaps much slower than Marx expected. The tendency for labor's share to fall in the pure model of mature capitalism has been counteracted in reality by several modifying factors. There have been (1) imperialist profits and cheap imports from colonial and neocolonial areas, some of which have dribbled down to the workers (see Chapter 10); (2) many capital-saving innovations, so that the ratio of fixed capital to labor required in production has not shifted as rapidly as expected; (3) the growth of labor unions; and (4) the growth of the socialist world, which makes it necessary for capitalist governments to see that concessions are given to the working class.

As soon as the analysis passes beyond the narrow confines of the "pure" economic issues of wages and employment in the advanced capitalist countries, the thesis of the increasing misery of the working class—at least *relative* to the affluence of the capitalist class—becomes a much stronger proposition. Radical and Marxist humanism pays much attention to the noneconomic aspects of the quality of life today.

Noneconomic misery may have increased with the elimination of the old middle class of independent artisans and small farmers, the degradation of culture, and the increase of alienation. Obviously, alienation is especially important in the evaluation of misery. We shall show (in Chapter 11) that alienation increases among the population because of (1) the greater division of labor and more routine nature of most jobs, (2) the dying out of independent artisans and the conversion of most people, including most professionals, into hired hands (no matter how well paid). Furthermore, a special degree of misery results from continued racial and sexual discrimination in America (see Chapter 11).

Finally, radicals evaluate the standard of living of workers not only in the advanced capitalist countries, but also in the immense populations of the underdeveloped two-thirds of the capitalist world. Here it does seem that "relative misery," and possibly absolute misery in several areas, has increased in the last century. It is a fact attested by every United Nations survey (and by almost every economist East and West) that the income levels of the underdeveloped capitalist countries fall ever further behind the levels of the advanced capitalist countries (see Chapter 10 for details).

Waste

It should be apparent by this time that radicals and Marxists, especially those who follow the humanist emphasis of the young Marx, do not treat the mere quantitative growth of the national product as the only or even the most important goal of political economics. In the first place, we emphasize the terrible inequality of income distribution as much or more than the problems of aggregate income growth. Secondly, we emphasize the *composition* of national product, the wasteful and harmful uses of it, as well as the very negative noneconomic consequences of the capitalist "automatic market" pattern of growth. Whole books have been written in political economics with the central focus on waste,[13] so this brief section can only outline the problems (with bare assertions to be developed and proven in later chapters).

The problem of waste has long been discussed under the heading of unnecessary or "nonproductive" labor (Appendix 2 to this book discusses this concept in Marx). The concept in present radical usage boils down to those activities under capitalism which simply squander resources or use labor and resources to produce products which contribute *neither* to the present consumption of the populace nor to future growth.

1. There is most of the expenditure for advertising, that part of advertising which gives no information, but is used to convince the consumer that one of two identical products is better. Closely related are huge sales forces (trudging from door-to-door as well as in stores), costly model changes in style back and forth each year, and "planned obsolescence" (the quaint task of engineers to design products so that they will not work after a short time). These practices are examined in detail in relation to the monopoly stage of capitalism in Chapter 8.

2. A high degree of monopoly will be found to result in restriction of output to obtain higher prices. It also means holding back new inventions and innovations to get longer use of present machinery. Thus, monopoly means misallocation of resources, even if the present manipulated consumer preference pattern is taken as the desirable allocation.

3. The still remaining competition is wasteful in other ways. For example, there is unnecessary duplication. Why do we need four gas stations at a single intersection (as is often the case in American cities)?

4. Capitalist competition is notoriously interested in short-run profit making, so there is little conservation, no care in preserving the natural resource base. "America was once a paradise of timberland and stream but it is dying because of the greed and money lust of a thousand little kings who slashed the timber all to hell and would not be controlled."[14] Of course, this behavior was not individual eccentricity, but is inherent in the profit motivation of capitalism.

5. Pollution of the physical environment (see next section) and deterioration of the social environment are normal aspects of capitalist economic growth. "I am not quite sure what the advantage is in having a few more dollars to spend if the air is too dirty to breathe, the water too polluted to drink, the commuters are losing out in the struggle to get in and out

of the city, the streets are filthy, and the schools so bad that the young perhaps wisely stay away, and hoodlums roll citizens for some of the dollars they saved in the tax."[15] It is strange that the liberal author of that quote (Galbraith) still believes in the reform and rescue of capitalism.

6. Part of the pollution is caused by the overwhelming outpouring of unnecessary and even harmful products, profitable because well advertised. For example, until recently the cigarette industry was renowned both for its large advertising expenditure and its very high profit rate.

7. There are also the extreme and even bizarre luxuries of the super-rich. Humanists are not against luxury living as an abstract principle. With our present highly unequal distribution of income, however, the extreme luxury living of the few super-rich means lack of necessities for many other people. In a world where many children lack sufficient milk, how can one fill a whole pool with milk for a party? And how can ideologists defend such "living" styles as merely necessary incentive for capitalist investment?

8. Considerable chronic unemployment and large-scale periodic unemployment is one of the more spectacular wastes of capitalism. The dry statistics translate into workers with poverty-level incomes and nothing to do, idle factories and products not produced, and "surplus" products (oranges, potatoes) destroyed.

9. Racial and sexual discrimination in America means that the talents of a huge bloc of humanity are wasted and prevented from expression.

10. There is also the incredible harm done to future human resources by allowing poverty to result in ill-fed and ill-housed children, with poor medical care and bad childhood environment.

11. The general alienation from the ugliness of American society causes some of our best students to drop out and causes a significant part of the population to take dope, or to consume large amounts of alcohol, or to reside in mental institutions. Surely these are wastes of human resources.

12. Overshadowing all the rest in the quantitative amount of wasted resources are the military expenditures of materials, labor, and lives for past, present, and future wars.

Pollution

Before the 1960's pollution was not a major concentration (nor even a footnote) in most works on economics. Our environment, however, has been declining in livability at an alarming pace. Air pollution is making it unsafe to breathe in most American cities. Water pollution is killing fish in rivers and even the life in the oceans (which had been counted as a vast reservoir of food for the future). Animal life and human life are both being hurt by nuclear radiation and pesticides. The worldwide intake of DDT by infants is double the maximum set by the World Health Organization.

All these facts of environmental destruction are recognized equally by liberals and radicals. The two part company, however, over the diagnosis of the problem. What is the cause of this vast pollution? "Who are the destroyers? . . . Who pollutes the air? Who fouls the rivers? Who cuts down the trees, builds houses on the stripped hillsides? Who poisons the sheep, shoots the deer, oils the beaches, dams, and rivers, dries up the swamps, concretes the countryside? Who bulldozes homes, builds missiles sites, pours poison wastes underground, poison gas overground, slabs over mountain tops, rocks the earth with explosions, scars the earth with stripped mines?"[16]

In the radical view, it is the businessman hunting for profit and the general planning bigger and better wars who cause this rape of the land. "It is the well-dressed, law abiding, patriotic, and upright citizens who are taking our country away from us."[17] Although these problems menace *any* modern urban and industrial complex, the intensity of the pollution, and the lack of action to stop it, seem directly related to the private profit-making motives of capitalism (and its military arm). "Look at the values which galvanize energies and allocate resources in the business system: pursuit of money, enrichment of self, the exploitation of man—and of nature—to generate still more money. Is it surprising that a system seeking to turn everything into gold ends up turning everything into garbage?"[18]

The problem is also closely related to the basic characteristic of capitalist society that it expands and promotes private consumption (especially by the rich), but it neglects many needed areas of public consumption. Both problems—the private-profit motivation and the difficulty of public action—may be seen in the facts about smog. Smog is the mixture of smoke and other noxious elements that makes breathing so unpleasant and makes the eyes tear in parts of America (for example, in the Los Angeles basin). Most of it is known to be the result of automotive fumes and industrial smoke. Yet it is almost impossible to get any rapid changes, for example, in the auto industry.

On the one side, smog "only" hurts the public and is not a cost directly affecting private profit, so the automobile companies have no monetary incentive to produce new types of smog-free autos, especially because these would require premature scrapping of much of their present plant and equipment. It is easier to spend a few dollars to influence legislatures not to take drastic action. On the public side, even if enough political pressure can get laws enacted in favor of purifying devices, the power of the vested interests involved is so immense that the laws are almost unenforceable.

"Throughout 1969, the Department of Justice in Washington held a secret hearing to discuss with industry lawyers its charge that automobile manufacturers had conspired to stifle the introduction of smog-control devices on automobiles. On September 11, the department announced that it had entered into a consent decree, allowing the companies to escape federal sanctions by promising that they would not conspire any more."[19]

Private transportation interests have also opposed tooth-and-nail all attempts to substitute public transport for private: that is, one electric train carrying 500 passengers to replace 500 cars each carrying one passenger, and each adding to smog and traffic congestion. In the radical view, it seems unlikely or impossible that much can be done to eliminate pollution or to expand public substitutes before capitalist private-profit–making is eliminated.

The liberal reformer's view of waste and pollution is really quite different. They may admit that a few unusually greedy capitalists put some harmful products on the market and also cause some pollution from lack of care. But the more "profound" problem, they say, is really (1) too many people for too few resources, and (2) too rapid use of resources and polluting processes by modern and newly developing technology.[20] Thus they argue that if all the underdeveloped world were brought up to the present American standard of living, it would require more than the known world supplies of metals such as copper, lead, and tin.

Moreover, the liberals claim that the most lethal threat is simply lack of food, since supply is limited, while population is doubling every thirty-five years.[21] Hence, they see population and pollution as threats to everyone. In this view, all classes (especially enlightened capitalists) have the same interests in rescuing the environment, conserving resources, and limiting population. It comes as no surprise that the ecology teach-ins and several "militant" books on pollution and population[22] have all been partly or wholly financed and promoted by the Rockefeller Fund and other "liberal" parts of the Establishment.[23]

A somewhat different liberal view comes in the vast literature of technocracy (dating all the way back to Thorstein Veblen's *Engineers and the Price System*). The modern technocratic argument is that, if it were all left to the engineers, technological solutions would be readily available to most of our problems, such as smog. This is a naive view of economics. *It is true* that engineering solutions already exist to many pollution problems. The problem is that these solutions require massive scrapping of present plant and equipment and massive investment, with no ready hope for profit. In the radical view, only a socialist framework could handle such a change.

The results of the difference in diagnoses become immediately apparent when we examine proposed solutions. The radical view is that the precondition for eliminating pollution and conserving resources is the abolition of the capitalist private-profit system and its replacement by a socially owned and directed system. The "liberal" part of the Establishment would pass a few reform laws on pollution, restrict output and technology, and —above all—*limit population*, especially among the poor in America and in all the underdeveloped countries. Even with population control, they contend, the underdeveloped countries must understand that resources are too limited for them ever to reach American standards of living, so they should begin to "reorient" and reduce their goals.[24]

Even some radicals have stressed the demand for no more economic growth at all (and add only incidentally that this "probably implies an end to capitalism")![25] They argue that the present American national product is enough if (1) waste and pollutants are eliminated, and (2) there is much more equal distribution of wealth. It is true that every American could be raised out of poverty if the present American production were rationalized and redistributed. But the stress is upside-down. Even in America we can only begin to plan and decide rationally on growth and other goals *after* the end of capitalism and establishment of a decent, human society. Furthermore, the underdeveloped countries clearly do need a great deal of economic growth.

Population

Is capitalism or sex the real enemy? The pious Reverend Malthus in 1798[26] and all his modern followers assert that mankind's sexual drive has produced too many children, and this is the main cause of poverty, pollution, disease, and even war. On the production side, this argument is buttressed by the concept of diminishing returns. The "law" of diminishing returns—a favorite proposition of neoclassical economics—states that, after a certain point, each additional worker adds less output than the worker hired before him.

This "law" holds true *only if* capital, natural resources, and technique remain unchanged (and after some minimum scale of employment is reached). Given these assumptions, the law of diminishing returns is a truism; it cannot be other than true. All other things remaining the same, it is obvious that if enough workers are crowded onto a single plot of land or even the entire world, the crowding alone will eventually cause the product of an additional worker to decline. But Malthus went much further than the truism embodied in the law of diminishing returns. He predicted that diminishing returns per worker in the economy as a whole *would* come about in actual fact. The Reverend Malthus reached this dismal conclusion on the grounds that population increase would be very rapid and would far outweigh the slow increase of capital, technology, and natural resources.

Malthus may be attacked on several grounds.[27] The gloomy long-run prediction based on Malthus's interpretation of the law of diminishing returns has not been borne out by the facts of historical progress. In the first place, it is not even clear that the world population is at that minimum level where further additions to the working force would bring diminishing returns, even if natural resources, capital, and technology were to remain constant. Second, labor itself improves in quality as scientific and technical education advance, although this may properly be classed as an aspect of technological improvement. Third, it was usual to argue that the earth is only so large and that its natural resources are slowly being depleted. The supply of *known* natural resources, however, is steadily expanding as a result of continuous geological discoveries of new reserves. Furthermore, there have been important discoveries of new uses for previously neglected materials—for example, coal was once merely a hard black stone of no use for fuel or heating purposes. Moreover, better ways have been found to use available resources—for example, power production by atomic fission or fusion, or food production by hydroponic farming. Of course, the last two means of resource expansion are again aspects of technological improvement.

Another reason why there have not been diminishing returns per worker in the economy as a whole is the increasing use of capital per worker, which allows a single worker to produce far more than previously. The final and most important reason for the defeat of diminishing returns is that development of technology in the last century has meant a much more efficient use of the available capital, natural resources, and labor. At the early date when Malthus wrote, it was still possible largely to ignore technological progress. Today, even the blindest economist is forced to consider the startling advances continually made in productive know-how.

Empirically, the evidence shows that the population in the developed countries has not outraced technology, natural resources, and capital, but that, on the contrary, product per person has grown enormously. Between 1870 and 1940, for example, employment in American agriculture rose by only 34 per cent, while output rose by 279 per cent.[28] The United States thus has no problem of lack of goods, but rather has surplus food relative to effective cash demand.

It may be concluded that in the industrialized capitalist economies the biological and technical problems have not been the *main* reasons for poverty, slowed growth, periodic depressions, waste, and pollution. It is rather the man-made economic institutions of capitalism itself that are

78

the main causes of the tendencies toward economic and environmental catastrophe. The advent of atomic energy makes it especially clear that the natural sciences have given us ample power to obtain in the future fantastic levels of abundance or to blow to pieces the entire world.

While Malthus generally assumed technology constant, his modern followers claim to allow for technological progress, but still reach the same gloomy conclusions on the basis of population forecasts.[29] They mechanically project the present world rate of population growth into the future and easily arrive at quite astronomical figures for total population in the near future. It was demonstrated above that, to date at least, capital and technology in the advanced capitalist countries have had no trouble keeping ahead of population growth, but there is, of course, some extreme level of population that would be impossible to handle.

The mechanical prognostications of vast population growth, however, do not seem to have taken into account the best present knowledge of population growth patterns. Malthus described people breeding like animals and population exploding with only a few kinds of checks to its expansion. Malthus speaks of "preventative checks" as those that cause lower birth rates. He recognizes only abstention from sex or vice and sexual deviation. He does not consider voluntary birth control through family planning and contraceptive methods. When preventative checks fail, Malthus believes the result will be "positive checks" to population, where "positive" means a higher death rate! Thus positive checks include wars, famine, and disease.

It is true that in many primitive economies at a low level of productivity there are often very high birth rates. At this stage, however, population may be constant for centuries since it is held in check by equally high death rates, caused indeed by wars, disease and starvation. A second stage of rapid population growth usually follows the beginnings of industrialization and the introduction of modern methods of public health sanitation. With better control of disease and enough food production, death rates decline. As long as birth rates remain high, the population soars (as in some of the newly developing countries today).

At the third stage, however, as the economy matures, the population discovers a wider range of choices. Knowledge of contraceptive devices for birth control spreads. There is also less and less possibility to put children to work at an early age, and more need to support them through a long education. Thus, all the more industrialized countries have shown some tendency toward lower and lower birth rates during the last hundred years, though there have been some upward spurts in the rate for short periods.

As we saw in the last section, the "liberal" cure-all is population control, with many advocates of *involuntary* birth control reported favorably in the

79

American press. One Rockefeller-financed study concludes that the American government should "discourage births among the socially handicapped."[30] In other words, this racist solution is that the poor, mostly black, should be pressured into having less babies. Naturally, the same study concludes that the American government should also "discourage" births in the underdeveloped countries. In Chapter 9 we shall try to prove that the primary problem of these countries is not population, but imperialism.

Certainly, radicals are in favor of the fullest spread of birth control information, so that women can control their own lives, if for no other reason. Certainly, some socialist countries (for example, China) will find it socially desirable to encourage voluntary birth control. In a better society "where there is a greater economic security, political participation, elimination of gross class division, liberation of women, . . . humane and successful population programs are at least possible. Without these conditions, genocide is nicely masked by the welfare imperialism of the West."[31] Moreover, more availability of birth control information and devices may reduce population growth in the socialist countries, and make for a more rapid growth of product per person (see Chapter 15). The point is not that rapid population growth is no problem, but that it is much less of a problem than many others, such as discrimination, inequality, unemployment, and imperialism.

NOTES

1. See, e.g., Wassily Leontief, "The Significance of Marxian Economics for Present-Day Economic Theory," *American Economic Review*, 28 (March 1938), supplement.

2. Paul Samuelson, "Marxian Economics as Economics," *American Economic Review*, 57 (May 1967): 616–623.

3. John M. Keynes, *General Theory of Employment, Interest, and Money* (New York: Harcourt, Brace and Company, 1936).

4. Simple and expanded reproduction (or static and dynamic equilibrium) are both presented in Karl Marx, *Capital*, vol. 2, part 3.

5. Some excellent Marxist contributions to growth economics can be found in Anonymous editor, *Problems of Economic Dynamics and Planning, Essays in Honour of Michael Kalecki* (New York: Pergamon Press, 1966).

6. Evsey D. Domar, "Expansion and Employment," *American Economic Review*, 37 (March 1947): 34–35.

7. Domar, "A Soviet Model of Growth," in his *Essays in the Theory of Economic Growth* (London: Oxford University Press, 1957). G. A. Feldman, "On the Theory of Growth Rates of National Income," transl. in Nicolas Spulber, *Foundations of Soviet Strategy for Economic Growth: Selected Soviet Essays, 1924–30* (Bloomington: Indiana University Press, 1964).

8. Take an example of the use of this equation of growth. If 9 per cent of output is saved and invested, and if the ratio of increase-in-output to increase-in-capital is one to three, then it can be calculated that:

$$\text{rate of growth} = (1/3)\ (0.09) = 0.03 \text{ or } 3 \text{ per cent a year}$$

Growth, Waste, and Pollution

This had been approximately the performance of the economy of the United States over a long period of time.

9. Milton Friedman, A *Theory of the Consumption Function* (Princeton, N.J.: Princeton University Press, 1957), pp. 69–79.

10. Marx, *Capital*, vol. I, pp. 707–709.

11. See data for Great Britain from 1870 to 1950 in Phelps Brown and Hart, "The Share of Wages in the National Income," *Economic Journal* 62 (June 1952): 276–277.

12. Data supporting this position may be found in Labor Research Association, *Trends in American Capitalism: Profits and Living Standards* (New York: International Publishers, 1948); with annual surveys in Labor Research Association, Labor Fact Books, nos. 1–17 (New York: International Publishers, 1931–1965).

13. See, e.g., Paul Baran and Paul Sweezy, *Monopoly Capital* (New York: Monthly Review Press, 1966).

14. Garrett de Bell, "Introduction" to *The Environmental Handbook* (New York: Ballantine, 1970), p. 3.

15. John Kenneth Galbraith in Congressional testimony, quoted in Michael Harrington, "Reactionary Keynesianism," *Encounter*, 26 (March 1966): 51.

16. Josephine W. Johnson, "Who Is Really Uprooting This Country?" *New York Times* (May 10, 1969).

17. *Ibid.*

18. Editorial, *Ramparts* (May 1970), p. 2.

19. de Bell, *op. cit.*, p. 269; also see the full-length exposé by George Laycock, *The Diligent Destroyers; A Critical Look at the Industries and Agencies that Are Permanently Defacing the American Landscape* (Garden City, N.Y.: Doubleday, 1970).

20. See, e.g., Paul and Anne Ehrlich, *Population, Resources, and Environment* (San Francisco: W. H. Freeman, 1970), *passim.*

21. See, e.g., Ehrlich, *loc. cit.*; see also Frederick Osborn, *Population: An International Dilemma* (New York: Population Council, 1958).

22. See, e.g., Ehrlich, *op. cit.*; de Bell, *op. cit.*; Osborn, *op. cit.*; and Paul Ehrlich, *The Population Bomb* (New York: Ballantine, 1968).

23. Steve Weissman, "Why the Population Bomb is a Rockefeller Baby," *Ramparts* (May 1970): 45–50.

24. A. and P. Ehrlich, *loc. cit.*

25. See, e.g., John Hardesty, "The Macroeconomics of Environmental Destruction," mimeographed paper at Conference of Union for Radical Political Economics, Berkeley, April 11, 1970.

26. Thomas Malthus, *Essay on Population* (New York: E. P. Dutton & Co., 1958, first publ. 1798).

27. The Marxist attack is stated in Ronald L. Meek, ed., *Malthus: Selections from Marx and Engels* (New York: International Publishers, 1953).

28. Arthur Burns, *Frontiers of Economic Knowledge* (Princeton, N. J.: Princeton University Press, 1954), p. 4.

29. See, e.g., A. and P. Ehrlich, *loc. cit.*

30. Osborn, *loc. cit.*

31. Weissman, *op. cit.*, p. 47.

CHAPTER
7

Cyclical Unemployment

In addition to a considerable "normal" long-run level of unemployment, the capitalist system periodically is subject to the peculiar disease of mass unemployment and depression. A time-traveler from the medieval or ancient periods would find everything upside-down in an *Alice in Wonderland* world. He would find output dropping and standards of living declining, but he could not believe that there were still plenty of factories and workers and bountiful harvests. He would assume that the cause of the severe decline in production is a natural calamity, such as flood or drought, or perhaps the destruction and loss of lives caused by war. How wrong he would be! In these modern capitalist calamities there is no problem of a shortage of supply. On the contrary there is "overproduction," too many workers and too much produced relative to the "effective demand" in the market. "Effective demand" means *money* ready to be spent, not mere desire or need, since the capitalist economy takes no notice of anything but money. And instead of war destruction causing the loss of production and poverty, production for war is often seen as the only solution to unemployment.

Although overproduction seems a strange and even absurd epidemic, its ravages among its millions of human victims are nonetheless very real. It is not merely that thousands of factories are idle and gather dust, but that millions of workers are involuntarily idle and gather frustration. In the Great Depression of the 1930's one out of every four workers was unemployed by official government statistics (which usually considerably understate the problem). Part-time unemployment, or less than full-time employment, was probably visited on another 50 per cent of all workers. The remaining 25 per cent suffered drastic cuts in wage levels. People traveled from place to place looking for work, subsisting on private handouts or government soup kitchens.[1]

Since the beginning of the Second World War, there have been no more major depressions (mainly due to monopoly capitalist wastes and unceasing military production, as we shall see). Periodic "minor" depressions have continued, with resulting full-time unemployment of "only" 6 to 8 per cent of all workers (and much higher percentages of unemployed women, Black, Brown, young, and elderly workers).

The Possibility of Unemployment

The discussion here is based on the insights of Marx, which foreshadowed most major cycle theories, but it is couched in the contemporary framework of analysis, which developed from the work of Keynes.[2] Both Keynes and Marx began their analyses with attacks on Say's Law, an assumption by which the classical and neoclassical economists denied the very possibility of insufficient demand or general unemployment.[3]

Say's Law has been stated in various forms. In its most common statement, Say's Law holds that "supply calls forth its own demand," so there can never be insufficient aggregate demand.[4] The argument in favor of Say's Law is that any output results in an equal income. When (and if) that income is spent, it will buy the same amount of output. This conclusion, while containing a grain of truth as a description of the "normal" circulation of money and goods, seems to be an unwarranted generalization from consideration of earlier and simpler societies.

Say's Law must be shown to be inapplicable before one can understand the phenomena of insufficient demand and unemployment in capitalist depressions. Of course, there are business cycle theories which accept Say's Law, but these theories all see cycles only in the *supply* of output, caused by factors external to the economy and not by lack of demand. On the contrary, it is asserted here that in capitalist economies there *is* a periodic lack of aggregate effective demand, generated by the internal mechanism of that system.[5]

It is characteristic of the modern capitalist economy that almost all production is directed solely toward its sale in the marketplace. According to most economic historians, this was hardly ever true of earlier societies. In very primitive economies the collective unit of the whole tribe carries on production for the collective use of the whole tribe; there can be no question of "overproduction" of all commodities in this case. Even in the ancient slave empires and in medieval feudalism, the basic production unit is the plantation or manor, which produces mostly for its own self-sufficient existence, though it may sell a small surplus. In some of these societies there was also a large, though not vital, trade in luxury goods.

In all these earlier societies, since most production was for the immediate use of the economic unit itself, the phenomenon of overproduction was impossible. Thus, the carpenter on the feudal manor would not produce more wagons than the manor would use. It is quite different when Henry Ford produces millions of autos, not for the use of Ford workers, but for sale in the market. It is certainly possible that Ford may produce many more cars than can be sold at a profit in the market. Furthermore, if Ford finds that he cannot sell so many cars at a profit, then he will reduce his production, and some Ford workers will be unemployed.

A second characteristic of modern capitalism is the regular use of money. The defenders of Say's Law always spoke of money as a veil over the process of exchange between two commodities; they held that the "essential" features of the capitalist economic process were the same as in a barter economy. In a barter economy, of course, every supply of goods to the market is at the same time a demand for other goods; there may be too much of single commodity and not enough of another, but there cannot be an excess of aggregate supply over demand. While many features remain the same in a money economy, there is an important difference because money is not only a medium of exchange between commodities, but may also be withdrawn from exchange and stored away for an indefinite time (as most commodities may *not* be). Thus, it is possible to have a monetary income in the capitalist economy that is hoarded and not immediately respent for the equivalent supply of products.

A third characteristic of capitalism is that the sole motivation for production is the private profit of the capitalist. Each individual enterprise makes its own plans on the basis of its own estimate of whether it will obtain a private profit by production. It follows that false profit expectations may lead the aggregate of all firms to produce more (or less) than the market will buy. If more is produced than can be sold *at a profit,* private enterprise will fire workers and reduce its investment spending, thus leading into a depression. Of course, this is still a very general statement because we are only concerned with the *possibility* of a depression, leaving the actual mechanics of the process for later.

By contrast, an industrialized socialist economy like the Soviet Union also has market exchange of commodities (at least, purchase of labor power and consumer goods), and it also uses money in almost all transactions, but the motivation for production is planned social use rather than private profit. In a planned socialist economy it is the same planning agency that decides both the aggregate supply of goods *and* the aggregate demand for investment (from the government budget) and consumption (by setting wages). Investment may be set at any desired level, regardless of the profit expectation. Therefore, most economists of business cycle theory admit the fact that industrialized socialist economies *do not* and *could not* have cyclical periods of insufficient aggregate demand (although their growth rates may fluctuate periodically for other reasons, such as inaccurate planning).[6]

Cyclical Unemployment

To show analytically the possibility of insufficient demand under capitalism, we begin by dividing all spending flows into personal consumption and investment (ignoring here all governmental and foreign transactions). Excess supply may occur if the value of goods supplied to the market exceeds the planned spending of all consumers and investors. Neglecting for the moment the long-run growth of productive capacity, we may argue that if all last month's income is always spent for this month's output, then the flow of circulation is continuous and full use of capacity prevails. If, however, some of last month's income is hoarded, then the total of consumer and investor spending declines, and there is relative "overproduction" this month (or "unintended investment" in excess inventories).

Suppose we add the distinction between wage and profit (including rent and interest) income. If all wages are spent for consumption (as a convenient simplification), then we may further locate the problem in terms of class behavior. Beyond their consumption needs and the profitable investment opportunities, capitalists may have additional money from profits. This excess of saving over investment means less effective demand for goods, so it results in unsold goods or overproduction. It is within this framework that we may construct a theory to account for the recurring depressions and mass unemployment found under capitalism. That there is hoarding of money and unwanted inventories of goods is merely a reflection of the problem; the task is to understand the processes that result in these phenomena.

Underconsumption Theory

The two most important themes of business cycle theory may perhaps be described as an underconsumption approach and an overinvestment approach.[7] The early and superficial underconsumptionist theories merely argued that workers are not paid enough to buy back all their products. These theories have been criticized by all sides,[8] even by those who have themselves advocated more sophisticated underconsumption theories.[9]

Whereas the earlier naive underconsumptionists had stated or implied that an absolute decline of worker's consumption caused the depression, more sophisticated theorists point out that both wages and consumption usually continue to rise right up to the peak of prosperity. We must then concentrate our attention on investment behavior. Although consumption continues to rise, its slow and limited rise may cut into the prospective rate of profit on investment.[10] The resulting decline in investment (and rise in excess saving or hoarding)[11] is the "immediate cause" of the depression, though we may say that its "ultimate cause" is the limitation of consumption. The word "cause" is in quotes because the economy is a single organism, in which each new condition is the result of all the conflicting forces at work within it in the preceding period, so we should speak not of causes, but of functional relationships.

This theory, which says that investment falls as a direct result of the slowed rise in consumption, is called the "accelerator" relation.[12] The "accelerator," which bases investment demand on the changes in consumption, is an objective relationship accepted more or less by many theories. Much more controversial are the different theories to account for the limited rise of consumer demand. The conservative (orthodox-Keynesian view) is that the relative decline in consumer spending merely reflects the psychological reaction of each individual by which he saves a large portion as his income rises above his traditional or habitual "needs." The radical (Left-Keynesian, Marxist) view stresses the fact that "prosperity" usually brings a shift in the distribution of income, with a reduction of the wage share and a rise in the profit share as the cause of limited consumption.[13]

Of course, total wages rise in expansion and fall in depression, but the wage *share* of national income *falls* in expansion and *rises* in depression. In other words, we assert that aggregate wages rise and fall proportionately less than aggregate income, and there is much empirical evidence to support this assumption. The aggregate data show, therefore, that the ratio of wages to national income falls in prosperity, but rises in depression. During the four business cycles from 1921 through 1938, the wage income (or aggregate employees' compensation) rose on the average in prosperity or expansion periods by only 19.8 per cent of its average value over the whole time. At the same time, the nonwage part of national income (profits, rent, and interest) rose by 23.3 per cent.

In these same four cycles, the wage income fell on the average in depressions or contraction periods by only 13.0 per cent of its average value, while nonwage income fell by 26.4 per cent.[14] The differences, while small in percentages, are very significant in billions of dollars. Furthermore, one of the single most important sources of saving today is corporate profits, either directly by corporate reinvestment or indirectly through capitalists' dividend income. In the years 1921 through 1938 the net profit of all corporations rose on the average in expansions by an astounding 168.8 per cent, and declined in contractions by an equally startling 174.6 per cent of its average value for the whole period.[15]

Specifically, to explain the Great Depression of 1929, there is plenty of evidence showing a shift of income in the 1920's from wages to profits, from poor to rich. For example, from 1919 to 1929 the share of the top 5 per cent of income receivers rose from 24.3 per cent of all income (*after taxes*) to 33.5 per cent. In the same period the income share of the top 1 per cent rose similarly from 12.2 to 18.9 per cent![16]

Why does the wage *share* of national income decline in an expansion (and rise again in the ensuing depression)? In the first place, as the economy advances, capitalists try to keep the average wage down at the level of the long-run habitual cost of living (or replacement "value" of the worker's labor power), even though new inventions—and speed-up—increase the worker's productivity.[17] During expansion the increased productivity means fewer hours required for the necessary labor to produce the value of the worker's consumption goods, and therefore more hours remaining for surplus labor going to produce profits. Second, capitalists use existing equipment more completely in an upswing in contrast to the underutilization of the depression. Therefore, more goods are produced (and at lower cost because of scale economies) with the same stock of capital, so the rate of profit rises. Third, during expansion capitalists try to meet the increased demand for output by technological innovations designed to use relatively less labor (and more machinery). This reduces demand for labor, and thus holds down wages. Fourth, at least at the beginning of recovery, the large numbers of unemployed hold down wages (and allow speed-up) by their potential competition for jobs. Finally, trade unions may have some power to influence the wage level.[18] Their bargaining position, however, is stronger in preventing wage cuts than in raising wages to keep up with rising prices.

What is the effect on consumption of the shift of income from wages to profits, or poor to rich, in the expansion phase? We emphasize that workers' wages are all or almost all spent for consumption, whereas most of the capitalists' profits are "saved" (that is, not consumed).[19] The empirical evidence even today indicates that most increases in workers' income do go for consumption, though perhaps not 100 per cent (as might have been true in Marx's day). Thus, a semiofficial model of the Dutch economy for 1947 to 1954 found that workers spent 85 per cent of additional wage income on consumption, while capitalists spent only 40 per cent of additional profits on consumption.[20] Similar results were obtained from a model of the British economy from 1947 to 1956,[21] and in a model of the United States economy for 1929 to 1952.[22] The percentage of consumption out of additional profits is based in these studies only on the personal income of capitalists. The percentage consumed out of additional profits would, in fact, be much lower if these studies included as capitalist income the retained profit of corporations. None of retained profit goes for consumption (although it is *all* invested in prosperous times).

The fall in the wage share of national income during expansion restricts the rise of consumption. The restricted growth of consumer demand lowers the rate of profit on sales, which eventually causes a fall in investment, and thus leads to a depression. This, of course, is *not* a permanent condition; the depression sets the stage for a recovery (notice how this is unlike the naive underconsumptionist view, which cannot easily explain a recovery). For one thing, the working class and its unions fiercely resist wage cuts, so when income falls in a depression, wages do not fall as rapidly, especially when wage rates move down toward the traditional subsistence level. The rise in the wage share, though total wages are decreasing, eventually slows the fall of consumption. This encourages investment to begin again until finally a full recovery is under way (other factors influencing the recovery, such as the wearing out of machinery, are discussed below).

Overinvestment Theory

In addition to the lack of effective consumer demand, there are other reasons why the rate of profit tends to fall at the peak of prosperity. We do not consider here the alleged "long-run" fall in the profit rate, where the long run represents an average tendency over several cycles (or long enough for investments to result in significant increase in capacity).[23] Even if such a long-run falling tendency of the profit rate could be demonstrated, it would still have little or no obvious connection with events in the business cycle, which are based on entrepreneurs' expectation of the most recent average or "normal" profit rates. Of much more importance to business cycle analysis are the reasons for short-run declines in profit rates and investment.[24]

A short-run rise in the cost of capital goods may lower the rate of profit. The phenomenon of rising costs may sometimes be due to natural calamities, such as flood or drought. Far more important, however, at the peak of prosperity the large profits may be translated into a very high rate of flow of money capital into investment. As a result, there is a vast increase in the demand for raw materials and machinery, which causes "a rise in the prices of all the commodities which enter into the formation of capital."[25] In other words, the rapid acceleration of demand for investment goods in the expansion phase outruns the actual production of investment goods. Therefore, in the usual expansion, the prices of investment goods rise far more rapidly than the prices of the products they are used to produce. As a result, even if consumer demand keeps pace with the supply of consumer goods, there is a squeeze on profits in consumer goods from the cost side.

Moreover, there are disproportionate price rises within the investment goods sector. Just as the demand for machinery rises faster than the consumer demand, so in turn the demand for raw materials grows faster than even the demand for machinery.[26] Each earlier stage of production derives its demand from a later stage in an accelerated manner. Thus, in the expansion phase the prices of raw materials rise more rapidly than any other category.

The theory of accelerated price increases in the earlier stages of production is borne out in a number of modern empirical investigations, especially in the careful study of price behavior by F. C. Mills.[27] His study includes data for several decades (up to 1938) on prices of twenty-two consumer goods, prices of forty-eight producers' goods (or capital goods other than raw materials), and prices of thirty-two raw materials. He finds that in the average prosperity period prices of consumer goods rise by only 12 per cent of their average value, while the prices of producers' goods rise by 21 per cent, and the price of raw materials rises by 23 per cent! Similarly, in the average depression the prices of consumer goods fall only 18 per cent, but the prices of producers' goods fall by 25 per cent, and the prices of raw materials fall by 26 per cent.

It follows that just before the peak of prosperity is reached, the rate of profit in consumer goods is being squeezed down because all the elements of cost (except wages) are rising more rapidly than the revenue from production. Falling profits in consumer goods depress the outlook for expected profits throughout the economy and cause falling investment, thus setting off the depression. Of course, when investment demand falls far enough, the prices of capital goods must decline drastically, or "adjust" themselves to the lower demand. This "adjustment" is then one aspect of the depression, but it does eventually lower costs (faster than prices), thus making production more profitable, and finally setting the stage for the following recovery.[28]

There has been some confusion, even among radicals, over the role that wages play in causing higher costs that lead to lower profits in the cycle upswing. At the beginning of an upswing, we have noted that the existing unemployment keeps wage costs low.[29] Of course, we must admit the hypothetical possibility that at the height of the boom with the existing supply of workers fully employed, the demand for labor accompanying new investment might run ahead of population growth.[30] In such an unusual case, as in the intensive railway expansion drives of the nineteenth century, the relative shortage of labor, high wages, and falling profits may set off a depression, in which production and demand for labor will decline until wages fall back to a lower level.[31]

Even some radical writers have laid great stress on the possibility of rising wages leading to falling rates of profit as the cause of depression.[32] This, however, seems to be an incorrect generalization from hypothetical, or at least very rare, cases. Wages do rise in the usual expansion, but we have demonstrated that they rise much more slowly than revenues (because wages tend to remain at the given standard of living, and because demand for labor is relatively lessened by substitution of machinery). This lag in wage costs, rather than lowering the profit rate, is a factor maintaining the profit margin in the face of other rising costs. Thus the *rate* of profit on capital falls *in spite* of the declining wage share (or rising rate of exploitation in Marx's terms).[33]

Most modern Keynesian as well as Marxist writers do see the wage share falling in the cyclical expansion. It might appear, however, that we are still left with two conflicting cycle theories: the underconsumptionist view of limited consumer demand caused by the too slow rise of wages, and the overinvestment view of lowered profit rates caused by rising costs of capital goods. Now we must clarify the relation of these two theories.

The Synthesis

Both underconsumption and overinvestment must be considered different aspects of a single cyclical process of expansion and depression. This "two-horned dilemma" is the explanation of our periodic depressions.[34] There are two distinct problems for capitalists to face. One is the *production* of profit, conceived as the margin of long-run price above labor costs and capital goods cost. The other problem is the *realization* of profit, by which we can mean the ability to actually sell the product at its long-run price (or "value").[35]

What is necessary is a consistent statement unifying the underconsumption and overinvestment aspects of the problem. Its essential features may be briefly stated here. During the expansion, wages rise more slowly than profit income, which causes consumer demand to rise more slowly than output. At the same time, costs of machinery and raw materials rise more rapidly than general prices, thus increasing the cost ratio, *even after allowing for the slower rise of wages*. As a result, profit (at least in consumer goods) is squeezed from both the cost and the demand sides, and this causes a pessimistic outlook for future profits in all industries which causes a decline in investment, which sets off the depression. Similarly, in a contraction period, wages and consumer demand fall more slowly than output, while costs of machinery and raw materials fall more swiftly than output. It follows that eventually the profit perspective looks more encouraging, investment picks up, and the recovery begins. Thus, the synthetic model argues that profits are squeezed at the peak of the upswing by *both* slowed demand and rapidly rising costs. On the other hand, profit prospects are aided at the trough of depression by *both* a slower fall of demand and a more rapid fall of costs. (All three theories of the cycle are presented in mathematical models in Appendix 5 to this book.)

Factors Intensifying Economic Instability

The unplanned competitive mechanism in the capitalist economy, as contrasted with planning inside the single factory, has often been called the "anarchy" of production. Some reformist writers allege that this anarchy of production is *the cause* of cycles, and that the most important difference from feudalism lies in the vastly increased complications of the capitalist economy.[36] Thus, Borchardt writes that

an exact equilibrium must exist between all the various branches of production. But this is impossible . . . because the process of production, in order to develop the productive forces, must obey its own laws, which derive from its own organization; and, therefore, it cannot accommodate itself to the requirements of the consumer.[37]

The reformists (such as Edward Bernstein) emphasized that these temporary and "merely frictional" disproportions could be ironed out in capitalism, partly by improvement of credit and worldwide communication, and partly by the increased planning that was taking place within each industrial monopoly.

Radicals may certainly recognize that the "anarchy of production" (or business competition) leads to temporary disproportions of supply and demand for individual products, but this constant frictional adjustment cannot be a major cause of periodic depressions.[38] The anarchy of competition may be viewed as one of the conditions allowing the possibility of depressions, and it certainly does intensify depressions once they begin. The radical point, however, is that since the depression is not merely due to frictional adjustment, no amount of improvement in or tinkering with the credit mechanism (or monopoly elimination of competitive friction) could pull all parts of the capitalist economy over the rough spots.

Certainly, in a context of unplanned competition, the irrational psychological responses of individual capitalists may drastically worsen the situation. In a boom, there will be a fantastic and irrational expansion in many areas, while in a depression, there is a similar irrational degree of contraction. But these one-sided errors of psychological expectations occur only *after* other basic factors have caused a sudden change in economic direction, say from boom to bust. While the economy as a whole is moving along ordinarily in one general direction, the irrational errors of competitors will usually cancel each other.

THE POLITICAL ECONOMY OF CAPITALISM

Money and Credit

We may look in a similar way at all the monetary institutions of capitalism. Their existence allows the possibility of depressions and greatly increases the intensity of depressions once they have begun, but they could not stand alone as a causal factor.[39] After a depression is begun, price deflation worsens the problems of capitalists. They cannot sell their existing inventories at a profit, and they cannot repay their debts—causing not only their bankruptcy, but that of their creditors (many of whom are banks).[40] Even if the credit system continued to work perfectly, there would still be depressions, though they might not be so bad if we were spared the financial panic and the bankruptcy of banks.

Of course, the problem in a depression is not that there is an aggregate lack of income (or "money"), but that the distribution of income is such that some few capitalists have vast savings, while most people have desires without the money to make their demand effective. The capitalists as a class hoard their money rather than investing it, not because of any psychological whim, but only after the outlook for further profit-making becomes dismal for quite objective reasons. Similarly, *after* the profit outlook brightens and recovery begins, it is easy to get loans of capital at low interest rates.[41] Easier credit and lower interest rates might somewhat ameliorate the worst of the financial crisis, but could not touch the basic causes of the economic crisis leading to a depression.[42]

Merchants and Inventories

The anarchy of capitalism shows up especially in the activities of merchants in retail and wholesale distribution. As long as conditions are good, merchants act as a smooth conveyor belt to the four corners of the world. The very fact, however, that they move goods so far may mean that the first signs of trouble are not transmitted very quickly to the producer. Thus, retail prices may fall while wholesalers are still optimistic, and are still increasing their stocks of finished goods. When the wholesalers can no longer sell enough goods to pay their bank debts, the banks may then recognize a crisis, try to restrict further credit, and set off the depression (though more rapid communication does lessen this problem).[43]

Furthermore, when retail sales even off or decline slightly, the purchase of new inventories may then decline by a drastic percentage, even to zero (because of an "acceleration" relationship). If a retailer is worried about future sales of his present stock, he will not load himself with a still greater stock of inventory. Hence, the shock of a decline in retail sales is eventually transmitted back to the manufacturer in an accelerated manner. It is not until all the present inventories are reduced to a very low level that any recovery of production is possible.[44]

Replacement Cycles

The *duration* of the business cycle is partly determined by the life-span of capital equipment and the need for its periodic replacement.[45] Nevertheless, the technological need for replacement investment cannot explain the turning points of the cycle as well as it explains its length (although the theory has sometimes been developed in this direction).[46] The importance of the "life-cycle" of machinery is that it begins for most machines in the same part of the expansion period, so its end for most machines is also bunched together, right when a new recovery is possible.

. . . This cycle comprising a number of years, through which capital is compelled to pass by its fixed part, furnishes a material basis for the periodic commercial crises in which business goes through successive periods of lassitude, average activity, overspending, and crisis. It is true that the periods in which capital is invested are different in time and place. But a crisis is always the starting point of a large amount of new investments. Therefore it also constitutes, from the point of view of society, more or less of a new material basis for the next cycle of turnover.[47]

There is a complicated two-way relationship between investment and the business cycle. In the expansion period, there is both replacement and new net investment. Moreover, the new investment is often qualitatively improved because it consists of technological innovations. The advent of prosperity and the upswing of demand witnesses an outpouring of new investments based on new inventions (causing long-run growth). Even so-called "replacement" is mostly for modernization, so a volume of investment just equal to the depreciation may actually lead to much growth in the economy. New investment proceeds over the whole expansion phase, so the average time of its introduction can only be roughly estimated.

During the depression, the existence of unused capacity acts as a depressing factor holding back further investment of any kind. As machinery (and plant) reaches the end of its useful lifetime, capacity is reduced, so a demand must arise after some years for replacement investment if nothing else. Yet this effect is very far from a mechanical certainty. In the first place, we already noted that the various capital goods were actually bought over a number of years, not at one time. Second, less use may

93

preserve machinery for a longer time than usual. Third, accounting and tax systems of reporting depreciation may hasten or retard the accumulation of funds for depreciation. Fourth, the rate of new inventions may be itself affected by the depression, which may hold back some kinds of research. If there are less new inventions, this may in turn affect the rate at which old machinery is considered obsolescent, a factor which is quite as important as physical depreciation. Finally, and perhaps most important, new inventions may not be introduced into industry (that is, entrepreneurs may not innovate) as long as the depression continues. So long as demand is too low to take the present supply, entrepreneurs may hesitate to make improvements that would increase their capacity. They may even hold off introducing cost-reducing inventions and new products during the general pessimism of a depression. Only after demand has begun to rise again is the flood of innovation released.

We must emphasize that new technological improvements result in higher output under capitalism *only if* demand rises sufficiently. With demand unchanged at the old level, new innovations in the automation of industry can only result in unemployment. In a depression, therefore, those innovations which do not affect demand may only serve to increase unemployment (although an innovation which speeded up the "replacement" of old capital might increase total investment demand). In a prosperity, when demand is racing ahead of supply, *then* a technological innovation would increase output.

Cyclical Growth

Here, we do not present a full theory of cyclical growth, but merely some of the relations of growth to cycles, especially to cycles of "increasing intensity." In the case of capitalism, we do not observe smooth and steady growth, yet neither do we find an end of growth or complete stagnation even in the long run.[48] A cyclical or *transitory* "overabundance of capital, overproduction, crisis, is something different. There are no permanent crises."[49] In other words, the growth of capitalism comes through temporary periods of prosperity, followed usually by depression periods (also temporary).[50] Nevertheless, the long-run economic trend of capitalism is one of growth. Of course, this does not mean that capitalism will last forever, but only that its demise is not likely to result from a slow and purely economic run-down into a stagnant state. We do not predict that there will be any automatic economic breakdown of capitalism, but rather assert that it will end through revolutionary struggles (as determined *in part* by the economic conditions).[51] Even the revolutionary Lenin ridiculed the idea of an automatic economic collapse, and noted the possibility of continued capitalist economic growth:

. . . There is nothing more stupid than to deduce from the contradictions of capitalism its impossibility, its unprogressive character, etc.—that is flight from an unpleasant but undoubted reality into the cloud world of romantic fantasies. . . . The contradictions of capitalism testify to its historical-transitional character, explain the conditions and causes of its downfall and its transformation into a higher form—but they exclude neither the possibility of capitalism nor its progressiveness in comparison with earlier systems of social economy.[52]

If capitalism were static and purely competitive, with unchanging technology, no monopoly, no government economic activity, and no international imperialism, *then* maybe there would be a long-run trend to underconsumption, worse and worse depression, and/or eventual stagnation.[53] The real world, however, is very unlike the pure capitalist model. There is no observable trend to worse depressions since the 1930's (the 1929 depression *was* the worst on record). Instead, we find that in any given crisis situation, a depression with mass unemployment may not be "inevitable." Crises of overproduction may be and have been resolved in many other ways. Private wastes, such as most advertising, competitive duplication of effort, large amounts of luxury consumption, monopoly misallocation and restriction, may use up part of the product.[54] Government wastes, such as war and war production, may use up much product and many lives. Monopoly power changes the business cycle; it is also closely related to our current American phenomenon of unemployment *and* inflation together. These issues are discussed in detail in succeeding chapters. (A mathematical model of cyclical growth is presented in Appendix 5 to this book.)

NOTES

1. The human tragedy of the 1930's is spelled out in David Shannon, *The Great Depression* (Englewood Cliffs, N.J.: Prentice-Hall, 1960); also in Studs Terkel, *Hard Times: An Oral History of the Great Depression* (New York: Pantheon Books, 1970); also Edward Ellis, *A Nation in Torment: The Great American Depression, 1929–1939* (New York: Coward-McCann, 1970).

2. John M. Keynes, *General Theory of Employment, Interest, and Money* (New York: Harcourt, Brace, and Company, 1936). Except for terminology, the basic framework of Keynes is mostly just an independent rediscovery of Marx's framework.

3. For Marx's attack on Say's Law, see his *Theories of Surplus Value* (New York: International Publishers, transl. 1952), pp. 368–415; also see Bernice Shoul, "Karl Marx and Say's Law," *Quarterly Journal of Economics*, 71 (November 1957): 611–629.

4. A strict and meaningless interpretation says that supply equals demand at every moment; the more usual interpretation is that demand automatically adjusts to supply

in a short time. The "Law" is sometimes stated as the truism that demand will eventually adjust to supply at *some* price level (and some unemployment level). Here we attack the mistaken notion (sometimes called "Say's Identity") that demand will adjust to supply at *any* price level and *any* level of employment, including full employment. For further clarification see Oskar Lange, "Say's Law: A Reinterpretation," in O. Lange, F. McIntyre, and T. Yntema, eds., *Studies in Mathematical Economics and Econometrics* (Chicago: University of Chicago Press, 1942), pp. 49–68.

5. Marx, *Capital*, vol. 1, pp. 26 and 695. Marx is cited in the footnotes to this chapter, not to prove anything, but for the convenience of those who wish to trace his views on each of the subjects covered here.

6. See, e.g., Gottfried Haberler, "Business Cycles in a Planned Economy," *Conference on Business Cycles, 1949* (New York: National Bureau of Economic Research, 1951), p. 385; also Abram Bergson, "A Comment on Business Cycles on a Planned Economy," *Conference on Business Cycles, 1949* (New York: National Bureau of Economic Research, 1951), p. 388. Contra, see David M. Wright, *A Key to Modern Economics* (New York: The Macmillan Co., 1954), Chapters 9 and 11.

7. See Gottfried Haberler, *Prosperity and Depression* (Cambridge: Harvard University Press, 1960), Chapters 5 and 3 respectively.

8. See, e.g., the sharp critique in Marx, *Capital*, vol. 2, pp. 475–476; yet Marx also said: "The ultimate cause of all real crises always remains the poverty and restricted consumption of the masses" (Marx, *Capital*, vol. 3, p. 568).

9. History of Marxist underconsumption theory is given in Paul Sweezy, *Theory of Capitalist Development* (New York: Monthly Review Press, first publ. 1942), with a formal model at pp. 186–189. That Marx had no underconsumptionist theory at all is asserted in Maurice Dobb, *Political Economy and Capitalism* (New York: International Publishers, 1945), p. 115.

10. *Capital*, vol. 3, p. 359.

11. *Capital*, vol. 1, p. 680.

12. For a full discussion of this relationship, see Howard Sherman, *Macrodynamic Economics* (New York: Appleton-Century-Crofts, 1964), pp. 65–74.

13. *Capital*, vol. 3, pp. 222–223; 568.

14. Data derived from Wesley Mitchell, *What Happens in Business Cycles* (New York: National Bureau of Economic Research, Inc., 1951), p. 155.

15. *Ibid.*, pp. 154–155 and 324; also see Simon Kuznets, *Shares of Upper Income Groups in Income and Savings* (New York: National Bureau of Economic Research, Inc., 1953), p. 55.

16. Department of Commerce, *Historical Statistics of the United States*, series 6, pp. 135–136.

17. Marx, *Capital*, vol. 1, p. 571.

18. See, e.g., Paul Sweezy, *op. cit.*, pp. 87–92, 181–189, and 273; also see Karl Marx, *Value, Price, and Profit* (New York: International Publishers, 1935).

19. *Capital*, vol. 2, p. 593; also vol. 3, pp. 286–287.

20. Lawrence R. Klein, *An Introduction to Econometrics* (Englewood Cliffs, N.J.: Prentice-Hall, Inc., 1962), p. 228.

21. *Ibid.*, p. 230.

22. L. R. Klein and A. S. Goldberger, *An Econometric Model of the United States, 1939–1952* (Amsterdam: North-Holland Publishing Co., 1955).

23. The falling rate of profit (long run?) is considered an important factor by Dobb, *loc. cit.*, and it is believed to cause worse and worse depressions by Joseph Gillman, *The Falling Rate of Profit* (New York: Cameron Associates, 1958).

24. See, e.g., Marx *Capital*, vol. 3, pp. 242ff. In fact, if one reads closely the famous chapter on "Unraveling the Internal Contradictions of the Law of the Falling Tendency of the Rate of Profit," in Marx *Capital*, vol. 3, chapter 15, it is amazing to find as much or more on short-run profit declines (with a constant amount of capital) as on the alleged long-run decline. In that chapter and elsewhere Marx seems to foreshadow Keynes's marginal profit (or "efficiency of capital") concept in the many useful things he has to say about the relation of short-run profit fluctuations to short-run fluctuations

in investment. Certainly, Marxists would meet a better reception among non-Marxist economists if they would completely disentangle the short-run and long-run analyses of profit behavior.

25. Karl Marx, *Theories of Surplus Value* (New York: International Publishers, 1952), p. 371.

26. *Ibid.*, p. 371ff.

27. Frederick C. Mills, *Price-Quantity Interactions in Business Cycles* (New York: National Bureau of Economic Research, Inc., 1946).

28. Marx describes this process of price-cost adjustment very colorfully. "The principal work of destruction would show its most dire effects in a slaughtering of the values of capitals. . . . One portion of the commodities on the market can complete its process of circulation and reproduction only by an immense contraction of its prices, which means a depreciation of the capital represented by it. In the same way the elements of fixed capital are more or less depreciated. . . . The depreciation of the elements of constant capital itself would be another factor tending to raise the average rate of profit. . . . And in this way the cycle would be run once more. . . . the same vicious circle would be described once more under expanded conditions of production, in an expanded market, and with increased productive forces." Marx, *Capital*, vol. 3, pp. 297–299.

29. Marx, *Capital*, vol. 1, p. 694.

30. Marx, *Capital*, vol. 3, p. 295.

31. Marx, *Capital*, vol. 1, p. 680.

32. See Paul Sweezy, *op. cit.*, pp. 148–149, where he incorrectly—I believe—attributes this theory to Marx.

33. "Nothing is more absurd, for this reason, than to explain a fall in the rate of profit by a rise in the rate of wages, although there may be exceptional cases where this may apply." Marx, *Capital*, vol. 3, p. 281.

34. See, e.g., John Strachey, *Nature of Capitalist Crisis* (New York: Covici-Friede, 1935). Also, see the hints in this direction by Marx, *Capital*, vol. 3, pp. 286–287, and *Theories of Surplus Value*, p. 407.

35. "The creation of . . . surplus-value is the object of the direct process of production. . . . But this production of surplus-value is but the first act of the capitalist process of production. . . . Now comes the second act of the process. The entire mass of commodities . . . must be sold. If this is not done, or only partly accomplished . . . the laborer has been none the less exploited, but his exploitation does not realise as much for the capitalist. . . . the realization of surplus value . . . is not determined . . . by the absolute consuming power, but by the consuming power based on antagonistic conditions of distribution, which reduces the consumption of the great mass of the population to a variable minimum within more or less narrow limits." Marx, *Capital*, vol. 3, p. 286.

36. See, e.g., Julian Borchardt, "The Essence of Marx's Theory of Crises," *Capital and Other Writings*, ed. by Marx Eastman (New York: The Modern Library, 1932), pp. 302–315.

37. *Ibid.*, p. 310. Sweezy notes that Borchardt's essay "had a wide currency in Germany and enjoyed the official approval of the Social Democratic party." Sweezy, *op. cit.*, p. 158.

38. Marx, *Theories of Surplus Value*, pp. 391–402. Also see the powerful attack on the reformist theory in Louis Boudin, *The Theoretical System of Karl Marx* (New York: Monthly Review Press, 1968, originally 1907).

39. Marx, *Theories of Surplus Value*, pp. 376–384.

40. "The chain of payments due at certain times is broken in a hundred places, and the disaster is intensified by the collapse of the credit system." Marx, *Capital*, vol. 3, p. 298.

41. Marx, *Capital*, vol. 3, p. 573.

42. Marx, *Capital*, vol. 3, p. 575.

43. Marx, *Capital*, vol. 3, pp. 359–360.

44. Marx, *Capital*, vol. 3, pp. 576–577.

45. Marx, *Capital*, vol. 2, Parts 1 and 2.

46. See, e.g., Johan Einarsen, *Reinvestment Cycles* (Oslo: J. Chr. Gundersens Boktrykkeri, 1938).

47. Marx, *Capital*, vol. 2, p. 211.

48. One careful discussion of long-term trends as seen by Marx can be found in Leo Rogin, *The Meaning and Validity of Economic Theory* (New York: Harper & Brothers, 1956), pp. 351–388.

49. Marx, *Theories of Surplus Value*, p. 373.

50. Marx, *Capital*, vol. 1, pp. 694–695.

51. A full history of the "breakdown" controversy in Marxist thought is presented in Paul Sweezy, *op. cit.*, pp. 190–213.

52. V. I. Lenin, *The Development of Capitalism in Russia*, quoted by Sweezy, *op. cit.*, p. 185. The reformist view, that capitalist economic conditions are getting better and better, is presented in Edward Bernstein, *Evolutionary Socialism* (New York: Schocken Books, 1961, first publ. 1899).

53. Sweezy, *op. cit.*, pp. 214–238.

54. Discussions of the countercyclical role of waste and nonproductive labor may be found in Sydney Coontz, *Productive Labor and Effective Demand* (New York: A. M. Kelly, 1966); Joseph Gillman, *op. cit.*, and Paul Baran and Paul Sweezy, *Monopoly Capital* (New York: Monthly Review Press, 1966).

CHAPTER

8

Monopoly Capitalism

The world of numerous, quaint, small competitive capitalist enterprises—which Adam Smith thought would produce the best result for all concerned—is gone forever. Since the period of the 1890's and early 1900's, we shall see that Western Europe and the United States have been characterized by the domination of a relatively small number of giant firms. This new stage of capitalism (monopoly capitalism) has not ended capitalism, but has intensified many old qualities and has added some entirely new (and unpleasant) ones.[1]

We shall see in this chapter that in the stage of monopoly capitalism the setting of prices and outputs is quite different, and the profit result is equally different.[2] The amount of waste, manipulation of the consumer, exploitation of the worker, and conflict with social needs (such as the need for a decent environment) will be shown to be on an entirely new scale. If Adam Smith's harmony of interests theory ever has a grain of truth, it is surely not applicable to monopoly capitalism. In further chapters we shall see the effect of monopoly capitalism on the capitalist state (Chapter 9), on the imperialist drive (Chapter 10), on discrimination and alienation (Chapter 11), and the prospects of revolution (Chapter 12).

An economy of pure competition would be an economy composed of individual business units competing with each other, where each is so small that its actions taken alone could not appreciably influence the quantity of goods or the price in the market. This description might have more or less matched the United States economy during the early nineteenth century. At that time small farms and small businesses produced most of the output, and there were no giant corporations dominating an entire industry (though there were many local monopolies). Since the 1890's or early 1900's, however, this picture no longer holds true.

Today, industry in the United State still has millions of very small enterprises, but a few hundred corporate giants hold most of the wealth and do most of the production. For all corporations, the picture of concentration is shown in Table 8–1.

TABLE 8-1
Distribution of Corporate Assets
(All U.S. Corporations, 1967)

SIZE (LOWER LIMIT)	CORPORA- TIONS %	ASSETS OWNED %
$ 0	59.01	1.5
$ 100,000	29.62	5.2
$ 500,000	9.71	9.5
$ 5,000,000	1.60	30.6
$250,000,000	.06	53.2
Total	100.00	100.0

Source: Reprinted by permission from Howard Sherman, *Profits in the United States* (Ithaca, N.Y.: Cornell University Press, 1968), p. 37.

This table reveals the extremely high concentration of assets within the corporate world. At the bottom, a large number of small corporations (906,458 or 59 per cent of the total) hold a tiny portion of corporate assets (31 billion dollars or 1.5 per cent). At the top a few giant corporations (958 or just 0.06 per cent) hold a majority of all assets (1,070 billion dollars or 53.2 per cent). That some 900 U.S. corporations should hold more than a trillion dollars of assets is incredible; that is more than the total value of all West European assets and in the same range as the value of all Soviet assets! Within those 958 corporations there is still a great concentration within just the top 200 or 300 corporations. Nor should these figures be dismissed because they include large sums of purely financial capital. Within the decisive sphere of manufacturing alone, the top 200 firms held 59 per cent of all manufacturing assets in 1967.[3] Moreover, it is these few large firms that control most research, and thus will continue to grow more rapidly. A 1960 survey showed that just four firms accounted for 22 per cent and just 384 firms accounted for 85 per cent of all industrial research and development.[4]

If we examine the individual industries, which are the arenas of most direct competition, the picture of economic concentration may be even more sharply drawn. In most individual industries, where an *industry* is defined so that there is easy substitution among the products of all firms within it and very little possible substitution with products of outside firms, the three or four giant corporations in the industry control most of its production. This domination of an industry by a few large firms is called an *oligopoly*. Many small firms also exist in most industries, but altogether they produce a small percentage of the total output. The economy of the United States has thus changed from a predominantly competitive to a predominantly oligopolistic production situation.[5] Finally, there is evidence that the trend toward concentration is continuing. For example, the 200 top firms held 49 per cent of all manufacturing assets in 1950, but that figure rose to 59 per cent by 1967.[6] Yet in that same period it is interesting that the average degree of concentration in each of the separate manufacturing industries changed very little. One reason is that the separate data on each industry are inadequate, mainly because they ignore the fact that the giant firms are increasingly acquiring and merging with firms in quite unrelated industries (called "conglomerate mergers").

Concentration may increase through rapid internal growth of firms, or by the merger of formerly independent firms. Mergers come in waves, the early one of the 1890's being rivalled by a new one today. In the period 1950 through 1959, there were an average of 540 corporate mergers a year. From 1960 through 1967 the average rose to 1,100 a year. In 1968 there were 2,655 mergers.[7]

More and more of these increasing numbers of mergers are conglomerate mergers between two giants in different industries. From 1948 through 1953 conglomerate mergers were 59 per cent of the total. From 1960 through 1965 they were 72 per cent of the total. In 1968 conglomerate mergers were 84 per cent of all mergers.[8] Thus, concentration of assets greatly increased in the economy as a whole, while it did not seem to change much when measured within each industry.

The Reasons for Monopoly

The fundamental cause of the emergence of the giant corporation is the economy of scale to be derived from large-size production units. Large-scale production turns out cheaper goods by using more specialized machinery, more specialized workers, and mass production assembly lines. "The battle of competition is fought by cheapening of commodities. The cheapness of commodities depends, ceteris paribus, on the productiveness of labor, and this again on the scale of production . . . it always ends in the ruin of many smaller capitalists, whose capitals partly pass into the hands of their conquerors, partly vanish."[9] The large firm gains a monopoly by selling at a lower price while making more profit. In addition to improved technology based on the economies of scale, there are other reasons for the greater profitability of huge firms such as General Motors. These firms grow internally or by merger far beyond the technologically necessary minimum because they wish to exercise monopoly power over the market. With small competitors eliminated or dominated, the few remaining giant firms can restrict output and set higher prices to make higher profit rates. Moreover, they can plan with more certainty over a longer period of time with less risk.

This elimination of risk and uncertainty entails not only control of their own industry's output but also (1) buying out of raw material suppliers, (2) buying out dealers and outlets for the finished product, (3) vast nationwide advertising, and (4) link-up with banks and other financial sources. In addition to nationwide advertising and control of retail outlets, there are other economies of scale in selling. For example, Litton Industries maintains a flock of ex–army officers, so they can sell to the Pentagon "more efficiently" than the small companies it bought up could do alone. With these motivations, there is no clear upper limit to desirable size. Their motto seems to be "the bigger the better."

Prices and Profit Maximization

What is the effect of monopoly on the price structure? The essence of the monopolist's position is his ability to keep competitors out of the market by greater efficiency, or by control of natural or financial resources, or by control of patents, or by any other legal or illegal methods. Thus, he can charge what the market will bear, and there is no competitive mechanism to bring his higher profit back down to the average rate of profit in all industry.[10]

Although the monopolist can make a higher than average rate of profit, he cannot make profit out of thin air. Total profit still remains within the limits of the total surplus value produced by the working class. Of course, in terms of the labor theory of value, monopoly power means that prices deviate still further from the values of particular commodities. The labor theory can be rescued, first, by arguing that monopoly does not affect aggregate prices nor aggregate profits, but only redistributes the aggregate profits. "The monopoly price of certain commodities would merely transfer a portion of the profit of the other producers of commodities to the commodities with a monopoly price."[11] From a given amount of aggregate profits (or surplus value), monopolists may take away part of the profits of small businessmen and small farmers by their competition for the consumer dollar, or by their power to buy raw materials and food at low prices and sell finished goods at high prices to these small entrepreneurs. Marx, however, immediately qualifies this statement by admitting that monopolists may also increase the total surplus.[12] They may do this by using their power to raise prices or to restrict money wages so as to lower the workers' real wages.

Monopoly Capitalism

While Marx thus retains clear, objective limits to monopoly power, various superficial Marxists have seen no limits, except demand, to the monopoly power to raise prices. For a long time, Marxists and radicals said very little about the quantification of monopoly prices. An orthodox Marxist writer of the 1950's merely wrote that monopoly prices are determined "in the manner with which we are nowadays made familiar in every economics textbook."[13]

The modern neoclassical textbooks give the following account. Monopoly price and quantity of production are set by the monopolist, but in order to maximize his profits he can only set the quantity at the point of greatest difference between total revenue (determined by demand) and total cost (determined by the cost of living labor plus material costs). Once the quantity is set, even a monopoly can only sell at a price determined by the demand at that point. The difference from competition is that *the quantity supplied is set lower so that the price is higher*, and, therefore, the short-run rate of profit is higher than average. The long-run rate of profit remains higher because capital cannot freely enter the industry.

Contrary to the elementary textbook view, many economists claim that modern capitalists do not always maximize profit. We should observe first that the capitalist today is not the individual businessman, but the corporation. Whether the businessman is rational and calculating in his private life is essentially irrelevant to the functioning of the system. In his company life there can be no doubt that the making and accumulating of profit hold as dominant a position today as they ever did.[14] The giant corporation today is still an engine for maximizing profits as were the individual enterprises of an earlier period, but it is used not merely as an enlarged version of the personal capitalist. There are two differences: (1) it has a much longer time horizon, and (2) it is a much more rational calculator.[15]

Having said that much, we must avoid a dogmatic notion that every corporate decision is made in terms of immediate dollars and cents returns. It is certainly true that corporate management may sacrifice short-run profits to the security of their market control, to the growth of their company, and even to the somewhat vague concept of "prestige." Thus, prices are *not* always set as high as the market will bear. We could say that they maximize a multiple set of objectives. Equally well (since the difference is only semantic), we could emphasize that each of the other objectives are merely rational ways of achieving maximum "long-run" profits, so that is really the sole objective.

The large corporations do prevent price competition (although they do compete through alleged quality differences and advertising). With no price competition, sellers of a given commodity (and its close substitutes) have an interest in seeing that the price or prices established are such as to maximize the profits of the group as a whole. In other words, each product is priced *as if* it were sold by a single monopoly corporation. This is the decisive fact in determining the price policies and strategies of the typical large corporation. And it means that the appropriate price theory of an economy dominated by such corporations is *not* competitive price theory, but monopoly price theory. What economists have hitherto treated as a special case is the general situation!

It is true that there is little open collusion in the United States because of the antitrust laws. Yet some kind of tacit collusion probably exists to a large degree in most industries. This tacit collusion reaches its most developed form in what is known as "price leadership." It is a mutual security in which no formal communication is necessary.[16]

In this situation, when one firm raises or lowers the price, if it is in the interest of all the others, they will follow. If they do not follow, the firm that made the first move will rescind its initial price change. It is this willingness to rescind if an initial change is not followed which distinguishes the tacit collusion situation from the price war situation. So long as all firms accept this convention, which is really nothing else but a corollary of the ban on price competition, it becomes easy for the group as a whole to feel its way toward the price which maximizes the industry's profit.

There is the qualification that in theory pure monopoly prices move upward or downward with equal ease, whereas that is not the case today. If one seller raises his price, this cannot possibly be interpreted as an aggressive move. The worst that can happen to him is that the others will stand pat and he'll have to rescind (or accept a smaller share of the market). In the case of a price cut, on the other hand, there is always the possibility that aggression is intended, that the cutter is trying to increase his share of the market by violating the taboo on price competition. If rivals interpret the initial move in this way, a price war with losses to all may result. Hence, everyone is more likely to be careful about lowering than raising prices. Under the present situation of oligopoly, in other words, prices tend to be stickier on the downward side than on the upward side, and this fact introduces a significant upward bias into the general price level in a monopoly capitalist economy.[17]

Who Controls the Corporation?

Liberals agree that monopoly is an evil aspect of capitalism, but they believe the evil can be ended without ending capitalism. Some rely on stricter enforcement of the antitrust laws. Others admit that the law is plainly inadequate on the basis of all our experience, but claim that the giant corporation is changing internally, so as to eliminate automatically most of its negative qualities while remaining large. Professor Galbraith, whose description of monopoly capitalism is otherwise excellent, is the leading spokesman of this latter view.[18]

Galbraith says there is a great contradiction between the notion that the modern corporation is mostly controlled by the management and that the modern corporation nevertheless ruthlessly tries to maximize profit for the stockholders. Furthermore, he argues that the most important factor of production is no longer capital, but the specialized talent of scientists and technologists. Therefore, he claims that real power passes from stockholders and top management to the members of the technical structure (scientists and technicians). Moreover, he says that the members of the technical structure do not get the profits that they are supposed to maximize. Since the technical structure supplies talent not capital, why should they worry about the return to capital? He says that the modern corporation has power to shape society, but this power is used, as might be expected, to serve the deeper interests or goals of the technical structure, for this structure possesses the power.[19]

Galbraith agrees that a few hundred giant corporations control the market, regulate output and prices, and exercise enormous political control. Yet by a wave of his hand, he eliminates class conflict, and puts the control of the corporation in the hands of all scientists and technically skilled workers. He then finds that they manage the corporation in the best interests of all society (this has been called the "soulful corporation" view). In other words, Galbraith is very critical of capitalism especially in the tremendous centralization of the means of production, but nevertheless is apologetic in the sense that he concludes that the "industrial system" has actually solved (or is solving) its problem.

The liberal view, as expressed by Galbraith, seems to ignore the real position of modern corporate management.[20] In the first place, the fact that so many top executives hold stock means their motivations cannot possibly be inconsistent with profit-making. For example, twenty-five General Motors' officers in early 1957 owned an average of 11,500 shares each.[21] They might not be able to affect policy even with that amount of stock in General Motors, yet each one owned roughly a half million dollars in the company, so their motivation was anything but nonprofit-directed. Moreover, a larger proportion of managers hold stock than any other group, and there are more of the managerial group in the stockholding class than any other group.[22]

Galbraith, of course, argues that it is not the motivation of the managers but the motivation of the technostructure that is decisive. Still, the goals of the technostructure would be the same as those of the managers, namely survival of the firm, its growth, its independence from outside control. All these demand profit-making. More importantly, it flies in the face of reality to think that the technicians control the corporations. The managers hire and fire the technicians, and not vice versa. In the end it is the boss, rather than his hired hand, who makes the decisions (and will use expert advice only to make more profitable decisions).

Monopoly Profit Rates
(and Income Distribution)

We have examined the monopoly structure of American capitalism, and have investigated the price-setting behavior of its management. Now we must see how the monopoly structure and behavior affect the performance of American capitalism. In this section, we examine its effect on profit rates. First, the sources of monopoly profit are briefly recapitulated in theory. Then the facts of monopoly profit are presented.

The whole point of monopoly (or oligopoly) control of markets is, of course, to restrict output and charge higher prices. Higher monopoly prices hurt all consumers (a majority of whom are workers). This source of extra profit may be called additional surplus value to the extent that it lowers workers' real wages. Second, higher monopoly prices for producer goods hurt all the purchasers of producer goods; and one may call this a shift of surplus value to the extent that it lowers the profits of small business and farmers. Third, if a large firm has some extra market power as a buyer of commodities (technically, "oligopsony power"), it may also shift some surplus value to itself by buying at a lower price from small business and farmers.

Fourth, if a giant firm has certain market power as a large buyer of labor (again, "oligopsony power"), it may also add to its surplus by buying labor at a lower rate than the average wage. This last factor may, of course, be somewhat offset by trade union action by workers. In the modern world of monopoly capitalism, wages are not determined simply by market supply and demand. We can no longer merely say that technological progress substitutes machinery for workers and the resulting unemployment keeps wages down to the habitual "subsistence" standard of living.

Marx's contention is that the mechanism of the reserve army of labour keeps wages within limits which permit the continuance of the capitalist system. An increase in productivity raises the upper limit of wages tolerable to capitalism. The development of trade-union power tends to push wages towards that upper limit, while the counteracting force of monopoly prevents them from rising above it.[23]

Monopoly Capitalism

Fifth, additional monopoly profits come from lucrative government military contracts—from the workers' tax money, thus again increasing surplus value (see Chapter 9). Sixth, additional monopoly profits come from imperialist returns from investments abroad, that is, extraction of surplus value from workers in foreign countries (see Chapter 9).

Turning to the facts, first, we may investigate how the profit rates of an enterprise are affected by the absolute size of the enterprise. The size of a business may be indicated by the total amount of its assets. The profit rate is the total profit divided by the capital investment of all the stockholders. Data for profit rates by asset size are available for all corporations since 1931. These data are shown in Table 8–2.

TABLE 8-2
Long-run Profit Rate by Corporate Size
(All U.S. Corporations, 1931-1961, Excluding the War Years 1940-1947)

	PROFIT RATE (PROFIT BEFORE TAXES DIVIDED BY STOCK-HOLDERS' CAPITAL)
$ 0 - 50,000	−7.1
$ 50,000 - 100,000	4.1
$ 100,000 - 250,000	5.9
$ 250,000 - 500,000	7.4
$ 500,000 - 1,000,000	8.3
$ 1,000,000 - 5,000,000	9.3
$ 5,000,000 - 10,000,000	9.7
$10,000,000 - 50,000,000	10.4
over $ 50,000,000	10.4

Source: Reprinted by permission from Howard Sherman, *Profits in the United States* (Ithaca, N.Y.: Cornell University Press, 1968), p. 41.

In an economy of pure and perfect competition, all profit rates should be equalized in the long run. The evidence, however, shows that in the U.S. economy the long-run profit rate is *not* the same for all corporations. On the contrary, the table shows that the smallest corporations have low or even negative profit rates. Then the profit rate rises with the scale of the corporation, although the differences are quite small among the largest size groups. These data are far from perfect, and many alternative definitions are possible; still, the general picture remains the same on any definition.[24]

Economic concentration, however, has another important aspect. The indicator of market power is the size and importance of a firm *relative* to other firms in its own industry. We may define a *concentration ratio* in each industry to be the percentage of sales controlled by the eight largest corporations in the industry. Several studies have found a definite relationship between the concentration ratio in an industry and the profit rates of an industry.[25] Further evidence is presented in Table 8-3.

TABLE 8-3

Profit Rates and Concentration Ratios by Industry Group
(All Manufacturing Corporations in 1954)

INDUSTRY GROUP	CONCENTRATION RATIO (% OF SALES BY EIGHT LARGEST SELLERS	PROFIT RATE (PROFIT BEFORE TAXES DIVIDED BY STOCKHOLDERS' CAPITAL)
Motor vehicles and parts	98.1	27.1
Tobacco	91.5	20.3
Transportation equipment (except motor vehicles)	75.6	29.8
Rubber	74.2	17.8
Primary metal	70.8	13.0
Chemicals	63.3	19.9
Electrical machinery	60.8	20.7
Petroleum and coal	57.7	7.7
Instruments	56.1	23.9
Stone, clay, glass	55.0	19.9
Food and beverages	45.7	14.4
Machinery except electrical	44.4	16.2
Fabricated metal	40.3	15.6
Paper	39.4	17.3
Textile mill	37.1	5.1
Leather	33.7	11.4
Furniture	23.8	12.8
Printing and publishing	21.5	15.1
Apparel	20.5	7.6
Lumber	15.5	12.2

Source: Reprinted by permission from Sherman, *Profit Rates in the United States*, op. cit., p. 85.

Table 8-3 shows the very high concentration of production that exists in many industry groups, reflecting the fact that in the majority of our industries the bulk of production is concentrated in a few giant corporations, with hundreds of smaller companies producing very little. Moreover, inspection of the table reveals a considerable rise of profit rates as the degree of concentration rises (the few noticeable exceptions are easy to explain from special causes). Thus the average rate of profit in the ten industry groups over the 50 per cent concentration level is 20 per cent; whereas it is only 12.8 per cent in the ten industry groups under the 50 per cent concentration level.[26]

This analysis may be extended to the trend of aggregate profits under capitalism.[27] There can be no doubt that, under monopoly capitalism, production costs per unit have tended downwards, and that there have been powerful impulses to innovation. Yet monopoly cannot be considered a rational and progressive system because, while it reduces costs, it continues to have extremely high prices. Moreover, its increased productivity does not go to everyone but to a few. Profit rates increase and the share of profit in national income rises. Contrary to the nineteenth century picture of falling rates of profit, under monopoly capitalism the giant corporations have been able to maintain high rates of profit.

Monopoly and Instability

When monopoly or oligopoly became the predominant forms of business enterprise in the 1890's and 1900's, many reformist socialists such as Eduard Bernstein predicted that careful planning by these large firms would end the periodic depressions of capitalism. Of course, if all competition were eliminated and there were only one big firm in each industry, then the business cycle *might* disappear; it would at least have an entirely different manifestation from what we know today. This, however, has never happened. In most industries there are a few large firms with most of the assets and sales, but a very large number of small firms continue in business. There is still violent competition (1) between small firms and large firms within the same industry, (2) between large firms with products that are substitutes, and (3) between all firms for the consumers' dollar. It can hardly be said that a situation of long-run industrial planning has replaced competition even if a few large firms do such planning for themselves. In this environment it is easy to understand why the prediction that the advent of trusts and oligopolies would completely eliminate the business cycle has proven false.

Lenin, in his work on *Imperialism*, made the opposite prediction: that the monopolistic structure of industry would increase instability and intensify the business cycle. Since we have so little concrete evidence concerning the earlier business cycles, it is very difficult to make a before-and-after comparison. About the most that can be said directly is that the depression of the 1890's (when monopoly was already very important) was one of the worst on record and that the depression of the 1930's (when monopoly had become the dominant form) was *the* worst on record. It is true that no serious depression has yet been seen in the post World War II period, but the period since 1940 really represents a still further structural stage in which the action of capitalist governments has again basically altered the economic environment. The tendency of monopoly to cause instability is, therefore, at most one set of pressures in a complex situation, overcome in recent years by other factors. Nevertheless, there is enough evidence to show that the underlying tendency does exist. First, we shall see that economic concentration may affect the *timing* of profit rate declines, with small business leading the downturn. Second, economic concentration may cause different *intensities* of profit rate fluctuation, with small business being hurt much worse in depressions. Third, we shall observe that small business investment declines usually set off the depression, and their catastrophic amount of decline makes it worse. All these reactions of small business can be traced to the pressures of the giant corporations. Finally, we shall see that the adverse effect of monopoly on income distribution may intensify the tendency to depression.

Timing of Profit Movements

Empirical evidence strongly suggests that the profit margin (profit divided by sales) of smaller corporations leads at the cycle turns by far more than the profit margin of the larger corporations, that is, it turns down earlier at prosperity peaks and turns up earlier at depression troughs. More precisely, let a "business cycle turning point" be defined as that month when the average of all economic indicators turns up or down. Then on the average at all turning points the profit margins of the smaller corporations (those under $100,000) lead the business cycle turning point by 7.35 months, but the profit margins of the largest corporations (those over $100,000,000) lead the business cycle turning point by only 2.7 months.[28]

We may also examine the profit data for manufacturing industry groups according to the degree of sales concentration. There is a statistically significant correlation between more competition and longer profit margin leads. In other words, earlier downturns are found in the less concentrated industries at cycle peaks (and earlier upturns at cycle troughs). From 1947 through 1963, the average lead in profit margins at all cycle turning points for the eleven most concentrated industry groups is only 2.16 months, but the average profit margin lead for the ten most competitive industry groups is 6.66 months.[29]

Why do the profit margins of the smallest firms and least concentrated industries show the earliest declines at business cycle peaks? First, it appears that prices in the more concentrated industries resist any decline for a longer time, and do not decline till after the peak. Second, in the usual business cycle expansion there is a great influx of new small firms into industry, many of which are very inefficient and can exist only so long as they make windfall profits from the general rise in prices. The increasing percentage of inefficient, high-cost, small firms means that the average cost of production by all small firms must rise, and their profit margins may be squeezed much before that of the larger firms.

Amplitude of Profit Movements

How does economic concentration affect the amount of change in business performance from prosperity to depression? A great deal of evidence shows that cyclical performance, as indicated by profit rates, is quite different for big business and small business. Specifically, annual data on the profit rates of all corporations from 1931 through 1961 reveal that larger corporations had much more stable profit rates than smaller ones. The smaller the corporation, the greater was the amplitude of rise and fall in its profit rate.[30]

More precise quarterly data for the postwar period are presented in Table 8-4. This table shows that the amplitude of rise and decline of profit margins decreases as the corporate size increases. In other words, the profit margins of smaller corporations are much more unstable (fluctuate more) over the business cycle than those of the larger corporations.

TABLE 8-4

Cyclical Changes in Profit Margins by Corporate Size
(Quarterly Data, All Manufacturing Corporations, 1947-1965;
Profit Margin Means Profit Divided by Sales)

ASSET SIZE OF CORPORATION	EXPANSION OF PROFIT MARGIN IN PROSPERITIES (AS % OF AVERAGE VALUE OVER THE WHOLE PERIOD)	CONTRACTION OF PROFIT MARGIN IN DEPRESSIONS (AS % OF AVERAGE VALUE OVER THE WHOLE PERIOD)
$ 0 - 250,000	83.1	82.7
$ 250,000 - 1,000,000	39.4	54.8
$1,000,000 - 5,000,000	37.2	51.3
$5,000,000 - 100,000,000	27.7	26.8
over $ 100,000,000	21.5	27.0

Source: Calculated and compiled by author from data of the Federal Trade Commission and Securities and Exchange Commission. Reprinted by permission from Sherman, *Profit Rates in the United States, op. cit.,* p. 169.

We also have available quarterly data on profit margins in U.S. manufacturing industries from 1947 through 1963. There is a tendency in these data for the industries with the lowest degree of concentration to have the greatest cyclical changes in profit margins.[31] For example, apparel and lumber are the two industries with the most competition; they have the highest cyclical changes in profit margins both in prosperity and in depression. On the other hand, tobacco is one of the more concentrated industries and has the lowest cyclical changes in its profit margin both in expansion and contraction. Of course, there are many exceptions. Nevertheless, if we average the eleven most concentrated industries, we find that the average decline of their profit margins in contraction is only 26.7 per cent. By contrast, the average contraction of the profit margin in the nine least concentrated (or most competitive) industries is 51.7 per cent. Similarly, in prosperity the average expansion of profit margins in the eleven most concentrated industries is only 30.9 per cent, but the average expansion amplitude of profit margins in the nine least concentrated industries is 58.3 per cent. The differences are statistically significant. We may therefore conclude that the highly concentrated industries have less cyclical instability of profit margins than the more competitive industries.

Why do small corporations and more competitive industries suffer more unstable profit rates than the giant firms? First, as we shall see below, the market power of oligopolies is sufficient to prevent or restrict price declines for the products of the oligopolies. Second, in depressions small businesses must still pay relatively high prices for oligopoly goods, but sell at relatively very low prices. Third, the small firms operate on a shoestring, keeping small inventories and small cash reserves, so they perform well in prosperity but at the first taste of bad times are in a crisis. Fourth, when the small firms go bankrupt, the giant firms acquire their assets for a song. Fifth, in a depression the small firms are forced to operate below the minimum technologically necessary scale of production, so they have relatively higher costs per unit. Finally, small firms are more loaded with debt; so when revenues drop in depression, the interest burden becomes relatively heavier, and the difficulty of repayment often leads to bankruptcy.

Monopoly and Investment Behavior

Investment behavior is closely related to profit rates and, thus, to industrial concentration. There is some (weak) evidence that new capital appropriations and actual investment expenditures on new plant and equipment begin to decline at the cycle peak significantly earlier in the more competitive industries. The evidence is much stronger that the amplitude of fluctuation in investment is affected by corporate size and degree of concentration. Thus one careful study found that small firms (under 4.9 million dollars in assets) had more rapid rates of capital growth during periods of expansion (in 1946–1948 and 1949–1950), but that the same small firms had much higher rates of decline during the recession of 1949.[32] It also appears (on the small amount of available evidence) that investment tends to be more stable in industries with a high degree of concentration than in the more competitive industries.

Conclusions on Monopoly and Instability

Under monopoly capitalism, we find, first, that the profit rates of the smaller and more competitive firms register the earliest declines in prosperity. The fact of their earlier decline in profit margins (as indicated in the evidence presented above) strongly implies *that it is these smaller, competitive firms that precipitate the depression,* since the decline in their profit margins is soon followed by a decline in their investment decisions and expenditures. The fact that the larger oligopolistic firms often maintain their own investment expenditures for some time, even after the cycle turning point, is not sufficient to stop the depression that is already under way and spreading to all areas of industry.

We have also seen that in depressions the profit margins of the small and competitive firms drop enormously, many turning into losses even in minor recessions. Moreover, we have noted that their large declines in profits are translated into very sharp declines in investment expenditures, which must considerably intensify the depression. Because of the cumulative and psychological effects of depressions, these losses and declines in investment in the competitive sectors cannot be fully offset by the comparative stability of profits and investment among the large oligopoly firms. Furthermore, we must always remember that the instability of the small competitive firms is largely caused by the pressures of the concentrated, giant corporations.

It must also be said that the monopoly sector achieves its "stability" of prices and profits by restricting supply of output, and hence by lowering employment. As we shall see in the next section, monopoly not only causes unemployment in its sector by restriction and in the small business sector by taking profits away; its rising prices are also a primary cause of inflation.

We also saw in an earlier section that monopoly power worsens the distribution of income. Therefore, it increases the shift that occurs in prosperity from wages to profits, from poor to rich. This has meant a further limitation in consumer buying power, with a greater tendency to depression. Moreover, in recent depressions, the stability of monopoly prices and profits has prevented much of a shift back to wages, thereby making recovery more difficult.

On the other hand, monopoly and government *do counter* the tendency

113

to "overproduction" and depression in their own ways. Later in this chapter we examine monopoly waste and restriction. In the next chapter we examine government waste, especially military waste.

Monopoly and Inflation

Keynesian theory (as presented in elementary textbooks) tells us that the price level rises when demand—in money terms—is greater than the value in present prices of the supply of goods at full employment. This situation arises in every major war because of the almost unlimited government demand for military goods. Thus, most of the rapid price increases of American history have occurred during wars: the Civil War, First and Second World Wars, Korean and Vietnam wars.

This Keynesian theory is called *demand-pull* inflation. It is often asserted that the United States has suffered recently from a great deal of *cost-push* inflation. The name "cost-push" comes from the idea that higher costs are pushing prices up, unlike the situation when a general excess of demand "pulls" prices up. It is alleged that a labor shortage raises wages, forcing entrepreneurs to raise prices, and thereby sets off a cost-push inflation.

It is true that back in the nineteenth century in the early stages of industrial development in the United States, during some of the railway booms, there may have been shortages of workers. These shortages temporarily caused an increase in wages and made immigration necessary to keep up with capital growth. Since that time, however, the opposite situation of labor surplus seems much more characteristic of the peacetime United States economy. Moreover, in all recent expansion periods, profits rose far faster than wages. Wage increases have only been *a pretext* for previously decided price increases; the cost-push theory of inflation has been used as a weapon against labor to hold down wages and increase profits.

The period since World War II in the United States has witnessed some long prosperities, but has been marked by a number of short recessions. It is, of course, normal during cyclical recovery to find prices rising as the demand for goods temporarily outdistances the supply. The important point to note is that price rises take place long *before* full employment is reached. In fact, in the period since 1953, even in the "prosperous" periods there have been chronic excess capacity and chronic unemployment of at least 5 or 6 per cent of the labor force according to official statistics. In this period the stage has been set for inflation by a fairly high level of demand. Demand, however, has still been below the full employment level, so it is not true that inflation has been caused by any real deficiency of labor supply relative to the demand.

This strange and very unpleasant phenomenon of unemployment *and* inflation is obviously not covered by the usual Keynesian analysis of inflation caused by the pull of excess demand. Yet the theory of wage or cost-push is factually untrue. Only one explanation remains to be considered. In this view, it is the oligopolistic freedom of price-fixing that causes the phenomenon of rising prices in certain industries in the face of declining demand, *with prices stable or rising even during recessions in recent years.* This phenomenon should be called "profit-push inflation," resulting from the exercise of monopoly power.[33]

This view accords with observations made earlier in this chapter. The relative stability of oligopolistic profit rates have been emphasized. These large corporations can afford to take a long view of profit maximization, and they have enough effect on the market through control of supply that they can set their prices at levels different from those that would result in a competitive market. Their profit rates fall relatively little in recessions because they maintain prices by restricting supply, but neither do their profit rates rise spectacularly in expansion. They increase production and hold on to their portion of the market in expansion, but they are cautious about raising prices and normally leave considerable slack below the price level that would be most profitable in the short run.

As expansion continues, all firms are faced by rising costs of both labor and capital goods. The small firm whose price is set by competition can only watch its profit margin decline, since demand is also limited. Not so the large oligopoly firm. Since it had intentionally set its prices below what the market would take, it may now use up part of the slack to raise its prices, often utilizing previous wage increases as an excuse. Higher wages may be part of the inflation spiral, being themselves a response to earlier price and profit rises. Higher wage costs, however, would have no direct effect on prices if it were not for the oligopolistic structure of industry that allows freedom of price-fixing within wide limits.

The market power of oligopolies to influence prices has been documented in several investigations. In the 1930's a famous study of price rigidity compared the drop in prices by industries during the Great Depression with the ratio of concentration of production by the four largest firms in each industry. It was found that the prices of the more concentrated industries fell much less than competitive prices.[34] The evidence from expansions in the 1920's and 1930's is less clear, with more equal price rises in competitive and oligopolistic sectors, or even a slightly greater rise in the competitive sector (so that the advantage merely seesawed to some extent cyclically, with only a very slow rise of oligopoly power).

In the United States in the period since the Second World War, the empirical data reflect a much more striking picture of the exercise of monopoly power, reflecting the accelerated trend toward concentration as well as the lucrative military contracts going to the giant corporations. In the 1948 recession, prices in the nine most competitive industry groups fell by 7.8 per cent, but prices in the seven most concentrated industry groups fell only 1.9 per cent.[35] In the recessions of 1953 and 1957, even the more competitive prices fell only slightly, but the prices in the more concentrated industries actually continued to *rise* during the recessions. Of course, this greater resistance of oligopoly prices to a decline in demand is a major cause of their more stable profit margins in depressions.

The expansions since the Second World War give even stronger evidence of the increase of monopoly power. From the trough of October, 1947, to the peak of July, 1953, the prices of the seven most concentrated industry groups rose 23.3 per cent, while prices in the nine most competitive rose only 12.4 per cent. Similarly, from the trough of August, 1954, to the peak of July, 1957, prices of the seven most concentrated groups rose by 16 per cent, while prices in the nine most competitive rose only 4.5 per cent. Thus, the cyclical pattern seems to have been changed (or exaggerated) by a long-run movement toward higher relative prices in the more concentrated industry groups.

What are the immediate policy implications for capitalist governments of the fact of profit-push inflation in the midst of unemployment? The Keynesian solution for unemployment has been to increase aggregate demand (by more spending and/or lower taxes), while the solution for inflation has been to reduce aggregate demand (by less spending and/or more taxes). These solutions are now clearly inadequate. A small increase in demand (usually by military production) does not necessarily stimulate output and employment, but is used by the dominant large corporations as a means of further raising prices for higher profits. A small decrease in demand (usually by cutting welfare spending or raising taxes) does not reduce most prices, but only leads to more unemployment.[36] In the context of the structure of political power in the capitalist state (see the next chapter), we shall find that direct wage-price controls are also not an adequate solution.

Monopoly and Waste

During the period since the U.S. economy has changed to a predominantly monopolistic structure, the rate of economic growth appears to have declined. Thus, the gross national product in constant prices grew by 4.31 per cent per year in 1839–1879, by 3.72 per cent per year in 1879–1919, and

2.97 per cent per year in 1919–1959.[37] To what extent, if any, this decline is related to the high level of oligopoly power is impossible to say because so many other factors have been operative.

We do know that production does not reach optimum efficiency below some crucial size. Thus, the increase in importance of large firms does mean that most of the economy has the ability to produce at lower costs than ever before. The data both on costs and on profit rates reveal the possibility of high efficiency at a fairly constant level beyond the minimum size firm.[38] Of course, the very large firms also have disproportionately larger research facilities and hold a very large proportion of all unexpired patents.[39] Therefore, they have the most potential for efficiency improvement. Moreover, many investment projects are simply too large for small firms.

On the other hand, the large, entrenched firm stands to lose most by the obsolescence of present machinery. It also loses most from such product improvements as will reduce the number of units that the customer need buy—for example, a longer-lasting light bulb. Therefore, if the large firm has an oligopoly position and faces no serious competitive pressure for improvement, it *may* hide away and not use many important new inventions. Oligopoly power may also be used to restrict supply in order to maintain prices. Oligopolies will expand production as rapidly as possible only in the unusual periods of unlimited demand, such as the Second World War. Monopoly capitalism has paradoxical effects on innovation; it has a rapid rate of technological progress, but retains a large amount of technologically obsolete equipment.

Moreover, we have seen that the existence of economic concentration may have increased the severity and possibly the number of depressions because of its destabilizing effects on the remaining small businesses. If this is so, then unless it has had a fully offsetting effect in increasing growth during prosperity, it would seem that this is another reason why the net effect of oligopoly may be to lower the rate of economic growth. This is not to say, of course, that breaking up large firms into smaller units would increase economic growth. Reduction of the American economy to all small firms would certainly cause a major decrease of economic efficiency, in addition to its probable negative effects on investment.

The rate of growth (and waste) under monopoly capitalism is also affected by the fact that the sales effort has greatly expanded. From being a relatively unimportant feature of the system, it has grown to the status of one of its decisive nerve centers.[40] Impact on the economy is outranked only by militarism. In all other aspects of social existence, its all-pervasive influence is second to none. In an economic system in which competition is fierce and relentless, but in which the fewness of the rivals rules out price-cutting, advertising becomes to an ever increasing extent the principal weapon of the competitive struggle. There is little room under atomistic competition for advertising, whereas in monopoly it is one of the most important factors in the firm's survival. Relatively large firms are in a position to exercise a powerful influence upon the market for their output by establishing and maintaining a pronounced difference between their products and those of their competitors. This differentiation is sought chiefly by means of advertising, trademarks, brand names, distinctive packaging, and product variation. If successful, it leads to a condition in which the differentiated products cease, in the view of consumers, to serve as close substitutes for each other.

Several studies have demonstrated that advertising involves a massive waste of resources, a continual drain on the consumer's income, and a systematic destruction of the consumer's freedom of choice between genuine alternatives.[41] Furthermore, advertising in all its aspects cannot be-meaningfully dealt with as some undesirable excrescence on the economic system which could be removed if we would only make up our minds to get rid of it. Advertising is the very offspring of monopoly capitalism, the inevitable by-product of the decline of price competition; it constitutes as much an integral part of the system as the giant corporation itself. The economic importance of advertising lies not primarily in its causing a real-location of consumers' expenditures among different commodities, but in its effect on the magnitude of aggregate effective demand and thus on the level of income and employment. In other words, it generates useless expenditures, both by capitalists and by consumers, that soak up part of the "overproduction" of monopoly capitalism.

Advertising affects profits in two ways.[42] The first effect is the fact that part of advertising and other selling expenses are paid for through an increase in the prices of consumer goods bought by productive workers. Their real wages are reduced by this amount, and profit is correspondingly increased. The other effect is that some capitalists make profits from the business of advertising. At the same time, advertising constitutes an expense for other capitalists. Thus, advertising costs redistribute profits from one capitalist to another. Some individuals living off profits are deprived of a fraction of their incomes in order to support other individuals living off profits, namely those who derive their incomes from the profits (and wages) in the advertising industry itself.

Advertising is therefore similar to government spending when the government spending is just balanced by taxes.[43] Both add to aggregate income and output by an amount just as large as the original revenue and outlay. Furthermore, in making it possible to *create* the demand for a product, advertising encourages investment in plant and equipment which otherwise would not take place. With regard to the division of total income between consumption and saving, the effect of advertising is not measurable, but clear in direction and probably very large. A main function of advertising, perhaps its dominant function today, is to wage a relentless war on behalf of the producers and sellers of consumers' goods, against saving and in favor of consumption.

Actually, much of the "newness" with which the consumer is systematically bombarded is either fraudulent or related trivially, and in many cases even negatively, to the function and serviceability of the product.[44] Moreover, there are other products introduced which are indeed new in design and appearance, but which serve essentially the same purposes as old products they are intended to replace. The extent of the difference can vary all the way from a simple change in packaging to the far-reaching and enormously expensive annual changes in automobile models.

Furthermore, most research and development programs, which constitute a multi-billion dollar effort in the United States, are more closely related to the production of saleable goods than to its much touted mission of advancing science and technology.[45] For example, if we exclude monopoly profit and dealers' markups, then the real cost of production of the 1949 automobile, built with the technology of 1956–1960, would have been less than $700. Moreover, it has been estimated that a rationally designed car could have been turned out at a cost of $200 less than the 1949 model. If we assume further the existence of an economical and efficient distributive system, we have to conclude that the final price to consumers of an automobile would not need to exceed something like $700 or $800. Total saving of resources would then be about eleven billion dollars a year. On this calculation useless automobile model changes alone amounted to about 2.5 per cent of gross national product in the late 1950's. Thus, the total amount of waste from all the time and effort devoted directly and indirectly to *selling* products under monopoly capitalism must considerably lower the rate of economic growth.

Not only does monopoly capitalism greatly increase the waste of capitalism, but it raises pollution and environmental destruction to a new level. In the competitive model, apologists could claim that what was produced was according to the consumers' preferences, so pollution was merely an unfortunate by-product of public demand (an "external diseconomy"). These unfortunate by-products of public preferences could be handled by some minor public action in beautifying the environment. Under monopoly capitalism the "preferences" are manipulated and directed toward whatever products are most profitable to produce. Therefore, under monopoly capitalism "environmental damage becomes a normal consequence of the conflict between the goals of the producing firm and those of the public."[46]

So far, only the unemployment, inflation, civilian wastes, and peacetime pollutions caused by monopoly capitalism have been considered. Its full effect cannot be appreciated until we analyze its political power and mili-

119

tarist trend (next chapter), international spread (Chapter 9), and social effects (Chapter 10).

NOTES

1. Marx was the first great economist to emphasize the trend toward extreme economic concentration—see Marx, *Capital*, vol. 1, pp. 681–689—but even he never thought that it might mean a whole qualitatively new stage of capitalism.

2. Western economics recognized these results in theory in the case of a pure monopoly as early as Augustin Cournot, *Researches into the Mathematical Principles of the Theory of Wealth* (New York: A. M. Kelly, 1960, first publ. 1838). Since, however, a pure monopoly is very rare, Western economics had little to say about (and largely ignored) the increasing concentration of ownership in a few giant companies in each industry. Not until the 1930's were there two pioneering works on this reality: Edward Chamberlin, *The Theory of Monopolistic Competition* (Cambridge: Harvard University Press, 1950, first publ. 1933); and Joan Robinson, *The Economics of Imperfect Competition* (London: Macmillan and Co., 1934).

3. Federal Trade Commission data cited in Federal Reserve Bank of Cleveland, *Economic Commentary* (May 12, 1969): 2.

4. See John K. Galbraith, *The New Industrial State* (Boston: Houghton Mifflin Co., 1967), p. 23 and sources cited therein.

5. For convenience, the terms "monopoly" and "monopoly power" are used in their common usages in this chapter to include (1) concentration of a large part of all U.S. corporate assets in 200 or 300 giant firms, and (2) oligopoly control of most individual markets. The meanings are differentiated where necessary.

6. Federal Trade Commission data cited in Federal Reserve Bank of Cleveland, *op. cit.*, pp. 1–2.

7. *Ibid.*, p. 3.

8. *Ibid.*

9. Marx, *Capital*, vol. 1, pp. 686–687. Empirical supporting evidence can be found in Joe S. Bain, "Price and Production Policies," in Howard S. Ellis, ed., *A Survey of Contemporary Economics* (New York: McGraw-Hill, 1948), p. 140.

10. Empirical data on the impact of monopoly power on prices through the prevention of entry by competitors can be found in J. S. Bain, *Barriers to New Competition* (Cambridge: Harvard University Press, 1956).

11. Marx, *Capital*, vol. 3, p. 1003.

12. *Ibid.*

13. Ronald Meek, *Studies in the Labor Theory of Value* (New York: International Publishers, 1956), p. 292.

14. This statement and the following argument relies on the sophisticated Marxist approach in Paul Baran and Paul Sweezy, *Monopoly Capital* (New York: Monthly Review Press, 1966), pp. 43ff.

15. In this respect, see James Earley, "The Impact of Some New Developments in Economic Theory: Discussion," *America Economic Review* (Proceedings), 47 (May 1957): 333–335.

16. See also Galbraith, *op. cit.*, p. 30.

17. This description does bear some resemblance to the earlier "kinked demand" theory; see Paul Sweezy, "Demand under Conditions of Oligopoly," *Journal of Political Economy*, 47 (August 1939): 568–573.

18. Galbraith, op. cit., Chapters 5, 6, 7, 8.

19. Galbraith, *op. cit.*, p. 127.

20. This critique follows the general views of Ralph Miliband, "Professor Galbraith and American Capitalism," Ralph Miliband and John Saville, eds., *The Socialist Register*, 1968 (New York: Monthly Review Press, 1968).

21. Gabriel Kolko, *Wealth and Power in America* (New York: Praeger, 1962), p. 13.

22. *Ibid.*

23. Joan Robinson, *An Essay on Marxian Economics* (New York: St. Martin's Press, 1966, 2nd ed.), pp. 32–33.

24. See Howard J. Sherman, *Profit Rates in the United States* (Ithaca, N.Y.: Cornell University Press, 1968), pp. 40–50.

25. See, e.g., J. S. Bain, "The Relation of Profit Rate to Industrial Concentration, American Manufacturing, 1936–1940," *Quarterly Journal of Economics*, 65 (August 1951): 292–324.

26. Such a difference is statistically significant, that is, it could occur by chance far less than 1 per cent of the time.

27. Baran and Sweezy, *op. cit.*, pp. 52–78.

28. Data calculated and compiled by author from the Federal Trade Commission and Securities and Exchange Commission. See Sherman, *op. cit.*, pp. 141–150.

29. Calculated from FTC and SEC data; see Sherman, *op. cit.*, pp. 151–155.

30. *Ibid.*, pp. 156–166.

31. See Table 7–8 in Sherman, *op. cit.*, p. 171.

32. John R. Meyer and Edwin Kuh, *The Investment Decision* (Cambridge: Harvard University Press, 1957), pp. 163–167.

33. See the similar conclusion in the staff report, U.S. Congress, Joint Economic Committee, *Employment, Growth, and Price Levels* (Washington, D.C.: U.S. Government Printing Office, 1959), p. xxii.

34. Gardiner C. Means, writing for the United States National Resources Committee, *Structure of the American Economy*, 1 (Washington, D.C.: United States Government Printing Office, 1939): 142. Also see John M. Blair, "Means, Throp, and Neal on Price Inflexibility," *Review of Economics and Statistics*, 38 (November 1956): 427–435.

35. The data given here are all adapted from a table by Robert K. Lanzillotti, in Hearings before the Joint Economic Committee of the Congress of the United States, 86th Congress, 1st Session, *Employment, Growth, and Price Levels* (Washington, D.C.: U.S. Government Printing Office, 1959), p. 2238.

36. Paul Baran in *Paul Baran: A Collective Portrait* (New York: Monthly Review Press, 1965), p. 15. Also see John Galbraith, "Economics as a System of Belief," *American Economic Review*, 60 (May 1970): 469–478. Government policy is discussed more fully in the next chapter of this book.

37. Joint Economic Committee, Congress of the United States, *Staff Report on Employment, Growth, and Price Levels* (Washington, D.C.: U.S. Government Printing Office, 1961), p. 34.

38. J. S. Bain, "Price and Production Policies," in Howard S. Ellis, *op. cit.*, p. 140.

39. W. Rupert MacLaurin, "The Sequence from Invention to Innovation, and Its Relation to Economic Growth," *Quarterly Journal of Economics*, 67 (February 1953): 106.

40. Baran and Sweezy, *op. cit.*, pp. 120–125.

41. *Ibid*, p. 122ff. Also Galbraith, *New Industrial State, op. cit., passim.*

42. Baran and Sweezy, *op. cit.*, pp. 124–126.

43. *Ibid.*, p. 127ff.

44. See Baran and Sweezy, *loc. cit.*

45. *Ibid.*, pp. 128–129.

46. Galbraith, "Economics as a System of Belief," *op. cit.*, p. 477.

CHAPTER
9

The Capitalist State
and Democracy

Previous chapters have concentrated on class divisions within the economic base of society. It was shown (Chapter 5) that the capitalist class begins with ownership of all output, by virtue of its ownership of the means of production, including machinery and other capital goods. Workers have nothing productive to sell but their own power to labor. Wages are held down by technological unemployment (Chapter 6), cyclical unemployment (Chapter 7), and monopoly power (Chapter 8). The result is considerable poverty and a very unequal distribution of income, particularly by class origin (Chapter 5), with the exact division between workers and capitalists being one of the focal points of social conflict.

In this chapter we first examine the effects of this socioeconomic structure on political structure and performance. Then, in the second half of the chapter, we investigate the feedback effects of the capitalist state on the economy in recent years.[1]

Two Conflicting Views of the Capitalist State

Here, we shall look at capitalist states with formal democracies, concentrating on the United States as the most important example. We leave for later the case of fascist and military dictatorships. Two extremely different views of capitalist democracy have been popularized in the world. In American Fourth of July speeches it is said that the United States is a pure democracy, everyone is equal in influence, everyone has one vote, and the majority wins (while the minority retain rights such as freedom of speech). On the other side, Marx oversimplified and exaggerated for propaganda purposes when he said, "The executive power of the modern state is simply a committee for managing the common affairs of the entire bourgeois class."[2] In the literal, dogmatic interpretation this says that freedom of speech does *no* good, that elections can change *nothing*, that workers can have *no* influence, that *no* reforms are possible, and so forth.

When serious scholars on both sides (certainly including Marx) have carefully analyzed real situations, they have always avoided these extreme assumptions. In reality, the United States is *not* a one hundred per cent pure democracy, *nor* is it zero per cent democratic (a pure dictatorship of the capitalist class). The truth lies somewhere between, and only empirical research can tell us where. Still, the "merely" empirical differences of factual evaluation have led to a continuing gulf between the conclusions of the two sides.

The dominant school in American political science is the *pluralist* school. The pluralists assert that the U.S. government is not a class dictatorship but a democracy reflecting many different interest groups, that power is not held by one group but plurally by many groups. They assert that the "power structure of the United States is highly complex and diversified (rather than unitary and monolithic), that the political system is more or less democratic. . . , that in political processes the political elite is ascendant over and not subordinate to the economic elite. . . ."[3] Notice that in arguing for the proposition that America is democratic in nature, the pluralists find it necessary to emphasize that political power is *to a large* degree independent of and superior to economic power. The reason of course, is that economic power is so extremely unequally distributed. If political power exactly followed economic power, the degree of inequality would leave little to be called "democracy."

The radical view, on the contrary, has emphasized that economic inequality does lead to political inequality. The institutions of the United States are democratic in form but not in content because of differences in economic power. Thus, a millionaire owning a newspaper chain has only the same formal political rights as an unemployed poor worker, but surely their actual political influence is very different. Thus a recent and careful study discovers "the existence of a national upperclass that meets generally accepted definitions of social class . . . that this upperclass owns a disproportionate amount of the country's wealth and receives a disproportionate amount of its yearly income, and that [its] members . . . control the major banks and corporations, which . . . dominate the American economy . . . that [its] members . . . and their high-level corporation executives control the foundations, the elite universities, the largest of the mass media, . . . the Executive branch of the federal government . . . regulatory agencies, the federal judiciary, the military, the CIA, and the FBI."[4]

How can one choose scientifically between these two views: the pluralist view and the ruling class view? The only scientific way is to look at the facts. But "the facts" are already suspect depending on who is giving them (not lies, but unconscious selectivity is the main problem). There is no definitive answer at present, but we may begin by noting that the present more sophisticated versions of each theory admit quite a bit of the other. Thus, the more nondogmatic pluralists say that the United States has considerable political democracy and political equality, yet they admit freely that socioeconomic inequality does lead to a large degree of political inequality and imperfect democracy (different interests are represented in disproportionate degree). Conversely, the more nondogmatic radicals and neo-Marxists argue that the American government is dominated by the capitalist class, whose political power is based on its economic power; but they also admit that formal democratic institutions do allow some working class influence, that the ruling class is often divided, and that, in many different ways, economic power does not directly and simply translate into political power.

The strategy adopted here will be to use *only* the admissions of each side contrary to their own basic theses as the "facts."[5] Thus, the "facts" of class bias and unequal political power based on unequal economic power will *all* be taken from a pluralist textbook. The "facts" as to necessary qualifications and limitations on the ruling class thesis will all be taken from a radical, neo-Marxist book.

No single book is exactly "typical" of either view. On the radical side, however, the most commonly used book on America is William Domhoff's *Who Rules America?*[6] On the pluralist side, one widely used text is Marian Irish and James Prothro's *The Politics of American Democracy*, which has all the standard references, and which is identical in all essential points to almost every other pluralist text.[7] So all "facts" in the next three sections will be based on references to Irish and Prothro and the references within it.

The Importance of Class

In Chapter 5 we defined membership in a class roughly according to the amount and type of income received—finding that most people earn low to moderate wage incomes from labor, while a few earn high incomes from ownership of property. While keeping this as a first approximation, we shall keep in mind in this section that many social and psychological factors may affect class identity (or at least self-identification).

A long string of American political analysts have stressed the importance of class interests in politics. James Madison wrote that "the most common and durable source of factions has been the various and unequal distribution of property. Those who hold and those who are without property have ever formed distinct interests in society."[8]

The Capitalist State and Democracy

More than a century later, while President of the United States, Woodrow Wilson wrote: "Suppose you go to Washington and try to get at your Government. You will always find that while you are politely listened to, the men really consulted are the men who have the biggest stake—the big bankers, the big manufacturers, the big masters of commerce, the heads of railroad corporations and of steamship corporations. . . . The masters of the Government of the United States are the combined capitalists and manufacturers of the United States."[9]

Today, the standard text by Irish and Prothro, summarizing a great deal of empirical data, says that "class, whether determined by personal feelings or by educational and occupational status, is an essential concept for understanding political differences."[10] Of course, a great many other socio-economic factors affect political differences, including racial and religious background, friends and community, union membership (obviously related to class), and simply family tradition and upbringing in one political ideology or party affiliation. Family influence has been shown in a study that found that 80 per cent of American voters cast their first vote for the same party as their parents did.[11] Furthermore, wives tend to follow their husband's voting behavior.[12] Finally, amount of education, which is partly determined by class, has a striking effect on opinions, changing them quite significantly.[13]

Class affects political behavior in many ways, of which the most obvious is voting behavior. A large mass of data shows that "members of the working-class typically vote Democratic, while middle-class voters tend to favor the Republicans."[14] More generally, a leading Western sociologist writes: "More than anything else the party struggle is a conflict among classes, and the most impressive single fact about political party support is that in virtually every economically developed country the lower income groups vote mainly for parties of the left, while the higher income groups vote mainly for parties of the right."[15]

In fact, class background goes beyond voting patterns to affect the entire political outlook. Class differences cut across regional and other lines. Thus, "the banker in California has more in common with another banker in New England than he has with a fruitpicker in his own country."[16] These general impressions are confirmed by all the available data.

In the late 1940's, a pioneering study (confirmed many times since) based social class on the respondent's own identification.[17] On this basis of "class consciousness" it was found that, on social welfare issues, class makes a vast difference. In the "upper" class 42 per cent were ultraconservative and another 24 per cent conservative, with only 17 per cent radical or ultraradical. In the "middle" class ultraconservatism declined to 35 per cent, but conservatism was a huge 33 per cent. In the "working" class, ultraconservatism was only 12 per cent, conservatism 23 per cent. In the self-defined "lower" class, ultraconservatism was far less than 1 per cent, conservatism 23 per cent, while radicalism and ultraradicalism were 46 per cent! (On the other hand, numerous studies show that working class people are much less interested in the traditional liberal middle class goals of civil liberties and freedom of speech for dissenters).

Just how class conscious are people, and how many people think of themselves as working class? Popular polls, such as Gallup, always report 80 or 90 per cent of Americans consider themselves "middle class." But these polls use loaded questions and have many other inaccuracies. Therefore, much careful research on the issue "tells quite a different story."[18] In a 1964 study 56 per cent said they thought of themselves as working class! Some 39 per cent considered themselves middle class. (It is true, though, that 35 per cent of all those questioned said they had never thought of their class identification before that moment.) In addition, 1 per cent said they were upper class. And only 2 per cent rejected the whole idea of class.[19]

How Economic Inequality
Produces Political Inequality

We have seen that an individual's political behavior is strongly influenced by class background. But that leads to a puzzle. If a majority identify with the working class, and everyone has one vote, how is it that parties favorable to the working class don't win every election? How come government policies usually do not represent working class desires, but, as Woodrow Wilson asserted, the overwhelming influence of the moneyed or capitalist class? More precisely, given formal democracy and capitalism, exactly how does our extreme economic inequality tend to be translated into inequality of political power?

In the first place, there is the simple fact that the degree of political participation tends to vary with class background. "The average citizen has little interest in public affairs, and he expends his energy on the daily round of life—eating, working, family talk, looking at the comics (today, TV), sex, sleeping."[20] More exactly, in a 1964 study, 86 per cent of those identified as middle class voted, but only 72 per cent of the working class voted. Similarly, 40 per cent of the middle class had talked to others about voting for a party or candidate, but only 24 per cent in the working class had. Among the middle class people interviewed, 16 per cent gave money to a political cause, 14 per cent attended political meetings, and 8 per cent worked for a party or candidate; in the working class, figures on the same activities were only 4, 5, and 3 per cent.[21]

Thus, political participation of all kinds rises in the higher income groups and drops in the working class. Some of the reasons are obvious. Lower income workers have less leisure time, less money above minimum needs, and more exhausting jobs. Furthermore, detailed studies show that the workers' lower participation also reflects less knowledge of how important the issues are because of (1) less education, and (2) less access to information. The same studies show more "cross-pressures" on workers—for example, the racial antagonisms which conveniently divide and weaken their working class outlook.[22]

Second, unequal political power is also achieved by control of the "news" media. Even if the average worker "had an interest in politics, he would have great difficulty getting accurate information; since the events of politics unfold at a great distance, he cannot observe them directly, and the press offers a partial and distorted picture."[23] Even the quantity of news is limited. Although 80 per cent of Americans read newspapers and 88 per cent have TV, political news is only 2.8 per cent of total newspaper space and less on TV.[24]

The quality of political news is worse than its quantity. The first problem is that only one view is available to most people because of increasing concentration of newspaper ownership. In 1910 some 57 per cent of American cities had competing daily papers, but in 1960 only 4 per cent had competing dailies! Furthermore, news media tend to have a conservative bias for three reasons. First, they do not want to offend anybody. Second, they especially do not want to offend major advertisers, all of whom are big businesses. Third, and most important, "since the media of communication are big businesses, too, the men who control them quite naturally share the convictions of other businessmen."[25]

A third factor in favor of unequal political power is the vast difference in the influence of different pressure groups according to their economic power. Thus the standard text by Irish and Prothro says that *status* is the most important factor in determining the influence of a pressure group. After listing other sources of status they conclude: "Finally, since status is so closely tied to money in the United States, the group with greater status will almost automatically be able to command greater financial resources. And it costs money to engage in pressure politics. . . ."[26]

Furthermore, advertising is now a vital component of politics: ". . . Pressure groups . . . are now spending millions of dollars every year on *mass propaganda*. Not only broad groups like the National Association of Manufacturers, but even individual companies maintain elaborate bureaucracies to sell 'correct' ideas on general policy questions along with favorable attitudes to the company."[27]

The vast amount of business advertising reinforces the general ethos of capitalism. It particularly tells us what a lovely country we have, says that material luxuries are the highest priority, and implies that everyone can have them. A certain percentage of advertising is also specifically devoted to political issues, as we saw above. Yet, *all* advertising is counted as a "cost," so it can be deducted from income when computing taxes! Of course, labor unions are not allowed this tax deduction for political advertising.

Specifically, the unequal distribtuion of economic power means a very unequal distribution of the power to control political parties and their choice of nominees, as well as to influence elections. Thus, in America upper income classes have a very disproportionate power in campaigns. Two other pluralist writers state that "because campaigns are exceedingly costly, the wealthier a person is, the more strategic his position for bringing pressure to bear on politicians."[28] Even more vividly, they conclude: "When it is remembered that a campaign for a congressional seat can easily cost $15,000–$25,000, and a senatorial campaign can cost half a million dollars or more, it is not difficult to see why 'money talks'."[29] The figures today are much, *much* higher; so money talks even more loudly in today's politics.

Today, the influence of money on elections has become still more obvious as politicians hire professional public relations firms to campaign for them. Who you can hire and how much they will do depends on how much money you are willing to spend.[30]

Another line of control of considerable importance in the modern United States are the private foundations, which spend money to support education and research. Naturally, the big businessmen who set them up have some say over the content of the education, propaganda, and research on which their money is spent. Moreover, many of these foundations get direct help from government, at least in their beginnings, and many of them are closely connected with the espionage and "intelligence" network.[31]

Finally, the fact that upper income groups exercise disproportionate political power naturally allows them to use the government itself to increase their power further. In a later section we shall examine these political feedback effects on political behavior and the economic structure. They include such things as the educational system, the police, the army, "intelligence" services, and even the announcements of the President. Also not to be overlooked is the effect on people's political behavior by the control over their jobs, both private and public.

Class Background of Political Leaders

Because of their disproportionate political influence, upper income individuals of the capitalist class have a disproportionate percentage of the top political positions. From 1789 to 1934 fathers of U.S. presidents and vice-presidents were 38 per cent professionals, 20 per cent proprietors and officials, 38 per cent farm owners, and only 4 per cent wage-earners or salaried workers.[32] Similarly, fathers of U.S. senators in the period 1947 to 1951 were 22 per cent professionals, 33 per cent proprietors and officials, 40 per cent farm owners, and only 4 per cent wage-earners or salaried workers. Finally, fathers of U.S. representatives in the period 1941 to 1943 were 31 per cent professionals, 31 per cent proprietors and officials, 29 per cent farm owners, and only 9 per cent wage-earners or salaried worker.[33]

In the executive branch outside the president and vice-president, upper income business-oriented individuals have had a majority of all the important positions throughout U.S. history. This includes the members of the Cabinet, their assistants and department heads, and heads of most regulatory agencies. They quite naturally, with no conspiracy, tend to consult big businessmen and groups as experts (such as the Committee for Economic Development or the Council on Foreign Relations). Wealthy families have also contributed a majority of our federal judges, top military men, and top leaders of "intelligence agencies." Lastly, we may note that there is much crossing-over at the top: ex-generals often get to be corporate executives, while corporate executives often get to be Cabinet members.

Qualifications to the Class Analysis

So far, we have stated the radical thesis that (1) class differences determine much of political behavior, and (2) the wealthy capitalist class has a disproportionate amount of political power, to the extent that (3) it occupies or controls most key political positions. All of this was shown relying solely on data given by the orthodox pluralist political analysts of the United States. Now we must turn to the very definite qualifications to this thesis admitted by most radical scholars.[34]

First, although the capitalist class has a strong influence on Congress, Domhoff shows that the Congress is *not* fully controlled or dominated by the capitalist class.[35] The direct representation of the capitalist class is disproportionate, but still a small minority. Influence must rather be exerted indirectly through pressure from the executive branch, paid lobbyists, and big campaign contributions to the parties and candidates.

Second, although strongly influenced by the capitalist class, most state governments and most city governments are *not* controlled or dominated directly by that class.[36]

Third, although the old middle class of independent small-farm owners, small businessmen, and self-employed artisans is no longer the vast majority, but only a tiny percentage of the labor force, U.S. society has *not* polarized into two classes with no middle. In addition to low-paid manual workers, there is a very large and growing percentage of high-paid technical workers—"a new working class" (or "new middle class" if you prefer) of engineers and teachers and such.[37] Even though they are "workers" in a purely economic sense, they see themselves mostly as "middle class," and their political behavior follows that pattern to some extent. On the other hand, teachers and even college professors are now organizing and even striking in some places, so the behavior of at least some of the new working class approximates that of the old working class rather than the old middle class.

Fourth, although the capitalist class controls some areas of government and strongly influences others, "the control is not complete; other groups sometimes have their innings, particularly when these groups are well-organized and angry."[38] Thus, farmers won reforms in the late nineteenth century against monopoly pressures, and angry workers won many reforms in the New Deal of the 1930's. The power of numbers and ORGANIZATION can defeat the power of money in some extraordinary circumstances.

Fifth, there is disagreement and factionalism within the capitalist class. "Nor is the power elite always united in its politics; there are long-standing disagreements between its moderate and conservative wings. . . ."[39] They disagree partly because of opposed interests. Thus, most large corporations benefit from and favor military spending, but a significant minority does not benefit from it and is opposed to much military spending.[40]

Sixth, they do not always have a perfect grasp of their own best interests: ". . . To read case studies of specific decisions is to be aware that lack of information, misunderstandings, and personality clashes may lead to mistakes on issues that must be decided in a hurry."[41] Thus, no one should predict that government policy will always represent an optimal solution from the capitalist view.

Seventh, critics of the class analysis sometimes point out that in America there are real conflicts over policies, that decisions are made by shifting coalitions, that these coalitions usually include some worker or farmer organization. True, but "the shifting coalitions are dominated . . . by members of the American upperclass."[42] Thus, one cannot simply say that a certain small capitalist group decides government policy. On the contrary, there appear to be several conflicting capitalist groups, and some of them are loosely allied with some farmer or worker groups. But the ruling coalition does always end up dominated by a major capitalist group— though, as in the New Deal, it may have to grant many reforms to its coalition partners. Whether it is hypothetically possible to win with a noncapitalist coalition under extraordinary circumstances—as in Chile?— is a question left for Chapter 12.

Eighth, another qualification to the class analysis is that "most businessmen are not part of the group that controls the government."[43] Certainly, most businessmen are small businessmen, and have little if any more power than workers or farmers. A ruling coalition may sometimes include small business, but it is usually dominated by a small group of big capitalists. In fact, as was demonstrated in Chapter 8, the American economy is dominated by very large corporations, exercising vast amounts of monopoly power. In this new stage of monopoly capitalism there is extreme concentration of income, wealth, ownership of the means of propaganda . . . and political power. Two mild liberal economists admit today that, "with every advance of monopoly toward greater economic power and more social acceptance, the federal government becomes more subservient to it, more dependent on it."[44]

Lastly, we noted much earlier that political behavior of individuals is guided at any given time by many factors besides pure economic motivations. A politician, such as Ronald Reagan (governor of California), may simply be power-hungry, rather than consciously acting in favor of class interest. A white worker, if he is infected with racism, may vent his anger at bad conditions against black workers rather than against the capitalist owner (some of this was evident in the 1968 support for George Wallace). Yet it may be that both power drives and racism themselves can be ultimately explained by the socioeconomic structure in many cases.

Feedback Mechanisms of Control

We have seen how—with many qualifications—extremely unequal economic power tends to lead to extremely unequal political power in the United States. Some political power may be exercised in class-neutral ways, that is, ways that benefit the whole society. For example, in ancient Egypt one reason a strong central state came into being was to practice flood control and irrigation on the Nile river.

On the other hand, once the state apparatus is controlled via economic power or other means, it may then function as a feedback mechanism to secure political power more firmly. Thus, the Egyptian slaveholders (including Pharaoh and the priests) used their control of the state apparatus —the police, army, courts—to control the slaves by laws supported by force.

Similarly, given a large measure of political control by those with the most economic power in America, the wealthy naturally tend to use the state apparatus to further strengthen their power. Thus, the police or the National Guard or the army may be directly ordered to support "law and order" by force, as law and order is interpreted by those with political control. The National Guard have killed students (at Kent State) demonstrating against the U.S. invasion of Cambodia. Police have killed Black Panthers who were organizing for self-defense against white violence. And many, many times in American history police, or even soldiers, have shot down strikers trying to organize American workers for better conditions (police have even been used recently against the relatively conservative construction workers). Most courts have always cooperated by issuing injunctions against strikes by labor unions.

There is also that means of feedback control which is a mixture of propaganda, terror, and force: namely, the various espionage and "information" agencies. These include in America the Central Intelligence Agency, Defense Intelligence Agency, National Security Agency, Army Intelligence, Navy Intelligence and Research, and the Federal Bureau of Investigation. "By 1964 the intelligence network had grown into a massive hidden apparatus, secretly employing about 200,000 persons and spending billions of dollars a year."[45] This so-called "invisible government" is still only an instrument of political power, but does exert its own semi-independent malevolent influence once it is activated, especially in foreign policy. Frequent publicized scandals have taught us that its corruption and paid agents reach down into every private organization (some outstanding cases being the subsidized leadership of the National Students Association and the subsidized foreign activities of the AFL-CIO).

Another important feedback is the use of the *prestige* of the state. Thus, while police assault students physically, Vice-President Agnew may assault them verbally. Similarly, while police try to break a strike by construction workers, President Nixon tells the nation that their wages are too high. Every department of the government, particularly the military, also does its own massive advertising in favor of business and government policies, particularly military spending.[46]

Education is the last avenue of feedback control considered here. Children are brought up to believe in the righteousness of a value system that preserves the status quo. Even if one looks at university boards of regents and trustees, it is astounding to find that they are almost wholly composed of capitalists, corporate lawyers, military officers, and their wives. Much of the funding (and direction) of research comes from military expenditure. The important schools of Law and Business Administration take the system for granted, and work to improve (or have their students improve) its efficiency—mainly in the making of private profits.

As if all these pressures were not enough, there are recurrent waves of repression against all radical thought in universities. This was very effective in America under the inspired leadership of the grand inquisitor, Joe McCarthy. A new wave of attacks on course content as well as on individual radicals (such as Angela Davis) is now beginning under such glamorous crusaders as Ronald Reagan.

Obviously, in spite of these attacks radicals persist in having an influence in universities. All radicals cannot be ousted without destroying the facade of democracy altogether. Moreover, every wave of repression gives rise to a sympathy with radicals by the large percentage of liberal-minded faculty and other intellectuals. Students also constitute a group not fully molded as yet by the establishment, not yet with a job to lose, and pushed together into very large concentrations. They thus constitute a fertile ground for mobilization into radical movements, similar in some ways to the large concentrations of workers in the factory system of the nineteenth century (the role of students is considered further in Chapter 12).

Militarism and Fascism

Although the power of the top military has certainly grown in America in the past thirty years, we have no serious fear of a military coup. Alas, many other countries have suffered from military coups and ended with military dictatorships. In a very large number of the underdeveloped countries of the "free" capitalist world, there are now such dictatorships, mostly dedicated according to their leaders "to the protection of democracy." (We shall examine this phenomenon further in the next few chapters.)

Also in the twentieth century a number of semideveloped capitalist countries (Spain, Mussolini's Italy, Portugal, Greece, Tojo's Japan) and at least one developed capitalist country (Nazi Germany) have had fascist or military-fascist dictatorships. In most cases, they were instituted because of the threat that the Left might win power in a peaceful democratic election (or in Spain after such an election).

In these cases, the feedback control of vested interests is manifested directly through the dictatorship of an extreme right wing individual or party (though they may claim to be anything but a class dictatorship). No working class organization is allowed, whether in unions or in political parties. Socialists are put in prison or are executed. No radical, socialist views are allowed in any newspaper, radio, or university. Votes do not count for anything, so the working class cannot peacefully pressure for reforms. Only violence can overthrow it, whether through war (the Allied defeat of the Axis) or revolution (Fidel Castro's ousting of the Batista dictatorship). Such military or fascist dictatorships point up the tremendous difference between a capitalist country that maintains formal political democracy and one that does not. Woe to any radical group that may ignore this difference!

Economic Behavior of the Capitalist State

We have examined the class bases of the capitalist state, and some of its poltical feedback mechanisms. We must now examine those political feedbacks that directly affect the economic structure itself.

The economic role of the government under capitalism has always been far greater than acknowledged by pure economic theory—especially during each war period. With the 1930's, however, the level of "peacetime" intervention began to reach a level which might be used to define a *new stage of capitalism*. The economy of the United States and Western Europe after World War II was not only characterized by monopoly power, but also by a great increase in government intervention and influence.

Government spending in the United States in 1929 was only 9.8 per cent of gross national product. By 1939 it had jumped to 19 per cent of national product. With the Second World War government spending rose to the incredible height of 41 per cent of national product in 1943 and 1944. After the war in 1946 and 1947 it fell to prewar levels. By 1949 it had again risen to 23 per cent of national product; in 1959 it was 27 per cent; and in 1968 it was back to 23 per cent.[47]

In a monopoly capitalist economy, in which a large sector is dominated by government spending, there is capitalist "planning" to mitigate depression, to avoid galloping inflation, and to stimulate economic growth. All these are goals to help all society, but always accomplished in ways limited by the necessity that the means used be favorable to the ruling class. The class limitations on economic policies will be found to be most obvious in the restriction on redistribution of income, but are reflected in many other ways in government policies.

A list of the functions of the modern capitalist state would include the following, all public in name but class-oriented in benefit.[48]

1. *Taxation*. Taxes are raised in a supposedly progressive manner. Yet the loopholes are such that the tax rate does *not* actually rise above the middle brackets. In 1957, for example, the highest tax rate was 91 per cent of income; yet taxpayers in that top category paid only 52 per cent to the government.[49]

One kind of loophole for the rich is "capital gains." Capital gains are the income derived from sale of a piece of property at a higher price than it was bought at. The increase in value of property (held more than six months) or Capital Gain is taxed at a maximum tax rate of 25 per cent, which is a lot less than 91 per cent. Of those taxpayers with income over $100,000 a year, over 20 per cent in 1957 was in capital gains. But it should be noted that this loophole does not save any money for the poor. For taxpayers in the $3,500–$4,000 income class, capital gains were only 0.3 per cent of their income.[50]

As a result of many such loopholes, some startling statistics have appeared. In 1960 a taxpayer had $20 million income, but no taxes! In 1959, five Americans had over $5 million income, but paid no taxes. In 1961 seventeen Americans had over $1 million income, but paid no taxes. One fellow has had over $2 million income a year since 1949, but has paid no taxes. It has been estimated that the total loss of government revenue from all loopholes in the income tax laws is about $40 *billion* a year.[51]

Whereas the rich with income from property can find many tax loopholes, there are none for the average worker with wage income. As a result we find that there is only the slightest redistribution of income as a result of the Federal income tax. The data for 1962 shows that the richest fifth (or top 20 per cent) of the population had 45.5 per cent of all income before taxes.[52] After taxes their percentage of national income had decreased by only 1.8 per cent. The poorest 20 per cent of the people had increased their share by only .3 per cent, the second fifth by only .6 per cent, and the third fifth by only .5 per cent. Thus *after taxes* the richest 20 per cent of the people still had far more income than the poorest 60 per cent of the people put together!

Even more important is the fact that the Federal income tax is only 40 per cent of all taxes, and is the only one that is progressive even to a slight extent. By "progressive" in taxation we mean that the tax falls more heavily on the upper income groups, while "regressive" taxes fall more heavily on lower income groups. The other 60 per cent of taxes are mainly "regressive" according to most observers, that is, they fall more heavily on the lower income groups. In 1958, for example, people with income under $2,000 paid 11.3 per cent of their income in state and local taxes; but each higher income group paid a *lower* and lower percentage, until those earning over $15,000 paid only 5.9 per cent of their income in state and local taxes.[53] "We might tentatively conclude that taxes other than individual income taxes do not reduce, and probably increase, income inequality."[54] So the entire tax system redistributes very little, if at all.

2. *Welfare.* Since we have seen that taxation does not redistribute income from the rich to the poor, the question is whether welfare programs have a significant effect in that direction. In the first place, expenditures for welfare have been fairly small.[55] In 1968 all welfare spending under all federal, state, and local programs was only $26.9 billion. This included public aid, unemployment payments, workman's compensation, health and medical programs, public housing, and educational aid to low-income

students. These payments do help the poor somewhat, but the effect is small, it has virtually no effect in altering relative position of the poorest segment, or of the richest segment of society. In fact, this $26.9 billion was only 3.82 per cent of the 1968 personal income, so while it could make a few people better off, it could not change things very much.

Furthermore, there are some qualifications even to that small apparent redistribution. Some of that 3.82 per cent does not go to the poorest groups. Welfare money spent on school lunches or university scholarships ends up going to the children of the middle class as well. Moreover, the poorest help pay for welfare by paying their share of taxes (as we saw above), so the net amount received is even less. Thus the percentage of income going in net welfare is even smaller than it looks at first. It is no wonder that our tax and welfare systems have not resulted in any significant redistribution of income.

It is interesting that this same pattern—of small effects and no significant reduction in income inequality over many decades—also holds true for the capitalist countries of Western Europe. A United Nations report covering all Western Europe reveals that "the general pattern of income distribution, by size of income, for the great majority of households, is only slightly affected by government action."[56]

3. *Farm Subsidies*. Farm subsidies were supposed to help the rural poor, but have mainly helped the rural rich. For background, note that economic concentration is now quite high among the business firms engaged in farming. At present the richest 10 per cent of farms produce over 50 per cent of all agricultural output. The poorest 50 per cent of all farms produce only 5 per cent of farm output.

On the whole, the farm support programs benefit mainly the richest farmers, and give very little support to the poorest farmers. Thus, in 1965 in sugar cane the poorest 20 per cent of farms received only 1 per cent of the farm subsidies, while the richest 20 per cent received 83 per cent of the subsidies.[57] In 1964 in cotton the poorest 20 per cent received 2 per cent of the subsidies, while the richest 20 per cent received 69 per cent of the subsidies. In 1963 in rice production the poorest 20 per cent received 1 per cent of the subsidies, while the richest 20 per cent received 65 per cent of the subsidies. In 1964 in wheat farming the poorest 20 per cent received 3 per cent of the subsidies, while the richest 20 per cent received 62 per cent of the subsidies. Aggregate figures are not available, but data for many other farm sectors in other years show similar patterns. Moreover, the subsidies to the poorest farms were even less than their percentage of other income, while the subsidies to the richest farms were even higher than their percentage of other income (at least in most of the cases studied), so the effect on farm income distribution actually may be regressive.

The Capitalist State and Democracy

These data show the regressive effects of the farm programs on farmers who own their own farms, but how about the effects on farm workers who own nothing but their power to labor? The answer is very simple. The two main farm programs pay farm owners—mainly the largest, richest farms—(1) price support to keep their prices up to a certain level above costs, and (2) pay to keep some land out of production, so as to reduce the supply of farm goods. No money from these programs goes to farm workers. In fact, the programs may hurt farm workers to the extent that they pay to keep land out of production, thereby increasing unemployment. "The State pays the *owners* of farm property not to produce, but pays virtually nothing to *farm workers* who become unemployed as a result of this dole to property owners."[58]

Finally, it should be said that the net result of this program—to help farm workers not at all, to help poor farmers slightly, and to help rich farmers very much—is not at all surprising. That has been the consistent pattern of subsidies in United States history. Large corporations have always been the ones helped by subsidies from the government. In the nineteenth century, for example, three-fourths of all railroad construction was paid for by the government, including the gift of huge amounts of land to the railroads.

4. *Education and Inequality.* Government subsidized education is often thought to decrease the inequality of incomes. Liberals argue that: "The government gives free education to all, so anyone can improve his station in life by going to school for a longer period."

Years of education *are* clearly correlated with higher income. Thus, the average individual with only 8 years schooling will have an average income of only $6,600 (the data is from 1968).[59] Someone with a high school diploma is associated with a median income of $11,800. In part, more schooling is the *cause* of better jobs and better pay for the individual. In part, however, better schooling is the *effect* of having parents with a high income.

It is a fact that individuals from high income families are able to get more schooling in the United States than individuals from low-income families. One study examined all 1966 high school graduates, grouped according to their family's income in 1965, to find out how many started college by February 1967.[60] It was found that only 20 per cent of those with a family income under $3,000 went on to college. Yet 32 per cent of those with family incomes from $3,000 to $4,000 went to college. In fact, the percentage of those going to college continued to rise in each higher income group: 37 per cent ($4,000–$6,000), 41 per cent ($6,000–$7,000), 51 per cent ($7,000–$10,000), 61 per cent ($10,000–$15,000) and fully 87 per cent in the over–$15,000 family income bracket! Thus, the higher one's family income, the more chance of starting college.

Children of richer parents get more schooling mainly because they can pay to stay in school longer than the poor. They can pay high tuitions in private schools that will admit students even with low grade averages. Even in the public universities, where the tuition may be much lower or non-existent, there are still living expenses. Many students must drop out of college or not start it simply because they have no money on which to live while in school.

Furthermore, children of richer families have a better chance to do well in school and learn more. They are better equipped by cultural opportunities at home and in their communities to study, and have been given very much motivation for many years. The cultural background is very important in IQ tests and College Board Exams. These examinations, which purport to test general ability, in reality are designed to conform to middle-class, white, urban experience. A student from a poor or Black or rural background will lack the necessary cultural references to understand the questions or have any intuition of the answers. This has been proven over and over again, but the tests are still used. They determine which "track" (see below) an elementary student is put into, and they determine who enters college. Thus, it is no surprise that only 7 per cent of college students come from the poorest 25 per cent of families.

Students in elementary and high schools are put into different "tracks."[61] One track is vocational training to prepare the poor for manual labor. Another track is college preparation to prepare the students from upper-middle and richer families to go to college, in order to get a high-income job (so that their children can go to college, and so forth). In elementary schools it is often called "ability grouping" of the bright and the stupid. The degree of ability, however, is determined by those same IQ tests. The tests do not assess any innate intelligence, but they are very good at reflecting the class background of the student—since they are designed for white, middle-class, urban background.

The system of different tracks exists partly also within high schools, where counselors push the poor and the minority groups into vocational training and the rich into college preparation. But it turns out that such pushing is hardly necessary within schools, because there is so much difference between schools. Schools in the Black slums give only "basic" or vocational training. Schools in the richest areas give only college preparation. These different tracks are enforced both formally by the tests given, and informally by counselors and by teachers. One investigation in New York found that middle-class white children were usually given voluntary classes in how to pass college exams—but that even seeing the old test was "against the rules" in Harlem.

We may conclude with certainty that our educational system does not reduce inequality from generation to generation. On the contrary, the

138

richer students have more opportunities to get a good elementary and high school education, to get into college, to remain in college, and so to get a high-income job after college—and then to send their children to college. Thus, the educational system seems to transmit inequality from one generation to the next.

5. *Labor Regulations.* Labor unions are restricted in the name of the rights of the individual worker, but actually such laws as the notorious Taft-Hartley Act mainly result in the reduction of the power of the unions in struggles with the monopolies. In the name of law and order, many strikes are postponed or broken by court injunctions or by police help to the scabs. Lack of space prevents further discussion of this important issue here, but there is an abundant literature on the past history of government bias against labor unions.[62]

6. *Regulation of Monopoly.* Anti-trust laws are weak to begin with and are poorly enforced, so monopoly keeps increasing. In fact, most of the cases under the Sherman Antitrust Act before 1914 were not against big business, but against labor unions! Again, there is lack of space here to go into the vast literature describing the weakness and perversion of anti-monopoly laws and enforcement.[63]

7. *Military Spending.* There is vast military spending for the avowed purpose of defending the "free world," mostly defending neocolonial areas that return high profits, and always resulting in very high profits to the producers of military goods.

As a result, the reality is that most of the massive government spending is for warfare, and very, very little for welfare. Thus, to some extent America may be a state-controlled economy, but the state itself is tightly controlled by a small number of monopolists. This is control to protect capitalism, not to abolish it. Even Roosevelt's New Deal was obviously designed to reform and revive capitalism, and only the blindest reactionaries could see it as a red menace.

All economists—even Marxists—know and agree that Keynesian measures of government intervention can *theoretically* prevent large-scale unemployment or run-away inflation (except when there is both unemployment and inflation at the same time). The basic fiscal formula (to which may be added certain monetary measures) is to raise taxes and lower spending during inflation; and to lower taxes and raise spending during depression.[64] Moreover, corporate executives and congressmen alike are by now well aware of and receptive to these techniques. But that by no means settles the issue.

What does remain a major . . . issue is to find suitable ways of spending the amounts of money that may be required to maintain . . . the present "comfortable" level of underemployment. All outlets that would be rational in the sense that they would contribute to the increase of human welfare, are more or

139

less incompatible with the vested interests of the ruling classes. Payment of doles tends to raise the wage level; government investment in steel, chemicals, public utilities, etc. tends to destroy carefully erected monopolistic fortresses. And so it goes. If the problem were to spend one or two billion a year, a solution could be found at the expense of less powerful interests. But with anything from $15 to $25 billion to be pressed into the income stream, the difficulties are well-nigh insuperable.

Or rather they would be if it weren't for the Cold War. The Cold War seems to solve this problem in a most admirable way. No interests that matter are violated as long as the money is spent on armaments and foreign operations. The short-run effect on employment and profits is the same as if the expenditures were of a "rational" type, and the long-run effect is even better since no new productive equipment is created to compete with existing facilities.[65]

Since that perceptive statement was made in 1950, the main change has been that the necessary addition to the income stream has risen to at least $70 to $80 billion per year. So the problem with stability under monopoly capitalism is primarily in the political sphere, rather than in any lack of economic analysis. One popular cure for depression is reduction of taxes to allow more money to flow into private spending. Given the composition of the U.S. government, however, tax cuts always end up mainly in benefiting the rich and the corporations. Even in the liberal Kennedy administration the tax reduction reduced the taxes of the poor very little and the rich very much, resulting in redistribution of income to the "deserving" members of the ruling class.[66] Especially in a depression, however, the capitalist class will not spend its increased income, since its consumption has remained at adequate levels, and it has no desire to invest in the face of probable losses. Hence, the political restriction as to *who* gets the tax cuts makes this policy economically ineffective.

Similarly, all economists (and even most businessmen) may see a need for more and more vast government spending under capitalism, but the prime political question is spending on what, for it is here that vested interests come into play. Thus, even small, vital expenditures on medical care have sometimes been defeated by the doctor's monopoly (the AMA). "In the case of almost every major item in the civilian budget, powerful vested interests are soon aroused to opposition as expansion proceeds beyond the necessary minimum."[67] What kind of interests must be defeated to have the necessary spending to fill a $70 to $80 billion deficiency in demand? There are constructive projects, such as a Missouri Valley Authority, that would develop dams, irrigation, and cheap power, but such would be fought tooth and nail by the private power interests (and indeed, might lower private investment by direct competition). There could be large-scale public housing, but private contractors have long kept such programs to a minimum.

There might be other welfare spending, such as hospitals and schools; but the ruling class sees these as subsidies to the poor for things that the rich could buy out of their own pockets, without the need for taxing them to provide support for every patient or student. Such items as increased unemployment compensation or lower taxes to the poor meet even greater resistance, because they would transfer income quite obviously from capitalists to workers. Likewise, many billions could usefully be spent in aid and loans to the underdeveloped world, including some socialist countries. That, however, could also not be passed with present political representation. If any of these measures are finally allowed to some extent, it is only after a long political fight, certainly not promptly enough to head off a developing depression.

It would be possible to run through the gamut of civilian spending objects and show how in case after case the private interests of the oligarchy stand in stark opposition to the satisfaction of social needs. Real competition with private enterprise cannot be tolerated, no matter how incompetent and inadequate its performance may be; undermining of class privileges or of the stability of the class structure must be resisted at any cost. And almost all types of civilian spending involve one or both these threats. There is just one major exception to this generalization in the United States today, and it is very much the exception that proves the rule: government spending on highways.[68]

Highway spending is actively promoted by the largest and most lucrative single industry after defense, the automobile producers.

The Military Economy

From the viewpoint of monopoly interests, major spending to avoid unemployment can only be military. But as the national product gets larger and larger—and the relative deficiency in buying power increases—military spending must not only remain high, but must continually increase if it is to fill the widening gap between effective consumer demand and potential supply. Bigger and costlier Vietnams are a necessary part of American economic stability.

Of course, military expenditure does *not* increase the amount of productive facilities available. Therefore, an economy at full employment with 10 to 15 per cent of the workers employed in military production will have a much lower rate of growth than an economy at full employment with no military production (assuming the same composition of civilian goods). There *was* a high growth rate in the 1960's because of full employment, but it would have been much, much higher without military spending. This negative effect on the long-run rate of growth is emphasized by Soviet economists—partly, at least, because of their understandable desire for effective propaganda in favor of disarmament.

141

The Soviets neglect, however, the main point of American radical analysis, that monopoly capitalism *normally* has a huge surplus, a huge potential unemployment (as we saw in Chapters 6 and 7). The potential unemployment is only prevented by vast waste, mostly military spending. For this reason military production is never said to be "enough." For example, America already has enough missiles to destroy the entire Soviet Union at least fifty times, but the supply is still being rapidly expanded.[69]

The political nature of the problem has become even more apparent in the inflationary situation of the last twenty years. The Korean and Vietnam wars caused so much government demand for military supply that inflation resulted (prices rising especially in 1950–1953 and in 1967–1970). To cure inflation, the simple Keynesian prescription is to increase taxes and reduce spending.

But *whose* taxes, *which* spending? Major increases in taxes on capitalists are not easily passed by capitalist governments. And there is not that much room for further taxes on the working class without rising discontent. So it is easier to reduce government spending. But not military spending; that would be terrible for "national security," that is, intervention in other countries. So we are left with cutting welfare spending. Already a tiny percentage of the American government budget, it was nevertheless cut further in the 1960's as a tool to fight inflation. Thus the burden of inflation falls on the working class in the forms of rising prices, rising taxes, and falling welfare spending all at the same time.

The economy in the 1950's and 1960's has in some periods also had an experience which is unique in American history: both unemployment and inflation at the same time! This situation appears impossible to elementary Keynesian analysis since inflation implies an excess of demand over supply, while unemployment implies an excess of supply over demand. The answer to the riddle lies in the monopoly power of American capitalism. In spite of a certain amount of unemployment, the largest corporations actually still have the power to continue to raise their prices, which we might call "profit-push" inflation. Thus, we saw in the preceding chapter that in the 1954 and 1958 recessions, although prices were constant or decreasing in the most competitive sectors, there were price *increases* in the most concentrated sectors. At present, prices and profit rates of the giant corporations for 1971 are rising in the face of large-scale unemployment, although profit rates of small corporations are falling.

No aggregate fiscal policy can remedy or prevent *both* inflation and unemployment in these circumstances. To end unemployment by increasing aggregate demand—sufficiently to affect output in all sectors—means to allow the monopoly sector to set off another inflation spiral. To end inflation by reducing aggregate demand—sufficiently to affect monopoly prices—means causing considerable unemployment in the whole economy.

142

The Capitalist State and Democracy

The capitalist governments of America (and England) have generally chosen to combat inflation at the expense of more unemployment of workers.

Since fiscal and monetary controls are inadequate to prevent both unemployment and inflation, it is natural to consider direct wage-price controls (as Nixon instituted in August 1971). We have observed, however, that "profit-push" by the monopoly corporations is the basic cause of present U.S. inflation. But the capitalist government is dominated by these same monopoly corporations. Therefore, such controls under any capitalist government (particularly the U.S. government under Nixon) tend to freeze only wages, while allowing plenty of loopholes for higher prices and profits. The results are naturally: (1) a lower share of wages in national income, a lower consumption percentage, and more unemployment; (2) continued inflation and excess profits in the monopoly sector, though some restriction of small business prices and profits; and (3) a swelled bureaucracy, more red tape and bribery, and more economic inefficiency.

These areas of government policy illustrate the strongest difference between conservative and even liberal Keynesian economics and radical, Marxist political economy. Diagnosis of the "purely economic" problems by the two schools differs only in emphasis, but the view of the political constraints is entirely different. Keynes speaks as if the problem is merely a rational one of finding the right answers. For example, if it is necessary that the state *should* increase spending to end unemployment, then he believes that the state *will* automatically carry out these policies (or as soon as legislators are well enough educated in economics). Thus one Keynesian critic of Marxism writes with great naivete:

> It must be admitted that Sweezy is right in saying hitherto massive government expenditures have had to be justified on the basis of military necessity. But the striking aspect of his analysis is the a priori conviction that the bourgeoisie will not help itself despite the advice of its *own* academic economists.[70]

He does not see that the simple economic prescriptions for nonmilitary spending may clash with the vested interests of the bourgeoisie in many respects. He also does not recognize the close relation of the capitalist state to the capitalists. Marx, on the contrary, has an integrated view of the state and the economy: the capitalist state does only what is in the *interest* of the capitalist class. Most welfare spending conflicts with these interests. Therefore, no significant Keynesian policies against unemployment are really carried into effect except military spending (and no significant price controls are enforced except on wages).

Suppose America agreed to complete disarmament in one year. What an economic catastrophe that would be under the present political (and economic) rulers! To measure the extent of the potential disaster, we must recall that the U.S. Defense Department is the largest planned economy in the world today outside the USSR. It spends more than the net income of all U.S. corporations. By 1969 it had 470 major and 6,000 lesser installations, owned thirty-nine million acres of land, spent over 80 billion dollars per year, used 22,000 prime contractors and 100,000 subcontractors, thus directly employing in the armed forces and military production about 10 per cent of the U.S. labor force.[71] Some key areas of the economy are especially affected. As early as 1963 before U.S. entry into the Vietnam war, studies show that 36 per cent of the output of producers' durable goods were purchased directly or indirectly by the federal government (mostly for military use).[72]

Recent studies quantify the impact of disarmament more precisely. In 1969 there were 3.7 million persons unemployed. Another 8.3 million persons were employed directly as a result of the military program. These twelve million were 14.3 per cent of the labor force. In addition, through expenditure of incomes earned in the military program (the so-called multiplier effect), it indirectly stimulated another 10 percent of employment.[73] Therefore, all other things remaining the same, the effect of total disarmament in that year would have been 24.3 per cent unemployment. Yet unemployment in 1932 in the worst year of the great depression was only 24.9 per cent.

This argument is denied, not only by Soviet economists, but by most American liberal Keynesian economists. They argue, first, that taxes could be cut to increase private spending to fill the whole gap. We have seen, however, that tax cuts have (necessarily under present political conditions) gone largely to the rich, increasing saving but not spending. The second, more popular argument, is that welfare spending could be increased to fully substitute for warfare spending. Certainly, this alternative is very desirable from the viewpoint of the majority of the American people and, just as certainly, it is technically feasible to substitute welfare spending for military spending. We have seen, however, that capitalists strive for maximum profits, that such a shift would drastically cut the profit rate while raising real wages, that capitalist oligopolies now have overwhelming economic and political power. Therefore, this tremendous substitution of welfare for warfare spending could not possibly occur in the United States under present political-economic conditions and institutions (unless there comes into being an effective new coalition against the military industrial complex).

The point should be emphasized that military spending not only benefits the capitalist system as a whole, but is crucial for the profits of the largest, oligopoly corporations. In the first place, the rate of profit on military contracts is twice that for peaceful production.[74] Second, between 1950 and 1967 Department of Defense reports show that the hundred largest contractors received two-thirds of the value of all military contracts;

and just ten firms received almost one-third![75] Furthermore, the giant firms require a stable market and a long period in which to develop new products, especially because of the rate of expansion of modern technology; and these benefits are provided by, and only by, government military (and space) spending.[76]

Non-Marxist economics has no theory of war, it sees war as a temporary disturbance to the peaceful course of economic development. But who can imagine what twentieth century economic development could have been without war? We have demonstrated here that war spending is a necessary and integral part of monopoly capitalism; without the stimulus of government military spending, the automatic functioning of the economic system would most likely generate frequent and deep mass unemployment.[77] We shall argue in the next chapter that the major wars of this century have been the result of imperialism, which itself is a necessary aspect of monopoly capitalism.

NOTES

1. The "state" is sometimes used by Marxists to refer only to the coercive apparatus of force, army, police, and so forth. "Government" may then be used to mean the coercive functions *plus* constructive functions, such as irrigation—but this distinction is not used consistently in the literature.
2. Marx, *The Communist Manifesto* (New York: International Publishers, 1948), p. 11.
3. Arnold Rose, *The Power Structure* (New York: Oxford University Press, 1967), p. 492.
4. G. William Domhoff, *Who Rules America?* (Englewood Cliffs, N. J.: Prentice-Hall, 1967), pp. 10–11.
5. This strategy was suggested to me by a few words about the "need to combine the two approaches" in Robert Heilbroner, *Between Capitalism and Socialism* (New York: Vintage Books, 1970), p. 257.
6. Domhoff, *op. cit.*
7. Marian D. Irish and James W. Prothro, *The Politics of American Democracy* (Englewood Cliffs, N. J.: Prentice-Hall, 1965 ed.).
8. Federalist Essay, No. 10 (Washington D. C.: Walter Dunne, 1901), p. 64.
9. Woodrow Wilson, *The New Freedom* (New York: Doubleday, 1914), p. 83.
10. Irish and Prothro, *op. cit.*, p. 175.
11. *Ibid.*, p. 170.
12. *Ibid.*, p. 171.
13. *Ibid.*, p. 174.
14. *Ibid.*, p. 177.
15. Seymour Lipset, *Political Man* (Garden City, N. Y.: Anchor Books, 1963), p. 234.
16. Irish and Prothro, *op. cit.*, p. 242.
17. R. Centers, reported in Irish and Prothro, *op. cit.*, p. 174.
18. Irish and Prothro, *op. cit.*, p. 37.
19. *Ibid.*, p. 38.

20. *Ibid.*, p. 165.
21. *Ibid.*, p. 38.
22. *Ibid.*, p. 193.
23. *Ibid.*, p. 165.
24. *Ibid.*, p. 183.
25. *Ibid.*, p. 184.
26. *Ibid.*, p. 245.
27. *Ibid.*, p. 249.
28. Robert Dahl and Charles Lindblom, *Politics, Economics, and Welfare* (New York: Harper & Row, 1953), p. 313.
29. *Ibid.*, p. 315.
30. Irish and Prothro, *op. cit.*, pp. 257–266.
31. David Wise and Thomas B. Ross, *The Invisible Government* (New York: Random House, 1964), *passim.*
32. Irish and Prothro, *op. cit.* p. 39.
33. *Ibid.*, p. 39.
34. See, e.g., Domhoff, *op. cit., passim.*
35. *Ibid., pp.* 111–114.
36. *Ibid., pp.* 132–137.
37. C. Wright Mills, *White Collar* (New York: Oxford University Press, 1956).
38. G. William Domhoff, in Domhoff and Ballard, eds. *C. Wright Mills and the Power Elite* (Englewood Cliffs, N. J.: Prentice-Hall, 1969), p. 277.
39. *Ibid.*, p. 277.
40. *Ibid.*
41. Domhoff, *op. cit.*, p. 277.
42. *Ibid.*, p. 3.
43. *Ibid.*, p. 154, where Domhoff attacks this argument.
44. Walter Adams and Horace Gray, *Monopoly in America* (New York: Macmillan, 1962), p. 35.
45. Wise and Ross, *op. cit.*, p. 4. Also see Fred Cook, *The Warfare State* (New York: Macmillan, 1962), *passim.*
46. Senator J. William Fulbright, *The Pentagon Propaganda Machine* (New York: Liveright, 1970), *passim.*
47. Data for 1929–1959 in Council of Economic Advisors, 1962 *Supplement to Economic Indicators* (Washington, D.C.: U.S. Government Printing Office, 1962), p. 3. Data for 1968 from U.S. Census Bureau, *Statistical Abstract of the United States, 1969* (Washington, D.C.: U.S. Government Printing Office, 1969), p. 312.
48. ". . . Unfortunately . . . economic prosperity is excessively dependent on a political and social atmosphere which is congenial to the average businessman." John M. Keynes, quoted by David Horowitz, "Analysis of Surplus," *Monthly Review*, 18 (January 1967): 55.
49. See Gabriel Kolko, "Taxation and Inequality," in R. Edwards, M. Reich, and T. Weisskopf, eds. *The Capitalist System* (Englewood Cliffs, N.J.: Prentice-Hall, forthcoming).
50. *Ibid.*
51. *Ibid.*
52. See Edward C. Budd, *Inequality and Poverty* (New York: W. W. Norton, 1967), pp. xiii and xvi.
53. Kolko, *loc. cit.*
54. F. Ackerman, H. Birnbaum, J. Wetzler, and A. Zimbalist, "Extent of Income Inequality in the United States," in *The Capitalist System, op. cit.*
55. See Richard Edwards, "Who Fares Well in the Welfare State," in *The Capitalist System, op. cit.*
56. U.N. Economic Commission of Europe, *Incomes in Postwar Europe: A Study of Policies, Growth, and Distribution* (Geneva: United Nations, 1957), pp. 1–15.
57. Data in this paragraph from James Bonnen, "The Farm Program and Inequality," in Edwards, Reich, and Weisskopf, *op. cit.*

146

The Capitalist State and Democracy

58. Howard Wachtel, "Looking at Poverty from a Radical Perspective," *Review of Radical Political Economics*, forthcoming.

59. All data in this paragraph is from F. Ackerman, H. Birnbaum, J. Wetzler, and A. Zimbalist, "Extent of Income Inequality in the United States," in Edwards, Reich, and Weisskopf, *op. cit.*

60. All data in this paragraph from *Ibid.*

61. The best description of "tracking" is in Florence Howe and Paul Lautner, "How the School System is Rigged," in *The Capitalist System, op. cit.*

62. See, e.g., Richard Boyer and Herbert Morais, *Labor's Untold Story* (New York: Marzani and Munsell, 1955).

63. See, e.g., the revelations of the former head of the government's antitrust division, Thurman Arnold, "Economic Reform and the Sherman Anti-Trust Act," in J. A. Garraty, ed., *Historical Viewpoints: Vol. II, Since 1865* (New York: Harper & Row, 1969), pp. 140–175.

64. These procedures are spelled out in a critical manner in Howard Sherman, *Macrodynamic Economics: Growth, Employment and Prices* (New York: Appleton-Century-Crofts, 1964), Chapter 10.

65. Historicus (Paul Baran), "Better Smaller but Better," in *Monthly Review*, 2 (July 1950): 82–86.

66. This is the usual result; see Michael Harrington, "Reactionary Keynesianism," *Encounter*, 26 (March 1966): 50–52. He shows the same tendencies in the "socialist" planning of Western Europe.

67. Paul Baran and Paul Sweezy, *Monopoly Capital* (New York: Monthly Review Press, 1968), p. 165.

68. *Ibid.*, p. 173.

69. Seymour Melman, *Our Depleted Society* (New York: Holt, Rinehart, Winston, 1965), p. 19. Also see Ralph E. Lapp, *The Weapons Culture* (New York: W. W. Norton, 1968), *passim*.

70. Murray Wolfson, *A Reappraisal of Marxian Economics* (New York: Columbia University Press, 1966), p. 160.

71. Source: United States Defense Department documents, reported and analyzed thoroughly in Seymour Melman, *Pentagon Capitalism: The Political Economy of War* (New York: McGraw-Hill, 1970), reviewed by Robert Heilbroner in *New York Review of Books* (July 23, 1970).

72. See sources and discussion in Harry Magdoff, "Militarism and Imperialism," *American Economic Review*, 60 (May 1970): 242.

73. *Ibid.*, p. 241.

74. H. Sherman, *Profits in the United States* (Ithaca: Cornell University Press, 1968), pp. 135–136. Thus, the profit rate on all military contracts in 1968 was 17 per cent! See *New York Times Magazine* (June 22, 1969), p. 11. An extensive report of the U.S. General Accounting Office published in December 1970 found a 56.1 per cent ratio of return on investment in military production! A very conservative view, based on very questionable evidence, still found a military profit rate twice as high as the average in the 1950's, but only equal to the average in the 1960's; see George Stigler and Claire Friedland, "Profits of Defense Contracts," *American Economic Review*, 61 (September 1971):692–694.

75. Galbraith, *New Industrial State* (Boston: Houghton Mifflin Co., 1967), Melman, *Pentagon Capitalism, loc cit.*

76. "That weaponry in the higher megaton ranges of destruction power has an organic relation to the performance of the economic system leads to unpleasant introspection," Galbraith, *op. cit.*, p. 229.

77. Some Marxists go further, claiming that, "except in war and periods of war-related prosperity, stagnation is now the normal state of the United States economy." Baran and Sweezy, *op. cit*, p. 76.

CHAPTER
10

Imperialism

Has there always been imperialism? Certainly, there has been colonial occupation and plunder since the days of the ancient Egyptians and Persians. The phenomena of modern imperialism, however, are quite new and different. The radical, Marxist definition of "imperialism"[1] emphasizes that the internal environment of modern imperialism is monopoly capitalism, which only became predominant in Western Europe and the United States in the 1880's and 1890's—so imperialism in the modern sense dates from that period. Furthermore, we emphasize that modern imperialism utilizes not only plunder and unequal trading, but especially vast amounts of international investment.

Definitions are arbitrary, of course, but the main characteristics of what we call imperialism—international trade and investment dominated by the giant corporations of a few countries—are the key to the modern world. Emphasis on these characteristics helps to explain why the change, from outright colonial control to "independence" in most of the underdeveloped world, made much less difference than most liberals expected. While the forms have changed, we shall probe in detail the thesis that the essential structure of imperialism persists (and the colonies become neocolonies).

To clarify and test these assertions, we shall begin with the facts of life in the underdeveloped countries, then discuss the obstacles to their development. We shall try to prove that imperialism hinders development by (1) supporting reactionary ruling classes, (2) imposing unfavorable trade patterns, and (3) extracting huge profits. Next we look at the forms of control and the role of the capitalist state in relation to the neocolonial countries. Finally, we look at the impact of imperialism on the imperialist countries, its benefits and costs, especially in terms of militarism and war. We shall try to prove that a few hundred giant corporations benefit greatly from imperialism, but that its net effects are negative for the rest of the population of the imperialist countries.

Facts of Economic Underdevelopment

There are at least two generally accepted definitions of an "underdeveloped" country—one based on an economic index and the other based on certain distinguishing characteristics. The economic index that is generally used is average income per person (gross national product divided by the number of the population). Under this criterion, a country with an average income per head of less than some amount, say $200 or $300 per year, is classified as "underdeveloped."

The word "underdeveloped" is used here because it is in common usage. We must be aware, however, that it has misleading sociological connotations. For example, there is no correlation between the level of income and the level of cultural or social development. Obviously, ancient Greece or Egypt or China had very highly developed cultures with very low average income levels. We should also observe that an average may hide wide disparities in individual incomes. For example, Kuwait has one of the highest levels of average income per head; but most of the income is concentrated in the hands of a few very rich persons, and there is an enormous gulf between the very rich and the very poor. The high level of average income per head in Kuwait is solely the result of the oil resources of this little country, and, therefore, one cannot assume that the country is highly developed in an over-all sense.

Dissatisfaction with the use of a single, purely economic measure of development has led some students of the subject to suggest a definition of underdevelopment based on several distinguishing characteristics of underdeveloped countries. The commonly found characteristics of underdeveloped countries are (1) low income per person, (2) the existence of a very high proportion (often 80 per cent or more) of the population engaged in agriculture, (3) a low level of techniques used in production,

(4) a low level of education, and (5) a low level of capital formation.

Any way that we define the underdeveloped and developed countries, *the fact is that more than 50 per cent of the population of the capitalist world lives in countries that can be classified as underdeveloped.* The enormity of the problem can be indicated by the estimate that to raise the incomes of that portion of the world's population living in nonsocialist underdeveloped countries to an average of only $200 per person per year (less than a tenth of the average American income), about $85 billion of aid per year would be needed so long as they remain at present production levels.[2]

Among capitalist (or capitalist-dominated countries) in the lowest category, with income per person less than $100 a year (and mostly agrarian, and lacking in technology, education, or capital) falls India, most of Asia, and most of Africa. In the second category between $100 and $300 a year (and still very underdeveloped in all other indices) are most of Latin America, North Africa, Indonesia, and the Philippines. In the third category of $300 to $600 a year (still very poor, but slightly developed in some aspects) are a few Latin American countries, Union of South Africa, Greece, and Spain. The fourth category of $600 to $1,500 (and well developed in many aspects) includes Israel, Australia, and New Zealand, Japan, and most of Western Europe. In a category by themselves are Canada and the United States with over $2,500 income per person per year. (Kuwait and Quatar are also listed above $2,500 income, but these are tiny areas sitting on top of oil wells with most of the income going to a few sheiks).

In the advanced capitalist countries it is true that workers' wages have grown greatly in the last hundred years. But conditions in most of the capitalist world—its underdeveloped part—have shown little or no improvement; and incomes remain at incredibly low levels. Most African and Asian incomes are less than a tenth, and most Latin American incomes about a fifth of the average incomes in the advanced capitalist countries. In fact, many of them are not only below poverty, but below subsistence levels. "Two thirds of the inhabitants of the underdeveloped countries of the Third World do not get the essential minimum of 2,500 calories per day; the expectation of life for many of them is less than half that in the highly developed countries."[3]

The gap between rich and poor is reflected in the fact that in 1964 two-thirds of the world's population produced only about 25 per cent of world output. At the same time the United States alone (with only 6 per cent of world population) produced about 30 per cent of world output.

Furthermore, the gap is getting larger; Marx might say the underdeveloped capitalist countries (or Third World inhabitants) are more and more relatively impoverished. In the whole period 1953 to 1964 the advanced capitalist countries showed rates of growth twice those of the underdeveloped capitalist countries.[4] Thus, the advanced capitalist countries outproduced the underdeveloped ones (in product per person) by 10 to 1 in 1950, but by 11 to 1 in 1960, and by almost 12 to 1 in 1969.[5]

Overpopulation?

In Chapter 5 we noted how many of the evils of capitalism are blamed (incorrectly) on overpopulation. If this apologia for the status quo is said to apply to the advanced capitalist countries, how much more is it said to apply to the underdeveloped capitalist countries. It is asserted as an axiom, which only crude and biased Marxists could deny, that people in the underdeveloped countries are hungry because there are too many people. Proof: just look at the vast number of poor and starving people, as in India. Thus that sophisticated and unbiased scholar, Robert S. McNamara (former President of Ford Motor Company and former U.S. Secretary of Defense) asserts that "the greatest single obstacle to the economic and social advancement of the majority of the peoples in the underdeveloped world is rampant population growth."[6]

The important point to note about McNamara's ideology is that it tells the hungry people that the "greatest single obstacle" to their development is their own animal sexual desires. The function of this ideology is thus identical to that of the theory that underdevelopment is due to racial inferiority, the laziness and/or stupidity of "the natives." It provides the perfect defense against the suspicion of these peoples that their problems are due to antiquated social systems, rapacious ruling classes, and—above all—foreign domination and exploitation.

If one turns to the facts, there is no evidence that high population density is the prime cause of underdevelopment. More precisely, there is *no* statistically significant correlation between high population density and low income per person.[7] On the contrary, many countries with high incomes per person also have high population densities. For example, Belgium has 816 people per square mile, West Germany has 624, and the United Kingdom has 588. India has only 406 people per square mile, and most of the underdeveloped countries have much lower population densities.

Another related "theory" of underdevelopment claims that the underdeveloped nations are all those who by accident have relatively few natural resources on their territories. Yet the underdeveloped countries in 1965 provided 37.5 per cent of the total output of raw materials in the capitalist world, including the bulk of many strategic materials. This is certainly a large enough absolute amount for a solid industrial base. Nor do the underdeveloped countries produce anything like 37.5 per cent of manufactured goods. In fact, we shall see that most of their raw materials are taken away to the advanced capitalist countries, and are there manufactured into finished goods(some of them being sold back at a high profit to the underdeveloped countries).

In the radical view, therefore, the main obstacles to development are *not* natural or biological factors inherent in the underdeveloped countries, and *not* sexual desires and procreation, laziness, low intelligence or lack of natural resources. The obstacles are in the present social relationships of man to man: the fact that all the peasants' and workers' surplus over immediate needs is extracted from them by the landlords, moneylenders, tax collectors, and foreign corporations. We shall show that the native ruling classes use their high incomes for luxury consumption, while most of the enormous profits of foreign corporations are removed from the country altogether.

As a result there is a lack of capital for investment in development. The lack of capital (and lack of nonhuman power per person) *is* correlated with low income per person.[8] The lack of capital means not only little construction, but also little new equipment and little technological improvement. It also means few funds available for education and training, let alone research. The lack of capital also means that millions of workers cannot be employed at a sufficient rate of profit, so they are left unemployed or underemployed. Thus, it is the social relations (and their consequences) that are the real obstacles to development.

As an example, let us take the present revolution in farming in several underdeveloped countries. In this "green revolution" new types of grains have been introduced, especially in India and Pakistan. They have brought much higher yields, so that the technical barrier to feeding the population seems to be falling. To make efficient use of the new processes and output, however, requires large mechanized farms. Indeed, small peasants are being evicted in growing numbers to make way for large agricultural enterprises. The dispossessed peasants are swelling the ranks of the unemployed in the cities. At the same time, complaints are heard from the large farm owners that there is overproduction of grain relative to the small money demand of the poor! Thus, the socioeconomic relationships form a barrier to technological development.

Obstacles to Development[9]

What keeps a country in an underdeveloped condition? It is a truism to say that growth would be faster if underdeveloped countries had more capital, more technology, and more education and training. In fact, for many underdeveloped capitalist countries the problem is not a low rate of growth of income per person, but no growth at all. The aggregate income does not grow much faster than (and maybe not as fast as) the population. Moreover, a complete change is needed from a rural, agrarian economy to and urban, industrialized economy. The issue, then, is how to *begin* to develop, how to start from little or no growth at all, and how to change the whole economic structure.

We shall argue that the obstacles are mainly institutional: (1) an internal ruling class that spends much of its income on luxuries and spends government revenues on unnecessary public monuments or military expenditures, (2) foreign trade on very poor terms, and which imports the wrong items for development, and (3) foreign investment in sectors least useful to development, with high profits sent abroad. Notice that this is quite opposite to most non-Marxist views. Some, we have seen, argue that the trouble is sex and too much population, or laziness, or stupidity.

Others argue a vicious circle in which poverty is the main cause of poverty: "the poor are considered the victims of their poverty. . . the poor society has nothing with which to buy growth. Having less that enough for its current needs for food, clothing and shelter, it has nothing for investment. . . ."[10] One wonders how the impoverished Soviet Union ever developed without foreign aid? The theory is a good apologia for the status quo, ignoring internal and external waste and exploitation.

Let us begin with the internal obstacles to development created by the social systems within the underdeveloped countries. The typical situation finds millions of peasants engaged in subsistence farming, obligated to pay high rents to landlords, high interest to moneylenders, and high taxes to local and national governments. From his original small net product, the peasant usually pays more than half to meet these obligations.[11] The peasant retains hardly enough for his bare subsistence, and has none left for major improvement or investment.

The landlords and moneylenders spend much of their share of the surplus taken from the peasant in conspicuous luxury consumption. If they reinvest any, their extreme conservatism prompts them to invest in more land or to send it to some safe foreign country; little if any is invested in industry. The governments are mostly dominated by a small elite of wealthy landlords and merchants (in turn often foreign-dominated, as we shall see), so they have little motivation to invest government funds in constructive projects—in fact, the advent of industrial capitalism would lose this elite their present power. Most government revenue is spent on military goods and services for the purpose of internal repression. Governments spend some on show-case projects, such as new sports arenas, or—as in Venezuela—in beautification of the capital city. The little that is spent constructively is usually for roads or ports to serve the needs of foreign investors.

One liberal view holds that the best panacea would be land reform, which would turn over the full ownership of their plots to the peasants, eliminating rents and landlords completely. The problem is that splitting up the estates into many small plots would make investment and technical progress even less likely. The peasant would still have very little income, and would tend to consume it all. The plots of land would be too small for the application of modern technology. This was exactly the case in the thorough-going Soviet land reform of 1917, which created twenty-six million tiny farms. Furthermore, the Soviets found that because the peasants were free to consume their own produce for the first time, they did increase their consumption, with the result that little remained on the market to feed urban workers or to export.

A related view (held by several Communist parties in Latin America) holds that the main obstacles to progress are the semifeudal forms and holdovers in the countryside. The key issue is again considered to be land reform to bring these countries at least into the age of capitalism. Although the problems of land reform are clearly important, this view probably gives too much weight to the few remaining leftovers of earlier systems. Throughout Latin America and much of the Third World, the web of capitalism reaches through the foreign enterprises in the ports and main cities via the native merchants and traders right down to the local landlords and moneylenders. In most of the underdeveloped areas agriculture is in fact highly commercialized; so that more commercialization and more capitalism does not seem to be the answer.[12]

Before discussing the obstacles presented by the present patterns of foreign trade and investment, we turn to the forms and methods of foreign domination of the underdeveloped countries.

Colonialism and Neocolonialism

From the fifteenth to the nineteenth centuries Europeans slowly took over the rest of the world. They plundered, enslaved, and ruled so as to extract the maximum from their subjects (all in the name of God and the spread of Christianity). Such havoc was created that ancient and culturally advanced civilizations disappeared, as in Peru and West Africa; and progress was set back hundreds of years by the destruction of native industries, as in India.

On the other side, the plunder was so great that it constituted the main element in the formation of European capital, and provided the foundation for prosperous trade and eventual industrialization. "The discovery of gold and silver in America, the extirpation, enslavement and entombment in mines of the aboriginal population, the beginning of the conquest and looting of the East Indies, the turning of Africa into a warren for the commercial hunting of black-skins, signalised the rosy dawn of the era of capitalist production."[13] It is important to remember always that the West industrialized with the help of loot from imperialism. By contrast, the present underdeveloped countries not only do no plundering of others, many of them are still being plundered.

By the end of the nineteenth century, almost all the present under- developed countries were under the colonial rule of the more advanced countries. The imperialist countries invested in the colonial countries at astoundingly high profit rates, primarily because of a cheap labor supply and an enforced lack of competition. The capital was mainly invested in extractive industries, which exported raw materials to the imperial country. In the imperial counrty, the cheap raw materials were profitably turned into manufactured goods, part of which were exported back (tariff-free) to the colonial country.

The tariff-free imports of finished goods from the imperial country generally completed by competition the destruction (often begun by plunder) of the manufacturing industries in the colonial country. An example of this destruction may be seen in colonial India, especially in its textile industry:

> Foreign trade statistics best show the effects of "deindustrialization." India, still an exporter of manufactured products at the end of the eighteenth century, becomes an importer. From 1815 to 1832 India's cotton exports dropped by 92 per cent. In 1850, India was buying one quarter of Britain's cotton exports. All industrial products shared this fate.
> The ruin of the traditional trades and crafts was the result of British commercial policy.[14]

The development of the colonial areas was thus held back by the imperialist countries, while the development of the imperialist countries was greatly speeded up by the flow of plunder and profits from the colonies. The exception which proves the rule is Japan, since Japan did escape colonialism. Thus, she was able independently to industrialize and develop her own advanced capitalism, alone among the countries of Asia, Africa, and Latin America, because the others had all been reduced to colonies and had their further development prevented.

From 1890 to the Second World War was the peak period of colonialism, when all the world was divided among the West European and North American powers. In the late 1940's and 1950's a new era begins, with formal independence achieved by hundreds of millions of people throughout Asia and Africa—as a result of struggles unleashed by the impact of two World Wars, the Russian and Chinese revolutions, and the long pent-up pressures for liberation. The day of open colonialism is over (except for southern Africa), but the pattern still holds by which the excolonial countries export food or raw materials. In fact, we shall see that they are often dependent mainly on exports of just one product; and they still import most of their finished goods. Foreign investment still dominates their industries. Moreover, most foreign capital invested in the less developed countries still goes into raw materials extraction,[15] in spite of the recent spread of some foreign investment to manufacturing in certain countries. Because of the continuance of the underlying colonial economic pattern, Marxists and other radicals call this situation "neocolonialism," in spite of formal political independence.

The point is that imperialism has changed in form, is supposed to smell better, but is still imperialism. On the one side are all the underdeveloped newly "independent" countries, still under foreign economic domination, still facing all the old obstacles to development. On the other side are the advanced capitalist countries, still extracting vast profits from the dependent Third World. The imperialist group includes all those who extract profits by trade and investment. Thus, it includes most of West Europe and the United States. After all, neocolonial profits from the underdeveloped countries flow even to countries such as Sweden and Switzerland, although they never held colonial power over any underdeveloped country.

Although there are still cases of direct occupation (for example, the Portuguese colonies in Africa), most imperialist control comes through economic and monetary penetration. This ranges from blatant forms such as subsidies and military supplies to highly complex monetary agreements. It also seems to be characteristic that "independence" is granted to small territories, tiny divisions of former colonial domains, for example, the many small countries made from the French empire in Africa. Thus they have no political or economic power with which to resist continued domination.[16]

It should also be noted that the economic control is often not direct, but built up in a complex pyramid. For example, some American companies directly invest in Northeast Brazil. More control of that area, however, is achieved through American domination of major Brazilian companies in the South, which in turn buy control in companies in the Northeast area. Still more control is achieved through American domination of some West European companies, which in turn own most of some major Brazilian firms, or which directly own some of the local firms in the Northeast area.[17]

Marx analyzed the relative impoverishment of the working class under capitalism. The more urgent issue today is the relative impoverishment of the vast neocolonial areas of the world. This is the breeding ground of wars of liberation from imperialism, all of which eventually tend to escalate under current circumstances into "limited" wars between the socialist and capitalist blocs.

Methods of Neocolonialism

In addition to economic penetration the methods of neocolonial subjugation extend from propaganda to assassination to coups d'etat by foreign-supported forces. One should also mention direct military force, as in the case of Vietnam. Short of that, treaties guarantee military bases (such as Guantanamo Bay in Cuba) and even grant exclusive rights to Western information services such as the U.S. Information Agency. Sophisticated imperialists naturally prefer control by propaganda in the broadest sense to armed intervention.

Under the category of imperialist propaganda, certainly, one must include the vast flow of Hollywood movies, Western books, and Western news services to the neocolonial areas. Another important agency of imperialist propaganda is the activity of missionary religious sects. The older ones would seem laughable and anachronistic in the twentieth century world of science. New ones with new techniques, however, are better prepared to attack the neocolonial world. These include Moral Rearmament, Jehovah's Witnesses, and even some forms of Zen Buddhism.

Closely akin is the evangelism, well subsidized by the CIA, of some American labor unions. American unions split the world unity of labor unions after the Second World War, and even then found their new restricted group of allies too far left. In international affairs American unions are one of the most reactionary forces, wielding major economic strength and utilizing a vast flow of money to buy propaganda and friends. Nor should the effective propaganda use of the U.S. Peace Corps be overlooked. If all other propaganda means fail, the CIA itself is clearly willing to use thirty pieces of silver in the case of important leaders.[18]

Finally, it should be stressed that the single most effective form of imperialist propaganda is racism, including the inflaming of religious and nationalist prejudices. By this disgusting means, imperialism has successfully practiced divide and rule in many areas. Instead of fighting imperialism, Jews fights Arabs, Catholics fight Protestants, Hindus fight Moslems, and so forth. Each is told that the other is the cause of his troubles, that the other is inferior, and anything else to prevent their unity. Yet it is the disunity fostered by racist filth which mortally weakens the position of both sides against imperialism.

Racism also operates to prejudice the working class of the imperialist country in support of military ventures against other peoples. At the end of the nineteenth century a leading European "socialist" could write: ". . . only a conditional right of savages to the land occpuied by them can be recognized. The higher civilization ultimately can claim a higher right."[19] Essentially the same racist thought was used to justify the attempt of Hitler's Aryan master race to conquer the world.

When beating the drums of war, racism is often called "patriotism." Such patriotism is used to justify the massacre of women and children in Vietnam by machine guns or by napalm. One general called for open provision of prostitutes (naturally Vietnamese women) to men at American Post Exchanges, all in the name of patriotism.[20] "Patriotism is an acceptance of national immorality."[21]

Foreign Trade

The colonial era left the economies of the underdeveloped countries very dependent on foreign demand, and consequently very sensitive to the foreign business cycle of expansion and depression. It is also a fact that international investments and trade in primary products (that is, in raw materials, both agricultural and mineral) show the greatest fluctuations. "It follows that any country whose economy is intimately dependent on foreign investment or whose trade is greatly dependent on primary commodities will be seriously affected by swings of business arising outside its own borders."[22]

This dependence is recognized in the underdeveloped countries. The government of Ceylon states: "The economy of Ceylon depends almost entirely on its export trade in tea, rubber and coconut products. . . . About 80 percent of the people are employed directly or indirectly in the production and handling of these exports."[23] The government of Burma says explicitly that "the most important source of unemployment in Burma is a decline in prices of raw materials caused by the depression generated elsewhere."[24]

The statistics for many countries, both developed and underdeveloped, show that (1) a high proportion of the demand for their national product is the demand for exports, and (2) the exports to the United States constitute a high proportion of the total export demand. Thus, the United States often absorbs more than half, and always more than a third, of the exports of Canada, Brazil, Chile, Mexico, the Philippines, and others.[25]

In addition to the special place of dominance of the United States vis-à-vis the underdeveloped Third World, there is some data bearing on the trade relations of all the imperialist groups with the Third World.[26] First, we find rapid growth in production in the underdeveloped countries *only* in those raw materials and food products exported to the imperialist countries. Goods for internal use in the Third World are growing very slowly, if at all.

Second, 73.5 per cent of the total trade of imperialist countries is with themselves. The continued dependence of the underdeveloped countries, however, is reflected in the fact that fully 74 per cent of *their* total trade is with the imperialist countries. Between 1948 and 1964, there were three important trends "(1) The commercial growth of the imperialist countries was much greater in value than that of the Third World. (2) The imperialist countries have come to depend less on the Third World for their exports, and (3) the latter has become more dependent on the countries of the capitalist group."[27]

These data also confirm the picture of the underdeveloped countries as raw material exporters and finished goods importers. Detailed examination "shows that the trade of the Third World is wildly out of balance: 85 per cent of its exports consists of raw materials and another 5 per cent of common metals, products of the first state of smelting. Only 10 per cent of the total consists of manufactured goods, most of which are textiles. Imports, on the other hand, are predominantly manufactured goods (60 per cent of the total)."[28] Since most of the manufactured imports are consumer goods, such a pattern can never lead to development, only to continued dependence.

The situation of dependence is still more exaggerated for each underdeveloped country taken by itself. Each of them tends to export only one or two goods and to trade with only one or two buyers (so that the buyers can easily exert monopsony power). "For the vast majority of Third World countries the range of products is as narrow as possible; one, or two, or three products often providing three quarters, or even more, of the trade of a country. The number of countries selling and buying is also very restricted; a single imperialist country usually occupies such a dominant position that it can exercise every kind of pressure."[29] It should be emphasized that most of the cases where the former colonial master has not retained control of the Third World countries are cases where control has shifted to the United States—for example, most of Latin America, Vietnam, and parts of Africa.

Another aspect of the worsening international payments situation arises from Western control of so-called "invisible trade" or services. "Over 90 per cent of world ocean shipping is controlled by the imperialist countries. They control shipping rates and, between 1951 and 1961, they increased them some five times in a total rise of about 60 per cent, the upward trend continuing. Thus, net annual freight expense incurred by Asia, Africa, and Latin America amount to no less than an estimated $1,600 million. This is over and above all other profits and interest payments. As for insurance payments, in 1961 alone these amounted to an unfavorable balance in Asia, Africa, and Latin America of some additional $370 million."[30]

We have noted that the value of the trade among the imperialist countries has grown much more rapidly than their trade with the Third World in recent years. As a result, the Third World's share in the trade of the imperialist countries has fallen from 32 per cent in 1948 to 23 per cent in 1964.[31] The question arises whether the imperialist countries really "need" the trade of the underdeveloped world as much today as previously.

The percentage decline in trade suggests a lessened importance. This was a period, however, of rapidly rising world trade, so the absolute amount of trade between the two groups *rose* from twelve billion in 1948 to more than twenty-five billion in 1964. Furthermore, almost all the increase in trade within the imperialist bloc was of manufactured goods. While some of these exchanges are urgent, most of them merely increase efficiency, so that more expensive substitutes could easily be arranged—not to speak of the heavy flow of luxury consumer goods, which would cause no permanent damage if ended. The situation is quite different in the trade of the imperialist bloc with the underdeveloped Third World. This trade is vital and irreplaceable. "It is not to satisfy whims that the imperialist countries import major food products and raw materials, but rather to meet the needs of their markets and factories for items which the former could ill dispense with and the latter not at all. On its part, the Third World buys the manufactured goods and machinery of the imperialist countries because it needs them desperately and does not produce them."[32]

Foreign Investment

Many economists, Marxists and non-Marxists alike, have argued that "the stability of capital-exporting countries with high rates of saving has . . . been dependent on the recurrent appearance of new opportunities for investment abroad."[33] During a depression a country may still have an intense desire to find or conquer new markets for goods and capital exports. Although Britain actually did this at times before about 1870, this easy road to recovery has seldom been open since then.

On the contrary, in the whole period since about 1870 we shall see that the net flow of capital has been into the imperialist countries! Imperialism still means a higher rate of profit from foreign investment. The flow of capital into the imperialist country, however, tends through competition to lower the domestic rate of profit (even though it raises the profit rate on all investments added together).

Foreign investment is very large today. Yet we can no longer say that it plays an important role as an outlet for an investment-seeking capital surplus. The reason is that the returns on it are greater than the new investment each year. Indeed, except possibly for brief periods of abnormally high capital exports from the advanced countries, foreign investment must be looked upon as a method of pumping capital *out* of underdeveloped areas, *not* as a channel through which capital is directed into them. Even in the years between 1870 and the First World War, Britain's income from overseas investment far exceeded her capital exports. Thus, in the years 1870 through 1913, net export of capital totaled 2.4 billion pounds, while income received from foreign investment came to 4.1 billion pounds.[34]

At any rate, in the present stage of mature imperialism, the situation is that the export of capital is exceeded by foreign earnings of the imperialist countries. For example, for the period 1950 through 1963, the United States had a net direct investment outflow of capital amounting to $17.383 billion. But for the same years the direct investment income was $29.416 billion.[35] Hence, we may conclude that monopoly capitalism tends to generate ever more surplus, yet it fails to provide the consumption and investment outlets required for the absorption of that product, so necessary for smooth working of the system.

In the private sector alone, the profit (and interest) payments from the underdeveloped countries to the imperialist countries are now clearly greater than the flow of investments (and loans) going the other way. The reason for this phenomenon is quite simple. Suppose the United States invests (net) $100 million in Latin America *each year*. Suppose the profit rate is 25 per cent. By the fourth year $400 million has been invested, so total profit is $100 million. In the fifth year total profit is $125 million, which is greater than the yearly investment of $100 million. For a profit rate as low as 10 per cent, the same phenomena occur; only profit does not begin to exceed investment until the eleventh year—the result, however, is the same.

Foreign aid, which is examined in a later section, only serves at best to fill up some of the gap between the profit outflow and investment inflow to the underdeveloped countries. The exact data are recorded, however, from the imperialist side in the most important cases. The United States from 1950 to 1960 received $5 billion more in private profits than was privately invested, while U.S. foreign aid amounted to only $4 billion more than government receipts from abroad.[36]

For the whole world there are only rough estimates for certain years.[37] For 1965, the estimate is that 4.8 billion dollars in profits were made by foreign firms in the underdeveloped countries. Of that total, $4 billion was sent back to the imperialist countries, while $0.8 billion was reinvested. New investment from the imperialist countries was 1.4 billion dollars. This means the outflow from the underdeveloped economies to the imperialist economies was $4 billion less $1.4 billion, or $2.6 billion in 1965. It may be added that there is also a large flow of money from the underdeveloped countries to the imperialist countries in the forms of salaries for foreign specialists and payments for foreign patents.

The U.S. Department of Commerce breaks some of the investment data for the United States into geographical areas, from which some interesting differences emerge for the period 1950 through 1965.[38] In Europe in that period U.S. corporations made direct investments of $8.1 billion, while transferring back to the United States income from investments in Europe of $5.5 billion; so there was a net flow of $2.6 billion U.S. into this advanced capitalist area. Similarly, in Canada in that period, U.S. corporations invested $6.8 billion while extracting $5.9 billion in profit; for a net flow of $0.9 billion U.S. into this advanced area.

In the underdeveloped Third World, the situation is different. In Latin America in those years American corporations invested $3.8 billion, but extracted in income $11.3 billion; for a net flow of $7.5 billion U.S. dollars from that area to the United States! Yet profit rates were so great that at the same time the value of direct U.S. investments in Latin America *rose* from $4.5 to $10.3 billion. In fact, in the period 1957 through 1964 only 11.8 per cent of direct U.S. investment in Latin America came from the United States, while 74.1 per cent was reinvestment of profits or depreciation funds from Latin American operations! Similarly, in Africa and Asia in the period 1950 through 1965 American corporations invested only $5.2 billion, while transferring to the United States $14.3 billion of profits, for a net flow of $9.1 billion to the United States! Yet, enough profit remained for reinvestment that direct U.S. investments in Africa and Asia rose from $1.3 to $4.7 billion.[39]

Two facts are blatantly obvious from the above data: (1) the rate of profit on U.S. investments abroad is several times higher in the underdeveloped than in the advanced capitalist countries; and (2) the underdeveloped neocolonial countries generously make a good-sized net contribution to U.S. capital accumulation! In other words, since the flow of profit out is more than the flow of investment into the underdeveloped countries, the net effect of the present situation is not a help to their development, but a drain on their capital.

Not only is aggregate investment less than the profit extracted, but the pattern of investment is very imbalanced. "Much of the foreign product capital investment in the underdeveloped countries takes the form of direct investment in primary production for export, especially in the oil industry."[40] The U.S. Department of Commerce figures show that in Latin America, Asia, and Africa, a large majority of all U.S. investment is in the extractive industries, especially petroleum. Thus, most foreign investment does not help the underdeveloped countries to industrialize, but only helps to deplete their raw materials. Only in Europe and Canada is the majority of U.S. investment in the nonextractive industries, mostly manufacturing, although there is a recent trend for more U.S. investment in manufacturing (or at least assembly parts) in some of the underdeveloped countries.

Multinational Firms

The form of surplus extraction has been changing since the Second World War. It used to be that most investment was in the form of loans or stock purchases in existing companies or the setting up of brand new companies (with or without native participation). Today, such purely financial movements are less important. Rather, the capitalist corporation simply sets up branches of its own firm or completely subordinates satellite firms. The day of the multinational firm is here.

The very dramatic example of Standard Oil of New Jersey typifies the trend. By 1962 Standard Oil of New Jersey had 33 per cent of its assets abroad, 20 per cent of its assets being in Latin America and 13 per cent of its assets in Europe and Asia. Furthermore, the importance of these areas is shown by the fact that Standard Oil's profit on equity amounted in the United States to only 7.4 per cent, but its rate of profit in Canada and in Latin America amounted to 17.6 per cent while the rate of profit in Europe and Asia amounted to 15 per cent.

Not only does the giant multinational firm operate equally well here and abroad, but its board of directors (and its control) usually has an inseparable mixture of financial and industrial interests. "One can no longer today speak of either industrialists or bankers as the leading echelon of the dominant capitalist classes."[41] In the fantastic size and complexity of their structure, which includes both finance and industrial capital, and the multiplicity of their interests which includes both domestic and foreign sales, the giant corporations of today are very different from either earlier banking or earlier industrial interests.

Through the multinational corporations, American capital thus directly owns a large chunk of West European industry, and the capitalists of all the imperialist countries together own the major industrial enterprises of the underdeveloped countries. "There are no reliable figures for the Third World as a whole which measure the extent of foreign economic intervention, but it is certain that many, perhaps even most, of the industrial undertakings of the underdeveloped countries are foreign-owned or controlled."[42] A careful investigation of one important neocolony concludes that "foreign capital can . . . be said to share the control of the Indian economy with domestic capital on what is very nearly a fifty-fifty basis."[43]

It should also be stressed that most of these multinational firms are none other than our old friends, the few largest American corporations. In the last official survey by size of firm using data for 1957, it was found that just 45 giants (each investing over 100 million dollars abroad) had 57 per cent of total American direct foreign investment; just 163 firms had 80 per cent; and just 455 firms had 93 per cent.[44] Certainly, any survey today would show increased concentration.

The concentration of profits is much greater. In 1966, more than half of American profits from abroad went to just sixteen firms (all among the top thirty according to the *Fortune* listing).[45] Moreover, these profits were not a small sum, even relatively to total American profits. From 1950 through 1969, profits from foreign investments were about 15 per cent of total American corporate profits, so half of that was still a tidy sum for a handful of giant corporations.[46]

One of the most important recent trends is the differential growth of domestic U.S. sales and sales abroad. These "sales abroad" do not include export sales, but are only the sales of the affiliates and subsidiaries of American corporations in foreign countries. From 1957 to 1962 total American domestic sales in manufacturing rose from $341 to $400 billion, while the sales of foreign affiliates of these same manufacturing corporations rose from $18.3 to $28.1 billion.[47] Thus, our foreign sales are growing much more rapidly than domestic sales.

This means that the United States is able to compete abroad not only by exports, but even more importantly by production of its subsidiaries within those countries. This trend is reflected in the fact that the sales of American owned plants abroad rose by 140 per cent in the last ten years, while exports from the United States went up by only 55 per cent. And this trend has certainly continued since 1960 as may be seen in the fact that in 1961 only 460 of the thousand largest U.S. companies had a subsidiary branch in Europe, but in 1965 over 700 of them had a branch in Europe.[48] This means, of course, that there is amazing concentration of capital in the few largest American firms, not only the capital of the United States, but the capital of the entire capitalist world.

All the largest American firms are on the road to being truly multinational, to think from a viewpoint based on their worldwide investments. Therefore, they are not merely interested, like the earlier industrialist, in the export of commodities nor, like earlier bankers, in the export of capital. Rather, many of them have some of their major assembly plants in foreign countries, and they export a great deal from those subsidiaries in foreign countries.

In 1966 a study found that 71 of the top 126 U.S. corporations (those for which data could be obtained) averaged one-third of their whole employment abroad.[49] Adding the multinationals of other capitalist countries, it now appears that approximately one-fourth of all capitalist production is in overseas plants.[50]

In fact, the foreign subsidiaries of many U.S. multinational firms are already large scale exporters to the market in the United States! For example, in 1967 the total sales of all U.S. enterprises abroad was $32 billion, of which 11 per cent was exported to the United States. That 11 per cent constituted a total of $3.5 billion of goods, which comes to the amazing percentage of 25 per cent of the total imports of the United States in that year.

As noted earlier, this especially means that profits can be transferred around within the corporation from a subsidiary in one country to the subsidiary in another. Therefore, we can no longer trust the reports of total profit remittances from the colonial areas to the United States as more than a general indicator. The total profits of an entire corporation are the crucial point, and they often include hidden profits in one subsidiary by reason of another selling to it more cheaply, or hidden losses in one subsidiary by reason of another selling to it more expensively than market price. For example, it appears that bauxite production in Jamaica, Surinam, and Guyana yielded to American corporations in 1961 a rate of profit of from 26 to 34 per cent. Yet this does not really give the total picture. Much of their costs "on materials and services" turn out to be exceedingly high payments to American corporations, also subsidiaries of the same major corporate group, at very high prices. On top of that, in the years from 1939 to 1959 the price of bauxite in the United States almost doubled, while the price of bauxite exported from Surinam and Guyana remained almost the same throughout the whole period. Thus, these firms' subsidiaries which were located in the West Indies overpaid for the supplies greatly and were underpaid for their finished product. (Notice that this also means more corporate taxes going to the United States, but much less going to the West Indies.)

It follows that "the multi-national companies often have conflicting interests when it comes to terms, export subsidies, foreign investment, etc."[51] They are absolutely united, however, in desiring that as many nations as possible should have laws and institutions that are favorable to the unhampered development of private capitalist enterprise. Thus, there is much intracorporate conflict over economic details, but there is no conflict over the main political and strategic issues concerning the defense of imperialism.

The United States, of course, is not alone in making foreign investments, yet its role has tremendously changed and it is certainly dominant at the present time. Thus, in 1914, the United States had only 6.3 per cent of all foreign investments of the capital exporting countries, whereas in 1960 it controlled 59.1 per cent of all foreign investments. In addition, the role of Canada increased. At the same time, the investments of the United Kingdom fell from 50.3 per cent of the total to 24.5 per cent of the total (though Britain remains the largest foreign investor on a per capita basis). Those of France fell from 22.2 per cent of the total to only 4.7 per cent. Those of Germany fell from 17.3 per cent to 1.1 per cent. Thus, it is clear that the total West European control of foreign investments fell drastically while American and Canadian investments rose fantastically.

What are the consequences of multinational firms? On the political side, we find an important and expected change. Under the old system there was conflict, direct and inevitable, between each of the investing countries. Under the new system, some of that conflict at least is eliminated. Thus a multinational firm has the interests of many different countries and many different investment bases to consider. On the other hand, most of the multinational firms have their home office in the United States. This, of course, greatly increases the dominance of the United States in the world scene. Thus, it provides one of the economic bases for the cohesion of the imperialist group against the socialist group and against the Third World—although this cohesion is also a natural political reaction to rising revolutionary movements.

Neocolonial "Aid"

During the period 1951 through 1959 average annual donations from the advanced countries to the underdeveloped countries amounted to $1.304 billion per year. The long-term public loans of capital amounted to $748 million per year. This gives a total of $2.052 billion per year.[52] Since these data include some aid and loans from the socialist countries, they over-state the amount provided by the advanced capitalist countries. For the year 1965, the Development Assistance Committee of the Organization for Economic Cooperation and Development calculates that public aid from the advanced capitalist (imperialist) countries to the underdeveloped countries was $6.270 billion. Even including private investments and loan funds, which were only $3.879 billion, the total comes to $10.149 billion for the whole year 1965. This is only 0.99 per cent of the national income of the imperialist countries.[53] Furthermore, this is a very generous estimate using extremely exaggerated figures. Such a small amount, certainly less than 1 per cent of the national income of the countries giving the aid, could not be considered much of a burden. And also, unfortunately, it is not much of a help.

As we saw, the private investment part is itself more than offset by the profit and interest returns on the investments. The small public aid

166

does not even offset the capital extracted by imperialism. That public aid which is (1) nonmilitary and (2) in the form of official donations or grants may be of some help, but it is not a large total amount. Even this "help" has extreme qualifications in that it is used to bolster repressive governments, to subsidize foreign investments, "to subsidize foreign imports which compete with national products, to introduce technology not adapted to the needs of underdeveloped countries, and to invest in low-priority sectors of the national economies."[54] The long-term public loans for nonmilitary purposes may also be of some help, but the necessity to return principle and interest is rapidly becoming a main worry of the underdeveloped areas. Thus, the United States officially admits that for all underdeveloped countries receiving U.S. aid, "the cost of maintaining such large indebtedness is at present eating up approximately 30 per cent of all new assistance."[55]

The basically political nature of this aid is clear: "Bi-lateral Public Aid, by far the most important, brings political servitude and economic subjection. It is given, received and applied in such a way as to strengthen business circles in the country giving it, and the local oligarchies in the country receiving it. International public aid is dispensed by international agencies dominated by the imperialist countries. It is technically better applied than bi-lateral aid but is, nevertheless, subject to one fundamental cause: anti-communism."[56] Certainly, one cannot find any specialist in foreign relations today who would claim that international public aid is given by any of the imperalist countries for purely charitable purposes. Obviously, it is given, and openly defended as such, for direct purposes of political domination and/or military support against the socialist bloc or against native liberation armies.

It is the declared policy of all the American agencies (for example, the Agency for International Development) that the countries that receive the aid shall use it primarily to beef up the private enterprise sectors of their economies, and shall not use it for public investment, which is often the most necessary in these countries for rapid development. Obviously, it goes without saying that the aid of the United States is directed to shore-up these countries against communism, and is not given for any pure, idealistic reason. In fact, the American aid agencies point out: "(1) Foreign aid provides a substantial and immediate market for U.S. goods and services. (2) Foreign aid stimulates the development of new overseas markets for U.S. companies. (3) Foreign aid orients national economies toward a free-enterprise system in which U.S. firms can prosper."[57]

The U.S. Agency for International Development boasts that "private enterprise has greater opportunities in India than it did a few years ago . . . fertilizer is an example of a field which is now open to the private sector, and was not in the past. This is largely a result of the efforts which we have made, the persuasion that we along with other members of the consortium have exerted on the Indian government."[58] A more blatant case of political pressure occurred in Brazil, where American aid fell from $81.8 to $15.1 million from 1962 to 1964 because the United States disliked the Goulart government. When "good" reactionary military officers overthrew Goulart, American aid jumped to $122.1 million in 1965 and $129.3 million in 1966.[59]

Nor are all the rewards of foreign aid purely ideological and in overseas areas. Just as the aid agencies claim, large parts of U.S. business benefit directly from the foreign aid program. Thus, 24.4 per cent of U.S. exports of iron and steel products are financed by the U.S. Agency for International Development. Similarly financed are 30.4 per cent of fertilizer exports, 29.5 per cent of railroad equipment exports, 11.5 per cent of non-ferrous metal exports, and 5 to 10 per cent of the U.S. exports of machinery and equipment, chemicals, motor vehicles and parts, rubber and rubber products, and textiles.[60]

The Importance of Imperialism
to the United States

Although everyone admits the importance of U.S. foreign investment and trade for the rest of the world, many economists consider that the effects of foreign trade and investment for the United States itself are negligible. This seems to be a misconception. It is true that our total exports normally run less than 5 per cent of our gross national product and that our foreign investment is normally less than 10 per cent of our domestic capital investment. The whole brunt of the argument for some pages previously, however, is the point that of very great importance today are the actual holdings of the United States through the means of multinational corporations which have branches in foreign countries (that is, the cumulative effect of all past investment). To emphasize this point once more, we may note that the "goods produced in enterprises owned by U.S. corporations in other countries now exceed 100 billion dollars yearly, or three times the annual export of goods from the United States."[61]

To find the total sales of U.S. corporations to foreign countries, we must add together exports and production of U.S. firms abroad. To make the most conservative estimate, we must eliminate some amount of double counting, since there is a certain type of overlap. If this is done, it is still found on the most conservative basis that the foreign market is something like 40 per cent of the domestic market for U.S. corporations.[62] Moreover, we saw above that the profit rate on U.S. foreign investment is much higher than the domestic rate, and that profits on foreign investment have averaged over 15 per cent of total corporate profits for the last two decades. We also mentioned that some raw materials from abroad are vital and not obtainable in the United States.

Finally, we saw in the last chapter the impact of military spending on the United States. Most U.S. military expenditures at home and abroad are directed to the aims of imperialism: protecting raw materials, foreign markets, commercial routes, spheres of influence of U.S. business, and U.S. investment opportunities (as well as capitalism in general). When we add together the profits from U.S. foreign trade, U.S. foreign investment, and from the military production to "defend U.S. interests," these profits come to about 25 to 30 per cent of all profits. When we also recall that most military and foreign profits go to the same few giant corporations, then we begin to have some idea of the importance of American international relationships.

Imperialism and War

Capitalism has always shown its aggressiveness in the international arena. Capitalist nations and their colonies have always been arranged in pyramid style, where the largest dominate the medium sized and the medium sized dominate the small ones. What has changed over time has been mostly the positions of leading capitalist countries in the international arena. From 1815 to 1914 the British Empire played a dominant, completely superior role to any other capitalist country. Germany, however, developed industrially at a much more rapid rate, so she soon demanded as her "right" a larger share of the colonial spoils than she had. The clash of the two countries (and their allies) over redivision of the colonies seems to have been the major cause leading to the First World War.

The Second World War might also be termed a clash of two sets of imperialist powers, each seeking added wealth and power. Yet it was also something more because of the fascist ideology of one group, because of the participation of the Soviet Union, and strong conflicting social forces within many advanced capitalist countries, as well as the beginnings of armed national liberation movements throughout Asia. It did, indeed, result in an expansion of various forms of socialism to a third of the world, and in struggles for independence over half the world.

In the capitalist sector the defeat of the fascist powers left the United States the single dominant force. Moreover, there was no complete American demobilization and demilitarization such as occurred for the most part after the First World War. The reason is that the United States, as the

169

dominant imperialist power, now attempts to maintain a clear military superiority as well as an economic superiority.

It maintains this military superiority both through the vast system of alliances in which it is the dominant power, and also through its own very much enlarged armed forces. By 1969, the United States had a total of 1,517,000 soldiers in 1,400 foreign bases of all types in seventy to eighty foreign countries. This military power plays the role of "the skeletal framework of the imperialist system in the absence of colonies."[63] These figures do not include the extra troops used in "police actions" or "limited wars," such as Korea and Vietnam (which are clearly also necessary for continuance of the U.S. imperium).

The major reason for this tremendous amount of armament is the need of control over the vast American empire. Notice in this connection that the decision to fight for a given area does *not* depend on the profits to be made from that area alone, but even more on its military-strategic importance to the structure of imperialism in a wider area. "Understood in these terms, the killing and destruction in Vietnam and the expenditure of vast sums of money are not balanced in the eyes of U.S. policy makers against profitable business opportunities in Vietnam; rather they are weighed according to the judgment of military and political leaders on what is necessary to control and influence Asia, and especially Southeast Asia, in order to keep the entire area within the imperialist system in general, and within the United States sphere of influence in particular."[64]

A secondary reason for armament is the need or desire to oppose socialism, especially because the expansion of socialism reduces the area of imperialist profit-making. It is certainly possible to trade with a socialist country; the United States could even become once again the major trading partner of Cuba if it wished. What is impossible, however, is to continue this trade in the old fashion with nonequivalent exchanges and the extraction of a tremendous amount of profit from privileged investments in these countries. Moreover, the success of development in socialist countries is one of the factors leading to the greatly increased revolutionary activity in the underdeveloped countries, where all strata are anxious for rapid economic development. (Also, in the sense that successful anti-imperialist revolution in one country sets an example for other countries, the U.S. State Department may be right about the "domino" theory.)

The third reason for armament is the fact, which we saw in the last chapter, that military expenditure is especially helpful to capitalism. It is unlike almost any other type of government expenditure in that it does not compete with any sort of private production. Furthermore, "the military plays the role of an ideal customer for private business, spending billions of dollars annually on terms that are most favorable to the sellers. Since a large part of their acquired capital equipment has no alternative use, its cost is commonly included in the price of the end product. The business of producing arms is therefore virtually risk free, in spite of which the allowable profit rates include a generous margin for a mythical risk factor."[65] Thus, the capitalist class tends to be strongly in favor of military spending (though particular capitalists may oppose any specific action or tactic).

Whereas education and welfare may redistribute some profits to the working classes and may even begin to allow some of these people to rise in the world and to gain new ideological understanding, militarization works in the opposite direction. Not only does it provide high rates of profit, but it also tends to kill "everything progressive and humane" and to "foster all the reactionary and irrational forces in society."[66] We saw in an earlier section that suddenly during a war the whole nation is made highly patriotic and chauvinist overnight by the vast outflowing of propaganda; and that patriotism kills off all reform, let alone radical sentiment for change in the society (aside from the unusual Vietnam war). Not only the military and the capitalist class are in favor of increased military spending, a large portion of the population is really convinced of the continued need for military spending. Only in the exceptional case of the Vietnam war has a large part of America been roused into opposition, many being radicalized by this exposure of one violent example of imperialism. Even a part of the capitalist class opposes it, mainly on tactical grounds (impossible to win, causing too much inflation).

The continued high military spending of the Vietnam war has made plain again that enough military spending will indefinitely stave off a major depression.[67] Under conditions of monopoly capitalism, however the increased military expenditure may also lead to significant inflation, less welfare spending, and aggravation of all social problems. Moreover, if the choice is between depression and war escalation (to get steadily increasing military spending), surely it is better to face directly the economic problems of depression than to have chronic "limited wars" and to run the risk of complete nuclear destruction. After nuclear destruction, there can be no saving the world. After the beginning of an economic depression, it is certainly possible to fight for a rational economic system that would get us out of the depression immediately and restore prosperity.

We may now make a clear evaluation of the costs and benefits of imperialism and militarism to the imperialist country, using America as the example. Military production and military service increase employment, assuming we begin with major unemployment. The large corporations make large profits on foreign investment. The flow of capital to the imperialist country (the excess of returns from foreign investment over current investment), however, must have a negative effect on domestic profits and employment through the competition of more capital.

The public at large, the taxpayer, pays the direct costs, including $115 billion in six years of fighting in Vietnam.[68] Non-Vietnam military expenditures continued at $30 to $40 billion a year. Since America began the war with a low level of unemployment, unemployment was not reduced (though *perhaps* a major depression was avoided at some point); but employment and demand remained high enough that monopoly power brought about price inflation, lowering the public's real income.

More than 45,000 Americans have been killed in Indochina, and more than five times that many wounded. (About 1,000,000 Vietnamese civilians have been killed, but that is presumably not a cost to America.)

The necessary climate of racism against the "inferior" Indochinese has also worsened racism at home (see Chapters 11 and 12 for more on this point). The need to limit opposition has increased repression and denial of civil liberties, and has especially hurt academic freedom in the colleges. The attempt to curb inflation by cutting all welfare spending increases the costs to the poor. For the public as a whole, therefore, the costs in blood and money are vast, and outweigh any slight benefits.

For the largest corporations, however, the balance is very different. They do pay some added taxes for the war, but they are able to pass on most of these to consumers and workers. They do have some higher costs from inflation, but their own prices rise faster. We saw that the sum of profits from military production and profits from foreign investment is about 25 to 30 per cent of all corporate profits. (Of course, there are also many small corporations and some large ones that participate neither in foreign investments nor in military production, and who therefore tend to oppose military adventures).

Furthermore, the largest 100 corporations receive more than half of that very large amount of profits. For them it is the difference between depression and very high profit rates. Therefore, for the giant corporations the benefits of the military-imperialist effort clearly outweigh the costs (whether they dribble down some of these benefits to the very top strata of labor, to keep labor content, is still highly controversial). Since these same corporate interests are dominant in the capitalist state, it is no wonder that militarism and imperialism continue to be American policy, regardless of the tremendous cost to the American people.

Yet war is not inevitable. Militarism and military actions are the "inevitable" *tendency* of imperialism. The American people have the power, however, *if* they will exercise it, to take over the state, to end imperialism, militarism, and wars. Even short of that, the situation is very different from the beginnings of the two World Wars. Within the capitalist world, America is so dominant that conflicts over imperialist spoils cannot conceivably come to the point of major warfare. Between the leading capitalist and socialist powers, one hopes that even the blindest "statesmen" on both sides recognize that all-out nuclear and biological warfare would cause the extinction of all human life on Earth within a few hours or days. Of course, increasing stockpiles of weapons by many countries make "accidental" war ever more likely.

We are still left with wars between the imperialist countries and the neocolonial countries, as the latter fight for their liberation (with varying degrees of support by the socialist countries). The question is whether these will remain "limited wars" or escalate to become the last World War. World public pressure, and especially American and West European public pressure, can at least limit these wars and make the liberation of the neocolonial peoples as quick and peaceful as possible.

The Cure for Underdevelopment

The cure for underdevelopment is socialism. Even liberal writers now recognize the appeal of socialism in the underdeveloped countries.[69] Socialist ownership means the end of foreign domination, the end of profit-outflow, and the concentration of resources and wealth on development.

The problem is whether socialism can come peacefully or not. The obstacles are internal reactionary power and foreign imperialism. This problem is explored in the next chapter.

NOTES

1. V. I. Lenin, *Imperialism: The Highest Stage of Capitalism* (New York: International Publishers, 1939, first publ. 1915).
2. Frederic Benham, *Economic Aid to Underdeveloped Countries* (London: Oxford University Press, 1961).
3. Pierre Jalee, *The Pillage of the Third World* (New York: Monthly Review Press, 1965), p. 8.
4. *Ibid.*, p. 11.
5. Jalee, *loc cit.*, and current United Nations' data.
6. R. S. McNamara, "Introduction" to H. Gray and Shanti Tangri, eds., *Economic Development and Population Growth: A Conflict?* (Lexington, Mass.: D.C. Heath, 1970). All the Western experts in the collection simply assume (or present inadequate proofs of) McNamara's ideology.
7. Paul Baran, *Political Economy of Growth* (New York: Monthly Review Press, 1957), pp. 237–248.
8. Baran, *op. cit.*, p. 246. Also David Landes, *The Unbound Prometheus* (Cambridge: Cambridge University Press, 1969).
9. See the Marxist view in Maurice Dobb, *Capitalism, Development, and Planning* (New York: International Publishers, 1967), part 2. Also Paul Baran, *op. cit.*
10. John Galbraith, *Economic Development* (Boston: Houghton Mifflin, 1962), pp. 25–26.

11. Baran, *op. cit.*, p. 165.

12. Andre Gunder Frank, *Capitalism and Underdevelopment in Latin America* (New York: Monthly Review Press, 1967), *passim*.

13. Marx, *Capital*, vol. 1, p. 823.

14. Charles Bettleheim, *India Independent* (New York: Monthly Review Press, 1968), p. 47. Also see Romesh Dutt, *The Economic History of England* (London: K. Paul, Trench, Trubner and Co., Ltd., 7th ed. 1950), pp. viii–x.

15. See, e.g., United Nations, *International Flow of Private Capital, 1948–1952* (New York: United Nations, 1954).

16. See especially Kwame Nkrumah, *Neo-colonialism: The Last Stage of Imperialism* (New York: International Publishers, 1965), *passim*.

17. Frank, *loc. cit.*

18. Nkrumah, *op. cit.*, pp. 245–250.

19. Edward Bernstein, *Evolutionary Socialism* (New York: Schocken Books, 1961, first publ. 1899), p. 179.

20. Brigadier General David Thomas, Surgeon General of the U.S. Army in Vietnam, reported in *San Francisco Chronicle* (October 24, 1969), p. 1.

21. Linus Pauling, speech on January 19, 1964, at a meeting of the Ethical Culture society in Pasadena, California.

22. League of Nations, *Economic Stability in the Post-War World* (Geneva: League of Nations, 1945), p. 103.

23. United Nations, Department of Economic Affairs, *National and International Measures for Full Employment* (New York: United Nations, 1949), p. 42.

24. *Ibid.*, p. 21

25. See annual reports for all countries in International Monetary Fund, *International Financial Statistics, 1950—*.

26. Jalee, *op. cit.*, pp. 25–55.

27. *Ibid.*, p. 32.

28. *Ibid.*, p. 33.

29. *Ibid.*, p. 43.

30. Nkrumah, *op. cit.*, pp. 243–244.

31. Jalee, *op. cit.*, p. 53.

32. *Ibid.*, p. 55.

33. League of Nations, Report of the Delegation on Economic Depression, *Economic Stability in the Post-War World* (Geneva: League of Nations, 1945), p. 92. Also see W. Bowden, M. Karpovich, and A. P. Usher, *An Economic History of Europe since 1750* (New York: American Book Company, 1937), p. 422.

34. A. K. Cairncross, *Home and Foreign Investments, 1880–1913* (Cambridge: Cambridge University Press, 1953), p. 180.

35. United States Department of Commerce, *Survey of Current Business* (November 1954, and the annual survey article in August of each year, 1955–1964).

36. Jalee, *op. cit.*, p. 74.

37. By the World Bank.

38. These data are also presented in detail in Harry Magdoff, *The Age of Imperialism* (New York: Monthly Review Press, 1969).

39. In other words, profit rates are so high that U.S. firms can both reinvest large amounts and still remit very large amounts to the United States.

40. International Monetary Fund, *Report*, 1963.

41. Paul Baran and Paul Sweezy, "Notes on the Theory of Imperialism," *Monthly Review*, 17 (March 1966): 18.

42. Jalee, *op. cit.*, p. 22.

43. Charles Bettleheim, *op. cit.*

44. U.S. Department of Commerce, *United States Business Investments in Foreign Countries* (Washington D.C.: U.S. Government Printing Office, 1960), p. 144.

45. Arthur MacEwan, "Comment of Imperialism," *American Economic Review*, 60 (May 1970): 246.

46. *Ibid.* Also data in Magdoff, *op. cit.*, p. 183.

47. Baran and Sweezy, *op. cit.*, p. 19.

48. All these data come from Baran and Sweezy, *op. cit.*, pp. 40–46.

49. Robert Heilbroner, "The Multinational Corporation and the Nation-State," *New York Review of Books* (February 11, 1971).

50. Louis Turner, *Invisible Empires* (New York: Harcourt Brace Jovanovich, 1971). Also Mira Wilkin, *The Emergence of Multinational Enterprise* (Cambridge: Harvard University Press, 1971).

51. *Ibid.*, p. 29.

52. United Nations, *The International Flow of Long-Term Capital and Official Donations, 1951–1959* (Table 7).

53. Jalee, *loc. cit.*

54. Theotinos Dos Santos, "The Structure of Dependence," *American Economic Review*, 60 (May 1970): 233.

55. Committee on Foreign Relations, U.S. Senate, *Some Important Issues in Foreign Aid* (Washington, D.C., 1966), p. 15. Also see Magdoff, *op. cit.*, pp. 52–57.

56. Jalee, *op. cit.*, p. 79.

57. Magdoff, *op. cit.*, p. 13.

58. Reported in Committee on Foreign Affairs, House of Representatives, *Hearings on Foreign Assistance Act of 1968*, p. 185.

59. Statistics and Reports Division, Agency for International Development, *U.S. Economic Assistance Programs, 1943–1966* (Washington, D.C., March 30, 1967), p. 28. Also see Magdoff, *op. cit.*, pp. 39–47.

60. Charles Hyson and Alan Strout, "Impact of Foreign Aid on U.S. Exports," *Harvard Business Review* (January–February 1968): 71. Also see Magdoff, *op. cit.*, pp. 32–39.

61. Stephen Hymer, "Comment on Imperialism," *American Economic Review*, 60 (May 1970): 244.

62. See estimate in Magdoff, *loc cit.*

63. Data and quote from Harry Magdoff, "Militarism and Imperialism," *American Economic Review*, 60 (May 1970): 237–242

64. Magdoff, *The Age of Imperialism, op. cit.*, pp. 14–15.

65. Baran and Sweezy, *op. cit.*, p. 207.

66. *Ibid.*, p. 209.

67. Contrary to the pre-Vietnam expectations of Baran and Sweezy, *op. cit.*, p. 217ff.

68. U.S. Bureau of the Budget.

69. Such as Robert Heilbroner, *The Great Ascent* (New York: Harper & Row, 1963).

CHAPTER
11

Racism, Sexism, and Alienation

Western economics ignores racism, sexism, and alienation as social phenomena, external to economics. These phenomena, however, have political-economic roots and, in turn, affect the political economy in important ways.

Racism

Racism involves prejudice and discrimination against many minorities in the United States. The white colonists in America stole the Indian lands and almost eliminated the Indians physically. Ironically, each succeeding wave of white settlers was met by a form of racism, nationalistic prejudice, from those who were already here. Thus, all East Europeans were held to be backward in culture, Italians were all lazy, Irish were all loud and uncouth.

Against Chinese and Japanese immigrants, there was a combination of nationalist and racist prejudice. This came out especially in the Second World War when all Americans of Japanese ancestry on the West Coast were confined to concentration camps (although German-Americans never were). Nationalist and racist prejudice also combines to support discrimination against Americans of Mexican descent (incorporated into the United States through imperialist expansion in the War against Mexico) and Americans of Puerto Rican descent (incorporated into the United States through imperialist expansion in the War against Spain). Finally, Black Americans are the largest oppressed minority and suffer severe racial discrimination, as we shall show below.

176

Racism, Sexism, and Alienation

Religious bigotry is another form closely related to national chauvinism and racial prejudice, all similar both in causes and effects. In Europe, Protestants and Catholics killed each other for some centuries (and still do in Ireland); and in America the Catholic minority is subjected to a certain amount of prejudice and discrimination. Much worse, of course, was the many centuries-long oppression of the Jews, forcibly converted, limited as to occupation, often taxed to bankruptcy, periodically massacred. Yet in the late nineteenth and early twentieth centuries it appeared that anti-Jewish sentiment was dying away—and it has never been severe in America, though it certainly exists. But just as the Jew felt secure, Hitler's fascism unleashed one of the worst racist atrocities in the history of the world. More than six million Jewish men, women, and children were tortured, gassed, burnt alive—all finally killed. It is surely one of the great ironies of history that some of the few survivors, now the leaders of Israel, themselves preach and practice discrimination, not only against the Arabs, but also against their "inferior" fellow Jews from Asia and Africa.

Another atrocity of racism was the enslavement of Africans for two or three centuries, and their shipment like cattle to various places of prison and work, especially the American South. This enslavement was not done in the name of Aryan domination, like Hitler's killing of the Jews and other inferior peoples, but in the gentle name of Christianity, it being the burden of the white man to bring civilization and the true religion to the Black man. One result of the slave trade was the killing of millions of Black people, both in their resistance to slavery and in the awful conditions of transportation. Another result of this enslavement is that Blacks today constitute the largest single minority in the United States.

When Blacks were slaves doing simple agricultural work in the South, racism played its usual function of explaining that Blacks were inferior to whites, that slavery was their natural condition, that such simple labor was all they could do, and that they were very happy in this condition. Now that Blacks are a large part or a majority of many American cities, and do all the complex tasks required to run American industry and urban life, the prejudices have changed somewhat but the discrimination is as fierce as ever.

The current data show that in 1968 the per capita income of whites in America was $2,616 but that of Blacks was only $1,348.[1] Only 8 per cent of white families were below the official poverty level (understated at $3,553 for an urban family of four), but 29 per cent of Black families were below the poverty level. Only 20 per cent of whites, but 47 per cent of Blacks were below $5,000 family income. Some 42 per cent of whites, but fully 71 per cent of Blacks were below $8,000 family income, while the Bureau of Labor Statistics computed at the much lower prices of 1966 that a "modest but adequate" family budget was $9,100. At the other extreme,

2.8 per cent of white families had incomes over $25,000, but only 0.4 per cent of Black families did.

The same dreary picture exists for unemployment statistics. In February, 1970 when white unemployment was officially at the very low figure of 3.8 per cent, nonwhite (92 per cent Black) unemployment was almost double that: 7 per cent by official data. Similarly, among married men white unemployment was a negligible 1.4 per cent, while nonwhite was 2.5 per cent. Among teenagers, white unemployment jumped to 11.7 per cent, while nonwhite unemployment was an incredible 25.3 per cent. Imagine the plight of Black youth when average white unemployment goes up to a 7 per cent level (the level of unemployment in California as this is written is 7.2 per cent).

Discrimination shows up in every other aspect of American life. Even the very conservative *Time Magazine* concludes that "Black Americans pay more than whites for comparable housing, and are four times more likely to live in substandard housing."[2] In fact, 25 per cent of Blacks report leaky ceilings, 26 per cent overcrowding, 29 per cent rats, 32 per cent faulty plumbing, 38 per cent cockroaches.

Time's survey (same issue) finds that in 1969 there were only nine Black representatives, and one Black senator in the U.S. Congress. Of 24,000 architects, only 450 are Black. Of 6,338 American radio stations, Blacks own 11. Of 690 TV channels, blacks own none. Of 300,000 American lawyers, only 3,000 are Black. Only 5 per cent of all reporters and photographers are Blacks. Blacks are 38 per cent of the population of Atlanta, but only 10 per cent of the police force there; 39 per cent of the Detroit population, but only 5 per cent of their police force; and 63 per cent of the Washington, D.C., population, but only 21 per cent of the police. Of 459 federal judges, only 22 are Black. Of 12,000 city and state judges, only 178 are Black. Blacks are arrested three to four times more often than whites, and of those arrested a larger proportion are jailed, a larger proportion convicted, and a larger proportion get stiff sentences. As of April 1970, more than 50 per cent of those condemned to death and awaiting execution are Black.

On the health scene Blacks constitute almost half of all American drug addicts.[3] The suicide rate in the ghetto is about twice the white rate. In 1967 for every 100,000 Americans there were 15.3 cases of tuberculosis among whites and 65.1 cases among nonwhites. The death rate from tuberculosis was 2.8 per 100,000 whites and 8.4 per 100,000 nonwhites. At birth the maternal death rate for whites was 19.7, but 37.5 for nonwhites. The death rate for infants in the first 28 days was 15 for whites, but 25 for nonwhites. The infant death rate for 1 to 11 months was 4.7 for whites, but 12.5 for nonwhites. Life expectancy for whites was 71.3 years, for nonwhites 64.6 years.

In education 73 per cent of whites complete 8th grade, but only 58 per cent of Blacks do.[4] And ¾ of Blacks in the South still attend (mid-1970) elementary schools that are at least 95 per cent Black, while ½ of all Blacks in the North attend elementary schools that are at least 95 per cent Black. High school is completed by 62 per cent of whites, but only 40 per cent of Blacks. Only 6.4 per cent of college students are Black: and half of these are in all-black colleges in the South. Blacks constitute only 1 per cent of all doctoral candidates; 3 per cent of all law students; 3 per cent of all medical students; and less than 1 per cent of the faculty at eighty public universities. Moreover, even if Blacks surmount all the barriers and get an equal education, they still face job and salary discrimination. Thus whites graduating from 8th grade have higher incomes than Blacks graduating from high school. And whites graduating from high school have higher incomes than Blacks graduating from college.

Finally, recent trends show the situation worsening rather than improving in several aspects.[5] The differences between Black and white incomes and between Black and white unemployment rates have been increasing in the last decade. Moreover, Blacks constitute a growing percentage of workers in "declining job categories," that is, unskilled jobs and industries with no employment growth. Blacks also constitute an increasing percentage (now over 25 per cent) of all the "long-term" or permanently unemployed. Furthermore, "patterns of residential segregation between Negro and white . . . are more pronounced than they were a decade ago."[6]

We need not detail the comparative facts for other minorities in America, since they are quite similar, though of somewhat less intensity. The intensity of oppression is perhaps closest in relation to the second largest minority group, the Americans of Mexican descent. Actually, although there might be some controversy over recent trends, every writer on the subject—conservative or liberal as well as radical—seems largely to agree on the present extent of discrimination. The argument comes over the causes and the solutions.

The most conservative view is now, as always, that there are inherited biological differences, making the Blacks (and Mexicans, Indians, Jews, Catholics, ad infinitum) intellectually inferior. The inferiority is the cause of lower income, less educational achievement, and so forth. Moreover, they are lazy and like to live in squalor. Since these arguments are not backed by any scientific evidence, and since refutations do not lessen the prejudice one bit, we may now leave aside this mud and muck. (Races are, of course, defined by their superficial physical differences, but there are *no* important biological differences among human races, much less any inherited intellectual differences.) It may be worth noting, however, that such views are not limited to the fascism of Adolph Hitler or the slave South of the pre-Civil War United States. Because, as we shall see, capitalism finds such defenses of racism useful. They pop up even among the most educated Americans.[7]

The usual liberal analyses see the problem as a vicious circle where the environment causes inferior performance, which leads to more prejudice, and which also leads to less achievement, so that they cannot leave their poor environment. For example, the problem is said to be that Blacks have "distinctive values" which isolate them culturally and hinder them economically. They have "a set of beliefs that favor a social dependency role for the Negro rather than one of independence; . . . female role dominance as against males; and low aspiration patterns that set limited achievement goals."[8] Although not necessarily saying that the problem is inherited inferiority, this "liberal" view still finds the problem located in the mind of the Black; so the approach is hardly different from that of the most conservative racist, except that they have added a sexist slander against the Black woman. In fact, this is a regression from the classic liberal analysis of Myrdal, who at least located the problem in the minds of the racist whites.[9] What a travesty of the truth to say that the problem is that Blacks want dependency or have "low aspiration patterns," when we have seen that discrimination is imposed on the Black by white society in every aspect of life, even against the minute few who struggle against the barriers to the highest levels of educational achievement.

The real causes of racist discrimination do not lie in inherent Black inferiority (because that is nonexistent), nor even in inherent white racism (since that has changed at different times, and can be changed further in the future). The real causes are the institutional relationships that give racism a useful function for ruling political and economic interests. In the pre–Civil War South racism was a useful apologia for slavery, so that the white Southern nonslaveowners would support slavery, the slaves might accept their lot more easily, and the Northerners would not interfere (since slavery was divinely ordained by God as a benefit to the inferior Black). Thus, its first function is to justify economic exploitation.

Its second function is to find a scapegoat for all problems. For example, the white is told that the dirt and violence of the modern city is all due to the Black. For example, the German worker was told that unemployment was all due to Jewish bankers, while the middle class was told that all the agitation was due to Jewish Communists.

The third function of racism is to *divide* the oppressed so that the elite can rule. For example, no one is more oppressed or poverty-stricken than the white sharecropper of the South (except the Black sharecropper). But he has always been told that he is still quite superior to all Blacks, so he has always fought against his natural allies, and supported the wealthy white Southerners to the extent that they not only monopolize Southern politics but achieve the chairmanship of most congressional committees by seniority. Similarly, the white worker is set against the Black worker, so that unionization is prevented altogether in many Southern areas, and each can be used as a strikebreaker against the other. The same kind of divide and rule tactic is used in Northern cities.

As we saw in the last chapter, racism is a particularly handy tool of imperialism. England especially has long used the strategy of *divide and rule*: Hindu against Moslem, Jew against Arab, Protestant against Catholic, Biafran against Northerner, Black against Hindu in Guyana. And America is quite willing to use the same tactic: Vietnamese against Cambodian, or Thai against Laotian. Moreover, we saw that inferiority, inherited or acquired, is still being given as a reason for lack of development where imperialism is the real reason. Finally, national chauvinism or "patriotism" always asserts that aggression comes from the other, evil people, so our own pure motives should not be questioned.

Within the United States we may say that blacks are exploited both as an internal colony and as workers. Blacks today are about a third of the entire industrial labor force, and an even larger percentage of the unskilled, manual laborers. Racial discrimination keeps them "in their place" as a large pool of unskilled and often unemployed workers, to be used to hold down wages in times of high demand for labor—while racial prejudice justifies that place. Thus, racism is in this respect only one more added apologia for intense exploitation of the lowest-paid part of the American working class.

Since that exploitation is at the heart of the system, legal reforms cannot give much help to most Blacks.

The system has two poles: wealth, privilege, power at one; poverty, deprivation, powerlessness at the other. It has always been that way, but in earlier times whole groups could rise because expansion made room above, and there were others ready to take their place at the bottom. Today, Negroes are at the bottom, and there is neither room above nor anyone ready to take their place. Thus only individuals can move up, not the group as such: reforms help the few, not the many. For the many nothing short of a complete change in the system—the abolition of both poles and the substitution of a society in which wealth and power are shared by all—can transform their condition.[10]

We have seen that Black people constitute the largest and most oppressed minority in the United States. As a consequence, they have played the largest single role in the radical movement in recent years. It follows that white radicals can only build a viable political movement if they fight against racism and unite with Black radicals. This is perhaps the prime political fact for the American Left. This section on racism has therefore been insufficient relative to the importance of the topic. For lack of space, it was limited to an introduction, so the reader is urged to make use of the references for further reading on it provided at the end of the book.

Sexism

Sexism, or the theory of male supremacy, is an ideology that serves in oppressing the majority of Americans—since women are about 51 per cent of the U.S. population. The pattern of discrimination—and the ideology itself—is quite similar to the effects of racism. In most aspects, but not all, racist discrimination is worse. Yet sexism is more pervasive, more deeply ingrained, and harder to combat. It is only clear that the black woman is doubly oppressed and faces the most discrimination.

The facts bear out these generalities. In 1966 in America only 5 per cent of all (four person) families headed by white males were below the official poverty income line. Of families headed by black males 20 per cent were below the poverty line. Of families headed by a white female 37 per cent were below the poverty line. And of families headed by a black female 62 per cent were below the poverty line![11]

The problem is no longer that women are not allowed to work outside the house. In 1968 women were 37 per cent of the whole civilian labor force. In fact, in 1969 some 48 per cent of all women twenty to sixty-four were in the labor force.[12] These figures could be higher, but that is not the main problem. The point is that over 90 per cent of these women work, not by desire, but by economic necessity; and they face discrimination on the job.

Thus in 1968 the average full-time employed woman earned only 58 per cent of the average male's salary. Specifically, the median salary of full-time workers was $7,870 for white men, $5,314 for black men, $4,580 for white women, and only $3,487 for black women. Furthermore, although women have a harder time getting an education, an equal education does *not* give them equal jobs or equal pay. Women with college degrees make just a little more than men with 8th grade educations! Of women with four years of college, 17 per cent take jobs as unskilled or semiskilled workers. Even among women with five years or more of college, 6 per cent take unskilled or semiskilled jobs.

Moreover, in 1968 in America women constituted only 9 per cent of all the professions, 7 per cent of the doctors, 3 per cent of the lawyers, and 1 per cent of the engineers. Women are only 5 per cent of all individuals with incomes over $10,000; only 2 per cent of business executives listed in Standard and Poors Directory; less than 4 per cent of all federal civil servants in the six highest grades; 1 per cent of federal judges; and 1 per cent of the United States Senate.[13] In 1968, California women with four years of college or more averaged only $4,151 a year, while California men with the same education averaged $8,108 a year. In fact, a 1961 poll of the National Office Managers Association found that ⅓ of the members admitted that they systematically paid women less than men for the same jobs.

Furthermore, more working women are unemployed. Typically, if white men are 5 per cent unemployed, black men will average 10 per cent unemployment, and black women will average 20 per cent unemployment (with unemployment among white women falling between 10 and 20 per cent). It might be added that discrimination against youth also shows in the unemployment figures, so that among teen-aged black women looking for jobs unemployment will run 40 per cent in that case. It should also be said that women face discrimination even in getting unemployment benefits; for example, in thirty-seven states a woman fired for pregnancy does *not* get the benefit of unemployment insurance.

Discrimination against women workers means a significant amount of extra profits to capitalist employers. In 1969 in America women's wages averaged about 40 per cent less than men's wages for the same job. On that basis, we can calculate that the extra profits from employing women at lower rates amounted to about 23 per cent of all manufacturing corporate profits.

The ideologies of racism and sexism are similar in many ways, both being based on the supposed inferiority of some groups of human beings to others: ". . . All discrimination is eventually the same thing—Anti-Humanism."[14] Women have long been alleged to be inferior both in intelligence and in physical ability to do hard work. Even in the present "enlightened" age, the ideology of sexism continues in unabated fury. Thus, reactionaries still justify lower pay for women: "If a woman were more like a man, she'd be treated as such."[15] This disgusting view ignores the main point, that millions of women get less pay for doing the same, identical work as men. Another attack on women comes from the crude Freudianism so frequent in the popular media and high school education. Woman suffers from penis envy, a lack which makes her innately inferior (but what about breast envy?). A more "scientific" statement of sexism comes from the noble Dr. Edgar Benson, member of the Democratic Party Committee on National Priorities and close personal friend of former Vice-President Hubert Humphrey, who says "that physical factors, particularly the menstrual cycle and menopause, disqualifies women for key executive jobs."[16] Isn't it fortunate that instead of nervous females, who might get us into wars, we have our destiny in the hands of such calm and pacific male thinkers as Johnson and Nixon?

All tests show that men and women are equal in intelligence, though they usually progress at different rates in childhood learning, with women leading in the early years.

Certainly, men and women have physical differences (*vive le difference!*).

With respect to working ability, however, it is by no means clear that the differences make women inferior. In fact, many modern tests indicate that women have more stamina as well as more patience, at least in Western society. There are some primitive societies where women normally carry heavier loads than men (and I have seen Russian rural women carrying loads I probably could not carry). The question is one of training and expectations. Listen to the lot of the slave woman of the American South as stated by the great Black abolitionist, Sojourner Truth: "Look at my arm! I have ploughed and planted and gathered into barns, and no man could head me—and ain't I a woman? I have borne thirteen children, and seen most of 'em sold into slavery, and when I cried out with my mother's grief, none but Jesus heard me—and ain't I a woman?"[17]

Even in social and sexual matters, it is not a given eternal fact that man must always dominate. There are some primitive societies where men and women appear to have about equal social and sexual roles (perhaps especially in those societies where the economic roles of the two are roughly equal in importance, as when women gather wild foods and men hunt). There are other primitive societies where women appear to play the dominant role. If nothing else can be said without controversy, at least modern anthropology makes clear that there are many types of family organization, not just one (including various kinds of group marriages).[18]

Only with the coming of "civilization"—meaning class distinctions, and the possession of property in land, cattle, slaves, or serfs—does the woman also become a piece of property. In fact, for purposes of clear inheritance of property, the woman of the upper classes is very well guarded; only the male may freely violate the theoretical monogamy.[19]

The particular attitudes of men and women in our society are not inherited, but carefully inculcated. "Women are taught from the time they are children to play a serving role, to be docile and submissive. . . ."[20] Women are taught to be ornamental, and we think of cosmetics as solely for women. Yet the French noblemen before the Revolution used plentiful cosmetics. And women in the West, except for prostitutes, did not use cosmetics before the nineteenth century.

What are the causes for the ideology of sexism and the discrimination against women? Some functions are similar to racism. First, it is an excuse for the superexploitation of women workers, a major source of extra profit as we saw above. Second, the division between male and female workers makes it possible to keep all workers weaker and ruled. The third function of sexism gets into a different kind of area. The stable family is considered to be an important basis for the stability of capitalism. "Thus [Talcott] Parsons finds sexual segregation 'functional' in terms of keeping the social structure as it is, which seems to be the functionalist's primary concern."[21]

Under capitalism the theoretically monogamous family provides the basis for holding and inheriting private property.

Furthermore, advertising has associated the number of gadgets in the household with the welfare of the family, so the family unit provides a powerful boost to the spirit of unlimited competition. Thus the women's magazines find the perfect heroine in the woman who says she is thankful for having a "wonderful husband, handsome sons . . . big comfortable house . . . my good health and faith in God and such material possessions as two cars, two TVs and two fireplaces."[22] Of course, most working class women don't have these material possessions, but they can have faith in God.

The drive to keep women out of public life and generally in an inferior position reached its heights in Nazi Germany—Hitler's recommendation for women was "children, kitchen, and church." In America it is interesting that a strong drive in that direction (by the media, by life adjustment courses, home economics courses, and many other channels) was recorded in the 1950's, just when there was a general drive in our society toward conformity and silence under Joe McCarthy, and toward justification of the new U.S. role as chief imperialist policeman of the world (with men in the army and women minding the home?). The drive was quite successful in that the proportion of women in college declined continuously during the 1940's and 1950's.[23]

It has often been said that the position of women in a society usually mirrors the general condition of human rights in a society. Even in the nineteenth century the connection was pointed out to those radicals who wished to ignore it: "Every socialist recognizes the dependence of workmen on the capitalist . . . but the same socialist often does not recognize the dependence of women on men because the question touches his own dear self more or less clearly."[24]

In the 1900's it was said that "notwithstanding all the laws emancipating women, she continues to be a domestic slave, because petty housework crushes, strangles, stultifies, and degrades her, chains her to the kitchen and the nursery. . . ."[25] Obviously, middle class women in America now have many gadgets to make their housework easier, and some women find aspects of housekeeping and child care pleasurable and creative. It is true that the average American housewife still provides 99.6 hours a week (or more than fourteen a day) of unpaid labor.[26] Nevertheless, in the words of one male advertiser: "Properly manipulated . . . American housewives can be given the sense of identity, purpose, creativity, the self-realization, even the sexual joy they lack—by the buying of things."[27] She shall have her gadgets, and they shall make her happy: or do they?

The middle class women's liberationists urge that women need more than housework; they also need productive, or artistic, or political activities. Moreover, the home could be better automated or supplied with outside services, such as better and cheaper nursery schools, restaurants, and laundries. We have seen, however, from the data that half of all American women in the working ages do work. The problem for the working class women—and especially the black working women—is discrimination at work, low pay, last hired and first fired and never promoted; and on top of that all the housework to do when she gets home.

There are many reforms on which all those fighting against sexism can agree. We need free child-care centers; equal pay to women for equal work; equal access by women to all education; equal access of women to equal kinds of jobs; free birth control information and devices, so that women can determine when they wish to have children, and as a last resort free and legal abortions. The problem is that even these reforms are still unlikely to change basic attitudes, nor is it clear that all these reforms can actually be won under capitalism. It is a fact that the lower wages of women are a source of additional profit. It is a fact—perhaps even more important—that the submissive attitude of women, encouraged by church and television "idiot box" alike, serves as an important prop to the status quo; and that the family socializes every child to acceptance of the status quo in the same way. There are thus strong and vested interests in favor of keeping woman in her present "place in the home."

Alienation

We Americans live as "alienated" strangers to each other and to society as a whole, with the feeling that we are pushed through life by vast social forces over which we have no control. Some problems of alienation are apparent in any large, complex, industrial society. Monopoly capitalism, however, greatly intensifies these problems. The very highly concentrated economic, political, and military power means that a few hundred men make most of the decisions vitally affecting the lives of the other two hundred million people. Is it any wonder that most people feel terribly alone and defensive in such a cold, money-and-power loving society?

It is possible to distinguish at least three different senses in which alienation is found in modern capitalist society.[28] First, the worker is dominated by his product. He produces consumers' goods, but they are taken away from him, so that much of his life is centered around earning enough money to run after consumer goods. He learns to relate to things, such as autos or TV sets, rather than to people. He produces producers' goods, which are taken away from him and become capital, with which he is then employed to work. He produces military goods, such as atomic bombs, and then they hang over his head like a Damocles sword, liable to destroy the whole world.

A second meaning of alienation is the separation of the worker from his production activity. He does not own the means of production with which he works—nor does he own the product of his labor. Thus, his working activity becomes "merely a *means* to satisfy needs external to it. Its alien character emerges clearly in the fact that as soon as no physical or other compulsion exists, labor is shunned like the plague."[29] The laborer sells his labor power as a thing to be purchased on the market. He has become dehumanized, a cog in a machine to make profit for someone else.

The worker no longer produces and sells a whole artifact, as in some precapitalist handicraft situations. He is therefore bored by the production process, and takes no pride in "workmanship" (as Veblen called it). Although the worker must be a small cog in a big machine in any complex industrial society, monopoly capitalism worsens the alienation because the production is carried on solely for the profit of a giant, faceless corporation. This fact also leads to political alienation, since the U.S. government stands to us as a vast and far distant institution, dominated by the large corporation, and dominating over the helpless individual.

A third aspect of alienation follows from the first two: namely the awful alienation of man from man. The ethic of capitalism is each man for himself, and the only honored goal is money. The result is a "lonely crowd," lack of communication, frustration, crime, and aggression.[30] As long as capitalism and private property exist, the individual must strive by competition to maximize his wealth; the competitive view isolates each individual in his or her lonely fortress. This alienation from fellow men and women, linked with a competitive dog-eat-dog drive, gives the United States its high rates of crime, prostitution, gambling, juvenile delinquency, alcoholism, drug addiction, divorce, suicide, and mental breakdown.

It comes as no surprise that big crime is closely linked to big business, both equally intent on making profits. And it is equally no surprise that pornographic magazines and other cultural trash are manufactured solely for profit—why else would anyone produce such stuff? It is also no surprise that advertising expenditures are about three times as high as all our expenditures on higher education taken together. The only surprise in American culture is that any marriages survive under these conditions: where the individual is trained to competition rather than cooperation; where the male is trained to dominate, the female to be beautiful but dumb, and both expect a Hollywood fairlyland of perfect lover and companion; where there is stress and tension in modern urban life; where no one stays put long enough to have a secure circle of friends and relatives; where the possibility of nuclear destruction is omnipresent. At the same time as the divorce rate soars, there is much preoccupation with sex today, partly because it seems the only real thing in a world where the old is collapsing and the new not yet built.

These conditions are, of course, much worse for low income and especially for Black families. A liberal writer laments: "The poor are always alienated from normal society, and when the poor are Negro, as they increasingly are in American cities, a double trauma exists."[31] True enough observation. But the word "normal" reveals an elitist, status quo view, and the word "trauma" conveys a feeling of paralysis, whereas Blacks today are angry and moving.

In some respects the subjective effects of the alienation of man from man make radical organization in America more difficult. In the early 1950's, at the height of McCarthyite repression, the seemingly insurmountable barriers to radicalism included "the still-vigorous belief in the possibilities of advancement within the framework of capitalist society. The deepseated acceptance of bourgeois values. . . . The . . . multi-pronged manipulation of the public mind. The heart-breaking emptiness and cynicism of the commerical, competitive, capitalist culture. The systematic cultivation of devastatingly neurotic reactions to most social phenomena (through the movies, the 'funnies,' etc) . . . the utterly paralyzing feeling of solitude which must overcome anyone who does not want to conform. The feeling that there is no movement, no camp, no group to which he can turn."[32]

This situation in the 1970's has changed very considerably. Most of the description still covers real problems, but there is now more of an anti-imperialist, anticapitalist movement to which one can turn, even in America. The American "New Left" has died as a unified movement, but there remains a changed atmosphere and a considerable and growing, if disunified, Left movement. The radical Left are those who react to oppression and alienation, not by apathy or withdrawal (or by following the "radical" antihumanism of a George Wallace), but by opposing the whole system with a vision of something better.

Liberals and radicals mostly recognize the same problems in America: the war in Vietnam, poverty, pollution, repression, unemployment, racism, sexism, and even alienation. They disagree over the causes. The liberal defenders of capitalism see each problem as independent. Some argue that each is a temporary accident of mistaken policy, like the "mistake" in Vietnam. Others believe that the problems are eternal, caused by unchanging human nature. Thus, there is the Freudian hypothesis of an innate tendency of aggression to account for war or racism; the smart aggressive character becomes rich and others stay poor because that's how it will always be; and women are naturally submissive, or protest because of penis envy. The liberals conclude, therefore, that better policies can remedy the random policy mistakes (like imperialist war or unemployment) without changing capitalism. Many other problems are seen as having no solution—certainly having nothing to do with capitalism—and subject only to some amelioration of their effects.

Radicals, on the contrary, see the problems all tied into the one institutional matrix. We find no evidence of innate inferiority in any group, poor or Black, Chicano or woman, but a great deal of evidence that all are exploited and manipulated by a relatively small class with vested interests in the status quo. We find no evidence of innate aggressive instincts, but a great deal of evidence that behavior is different under different social institutions—and that present American militarist aggression stems from the interests of a small number of oligopoly corporations. Our psychologies, too, are formed by this milieu of waste and aggression. "For behind the emptiness, the degradation, and the suffering which poison human existence in this society lies the profound irrationality and moral bankruptcy of monopoly capitalism itself."[33]

Alienation of Youth

Youth, and particularly students, have suffered a higher intensity of alienation than the older generations. (We speak here of America, but most of the phenomena are worldwide). In discussing sexism, it was mentioned that a large stratum of American women (mostly middle class) see the home and family as their sole vocation, they are devoted to their gadgets and possessions, and see their children as their most valuable possession, even ahead of the TV set. The mother tries hard to hold on to the child, the result being either submission and arrested development or psychological alienation in the form of rebellion from the family.

In addition to that home background, students today face a world with some unique and overwhelming problems. This generation has grown up in the shadow of nuclear weapons, in a world continually on the brink of total destruction. They know there is a chance that, even without nuclear war, man may irretrievably damage his environment, where youth has always reveled in the open beauty of lake and mountain and forest. They are witnesses to a rising of minority groups and neocolonial peoples met by cynical racism and militarism—and the stink of it is particularly disgusting to the idealistic expectations of youth. They have all suffered from, witnessed, or heard of police repression and official McCarthyism.

Moreover, many of the social evils and discrimination hit hardest against youth. The unemployment rate is twice as high among youth (and again twice as high among minority youth) as among the general population.

At an age when they have just completed their years of education and are most filled with energy and enthusiasm, they cannot get a job or can only get routine, tedious jobs (in industry or home). The individual frustration is equalled only by the social waste. Yet, in the face of their great expectations, one job is forced on youth: military service and the "duty" to kill other youth. At the same time as they could kill and be killed in the army, they were not yet allowed to vote before the age of twenty-one until recently.

Is it any wonder that today's youth are alienated? They show the alienation in many ways, some by the hippie life-style and appearance, by drug addiction, and by complete drop out from the competitive race. A minority reacts by a militant fight to change the society. A typical militant student view in the mid-sixties said: "What, beyond economic, political, and racial inequality, is wrong with this country? The New Left's answer is that there is plenty more wrong, that the standard American way of life is incompatible with a decent human existence."[34]

NOTES

1. United States Department of Commerce, various publications, such as the United States Statistical Abstract, 1970.

2. *Time Magazine* (April 6, 1970), p. 53.

3. Data from *Time*, obtained by them from U.S. Department of Health, Education, and Welfare.

4. *Time, op. cit.*, p. 194.

5. See data and analysis in Louis Ferman, Joyce Kornbluh, and J. Miller, eds., *Negroes and Jobs* (Ann Arbor: University of Michigan Press, 1968).

6. *Ibid.*, p. 194.

7. For example, some erroneous and unscientific articles have been written on this theme by Professor Arthur Jensen of the University of California, Berkeley and by Professor William Shockley of Stanford, and have been discussed "objectively" by the U.S. National Academy of Sciences. See *Newsweek* (May 10, 1971): 69–70. On the contrary, careful studies have shown that all racial groups have approximately the same intelligence as proven in I.Q. tests, once the racial bias of the test is eliminated; evidence is presented in excellent papers by George Mayeske and by Jane Mercer at the meetings of the American Psychological Association, Washington, D.C., September 1971.

8. Ferman, Kornbluh, and Miller, eds., op. cit., p. 108

9. Gunnar Myrdal, *The American Dilemma* (New York: Harper & Bros. 1944).

10. Paul Baran and Paul Sweezy, *Monopoly Capital* (Monthly Review Press, 1966), p. 279.

11. U. S. Bureau of the Census, *Extent of Poverty in the United States 1959 to 1966*, Current Population Reports Series p–60, no. 54 (May 1968).

12. Department of Labor data, cited in Mickey and John Rowntree, "More on the Political Economy of Women's Liberation," *Monthly Review*, 21 (January 1970): 26–32.

13. Caroline Bind, *Born Female: The High Cost of Keeping Women Down* (New

York: Pocket Books, 1969), p. 82. This book gives an excellent factual survey, including most of the material cited here.

14. Shirley Chisholm, "Racism and Anti-Feminism," *The Black Scholar*, 1 (January–February 1970): 45.

15. Angus Black, *A Radical's Guide to Economic Reality* (New York: Holt, Rinehart and Winston, 1970), p. 37.

16. Quoted in *San Francisco Chronicle* (July 27, 1970), p. 9.

17. Quoted in Bind, *op. cit.*, p. 25.

18. See, e.g., the interesting case study in E. Kathleen Gough, "The Nayars and the Definition of Marriage," in Peter Hammond, ed., *Cultural and Social Anthropology* (New York: Macmillan, 1964), pp. 167–180. For a description of all known kinship structures, see G. P. Murdock, *Social Structure* (New York: Macmillan, 1949), *passim*.

19. Although based partly on incorrect data, some penetrating and caustic insights are given by Frederick Engels, *The Origin of the Family, Private Property, and the State* (New York: International Publishers, 1942, first publ. 1884). Also see the interesting discussion in Bernhard J. Stern, "Engels on the Family," *Science and Society*, 12 (winter 1948): 42–64.

20. Marilyn Goldberg, "The Economic Exploitation of Women," *The Review of Radical Political Economics*, 2 (Spring 1970): 35.

21. Critique of Parsons, the leading light of Western sociology, by Betty Friedan, *The Feminine Mystique* (New York: Dell, 1963), p. 122.

22. *Ibid.*, p. 64.

23. *Ibid.*, p. 153.

24. Statement in the 1890's by August Bebel, in *Women and Socialism*, quoted by editors in *Monthly Review* (September 1969): 27.

25. V. I. Lenin, *On the Emancipation of Women* (Moscow: Progress Publishers, n.d.).

26. Estimate by Chase Manhattan Bank.

27. Quoted in Friedan, *op. cit.*, p. 199.

28. This exposition follows Karl Marx, *The Economic and Philosophical Manuscripts of 1844* (New York: International Publishers, transl. 1964). The humanist indignation over alienation expressed by the young Marx was not made explicit in Marx's later works, but shines as a strong illumination implicitly in all of them. For a century or more Marx's followers did not emphasize these human aspects of political economy. It is to the honor of the existentialists, such as Jean Paul Sartre, that they did bring these individual human problems to the fore. Even now, only the most nondogmatic Marxists have seriously returned to these issues; see e.g., Leszek Kolakowski, *Toward a Marxist Humanism* (New York: Grove Press, 1968).

29. Marx, *Economic and Philosophical Manuscripts*, op. cit., p. 111.

30. A good example of the alienation of man from man in recent art is in Fellini's *La Strada*. The heroine, Quelsimmina, never really has any contact with her family, nor even with the performer she goes off with. In most of the movie she is not physically isolated, but is with other people. Yet she doesn't relate at all. There is little communication of any kind, and no attempt at deep, affectionate communication.

31. Kenneth Clark, *Dark Ghetto*, cited in Ferman, Kornbluh, and Miller, *op. cit.*, p. 110.

32. Historicus (Paul Baran), in *Monthly Review* (July 1950): 82–86.

33. Baran and Sweezy, *op. cit.*, p. 363.

34. Mitchell Cohen and Dennis Hale, *The New Student Left* (Boston: Beacon, 1967), p. xxvi.

CHAPTER

12

Reform or Revolution

You will print such books as these!
Then you're lost, my friend, that's certain.
If you wish for gold and honor,
Write more humbly—bend your knee!

Aye, you must have lost your senses
Thus to speak before the people;
Thus to dare to speak of Preachers
And of Potentates and Princes.

Friend, you're lost—so it appears—
For the Princes have long arms,
And the Preachers have long tongues,
—And the masses have long ears!

HEINRICH HEINE, "A Warning"*

A revolution may be defined as a basic change in political, social, and economic institutions and relationships among humans. Of course, the word "revolution" is also applied to many other changes, such as the industrial revolution, which involved important technological and organizational changes in economic activity; in this chapter, however, the word is restricted to fundamental changes in the whole social-political-economic web of human relations. Smaller changes in institutions, not changing the fundamental relationships, may be referred to as "reforms."

Reformism

Revolutions—and even reforms—may be accompanied by violence, or they may be peaceful. At least, it is logically possible that a revolutionary change may be peaceful; and it is very confusing to rule out a peaceful revolution-

* Translated by Louis Untermeyer, *Heinrich Heine: Paradox and Poet* (New York: Harcourt Brace Jovanovich, 1937). Reprinted by permission of the publisher.

ary change by definition, since this is one of the problems to be discussed. For example, one writer speaks approvingly of "uncompromising public commitment to revolutionary goals while practicing . . . reformist tactics."[1] By "reformist" he appears to mean someone who advocates peaceful change, concentrating on immediate issues, while also arguing for revolutionary change. This does not seem to draw the line clearly enough between reformist and revolutionary positions, since we shall see that revolutionaries may also differ among themselves on tactics.

The clearest position of reformism admits some problems, but claims that they can be solved without revolutionary change (even peaceful revolutionary change). The reformist socialists in Germany of the 1890's, for example, argued that capitalism was steadily improving in many ways, such as rising workers' incomes and a stable economy under the giant corporations. Therefore, they said, only certain reforms for welfare and redistribution are now necessary; and it doesn't matter if we never reach socialism for a thousand years, so long as gradual reforms are continued.[2]

It is interesting that their descendants, the German socialists of the 1970's, have gone even further to say that the present mixture of capitalism and state regulation is just about right, or needs very little change. Of course, most American liberals are not even socialist in name, so their reformism is still clearer. For example, two liberals write: "Patching up an old system is the most rational way to change it, for the patch constitutes about as big a change as one can comprehend at a time. . . . Capitalism was only a series of patches on feudalism."[3] They not only deny the possibility of future revolutionary change, but also deny the reality of past revolutionary change.

Naturally, with this outlook which is widespread in non-Marxist social science, they consider *any* analysis of real revolutionary changes as unsophisticated, and limit themselves to suggestions for marginal changes in administration. Thus another conservative political scientist says: "I retain the conviction . . . that revolution is always avoidable if only the creative potentialities of political organization can be realized."[4]

Radicals and revolutionaries, on the other hand, begin with the facts of the problems of capitalism enumerated in previous chapters: poverty, exploitation, waste, pollution, unemployment, monopoly, political repression, imperialism, war, racism, sexism, and alienation. Obviously, not all these problems can be ended overnight, though some can. But none of them can even begin to be really cured without a revolutionary change, namely, an end to capitalism itself.

Peaceful Revolution?

What are the possibilities of a revolutionary change being peaceful? The liberal, pluralist view says that the state stands above classes, responds impartially to all pressures, and could be peacefully changed. The Marxist view is that the capitalist state is controlled by the capitalist ruling class, which has an interest in maintaining the status quo and preventing revolutionary change. The dogmatic Marxist view therefore says that revolutionary change can *never* be peaceful.

In a more nondogmatic view it would seem that the possibility of peaceful change cannot be flatly denied or asserted for all capitalist countries at all times. We saw in Chapter 9 that political actions of the working class under capitalist democracy may sometimes force reforms. Certainly *some* of the reformers may remain honest and sincere in office. Certainly *some* reforms may actually be carried into effect by the bourgeois bureaucracy, bourgeois police, and bourgeois courts. But is there any historical case of very gradual reforms actually leading to a complete change in the basic class relations with respect to the means of production?

Reformist socialists object, however, that with universal suffrage in a capitalist "democracy," the workers and friendly intellectuals can elect a majority of socialists and the majority can simply legislate socialism. There is no formal, constitutional reason why this couldn't be done in most of the bourgeois democracies. Nevertheless, in Chapter 9 we noted a long list of obstacles to peaceful change to socialism (summarized briefly here): (1) low political participation of low income groups; (2) the built-in conservative bias of mass media; (3) political advertising; (4) power of money in party primaries; (5) power of money in general elections; (6) conservative bias of religion; (7) big-business control of boards of regents of universities; (8) as a feedback, use of the state against socialist movements; (9) buying out a few (key) socialist or radical politicians.

For underdeveloped countries, we may add external economic pressures, such as flight of capital and decline of exports—for example, in copper in Chile. If Chile should actually maintain a socialist-communist government in office for any length of time, and if that government really enacts and carries out radical measures, then this kind of economic pressure is very likely. Then either the socialist government must surrender (as is the natural inclination of all reformist socialists), or else it must go on to more thoroughly revolutionary measures.

Furthermore, the old state apparatus—the army, police, judiciary, government bureaucrats—has *never* been known to obey a simple legal order to socialize the economy. In the Russian Revolution of 1917 the old state

apparatus did its best to sabotage the new government. The Russian socialists kept political power only through a civil war in which they fought
parts of the old army and police, dismissed the old judiciary, and tossed out
most of the old government bureaucrats.

The Use of Violence

This brings us to the last barrier to the peaceful election and maintenance
of a government fully committed to socialism. All historical experience
indicates that any ruling class will in the end use force and violence to
protect its vital interests against radical change. For example, the French
feudal ruling class used force to try to prevent a bourgeois revolution
(which began in a peaceful and parliamentary way) in 1789–1812. The
American slaveowners used force to protect slavery (against a possibility
of peaceful legislative abolition) in 1861–1865. The Russian feudal and
capitalist forces joined hands with foreign allies to attack the new socialist
state in 1917–1921. Fascism in the 1920's and 1930's used force and violence
to prepare for an attempt at world conquest and to forestall the possible
democratic advent of socialism in Germany, Italy, and Spain. In the present
period a military coup prevented an election in Greece because a Left
government might have won it.[5] In the present period the legal governments of Guatemala, Iran, Guyana, Brazil, Ghana, Indonesia, and so many
others, when they began to introduce mild anti-imperialist reforms, were
overthrown by capitalist and imperialist force.

Eisenhower admitted that 80 per cent of the Vietnamese in 1954 would
have chosen Ho Chi Minh in a free election.[6] Yet America prevented that
election by force in South Vietnam. The State Department's ingenious
apologia said that "it was the Communists' calculation that nationwide
elections scheduled in the accords of 1956 would turn all of South Vietnam over to them. . . . The authorities of South Vietnam [with American
support] refused to fall into this well-laid trap."[7] So a free election becomes
a well-laid trap when the results may be contrary to U.S. desire.

Violence is used not only to prevent socialist revolution in the final
analysis, but also day-to-day to prevent radical causes from ever gaining
strength. For example, there were the police riots against the protesters at
the 1968 Chicago convention of the Democratic party. Special riot police
are given training in particularly nasty weapons for use against student or
Black demonstrations. There are also National Guardsmen, who have been
used to shoot down students, as at Kent State in 1970. In addition, the
campuses and the Black ghettos have both been invaded by hordes of
FBI agents, CIA agents, and other varieties of secret thought police.

Instead of improving conditions, there has been in some ways an increase of repression and violence in class strife since Marx wrote that "direct force, outside economic conditions, is of course still used but only exceptionally."[8] American labor history records thousands of instances of police violence against workers to prevent successful strikes (as well as the use of private armies, such as the Pinkertons). Only the reduced militancy of American labor in recent years has brought a reduced number of cases of police violence against labor, but it is still found in many strike situations, especially those where workers are predominantly composed of minority groups, such as blacks or Chicanos. As students have become more politically active, their demonstrations have been met with increasing violence (this author was tear gassed during indiscriminate police attacks on students and faculty in Berkeley in 1970). Especially hit by violence have been black groups, as in the police murders of Black Panthers in 1969–1970, and in the continued police violence against ghettos such as the Watts area of Los Angeles.

There have been innumerable documentations of the fact that the violence stems from the rulers, not the ruled. For example, in Berkeley in 1969, "something on the order of 90 or 95 per cent of the violence that took place on campus was initiated by the police."[9] In a common incident at Berkeley happening to a student (hitherto nonpolitical, who got involved for the first time as he was defending a fallen reporter), a Visiting Professor wrote: "Suddenly four policemen . . . knocked him to the ground and began beating him. One knocked all his front teeth out with a club. After a while they dragged him—blood pouring from his mouth, screaming in mingled pain and terror—into the administration building itself."[10]

In an instance of unwarranted optimism Marx said: "The superstition that used to ascribe revolutions to the ugly intentions of agitators is a thing of the past. Today everyone knows that whenever a revolutionary upheaval takes place, its source lies in some social need that outdated institutions are not meeting."[11] Alas, that Marx should be so wrong; more than a hundred years later, the superstition still prevails. The State Department tells us that South Vietnam is aflame only because of agitators from the North. The vulgar Marxists of the Soviet Union tell us that Czechoslovakia began a revolutionary experiment in humanist socialism because of the influence of America and West Germany. The vice-president of the United States, the head of the FBI, and the governor of California tell us that campus disturbances are not caused by concern for social issues, but by outside agitators and conspirators.

It must be admitted that there are a few sects of radicals—mainly those influenced by a resurgence of anarchist thought—who themselves advocate and practice the use of violence. In a broad sense we may still defend their actions as the reactions of the oppressed to ruling class violence. Yet, they are clearly using violence beyond self-defense. For some of them, the argument for violence is their despair at ever convincing the majority of workers of the socialist program; immediate violent acts are "easier" than long-run education. For others, they believe that the consciousness of men will only really be changed by violence; that the "socialist man" will only be tempered by such a violent struggle. This line of thought is uncomfortably like Mussolini's notion that man only achieves really full living in warfare. It is true, of course that whole peoples such as the Vietnamese or Algerians have been raised several levels of social understanding by their struggles with imperialism, but this is violent *resistance* to violent oppression. Unfortunately, we will probably need a great deal more such resistance before socialism is achieved, but that is very different from a small minority going out to perform violent "propaganda of the deed."

Revolution in the Advanced Capitalist Countries?

It is a fact that the majority of the working class in America, Canada, and West Europe is nonrevolutionary, although they are for some kind of socialism in Western Europe. These countries all have advanced, developed capitalist economies, and are all involved to some extent in the imperialist domination of the underdeveloped countries. Why are the workers in developed capitalism, particularly America, nonrevolutionary?

Marx saw revolutionary potential in the terrible conditions of industrialization in the early nineteenth century, but technological development (and imperialism) has changed the situation. American workers are now much less in blue collar, and many more in white collar, scientific, and teaching jobs. They are also less in industrial production, and more in service jobs, from beauticians and TV repairmen to ball players. These jobs are mostly more pleasant and interesting. The working class is much more differentiated occupationally (though various national groups with different languages and traditions have been integrated) and less easily united on any single issue. Moreover, absolute income has risen very, very considerably, although the share of wages relative to total income has fallen.

Imperialism has also adversely affected revolutionary potential. While its effect on most workers is to lower their real wages through inflation and taxes (and to kill their sons in wars), it is also true that militarism increases employment, and—probably—imperialist profits are used to bribe the top technical workers. Its ideological effect is even clearer. Imperialist wars are always a time of "hooray for my country, right or wrong." The clash of rival imperialisms in the First World War lined up the workers and their socialist parties on opposite sides, thus destroying the Second Workers' International.

Imperialist warfare not only stirs up nationalism and superpatriotism, but also racism. American soldiers in Korea and Vietnam have been taught to despise these "inferior" peoples, and always refer to them with derogatory names. The racism naturally carries over into America itself, reinforcing our usual level of chauvinism. Moreover, warfare means millions of men trained to think of the highest good as the murdering of their fellow human beings; training is designed, as the army often tells the soldier, to produce killers. Such attitudes also carry over into civilian life, increasing mental instability, and increasing the masculine view of superiority over the peace-loving woman. Thus, imperialism tends to split the working class of the advanced capitalist countries into black and white, Jew and Christian, Protestant and Catholic, male and female, and a hundred other irrational divisions.

Under these circumstances the majority of American workers are employed at wages considerably above poverty levels and are separated from militant minority groups. They are still, though, alienated in many ways —for example, seeing the giant corporations and the state as far-away dominant masters. Youth and students have more reason to be militant because they are more directly affected by war and alienation (and French students in May, 1968, did succeed as a catalyst in putting workers into militant action). Moreover, minorities such as the Blacks and Chicanos suffer the full brunt of racist discrimination, including low wages and high unemployment, so they certainly do have a revolutionary potential. Admittedly, however, this leaves a very large majority of Americans with no immediate revolutionary potential, at least so long as the United States continues to sit atop the world. As a consequence, patient, nonviolent, socialist education seems the only useful radical tactic in America (though this educational process will include strikes, sit-ins, marches, and other practical activities).

Revolution in Underdeveloped Capitalist Countries

The situation is quite different in the underdeveloped countries of the capitalist world. This area, the Third World, is kept underdeveloped by the neocolonial economic exploitation and political domination of the imperialist countries. Even the most conservative economists agree that their income levels are falling ever further behind those of the advanced capitalist countries. Moreover, their absolute income levels are abysmal, and may even be falling in some areas. Thus, their economic situation is closely akin to that of the West European workers in the early nineteenth century. Their political-social situation is much worse, since they feel themselves to be, and are, dominated by a small elite stratum supported and directed by foreigners, who look down on them as inferiors.

The result is quite naturally that the peoples of the Third World are very revolutionary-minded, desiring real independence and socialism. This is especially the case because they are coming to realize that the peaceful road of economic evolution to a level above poverty for most workers, that was followed by Western Europe and the United States, is not open to them. It is closed by the barriers raised by imperialism: the outflow of capital in the form of profits and interest, the export trade dependent on one or two food or raw material products, the investment mainly in extractive industries or very light consumer goods industries, the all-out military support for the most reactionary governments and forms of land ownership (and lack of taxation of the rich).

The tactical situation is made even clearer by the fact that most of these Third World countries in the "free world" are dictatorships, military and otherwise. Thus, fifteen or sixteen of the twenty-two Latin American countries are dictatorships; perhaps twenty-five or twenty-six of the thirty-two African countries are dictatorships; and something like sixteen or seventeen of the twenty-one underdeveloped capitalist countries of Asia are dictatorships.[12] Even in the semideveloped areas of Western Europe, in Spain and Portugal and Greece, there are uncompromising dictatorships. There is no implication here of a simple connection between low income and dictatorship. But when there is underdevelopment, imperialist domination, and revolutionary sentiment, then there is a strong tendency to handle the "restless natives" by a dictatorship.

To talk about making the fundamental changes needed for development in a peaceful, parliamentary way in these countries is worse than sheer nonsense or dreaming. It can only lead to the whole movement, usually including the theorist who proposes it, getting jailed or executed. When faced with a violent reactionary dictatorship, how can anyone consider nonviolence?

In the case of a reactionary dictatorship, where the people are quite ready for revolutionary leadership, a secret and highly disciplined party fits the bill. In fact, since these are often countries spread out through jungle and mountains with poor communications, and with more radical peasant populations, it is possible to go beyond an urban-based party and unite with—or even make the core of the revolution—rural guerrilla groups based on the peasantry.

There are, of course, exceptional cases among the neocolonial countries, such as Chile, where there is a long democratic tradition and the continued existence of formal democracy. In these cases it would seem sensible and necessary to pursue nonviolent tactics, to educate and gain majority support, and to fight peacefully for election. It is a different question as to whether the election of a radical government could be followed by a peaceful evolution to socialism. Chile has a radical government at this moment, but the question of a military coup is still open. The problem is complicated by the fact that the neocolonial armies, as in Chile, do not exist in a vacuum. The Chilean ruling class and the Chilean army has long been supported and dominated by the United States. The United States is not likely to stand by and see her corporate interests confiscated, so she may decide to intervene in the guise of civil war—as was done in Guatemala or in the Dominican Republic.

In this perspective, we can examine the Soviet and Chinese positions on reform and revolution. The Soviets focus on the advanced capitalist countries, and therefore conclude that peaceful, parliamentary advance toward socialism is the wisest tactic. Surely, anyone who sets up bomb factories and supports urban guerrillas in the United States should have his head examined before it is blown off.

The Soviets, however, then seem to extend their analysis in an incorrect generalization to the underdeveloped countries. According to the Chinese, the Soviets urge restraint in those areas and give liberation armies little support because of the extreme Soviet timidity and caution before American arms. Since they have a degree of affluence and something to lose, they hesitate to see the world destroyed in a nuclear war. The hesitation is understandable (as is their commitment to peaceful coexistence), but they could still recognize and give more support to the peoples who are revolting against native dictatorships supported by foreign imperialism.[13]

The Chinese focus on the underdeveloped countries, with their native dictatorships and imperialist domination. Therefore, they urge armed struggle by liberation armies. Surely, anyone who goes around urging peaceful, parliamentary advance to socialism in Brazil or Greece should have his head examined, if he can be reached before he is tortured or executed. The Chinese then incorrectly extend their analysis to the whole world. Thus, in the advanced capitalist countries their adherents tend to favor violence when peaceful tactics are much more productive. And they extend the analysis of internal liberation warfare even to the possibility of international warfare. They reflect their underdeveloped economy and the feeling that they have nothing to lose (and that some will survive), accusing the Soviets of timidity and unwillingness to take the calculated risk of world war in order to support national liberation fights.[14]

The Chinese emphasize that "it should never . . . be asserted that peaceful coexistence is mankind's road to socialism."[15] But should it not be asserted that nuclear warfare is mankind's road to total destruction? Can't there be peaceful coexistence among the major capitalist and socialist powers while, at the same time, liberation wars are fought in the neocolonial areas, and socialist revolutions (some peaceful?) take place country by country? This solution is complex, and perhaps not the most "radical" sounding, but at least it gives mankind a chance to survive into the era of socialism.

NOTES

1. Raymond Franklin, "Party and Class," in Franklin, ed., *State and Revolution* (New York: New Critics Press, forthcoming), p. 27.
2. See, e.g., Edward Bernstein, *Evolutionary Socialism* (New York: Schocken Books, 1961, first publ. 1899).
3. Robert Dahl and Charles Lindblom, *Politics, Economics, and Welfare* (New York: Harper & Row, 1953), p. 86.
4. Franklin, *op. cit.*, p. 28.
5. See Andreas Papandreou, *Democracy at Gun Point: the Greek Case* (New York: Doubleday, 1970).
6. Dwight Eisenhower, *Mandate for Change* (Garden City, N.Y.: Doubleday, 1963), p. 372.
7. U.S. State Department, "A Threat to the Peace: North Vietnam's Effort to Conquer South Vietnam," *Blue Book on Vietnam* (1961).
8. *Capital*, vol. 1, p. 809.
9. John Holt, "The Radicalizing of a Guest Teacher at Berkeley," *The New York Times Magazine* (February 22, 1970), p. 57.
10. *Ibid.*, p. 60.
11. Marx, *Enthüllungen über den Kommunistenprozess zu Köln* (Basel and Boston, 1853).
12. These figures exclude developed capitalist countries, socialist countries, and direct colonial dependencies.
13. An interesting and slightly different critique of the Soviet position is given in Herbert Marcuse, *Soviet Marxism* (New York: Vintage Books, 1961).
14. The Chinese put it more strongly that the Soviets have "withdrawn support from national liberation movements all over the world and called off the struggle against imperialism." Joan Robinson, *Notes from China* (New York: Monthly Review Press, 1964), p. 7.
15. Central Committee of the Chinese Communist Party, "A Proposal Concerning the General Line of the International Communist Movement," *Peking Review* (June 21, 1963), p. 15. Also see "Peaceful Coexistence—Two Diametrically Opposed Policies," *Peking Review* (December 20, 1963). Also see Yung Ping Chen, *Chinese Political Thought* (The Hague: M. Nijhoff, 1966).

PART III

THE POLITICAL ECONOMY OF SOCIALISM

CHAPTER
13

Origins of Socialism

In this chapter we will first outline *very* briefly the origins and development of the socialist movement. Then we will discuss the early economic development of two "socialist" countries, the Soviet Union and China. "Socialism" will be defined more carefully in the next two chapters. Here it is enough to say roughly that it is (1) a political movement trying to replace capitalism with a better system, and also (2) that system wherein exploitation and alienation are replaced by human cooperation, *one* of its characteristics being the shift from private to public ownership of capital goods.

Marx

Radical critiques and visions of socialist utopias have existed for several centuries, but the first serious attempt to produce a comprehensive radical social science was made by Karl Marx. Karl Marx was born in 1818 in Trier, Germany. Although his family wished him to be educated as a lawyer, he chose to obtain his doctorate in philosophy. Because his views were already "too liberal," the German government prevented the young Marx from obtaining a job in a German university. Perhaps if the witch-hunters of that day had not been so careful, Marx would have settled down to become a brilliant, but eventually forgotten, German professor. Nevertheless, Marx carried the imprint of the predominant Hegelian philosophy throughout his life; for example, Marx made a modified form of Hegel's concept of alienation the basis of his humanist critique of society.

Marx turned to journalism and ran a liberal newspaper for a time, until he was exiled to France for his republican ideas. In Paris Marx learned the views of the French socialists and the tradition of the French Revolution. His conversion to socialism was also aided by his friend, Frederick Engels, who reached a socialist position before Marx. Eventually the

French government also decided that Marx was too radical for it, and he was exiled to Belgium. He returned to Germany to take part in the revolution of 1848. When that revolution failed, Marx emigrated to England. He spent most of his life in England, from 1849 until his death in 1883.

In London Marx spent several decades studying classical political economy, from the works of Adam Smith to those of Ricardo and Malthus. In addition, he read the reports of the factory inspectors and made much use of the official parliamentary investigations.

Thus the intellectual heritage of Marxism was derived from three main sources: German Hegelian philosophy, French revolutionary socialism, and English classical economics. Marx fused these divergent views into one unified social science.

1848 to the Paris Commune

After the collapse of the 1848 revolution, Marx led the inactive life of the political exile for many years. In 1864, however, he joined with British trade unionists and some French and Belgian unionists, as well as certain sects of anarchists, to form the First International (officially called the International Workingmen's Association). The International did succeed in coordinating the efforts of unionists in several countries, in preventing strike-breaking by workers of adjoining countries, and in giving support to the revolutionary nationalist movements of Poland and Italy. The International also supported the North in the American Civil War against the slaveholders. In this action it succeeded in rallying large numbers of British workers against the views of the British government and the conservative ruling classes, who might otherwise have intervened on the side of the South.

The First International lost much of its strength in intense factional struggles. The socialists, led by Marx, and the anarchists, led by Bakunin, clashed over basic theoretical and tactical issues. How disciplined should the workers' movement be? Is a state apparatus necessary after the revolution? On the other side, Marx had to debate with conservative unionists, who wanted less interest in revolution, and more attention to bread and butter issues.

Although the International was already in decline, the final blow was the advent of the Paris Commune, which split its ranks wide open. In 1871 when the French armies had been defeated by the Germans, Napoleon III was dethroned and a republican government came into being. The republican government, however, was quite reactionary, and also was unpopular because of its forced concessions to the Germans. The Parisian populace then took matters into its own hands and elected its own government, the famed Paris Commune. An overwhelming majority of the delegates were socialists, though not members of the Marxist International. The Commune lasted but a few months, and then was drowned in blood by the reactionary French government. All Europe was aghast at the red Commune of Paris; and just as horrified were the respectable British unionists who constituted the base of the International in England. When Marx wrote a flaming defense of the Commune, the end of the International was made certain. The International formally died in 1876.

The Paris Commune to the Russian Revolution

Marx continued working and writing until his death in 1883. The early 1880's witnessed at the same time the beginnings of strong Socialist parties in France, Germany, and much of Western Europe. In spite of much initial persecution, the German Social Democratic Party eventually came to be a very large and highly respectable party. The various Socialist parties together formed the Second International in 1889.

Although the Second International continued to use revolutionary Marxist language, the content of its actions grew less and less revolutionary as its member parties grew more and more respectable. The various socialist parties of Europe and the United States drew large numbers of votes, ran their own newspapers, controlled most of the trade union apparatus, and acquired many vested interests in the continued operation of capitalist society. During the 1890's the chief spokesman of orthodox socialism was Karl Kautsky, who used suitably revolutionary language while defending a peaceful evolutionary view of socialism.

Kautsky was challenged from the right by Eduard Bernstein. Bernstein contended that the Socialists continued to repeat Marx's revolutionary phrases, but that in reality they pursued a much more practical policy of gradual reforms. Bernstein wished to explicitly *revise* Marxist theory to make it accord with the new *reformist* practice (hence the labels "revisionist" or "reformist"). He believed that things were slowly getting better even under capitalism, and that democratic parliamentary pressure by Socialists would lead to a *very* gradual evolution toward socialist ideals.

Kautsky answered in orthodox Marxist language that a "revolution" was necessary to introduce full socialism against the opposition of the old ruling classes. The Socialist parties then interpreted "revolution" to mean a fundamental social change, but assumed it could be achieved through a majority in parliament by democratic means. So in practice they continued a policy of gradual reforms by gradual election victories. By the 1920's the official Socialist parties came to accept almost all Bernstein's revisionist position. In fact, at the present time the major West European Socialist and Labor parties no longer advocate complete public ownership in industry, much less revolution to achieve it.

As the official Socialist parties swung to the right, there arose a left opposition, which became ever more vocal and important. It was led by such striking personalities as V. I. Lenin and the fiery Rosa Luxemburg, whose powerful oratory moved thousands of workers. Lenin and Luxemburg agreed that real revolutionaries needed practical action as well as Kautsky's revolutionary words and gestures. They emphasized that imperialism was leading to war, and that the Socialist parties must take united revolutionary action in that case.

In 1914 when the First World War broke out, the Second International was put to the test. The question was whether the socialists of all countries would stand together against the war, or whether the socialists of each country would support their own ruling class against the opposite group of countries. The Second International flunked its test, and thereafter was terminated in all but name. Officially it has continued to this day, but in practice it split into warring groups: the German and Austrian Socialists fought against the British and French Socialists, while each of the Socialist parties split into right, center, and left factions. The right wing supported its own government in each of the warring countries. The center was pacifist, advocating a negotiated end to the war. The left wing of the Socialist parties continued to advocate workers' revolution against each government. The left wing eventually split off to form a Communist party within each country.

In 1917 the Russian Revolution broke out. Its first phase was the so-called February Revolution of March 1917, which put the liberals and moderate socialists (called Mensheviks) into power. The Russian peasants were represented by the Socialist Revolutionary Party, which stood for a populist type of agrarian socialism. In November 1917 there occurred the famous October Revolution (October on the old Russian calender) led by the Bolsheviks, who had constituted the left faction of the socialists in Russia, and who later were to be called the Communist Party.

Under the leadership of Lenin, the Bolsheviks attempted to transform Russia into a socialist country. Their attempt was opposed not only by the forces of reaction, but also by all the old Socialist parties. As a response, Lenin in 1919 gathered the Communist parties of the world into the new Third International or Communist International (called, for short, the Comintern).

From the Russian Revolution
to the Death of Stalin

In the 1920's, especially after Lenin's death in 1924, the Communist Party of the Soviet Union divided into a "left" faction under Leon Trotsky, a "right" faction under N. I. Bukharin, and a "center" faction under Joseph Stalin. Of course, "right" and "left" here are only relative and somewhat misleading. All factions considered themselves to be revolutionaries and good Communists. All of them denied any "revision" of Marx or Lenin, but each argued that their opponents were revisionists. (But what is a "revisionist"? Lenin, for example, made more fundamental additions to Marx than anyone else who claimed to be a Marxist. Does that make him a revisionist?)

All factions agreed on industrialization of the Soviet Union and advocacy of world socialist revolution, but with very different tactics and emphasis. Bukharin (joined by Stalin for some years) advocated a firm alliance with the peasantry, eventual enrichment of the peasants through private trade, and cautious industrialization through moderate taxes and investment. On this basis, socialism would slowly be built in one country, the Soviet Union, which would eventually serve as a powerful support for the world revolution.

Trotsky, on the contrary, advocated rapid industrialization by taking the necessary resources from agriculture, even if most peasants were temporarily displeased (the details of this economic debate are discussed later in this chapter). Trotsky also wanted to commit this rapidly growing industry of the USSR to the all-out support of the world revolution, even at the risk of temporarily losing control of the USSR itself. The point is that Trotsky did not believe the USSR could achieve full socialism without the success of the socialist revolution in the advanced countries.

After a struggle lasting from 1924 to 1928, Stalin won undivided power. Trotsky was exiled in 1928, and finally murdered in Mexico in 1940. The other old Bolshevik leaders continued to work under Stalin's direction until they were mostly killed in the purge trials of 1936 to 1938. During the Stalin era, the Trotskyites became a small sect, the Bukharinites disappeared, and the Soviet Union was rapidly industrialized. The industrialization was carried out on the basis of restricted consumption enforced by extreme repression.

After 1928, Stalin ruled alone from his lofty eminence until his death in 1953. He ruled not only the Soviet Union but also the other Communist parties of the world, including the new rulers of Eastern Europe. In theory, the Comintern (or Communist International), was dissolved in 1943, but in practice Stalin continued to direct the other parties with an iron fist. Only Tito of Yugoslavia dared to defect in 1948. Stalin kept the other Communist parties in line partly by means of the new Communist Information Bureau (or Cominform), set up in 1947.

Soon after he took power, Stalin transformed Marxism-Leninism into a divinely given rigid doctrine. Only Stalin could make new interpretations, which he did only to suit his needs, with little regard for theoretical niceties. All dissent was met with prison or murder, and silence descended on the theoretical stage. Through his hold on foreign Communist parties, and through their position in each country, Stalin dominated international Marxist thought from about 1926 to 1956 (even though he died in 1953). This was a period of utter sterility in Soviet Marxist thought, with few major contributions, either by those who idolized Stalin or by those who hated Stalin. No serious attention was paid to Western social science, except to criticize it.

After the Death of Stalin

Even when Stalin was laid to rest in 1953, he was still venerated in Red Square with Lenin. The Communist leaders, always with the exception of Tito, continued to act in Stalin's image with apparently iron discipline and a monolithic face towards the outer world. In 1956, however, Khrushchev, who was then the leader of the Soviet Union, disinterred the old bones of Stalin along with the old ghosts of Stalinism. He achieved popularity at the Twentieth Congress of the Communist Party of the Soviet Union by denouncing the evils and murders of Stalin's day and promising a new era of freedom. His denunciation of terror and dogmatic thinking had a thrilling and profoundly traumatic effect on Communist intellectuals the world around. Some of them escaped from the heavy chains of Stalin's irrational and dogmatic orthodoxy. Many proclaimed a renaissance of Marxist thought, and began to take seriously Marx's injunction to "doubt everything." The frozen thinking of the Stalinist bureaucrats was challenged from many sides at once.

De-Stalinization, however, went far beyond what Comrade Khrushchev had anticipated. Eastern Europe took Khrushchev's teachings to heart and showed a restless independence. Poland in October, 1956, ousted its own Stalinists and established a more liberal Communist regime under Gomulka, barely avoiding the violence of civil war in the process. Poland, however, continued to have internal Communist rule, though with much freedom of discussion, and largely followed the leadership of Soviet foreign policy. Finally, the pot boiled over in Hungary in November 1956. A brief attempt at a more tolerant Communism, followed by widespread organized opposition stretching to the extreme fascist right, led to the bloody intervention of the Soviet army.

The genie of independent thought, once unleashed, was not easily put back into the bottle. The Italian Communist leader, Togliatti, voiced the thoughts of many when he said that this was to be an era of "polycentrism," that is, of many divergent national paths to socialism. The many rumblings within the Communist movement were kept under cover for some years, but then broke into the open in 1959 with the leftist defection of tiny Albania. Albania, with the friendly hand of 700,000,000 Chinese, thus formed a balance against right-swinging Yugoslavia.

There were constant ideological arguments between the Soviet and Chinese parties. The crucial point of no return in the split came in 1960, when Khrushchev went from words to deeds by recalling from China all Soviet technicians (and their blueprints and plans)! Finally in 1963 came an open break between the Chinese Communists and the Soviet Communists. To some extent, the split reflects the fact that the Chinese are still attempting to break the chains of economic underdevelopment while the Soviets are now a developed industrial power.

Last but not least, in 1968 the Czechoslovak people lifted their heads, ousted the old leadership, and began to build a socialism with a human face. This was the most important experiment in democratic Communism to date (discussed in detail in a later chapter). It was led by Alexander Dubček and the Czechoslovak Communist Party to their eternal credit. It was crushed by the Soviet army to its eternal shame.

Communists, themselves, are thus divided among "right" and "left" today. The labels used here are very confusing. Is it "right wing" to advocate more democracy, and "left wing" to advocate Stalinist dictatorship, or vice versa? What should we call the new breed of radicals who advocate both full socialism and full political democracy? They cannot be called social democrats because they do call for an immediate and complete socialist revolution. Yet they cannot be called Communist if that refers only to the Stalinists who are in favor of political dictatorship. Perhaps those who advocate both political democracy and a completely socialist economy should be called "Democratic Communists."

Economic Development under Socialism

We have considered the origins of socialism in terms of the growth of the socialist political movement. We turn now to a very different aspect, its economic beginnings; that is, the question of the *initial* construction of socialist industry, especially in a country with only an underdeveloped agricultural economy. We begin with the Soviet case, then consider the quite different Chinese case.

The whole period of the 1920's in the Soviet Union was witness to a violent debate on methods of rapid initial development.[1] Immediately after the Revolution, from 1918 to 1921, the Soviet government had practiced the policy called "war communism." Under that policy, all enterprises and all trade were nationalized, central directives tried to cover all economic activity, and food was simply requisitioned from the peasantry. In 1921 Lenin led a "temporary" retreat to the New Economic Policy (NEP), which allowed a return to the use of the market to sell peasant goods, and a return to private enterprise for merchants and small businessmen.

After Lenin died in 1924, the left wing of the Communist Party, led by Trotsky, took the view that the NEP must be quickly ended and a transition made to the rapid growth of socialist industry. They considered it necessary to build large-scale industry on the basis of modern technology, but also considered it necessary for such modern technology to be extended into the countryside by the fullest encouragement of agricultural cooperatives to replace the tiny peasant farms. Yet Trotsky considered that the international political situation would prevent such a development until the revolution could spread to more advanced economies, capable of furnishing political support and economic aid to Soviet Russia. In this context, he denied "the possibility of socialism in a single country." Trotsky argued instead that

the contradiction inherent in the position of a worker's government functioning in a backward country where the large minority of the population is composed of peasants, can only be liquidated on an international scale in the arena of a worldwide proletarian revolution, [and that] the real growth of the socialist economy in Russia can take place only after the victory of the proletariat in the more important countries of Europe.[2]

Although Trotsky was the main proponent of the notion that socialist industry could not really expand rapidly in the Soviet Union until after the revolution triumphed in Europe, he nevertheless was also the main proponent of the attempt to industrialize as rapidly as possible, while recognizing the difficulty of accomplishing this under the existing conditions. (In fact, it seems that Trotsky later came to believe that economic growth was possible under these conditions, but that such forced industrialization would lead to harsh political dictatorship *over* the proletariat.) The argument in favor of the all-out expansion of industry at the expense of agriculture came to be the principal economic plank of Trotsky's opposition faction in the Party. He conceived that it was unfortunate but true that rapid industrialization under the existing circumstances could only come at the expense of the peasantry. Furthermore, Trotsky argued strongly that such industrial expansion could be achieved only by detailed and comprehensive economic planning under the direction of the state planning commission.

The more systematic economic analysis of the left wing position was most clearly stated by the very original Soviet economist, Preobrazhensky.[3] Preobrazhensky spoke of the need for "primitive socialist accumulation." Marx had described "primitive capitalist accumulation" as the period in which "capitalist" countries first acquire the initial capital for rapid industrialization.[4] They acquire most of it by piracy or colonial plunder or the slave trade, or some other means of extraction from other countries. Primitive socialist accumulation, according to Preobrazhensky, means the accumulation of capital for socialist industry from "the surplus product of all pre-socialist economic forms." Of course, when socialism comes to an advanced capitalist economy, the primitive accumulation will be completed by the revolutionary acquisition of all large firms. In a relatively underdeveloped economy, however, there is little to take over, so the problem is one of constructing industry from scratch.

Where could capital be obtained? The Soviet Union in the 1920's had neither the desire nor the strength to engage in the imperialist plundering of other countries. It was also impossible to obtain large foreign loans or investments. Most foreign governments still backed the return of the pre-Soviet government or even the Tsars. Moreover, they feared that the Soviets might confiscate any new loans and investments just as they had done the old. At any rate, they were more willing to hinder Soviet development than help it.

Thus, the Soviet Union would have to develop solely from its own meager resources. Preobrazhensky argued that up to a half of all the profits of Soviet trade and industry were going into private hands under the NEP. He advocated nationalizing these enterprises so as to increase the profits available for government investment in industry. Yet Preobrazhensky pointed out that Soviet industry was still so small that, even including private profits, the internal reinvestments of its surplus product (above workers' wages and replacement costs) would mean only minute amounts of new capital each year. A "big push" in investment was necessary, however, to create new factories in the many related industries all at once. Without this initial surge of capital creation, development could never get off the ground, let alone gain momentum.

Since sufficient capital could not be obtained from foreign countries or from the infant Soviet industry, the only remaining possibility was to extract it from agriculture. In agriculture presocialist private ownership prevailed. In fact, in 1928 there were still twenty-six million private farms in the Soviet Union. The left wing urged that the agricultural surplus be extracted by high taxes, and by setting high monopoly prices on the industrial goods that farmers must buy (which amounts to the same thing as taxation of the product of the private farmers).

The right wing of the Communist Party, led by Bukharin, criticized this policy on several grounds.[5] First, they argued that it would not succeed because the farmer would either cut back production or use his ingenuity to hide his products, and either consume them himself or sell them on the black market. Second, Bukharin argued that such a harsh policy would break the vital political alliance between the workers and the farmers.

Third, Bukharin presented his own policy, which he believed would reach the same goal more easily. He had been impressed by the results of the NEP, which had allowed freedom for private trade and private agriculture. Under the NEP, large-scale industrial output had tripled from 1920 to 1924, although this was reconstruction and not new expansion. So Bukharin recommended more of the same, allowing the farmer to prosper and grow rich. Eventually he would use moderate taxes on the farmer to build industry, while very gradually forming voluntary farmer cooperatives to end the rule of rich farmers. In his own words, Bukharin wrote:

. . . The ideologists of Trotskyism believe that a maximum annual transfer from peasant agriculture into industry secures the maximum rate of development of industry in general. But this is clearly incorrect. The maximum continued rate of growth will be experienced . . . when industry will advance on the basis of rapidly growing agriculture.[6]

Another right wing writer, Rykov, expressed the idea that industry would eventually acquire the capital for expansion simply out of the continually increasing turnover of goods traded between agriculture and industry.[7]

Preobrazhensky and Trotsky countered with three arguments. The political argument was given that the right wing policy would strengthen the rich farmers and thereby weaken the Communist political base. Furthermore, the Left argued that their own policy of rapid industrialization would eventually result in an increased flow of manufactured consumer goods to the villages, which would finally solve the scarcity problem and peasant dissatisfaction once and for all. Finally, they claimed that small amounts of resources drawn very gradually from agriculture would *never* get industry moving on a basis of self-sustaining expansion (because of the necessity for an initial "big push" to development).

Stalin, leading the center faction, first joined with the right to defeat the left and to exile Trotsky. Then he swung over to an ultraleft program, and used the remnants of the left to help defeat the right wing. Finally, when Stalin became sole ruler, he "solved" the problem.

The Stalinist Solution

Stalin claimed that industry had recovered the prewar level by 1926, and had surpassed it by 18 per cent in 1927. Whereas industry was doing well, in agriculture the total harvest was barely above prewar. Thus, the crucial grain production was only 91 per cent of prewar production, and the marketed surplus of grain was only 37 per cent of prewar surplus. He concluded that collectivization was necessary: "The way out is to unite the small and dwarf peasant farms gradually and surely, not by pressure but by example and persuasion, into large farms based on common, co-operative cultivation of the soil, with the use of agricultural machines and tractors and scientific methods of intensive agriculture."[8] He defended this sudden policy shift by arguing that conditions had changed considerably since the last Party congress, that now the peasants were in a mood favorable to collective farming, that the Party was now strong and capable enough to lead the change, and that industry was now enough developed to supply the new collective farms with sufficient machinery and tractors. Whether this argument was true or merely politically convenient, the Fifteenth Party Congress (packed with Stalin's supporters) agreed "to build the industrialization program upon the introduction of large-scale farming on cooperative lines as its cornerstone."

Stalin's solution to economic development was bloody and costly, but it did accomplish its objectives. He "persuaded" the unwilling farmers (and not only the small farmers, but especially the richer farmers) to give up their private farms and livestock and to join collective farms. These collectives were supposed to be cooperative ventures, but were actually under strict central control. It should be noted that the earlier proposals by Bukharin had only casually mentioned peasant cooperation and collectives, and even Trotsky had thought of the process as a very long and gradual one, not an overnight collectivization. Thus, until Stalin acted in favor of collectivization in 1928, no one else had seriously considered it as more than a minor component in raising the marketed agricultural surplus. Even Stalin started very slowly, and only intensified the program in later years as a result of unforeseen emergencies.

Stalin's "persuasion" to collectivize, which began in earnest in the fall of 1929, was marked by a civil war in which large numbers of peasants were killed or exiled to Siberia for resisting collectivization. Livestock was slaughtered by the farmers, and the crop production fell. Yet Stalin succeeded in three objectives. First, he eliminated the rich farmer and strengthened socialism politically. Second, the large size of collectives

215

eventually allowed the introduction of machinery and more efficient farming (though they were anything but efficient in the first few years). Third, and this was most important, in spite of the lower total production, he greatly increased the amount of grain actually marketed and available for government use as "capital."

That Stalin succeeded in increasing grain collections is clear from Table 13-1.

TABLE 13-1

Output, Procurement, and Exports of Grain,
1928-1932, USSR (Millions of Tons)

	OUTPUT	COLLEC-TIONS
1928-1929	73.3	10.8
1929-1930	71.7	16.1
1930-1931	83.5	22.1
1931-1932	66.0	22.8

Sources: Naum Jasny, *Soviet Russian Agriculture,* Appendix. Also USSR Central Statistical Agency, *Foreign Trade Handbook.*

Procurements of grain doubled from 1928–1929 to 1930–1931. Then, despite the terrible famine in 1931–1932, procurements actually increased slightly. This would have been impossible to achieve had peasants not been collectivized. But in collective farms and under strict government control, they were no longer in position to withhold grain either for speculation or for their own use. The government levied upon the farms so-called "obligatory deliveries"—in effect, a tax in kind—which had first claim on whatever output was produced. The amount of deliveries was based on the number of acres owned by the farm or in cultivation. Thus, it did not matter how much the farm produced, or whether or not there was a famine; the state's share remained stable since it was based on acreage, not output. The state did pay the farms for these deliveries, but at a fraction of their true cost of production, not to mention the high prices at which grain products were eventually sold in state stores. It was this tax in kind which provided the bulk of the "capital" for the industrialization drive of the first two five year plans.

How can farm products become "capital"? First, note that some farm products, such as industrial crops and raw materials, are directly useful in industry. Second, farm products can be exported in exchange for machinery. Third, and most important, farm products can be used to feed industrial workers while they build new factories and basic utilities (or infrastructure). Fourth, food must be sent to those other rural areas which specialize in the production of nonedible industrial crops and raw materials.

Farmers then constituted the majority of the Soviet population, as in most underdeveloped countries. Stalin's solution therefore amounted to keeping most of the population at a very low level of consumption, while using their "surplus" product for investment purposes. Since investment reached 25 to 35 per cent of national income, this naturally resulted in a very rapid economic growth. Once industry got under way, the problem became a little easier since more of industry's own resources could be reinvested for further expansion. This meant high profits and restriction of wages, again postponing the increase of current consumption, though this time at the primary expense of the urban worker.

Obviously, this model of economic development not only presumes heroic sacrifices in present consumption initially and for many years to come, but it also continues to reinforce the arguments for one-party dictatorship. No people will freely vote for such unpopular and drastic development measures. Only a one-party dictatorship allowing no opposition could possibly enforce these "temporary" measures for the development of an "infant" economy. This situation was surely a basic ingredient prolonging the Stalinist dictatorship in its protection of the "infant" industries of the USSR against temptations of its own populace (who were in favor of more present consumption). But, one wonders, who decides when the infant is grown up enough to restore democracy?

The Maoist Solution

The Chinese have approached the question of economic development somewhat differently from the Soviets. They do stress the need to raise the material welfare of the nation. They also emphasize, however, that it must be done on the basis of roughly equal progress for all, and must be accompanied by the development of better human beings. It is true that in any underdeveloped country dedicated to rapid industrialization, the average worker must remain poor for a long time, while resources are devoted to building up industrial capacity.

Yet the hard fact of continued low consumption leaves two alternative paths of development. *Either* a few skilled engineers and managers can be given high material incentives, *or* (small) equal material incentives can be given to all. The Soviets under Stalin clearly opted for high material incentives to a small elite. The Chinese have taken the opposite decision (including even more propaganda on moral incentives than the Soviets use), which may also be a logical strategy of development. They use both propaganda and deeds in carrying out this policy. The deeds include a relatively low pay for managers and engineers, only slightly above other workers. Moreover, the manager is expected to do manual labor at times, even sweeping out the factory floor with a broom.

The Chinese thus argue that collective incentives are necessary for development. They deemphasize individual incentives and allow only a small range of inequality of incomes. The logic of this is that it presumably enables them to mobilize vast numbers of people with a high degree of enthusiasm, rather than to mobilize only a small elite to outstanding work with millions of less enthusiastic followers. Western observers have indeed noted that there is a much closer and more amiable tie between the Chinese factory worker and the Chinese factory manager than in most other countries.[9] Furthermore, the necessary policy of national saving and investment, with restricted consumption, hurts less psychologically if everyone sacrifices about the same.

The Maoists urge investment in human capital—that is, education and health—with a large part of national resources. They also urge major campaigns to change men's ideas, in the form of ideological training. The ideological training concentrates on (1) overcoming selfishness and promoting unselfish behavior for the good of the nation; (2) not passive listening, but active participation as the only way to learn; and (3) general, nonspecialized learning. Nonspecialization means the attempt to acquire a broad range of skills, to do manual as well as mental labor, to rotate jobs from leadership positions to rank and file positions, and from urban to rural and back to urban jobs.

These prescriptions undoubtedly mean initial dislocations and initial slow economic development, since individuals may perform less well in any given job. But again, it has a kind of logic to it which may eventually speed development (besides doing it in a happier way). It is true that spending time in much political education on the job means less hours of work. Yet if the Chinese are succeeding in mobilizing hundreds of millions of people in the tasks of development, then it will soon pay off. They will then leave far behind a country such as India where the masses of people are not involved in development and even oppose many modernizing measures on the basis of tradition and inertia (not to speak of the opposition by elite classes with vested interests in the old society).

Moreover, even the idea of nonspecialization may make a good deal of sense in a rapidly developing country. If a large number of people are educated to be flexible and to be qualified for many kinds of trades and positions, then they may be able to meet the many emergencies and sudden needs that often confront a country in the midst of extensive industrialization.

Similarly, the Chinese are striving for balanced development in some ways that are often neglected by other societies. They are attempting a generalized progress in many areas at once: less reliance on expert decisions, more mass participation in decision-making; new industries in rural areas, rather than ever larger cities; education not just for the brightest, but especially for the most culturally deprived. They claim that all this "will eventually pay off not only in economic ways by enormously raising labor productivity but, more important, by creating a society of truly free men, who respond intelligently to the world around them, and who are happy."[10]

Of course, the Chinese model is designed only for a developing socialist country. Its claims and propaganda may be doubted, and have been by many of the Western and Soviet "experts." Yet the important point remains that it does provide another approach to development, perhaps much less painful than the Soviet one, and perhaps less prone to produce a bloody dictator. One should *not* generalize from the Chinese model as to what may be done—or should be done—in an advanced socialist economy. The traditions as well as the conditions of Eastern Europe and the Soviet Union, for example, are enormously different, and they face entirely different sets of problems. Even the Chinese may well have to take quite different approaches to economic activity when they reach a more complex industrial society at a higher level of consumption. Their example remains of utmost importance to the whole underdeveloped world (and may be joined by the somewhat similar example of Cuba), and merits more study even in relation to the more developed countries.

NOTES

1. For a discussion of the historical context of the debate, see Maurice Dobb, *Soviet Economic Development since 1917* (New York: International Publishers, 1966), Chapters 7, 8, and 9. Also see the non-Marxist discussion in Alexander Ehrlich, *The Soviet Industrialization Debate, 1924–1928* (Cambridge: Harvard University Press, 1960).
2. Cited in Dobb, *op. cit.*, p. 178.
3. E. A. Preobrazhensky, *The New Economics* (Oxford: Clarendon Press, 1965, first publ. in Moscow 1926). Also see the other positions translated in Nicholas Spulber, *Foundations of Soviet Strategy for Economic Growth: Selected Soviet Essays, 1924–1930* (Bloomington: Indiana University Press, 1964).
4. Marx, *Capital*, vol 1, part 8.
5. See, e.g., N. I. Bukharin, "Notes of an Economist" (first publ. 1927) in Spulber, *op. cit.*, pp. 258–265.
6. Bukharin, *op. cit.*, p. 260.
7. Dobb, *op. cit.*, p. 187.
8. Stalin, quoted in Dobb, *op. cit.*, p. 222.
9. See, e.g., Barry M. Richman, *Industrial Society in Communist China* (New York: Random House, 1969), Chapter 9.
10. John Gurley, "Maoist Economic Development," *The Center Magazine*, 3 (May–June 1970): 25–33.

CHAPTER
14

Value and Plan

Just as Marx began with the study of the value of commodities under capitalism, so here we must begin with the question of value and its relation to planning under socialism. We assume for the time being that the centralized Soviet model (with its political dictatorship) represents a kind of "socialism." In every later chapter that definition will be examined and challenged. For example, in the next chapter we will ask to what degree exploitation still exists in the Soviet Union. Here, however, the Soviet case is considered simply because it shows the longest experience with some kind of "planning" under some kind of "socialism."

The Soviet Economic Model

In the capitalist United States, most land and factories are privately owned. In the socialist Soviet Union, most land and factories are publicly owned. The public ownership, of course, tends to mean public direction, and therefore usually means planning. The principal type of household income in the Soviet Union is wage income for labor. On the other side, in the United States income consists not only of wages, but also of profit, rent, dividends, and interest. These latter incomes are derived basically from private property; thus most U.S. planning is necessarily limited in scope to the confines of single enterprises, in which decisions reflect the search for private profit.

Most Soviet industrial enterprises are owned and operated by the "public," with the Soviet government claiming to represent the public. The only exceptions are a very small percentage of industrial enterprises that are cooperatives, mainly composed of handicraft workers, and the many "collective farms" in agriculture that are supposed to be cooperatives. In the public enterprises, the government, or some agency of the government, appoints a manager. He is solely responsible for the performance of the factory, and his bonus is based on how well it performs. His performance and his conduct are checked by numerous agencies, and he may be promoted, transferred, or fired at any time. In turn, he hires and fires all the other workers at the enterprise.

The government grants the enterprise its plant and equipment and initial working capital, although it is now beginning to charge interest on capital. After the initial grant of capital, however, the enterprise is then made financially independent. It must meet all costs of wages and materials out of current revenue. It must also replace or repair depreciated and broken capital out of its revenues from sales. And it is normally expected to show a profit above all of its costs.

The Soviet economy is centrally planned. The most important economic orders originate from the USSR council of ministers, but additional orders to the enterprise may come from regional or local government bodies. Further orders may originate in or be transmitted through the agency directly supervising the enterprise, whether that agency is associated with a regional governing body or with the ministry directing some industrial area. Finally, all these orders from governmental or supervisory bodies are supposed to be in accord with the plan, which emanates from the Central Planning Commission or its subordinate agencies. The enterprise manager is solely responsible for the performance of the factory, then, only in the sense that he must execute all the orders he has received within the constraint of the resources allocated to him.

The Central Planning Commission first collects information up the ladder of agencies from the enterprise in order to evaluate the last year's performance and the present conditions and possibilities. Then the commission is told by the Council of Ministers what goals it must strive to meet. On these bases, it draws up a general plan for the whole economy, although details of production and allocation are provided only for a couple of thousand commodities. The draft plan is then shown to all agencies in the hierarchy from the Ministry to the enterprise. After all these units have added their detailed modifications and suggestions, the Central Planning Commission draws up the final draft.

The plan is supposed to provide sufficient investment for the desired rate of growth, guarantee balance among all the industrial needs and outputs, and choose the "best" assortment of goods. At any rate, the Central Planning Commission hands the plan over to appropriate government bodies to enact into law, and it is then passed on with detailed expansions at each intermediate level until the enterprise receives a formidable document. This document is supposed to tell the enterprise for a year, or some other period, exactly what to produce, how to produce it, what prices to charge, and what funds it may use. Again, the manager is judged on how well he follows these commands, though he has always had some local decision-making power. The economic reforms of 1965 give the manager an expanded area of decision-making, as will be seen in a later chapter.

History of Soviet Planning Theory

In the theory of economic planning and economic organization under socialism, Soviet economics has made ten times as much advance in the last decade as in all the dreary years of Stalin's dictatorship. This "revolution" is fully as great as the Keynesian "revolution" in Western economics, and has suddenly removed Soviet economists from the stagnant backwaters of dogma to the most advanced and exciting pioneering research and debate. To understand the present Marxist view of optimal economic planning, we must examine briefly the evolution of non-Marxist planning theories as well as the long development of Soviet theory leading up to their recent revolution.

Marx assumed without proof that it is possible to plan rationally in a socialist society—"socialism" being defined here simply as public ownership of all means of production. He considered it impractical utopianism to describe in detail the problems of the unborn socialist economy.[1] Since the planned economy of the Soviet Union has survived and has developed for a significant length of time, detailed planning can no longer be called a "utopian" project. Soviet Marxists, indeed, consider that the *possibility* of rational, efficient planning has now been proven in practice, so need not be proven theoretically. Whatever the merits of this squelching answer, the theoretical debate about the possibility of rational planning in socialism teaches many lessons, and will serve as a very useful background to the Marxist study of optimal planning.

Need for Rational Prices

The most famous denial of the possibility of rational planning came from Ludwig von Mises in the 1920's.[2] Von Mises argues that the calculation of economic choices requires a knowledge of "rational" prices for both inputs and outputs. For example, if a farmer wishes to know whether to produce oranges or apples, he must know their relative prices at the time in order to maximize his revenues. Or, if a planner wishes to decide whether railroad locomotives should use coal or oil, he must know the relative prices of coal and oil in order to minimize costs.

In socialism, however, the government owns the coal and oil as well as the locomotives. Therefore, says von Mises, since there is no market and no competition between producers, there can be no rational prices. If the coal and oil producers are merely commanded to turn over a certain physical product to the locomotive makers, no one can know which kind of fuel will cost more. In short, there is no free market in socialism, so there are no rational prices, so there can be no meaningful calculation or rational planning of the allocation of resources.

Optimal Calculation

It has long been known[3] that economic calculation of optimal allocation of resources does not require "prices" in an actual market. We only need three kinds of information. First, we must know what resources are available, including men and machines as well as raw materials. Second, we must know the preference scale of "consumers," whether these are individuals or planners or politicians or some weighted sum of these. Third, we must know the "production function" of each output; that is, what combination of resources is necessary to produce each output at the present level of technology.

In both a private enterprise economy and in socialism the third kind of information (about alternative production possibilities) is furnished by engineers, although the final choice among technologies is an economic problem depending on the costs of various inputs. In a competitive private enterprise economy, however, market prices *automatically* reflect the first and second types of information, that is, the relative scarcity of different resources as well as the relative preference of consumers for different products (though these rational prices do not exist under monopoly capitalism). If a knowledge of the actual information of resource scarcities and consumer preferences can be obtained, however, then socialist planners will be able theoretically to calculate rational "prices" for all resources and for all products. These "prices" would be merely data for planners to use, and need not ever be paid to anybody.

If this information were available, the planners of socialist industry would then have the same information as the private enterprise managers. They could then presumably calculate the optimal choice of technologies and allocation of resources for the goal of the maximum welfare of all society in much the same way as private enterprise managers calculate for the maximization of profit.

Information and Computation Problems

In the next stage of debate the conservative economist, Hayek, admits that *in theory* the planners might accumulate all the millions of pieces of necessary information and might then solve all the millions of equations necessary to make an optimal decision.[4] *In practice*, Hayek argues, no conceivable force of planners could actually gather all the various kinds of information from every factory and farm, and from every private and public consumer. Furthermore, *in practice*, even with all the information, it would take hundreds of years to solve correctly all the equations for just one year's plan.

Hayek does not directly refer to Soviet experience, but it is clear that he believes that *any* centrally planned economy must be terribly inefficient. While conceding its theoretical possibility, he argues that any planned economy must base its decisions on only partial bits of information and very rough calculations. The result, he predicts, is far below the optimal efficiency of allocation of resources compared to that of a competitive private enterprise model.

Nor are these purely academic problems to be dismissed by any socialist. The high rate of Soviet growth proves the possibility of planning; however, it *does not* tell us how much is lost by the inefficiency of Soviet planning. Even Soviet economists have admitted that with the continued use of present methods and with increasing economic complexity, the Soviet Union would eventually need more than its total population just for management of the planning process. Many have argued that this problem could be solved by automated information-collecting and the use of computers. Yet others argue that even these improvements will not suffice to maintain, much less raise, the level of efficiency in Soviet planning.

Central and Decentralized Solutions

The most famous answer to Hayek's criticism of the practicability of socialist planning was given by Lange.[5] He replies that a decentralized or market socialism would have no more trouble than competitive private enterprise in reaching rational prices and optimal allocation of resources. He refers to a system in which the public owns all firms, but each firm *acts* as an independent unit. The manager is instructed to set his prices and output so as to maximize firm profit, and may receive a bonus for making more profit, though the profit itself goes to society.[6]

Lange also explored a socialist model of intermediate decentralization in which planners set prices, but managers still control production (and their bonuses are based on profitability). Suppose that the planners begin by setting arbitrary prices. He argues that the prices could still be rational guides for managers if the central planners react promptly to any shortage of supply by raising prices and to an excess of supply by lowering prices. The planners thus simulate market prices by trial and error. These moves will induce the managers to increase or reduce the outputs, respectively. Both this and the preceding model are now being followed to some extent in Eastern Europe.

Central planning has been most fully defended by the British Marxist, Maurice Dobb.[7] Dobb points to the existence and rapid growth of the planned economies. He considers the problems of growth, balance, and efficiency, and concludes that all three could be better solved under central planning than under capitalism, even though he admits that the planners may have far from rational and accurate price data.

First, Dobb argues that growth depends primarily on the ratio of new investment to national product. He maintains that the decision on this ratio does not depend on relative prices because it is not an economic problem, but is primarily political. He believes that the choice made by a centralized socialist government will be more conducive to growth than the choices made by multitudinous private capitalists.

Second, Dobb contends that the problem of a consistent (*not* necessarily optimal) balance of physical goods and actual money flows can be solved with any constant but arbitrary prices. Thus, a socialist economy can and does ensure continuous full employment of men and resources, while capitalist economies periodically suffer unemployment.

Third, Dobb admits it is true that rational prices are necessary for static optimal efficiency, but argues that this criterion is much less important in economic practice than balance and rapid growth. Anyway, he argues, new computing methods and machines now permit fairly good planners' calculations of the equations for prices and outputs. Moreover, he maintains, capitalist prices are also far from perfectly rational, since there is monopoly on the sellers' side and irrational advertising pressure on the consumers.

The "Law of Value" in Socialism

Soviet economists have not discussed efficiency planning in terms of welfare economics until recently, but have often discussed many of the same issues in the dogmatic form of a debate about the applicability of Marx's "law of value" to a socialist economy. The debate over the "law of value" has a long history in the Soviet Union and it may help to give that setting before we examine the issues as they actually affect present day planning. The Marxist "law of value" states roughly, as we saw in Chapter 4, that the value of any commodity is equal to the amount of average socially necessary labor embodied in it—that is, the amount of labor necessary under present technological conditions.

During the period of "war communism" from 1917 to 1921, the Soviet Union did not in practice make much use of prices or of money. This lack of prices and money was idealized in theory as a true state of communism. During this period, therefore, it was held very dogmatically that the "law of value" has no application under socialism, but is only a description of the situation under competitive capitalism. Then, in the period of the New Economic Policy of the 1920's, trade and exchange became general and the use of money permeated the economy. In this period there ensued a great deal of interesting debate over the uses of prices in socialism and over the methodology of planning, but without much clarification of the use of the Marxist "law of value."

Unfortunately, Stalin killed off this promising discussion (and some of the discussants as well), and attacked all model-building as "bourgeois, mathematical formalism." As a result, the years of Stalin's dictatorship from 1928 to 1953 were uncreative and terribly dull in economics.[8] The tasks of Soviet economists in these years were characterized by one harsh critic as "perpetual propagation of Marxism, peremptory assessment of the processes of disintegration in capitalism, and exorbitant praise for the success of Soviet industrialization."[9] At any rate, it is a fact that in all those years there were no translations and few discussions of Western economics. It is a more damning fact that in all those years there was published *no* new textbook of economics and planning; the first weak effort toward a new Soviet textbook was published in 1954. Available statistical data were greatly reduced in the late 1930's, and their publication almost ceased after 1937; Soviet statistical yearbooks began to appear again only in 1957.

During the five year plans of the 1930's Stalin stressed that there were no limits to what could be done: there was neither need nor possibility for the operation of an authentic "law of value," but room only for the law of the "plan." Soviet economics in this period reverted to a loose Marxist formulation that "value" would disappear in socialism, which was taken to mean that the planners could do anything that Stalin desired. In fact, the official Soviet view urged planners "not to study, but to change economics, to disregard economic laws."[10] Stalinist planning was mostly empirical, using little theory and no attempt at optimal efficiency, but simply pushing as much investment as possible. At that period, Soviet planners merely used the rule of thumb in basic industry that it is wisest to follow the technology and output mix of the United States (since they had developed no other method of choice).

The Soviet economists of that period used the concept of "law of value" in a very peculiar fashion. For them the "law of value" meant that prices are formed by the unconscious and automatic working of the competition of independent units. It is obviously true that in this sense the "law of value" does not exist in pure centrally planned socialism. Yet by the operation of a law of value in socialism most economists would mean merely that prices *should* exist and that these prices *should* somehow reflect reality. We say "should" here to express a normative (or policy) judgment that such use of prices and values will be a necessary aid to optimal planning. Obviously, in the latter sense the "law of value" not only exists in socialism but is absolutely necessary and compatible with planning.

It might also be noted that while Stalin was rejecting any but purely empirical methods of planning, various important theoretical advances were beginning to poke their heads up from the practical operational fields of Soviet engineering and project-making. For example, it was in 1939 that the Soviet mathematician, Kantorovich, was employed by an engineering firm to advise on the optimal use of their machinery. As a result, he published the first paper on what has become the most famous of all planning methods, the method of linear programming. Yet this discovery, too, was buried under the heap of ideological trash produced under the Stalinist dictatorship. It is true that U.S. economists took several years to recognize the importance of linear programming after its first appearance in America, but in the Stalinist atmosphere any general utilization of such a radically new economic concept was simply inconceivable. Not only was an official dogma promulgated in scholastic detail, but Stalin executed or imprisoned several of the most brilliant and daring economists of the 1930's.

In 1943 came the first official breakthrough and recognition of value problems in the Soviet Union. At that time, in a famous article first appearing in a Soviet journal, there appeared a vague but definite statement that the "law of value" does apply under socialism.[11] Nothing more concrete, however, evolved in the Soviet discussions until Stalin himself took a hand in the discussion. Stalin in 1952 made his last authoritative pronouncement on the subject, leading to a major debate throughout the socialist countries and the ranks of Marxists throughout the world.[12]

Stalin argues that "wherever commodities and commodity production exists,"[13] there the law of value will operate. By commodity production he means production for sale in the competitive marketplace, just as Marx described competition in the marketplace of capitalism. Stalin saw commodity production in the Soviet Union existing almost exclusively in the collective farm markets and in the exchange of goods between the collective farm and the government-owned factories. In other words, Stalinist economic theory (really a theology) could admit only that *some* manufactured goods are "commodities" because they exchange on the market with some agricultural goods, although this is a very small peg upon which to hang a value theory. It was still argued that there is no possibility, or perhaps no need, to plan prices within the manufacturing sector in accordance with value. This very limited recognition of the importance of economic value did very little to improve the quality of the Soviet debate.

It was not until Stalin's death, and especially after the severe and public criticism of Stalin in 1956, that Soviet economists once again felt really free to discuss the importance of money and prices. After 1956, almost all Soviet economists did come to agree that the "law of value" has great importance in socialism; that is, that planning must be based on the objective facts of social needs and costs. And it was only at this time that official Soviet recognition was given to Leontief's input-output discovery and Kantorovich's linear programming discovery—indeed, claiming both as purely Soviet achievements. This claim was made in spite of the fact that, although the work of both was begun in the Soviet Union, their theories had been ignored and had returned to the Soviet Union only via the extensive research and writings of non-Soviet economists.

After it was admitted that the "law of value" does apply to a socialist economy, there arose in the Soviet Union three different views of the value of manufactured means of production.[14] The first, and most conservative, view assumes, like Stalin, that the "law of value" only operates under socialism where there is market exchange.[15] But means of production are owned and exchanged only between government firms and the collective farms, so "value" exists only in the market exchange between manufacturing and these agricultural units, but nowhere else. This is naturally a very limited view of the role of value, and does not allow the rational calculation of values or prices of the manufactured means of production exchanged by government firms.

The second view of value assumes that "value" operates wherever there is "exchange," but it argues that government enterprises (1) do exchange goods, (2) are autonomous units and may not be treated as one big firm, and (3) must exchange equivalent value products in order to provide material incentives for the workers of each enterprise.[16] Therefore, it concludes that the "law of value" does operate in the government sector of the economy. By contrast, the third and most radical view argues that value does *not* arise from exchange in socialism at all, or from any automatic market process.[17] Rather, in socialism, value, or the need for valuation, arises from the necessity in the planning process of measuring the amount of labor expended on each product and in the aggregate. This view obviously sees the need for a rational calculation of value on all products coming within the plan.

These more progressive or radical Soviet views stress, as will be seen below, that the current Soviet price structure is highly irrational and misleading. Soviet prices omit rent, interest, and any meaningful category of profits, although they include a fixed and arbitrary profit rate. Moreover, prices remain set for many years, but since supply and demand conditions are constantly changing in any dynamic economy, this implies that prices are far out of line during much of this time. One reflection of this distortion is that many commodities must be subsidized for long periods, while others carry heavy sales or turnover taxes. Most chaotic of all are agricultural prices. Even Stalin once cited a case in which the price of bread was lower than the price of the flour it contained.

It may be asked why in more recent years not only the progressives, but even the Stalinists, began to talk about the need for rational valuation and calculation in the Soviet economy. The increased need seems to grow out of the increased complexity of the Soviet economy. For one thing, it has many more enterprise units and more varied products than it did in earlier days—at the present time over 200,000 separate enterprises and over 2,000,000 different products. Second, there are many more technological possibilities and variants open to the Soviet planners in each industry. Third, there is a much wider variety of consumer goods to choose among, and the average income now puts the Soviet consumer far above the level of absolute biological need. After 1956, the new political atmosphere emphasized prompt satisfaction of the wide variety of consumer needs. Fourth, although there had been plenty of reserve labor in the rural areas in the 1930's, the terrible losses of the Second World War made it urgently necessary to use labor most efficiently. Fifth, the problems of an increased international trade began to call most urgently for more rational calculation.

The more progressive Soviet writers emphasize the enormous losses in each of these areas caused by an irrational price structure. The seriousness of the problem not only has been stressed by U.S. critics,[18] but was recognized in print by Soviet critics at least as early as 1957.[19] All the defects in the price system add up to the net result that relative prices do not correctly reflect "value," scarcity, or consumer demand. Since society is very complex, planners have to make many decisions in ignorance of the information which a rational price system would provide them. One famous progressive Soviet writer says that more efficient planning could increase output by 40 to 50 per cent.[20] This is no small matter.

Marxist Economic Laws and Planning Models

Is there a conflict between the Marxist economic "law of value" and the modern methods of planning, such as linear programming? Specifically, can the Soviet Union continue to promote Marxist economics while using the latest planning devices? There are three opposing views. First, most Anglo-American experts, such as Campbell, believe that there is indeed a conflict between Marxism and modern planning theory.[21] An extreme view is expressed by Zauberman, who claims

that the price arrived at in the calculus [of the new Soviet mathematical model] . . . turns out to be in unmistakable conflict with that derived from Marx. Marx's price is a cost price, while the conservative Soviet critics of the . . . mathematical scheme . . . correctly identified . . . [its] value-weights as scarcity prices, typically marginalist in their nature. Many of these critics . . . have rightly pointed to the deep roots of the mathematicians' price in the subjective value concept, and to its incompatibility with Marx's objective value, reducible to "congealed" socially necessary labor.[22]

It follows, according to this argument, that Marxist value economics must be eliminated if the Soviet Union is to plan rationally.

Strangely enough, the major premise of this argument is accepted among the second group, the more dogmatic (orthodox?) Soviet Marxist economists.[23] They agree—that there *is* a conflict between Marxist economics and certain modern theories of planning. Since they believe in the absolute truth of Marxism, however, their conclusion is directly opposite to that reached by Zauberman. They conclude that these planning theories must not be followed in the Soviet Union. Particular devices, such as input-output or linear programming, may be used if they are first completely purged of their marginal utility taint.

A third position is that of the less dogmatic Marxists in the Soviet Union, such as Novozhilov[24] or Kantorovich.[25] They hold that modern theories of economic planning are quite compatible with Marxism, and that the modern instruments of rational planning should be used to the fullest extent. Novozhilov and Kantorovich advocate a price formula based on the imputation of prices from the objective facts of social costs and social needs. Costs are calculated to include "indirect" labor costs resulting from the use of limited capital and natural resources in one project rather than any other. The other projects, lower in social priority, will have to switch to the use of more labor and less capital, thus "indirectly" causing an increase of labor costs. This is similar to the Western concept of the "opportunity costs" of using scarce resources.

For these views, Novozhilov and Kantorovich have been labeled as revisionists of Marx both by their own dogmatic Soviet colleagues and by most Anglo-American experts. In fact, Novozhilov himself admits that some of his categories of calculation under socialism, such as marginal costs, marginal benefits, and marginal profits, are semantically similar to those used under capitalism, but he argues strongly that this is due only to the mathematical similarities in all optimization problems.[26] Novozhilov alleged that it is possible to present all the specific methods of rational planning within a Marxist framework, regardless of whether or not neoclassical economics reaches the same conclusions.

Value and Plan

A great many of the Soviet writers now argue that there is no conflict between Marxism and the modern neoclassical theories of rational allocation of resources.[27] Specifically, the more progressive Soviet writers point out that to advocate a mathematical device (like a rate of interest) for rationally allocating capital in a planned economy *is quite different from advocating that any profit (or interest) be given as individual income.* If the neoclassical theory of allocation, which has largely been concerned with the allocation of scarce resources in capitalist firms, also happens to meet the similar problems of socialist firms, there is no reason not to use it.

The progressive Marxists of the West, like the early Lange, argue that there is a qualitative difference between the technical problems of planned allocation of resources and the political-ethical problems of class ownership and distribution. They agree that the technical problems of socialist planning may be best discussed in terms of "bourgeois" neoclassical economics. Yet they still believe that the political-ethical questions of income distribution by classes, as well as the macro economic problems of capitalism, are to be understood in terms of Marxist political economy.[28]

If the more progressive Marxist attitude were accepted, then there would be no conflict between Marxism and any prospective tool of Soviet economic planning. Since it is far from fully accepted, each tool of Soviet planning is still gauged by the politicians in terms of a very dogmatic interpretation of Marxism.

The really difficult problem is not how to justify the use of neoclassical marginal concepts; the difficult problem is that the neoclassical marginal concepts are much too abstract and complex for actual socialist price-setting. Even the very crude Marxist "price of production" theory is better because it can be, and has been, used for practical price-setting in the socialist countries. Much better in theory and more usable in practice are the techniques of linear programming and input-output. It is interesting that both of these techniques grew out of practice. Only later were they rationalized by theory; and it turns out that they are quite consistent with either neoclassical or Marxist value theory.

NOTES

1. All the pre-1917 discussions by socialists and antisocialists on this problem are discussed in Carl Landauer, *European Socialism*, vol. 2 (Berkeley: University of California Press, 1959), pp. 1602–1635.

2. Ludwig von Mises, "Economic Calculation in the Socialist Commonwealth," in F. A. Hayek, ed., *Collectivist Economic Planning* (London: Routledge and Kegan Paul, Ltd., 1935). A brief history of the whole debate appears in Abram Bergson, "Socialist Economics," in Howard Ellis, ed., *A Survey of Contemporary Economics*, vol. 1 (Philadelphia: Blakiston, 1948), pp. 412–448.

3. First stated in 1908 by E. Barone, "The Ministry of Production in the Collective State," reprinted in F. A. Hayek, ed., *Collectivist Economic Planning, op. cit.* For a recent discussion of optimal conditions from the Western view, see E. J. Mishan, "A Survey of Welfare Economics," in American Economic Association and Royal Economic Society, eds., *Surveys of Economic Theory*, vol. 1 (New York: St. Martin's Press, 1966), pp. 154–222.

4. F. A. Hayek, ed., *Collectivist Economic Planning, op. cit.*, pp. 24–49.

5. Oskar Lange, *On the Economic Theory of Socialism* (Minneapolis: University of Minnesota Press, 1938).

6. This use of an actual market in socialism was first considered thoroughly by Abba Lerner, *Economics of Control* (New York: Macmillan, 1944).

7. See, e.g., Maurice Dobb, *Economic Theory and Socialism* (New York: International Publishers, 1955), pp. 55–93. But also see the Marxist analysis by Paul M. Sweezy, *Socialism* (New York: McGraw-Hill Book Co., Inc., 1949).

8. For a feeling of the enormous difference that the change in political atmosphere made, read the drivel written on planning in the Soviet textbook of *Political Economy* (USSR Academy of Sciences, 1954; English ed. publ. by Lawrence and Wishart, 1957) produced collectively under Stalin's direction. Then compare the brilliant collection of articles issued just five years later in the Khrushchev era by the more progressive Soviet economists, called *The Uses of Mathematics in Economics* (ed. by Nemchinov, Moscow, 1959, English ed. publ. by Oliver and Boyd, 1964).

9. Vladimir Treml, "Revival of Soviet Economics and the New Generation of Soviet Economists," *Studies on the Soviet Union*, 5, no. 2 (1965): 4.

10. S. Strumilin, quoted in Treml, *op. cit.*, p. 3.

11. "Some Problems in the Teaching of Political Economy," transl. in the *American Economic Review*, 34 (September 1944): 501–530.

12. Joseph Stalin, *Economic Problem of Socialism in the U.S.S.R.* (New York: International Publishers, 1952.

13. *Ibid*, p. 18.

14. These three views are discussed in detail in Gregory Grossman, "Gold and the Sword: Money in the Soviet Command Economy," in H. Rosovky, ed., *Industrialization in Two Systems* (New York: John Wiley, 1966).

15. Ostrovitianov, *Stroitelstvo kommunizma i tovarno—denezhnye otnosheniia* (Moscow, 1962).

16. I. A. Kronrod, *Dengi v sotsialisticheskom obshchestve* (Moscow, 1960).

17. I. S. Malyshev, *Obshchestvennyi uchet truda i tsena pri sotsializme* (Moscow, 1960).

18. See, e.g., Jere L. Felker, *Soviet Economic Controversies, the Emerging Marketing Concept and Changes in Planning, 1960–1965* (Cambridge: MIT Press, 1966), *passim.*

19. See, e.g., I. Malyshev, *Voprosy ekonomiki*, 3 (March 1957), p. 32.

20. L. V. Kantorovich, *The Best Use of Economic Resources* (Cambridge: Harvard University Press, transl. 1965, first publ. 1959).

21. See, e.g., Robert W. Campbell, "Marx, Kantorovich, and Novozhilov," *Slavic Review*, 20 (October 1961): 402–418. A discussion of more general conflicts is given by Joseph Berliner, "Marxism and the Soviet Economy," *Problems of Communism*, 13 (September–October 1964): 1–10.

22. Alfred Zauberman, "Revisionism in Soviet Economics," in Leopold Labedz, ed., *Revisionism* (New York: Frederick A. Praeger, 1962), p. 276.

23. See, e.g., A. Y. Boiarskii, "On the Proper Relationship between Mathematics and Economics in a Socialist Society," transl. in *Problems of Economics*, 4 (January 1962): 12–24. Also see the similar views in A. I. Kats, "Concerning a Fallacious Concept of Economic Calculations," transl. in *Problems of Economics*, 3 (November 1960): 42–52. A history of the various viewpoints in the Stalin era is available in Gregory Grossman, "Scarce Capital and Soviet Doctrine," *Quarterly Journal of Economics*, 67 (August 1963): 311–343.

24. See, e.g., V. V. Novozhilov, *Problems of Measuring Outlays and Results under*

Optimal Planning (White Plains, N.Y.: International Arts and Sciences Press, transl. 1969).

25. See, e.g., L. V. Kantorovich, *op. cit.*

26. Novozhilov's article in V. S. Nemchinov, ed., *The Use of Mathematics in Economics* (London: Oliver and Boyd Ltd., 1964 ed. in English, first Russian ed. 1959), p. 189.

27. See, e.g., A. Postyshev, "The Labor Theory of Value and Optimal Planning," transl. in *Problems of Economics*, 10 (December 1967): 3–15. He identifies the famous "shadow prices" of linear programming with Marx's value in terms of labor.

28. This view of the distinction between Marxist political economy and technical bourgeois economics is presented by the Marxist writers, Paul Baran and Paul Sweezy, in "Economics of Two Worlds," in *On Political Economy and Econometrics: Essays in Honour of Oskar Lange* (New York: Pergamon Press, 1965), pp. 15–29.

CHAPTER
15

Exploitation in Socialism?

How do we define socialism? Does it exclude exploitation by definition?
Is the Union of Soviet Socialist Republics socialist?

What Is Socialism?

The contemporary American Marxist, Paul Sweezy, wrote that "the *differentia specifica* of socialism as compared to capitalism is public ownership of the means of production. This does not mean *all* the means of production: what it does mean is that those branches of the economy which are *decisive* for its fuctioning must be in . . . the 'public sector.' "[1] Yet Sweezy now comments on this definition, "I no longer think that this goes to the heart of the matter. But I have no neat formulas or definitions to replace it with."[2] Why are contemporary Marxists questioning the traditional definitions?

One problem is that there are now a variety of nations with different political-economic models, each claiming to be socialist, and each claiming that several of the others are not socialist. Another problem is that recent socialist writings, especially since the discovery of the writings of the young Marx, have emphasized spiritual values beyond the neatly defined economic models. Our final goal is the abolition of alienation, to abolish "labor as toil" and make the remaining labor desirable, to achieve a nonalienated, "free," human society. All the existing "socialist" societies are far from these goals. We don't seriously expect to achieve these goals immediately, yet we hesitate to call "socialist" a society that is very, very far from them.[3]

The variety of different "socialist" economies has also raised the question of the meaning of public ownership. On one side, the Soviet Union controls all economic activity from the central government offices with the aid of a huge bureaucratic machine. But surely "there is nothing more distant from Marx's concept of communism than bureaucratic centralism in which the very top of the social pyramid makes all the decisions and the individual becomes only an instrument."[4]

On the other side, the Yugoslav economy is run by autonomous local enterprises directed by workers councils. In so far as workers councils bring more democratic participation and less alienation in the production unit, this seems quite in line with socialist goals. It also means, however, extensive use of the market and material incentives, growth of acquisitive psychology, *and* ownership, control, and profit-making by a local collective rather than all of society (and sometimes at the expense of the rest of society through monopoly pricing).[5]

It is also unfortunately true that the Soviet Union came into being in a backward economic situation, isolated and under attack by the advanced capitalist countries. Hence *Soviet socialism has been a backward socialism.* This meant a high degree of bureaucratic centralism and alienation during the drastic process of industrialization. It also resulted in an arbitrary dictatorship over the working class by a few leaders during that period. Perhaps this was the only way to enforce grim sacrifices for the future on much of the population. Still, it meant high incomes for a few, and political determination of who should get what incomes. It meant economic privileges to the few, determined as a "just" return to their labor only by the decision of a self-perpetuating political leadership.[6]

And here we do begin to come to the heart of the problem. Marx spoke of a brief transitional period between capitalism and communism, in which there would be public ownership, but bourgeois morality would still govern in the distribution of income.[7] That is to say, private profit would be abolished, but wages would still be paid according to work done, rather than according to need (as it would be in full "communism"). Lenin emphasized this distinction, and called the transitional period "socialism."[8]

So the transitional period, the "socialist" period, came to mean public ownership *and* payment of differential wages according to differences in the quantity and quality of work done. Both Marx and Lenin acknowledged that this would still be catering to a bourgeois notion of equity, rather than a communist notion of equity. This transition, however, would be brief, and we would soon pass to a society in which people would work without pay, and goods would be free and taken according to need. Alas, the transition—at least in backward, underdeveloped countries—has proven to be very long and bloody.

The worker does not receive his full product in the Soviet Union. Yet even Marx recognized that that does not necessarily mean exploitation. Some of the workers' product *must* be used for replacement of depreciated capital, investment in new capital, government welfare spending, and government military spending.

It *is* exploitation, however, even according to the "transitional, socialist" morality, if some of the remaining product goes to the Soviet elite beyond their own contribution by labor to the product. Given the fact that the elite is rewarded by a leadership that chooses itself to continue in office, picks its own successors, and allows no criticism of itself (although criticism is allowed on the local level), it is hard to believe that all rewards are strictly according to work done. Rather, it appears—as is "natural" in this institutional situation—that the elite exploits the ordinary worker to some extent by giving some of his product to the elite.

Thus, the Soviet elite's income is all called labor income, but it is doubtful that all of it is. The exploitation results, not from private ownership of the means of production, but from control of the "public" means of production by an elite operating through an undemocratic control of the Soviet state. It is true that only public ownership and control provides the possibility of doing away with exploitation, but that result may not follow. If economic backwardness and underdevelopment lead to a dictatorship that can take the drastic measures required for initial industrialization, then the control of the means of production resides in a small political elite, who may use that control for exploitation.

Income Distribution in the USSR

Exploitation in the United States and other capitalist countries is reflected in a very unequal income distribution, with vast wealth and high incomes concentrated in the capitalist class. Among the socialist countries China and Cuba claim to have gone very far toward income equality, but there is still insufficient data to investigate their situations. Instead we confine ourselves to the income distribution of the Soviet Union.

Wage differentials are used in the USSR to allocate labor to different geographical areas and to different industries, and to provide a major incentive to acquire new skills and to use old skills as fully as possible. In order to provide the incentive for labor in a rapidly expanding economy, the Soviet economy has generally had even wider range differentials than the U.S. economy. Thus, in 1956 it is reported that the ratio of wages among the third quartile (relatively skilled) of Soviet workers to the first quartile (relatively unskilled) was 1.85 to 1.00.[9] In the same year the corresponding U.S. ratio is reported as only 1.37 to 1.00. There are some very difficult statistical problems with the comparison, so the exact figures should not be taken too seriously, but the fact does remain that Soviet wage differences are as great or greater than U.S. wage differences.

Exploitation in Socialism?

The conclusion is quite different when a comparison is made of the distribution of total income in the two countries. The official Soviet distribution shows that in 1960 the top 10 per cent of families had a total of only 4.75 times as much income as the total of the bottom 10 per cent, and the Soviets claim that this ratio will move down to only 3 to 1 in the near future. Conservative U.S. experts place the present Soviet ratio much higher. But even these adjustments would put the Soviet differential far below the U.S. ratio, which in 1960 revealed the top 10 per cent as having thirty times the total income of the lowest 10 per cent.[10] The reason for the much higher income inequality in the United States lies in the fact that the Soviet Union has only wage or salary income, whereas in the United States we also find the categories of rent, interest, and profit income. These latter categories, in which a few U.S. citizens have the very highest incomes, therefore create the over-all greater inequality of United States incomes (in spite of the equally wide spread of Soviet wage incomes).

In order to place present Soviet wage differentials in their proper perspective, we must consider briefly the historical evolution of Soviet wage policy. Immediately after the 1917 revolution, wages were very much equalized in accordance with old socialist ideals. During war communism, 1917 to 1921, wages were initially equal for all but the most difficult and exhausting jobs, in which cases the ratio was increased as a result of absolute necessity. During the New Economic Policy (1921–1928), wages were again very much differentiated. The trade unions, however, often fought for more wage equality and obtained considerable equality from 1926 to 1931.

In the 1930's, in order to push rapid industrialization, Stalin kept the average unskilled wage very low to avoid pressure for more consumer goods and to free resources for investment. At the same time, the industrialization drive made it all the more important to foster workers' incentives to obtain better skills and to work hard. Therefore, while the real wages of the millions of unskilled workers were kept very low, the real wage rates of the most skilled workers were being raised. Under Stalin's direction in the 1930's the ratio of most skilled wage rates to unskilled wage rates stood at 3.5 to 1 in the officially prescribed wage scales, and piece-rate bonuses undoubtedly increased this ratio in practice. This is a much higher wage differential than prevails currently in the United States. Of course, the United States also had much higher wage differentials during its own period of rapid industrialization. Thus, many economists argue that U.S. wage differentials for skills were approximately comparable with Soviet differentials when we were at comparable levels of development.

To allow Soviet workers in the 1930's to achieve their desires to increase skill and earnings, the government provided a multiple-level educational system for adults as well as young students. Included within it were on-the-job individual and group training, full time factory schools in methods of mass production, secondary and advanced technical training schools, and the higher institutes and universities. When the supply of unskilled workers from the farms into industry was tripling in the 1930's, the worker training program was very active, and millions of adult workers participated in it.

In any event, from 1931, during Stalin's drive for industrialization, until 1956, when Stalinism was attacked at the Twentieth Party Congress, Soviet slogans continuously denounced "wage equalization." It was maintained that socialism means payment according to the work done by the individual, whereas wage leveling is only a utopian, unrealistic, and petty bourgeois policy. Since 1956 the more liberal influence has prevailed, and Soviet wage policy has emphasized more equality of high and low wages as a step toward communism. By 1958 the official differential in the wages of the most skilled and the unskilled had already fallen to 2.8 to 1, a considerable decline from the 3.5 to 1 of the 1930's. Party programs and economic plans now envisage a more rapidly rising minimum wage that will reduce the official wage differential to 2 to 1 in the near future.

The changes may be traced more precisely in the ratio of the wages of the highly skilled workers in the ninth decile (80th to 90th percentile of earnings) to the wages of the unskilled workers in the first decile (the lowest paid 10 per cent). In 1929 this ratio of the wages of the highly skilled to the wages of the unskilled workers was 3.15 to 1. This ratio had risen to 3.88 by 1956 at the time of the Twentieth Party Congress, but declined to 3.28 by 1959.[11] Since 1959 we have further evidence of reduced wage inequality in that (1) as noted above, new wage scales already show a lower ratio of skilled to unskilled wages, (2) minimum wages have risen considerably, (3) there is a continuing switch from piece-rate wages to the more equalizing time-rate wages, and (4) there is an increasing area of free goods for public consumption (such as free health and education services). Further, the Party and government promise continuance of these trends into the 1970's.

What are the economic reasons (partly reflected in the political changes) for this important switch in Soviet policy? In the 1930's, most workers were unskilled and there was a tremendous relative shortage of skilled workers. Managers bid up wages of skilled workers simply to get them, and Soviet leaders felt that high payment for skilled work was a necessary prod to further acquisition and use of skills. By the early 1960's, there was already a very large reservoir of highly trained and self-disciplined workers, and there were even shortages of unskilled workers in some areas. Thus, the extreme differentials had become unnecessary to attract skilled workers, and Soviet leaders preferred to cultivate a more popular, equalitarian image.

238

Exploitation in Socialism?

In addition to wage workers, the Soviet income distribution includes salaried white-collar employees and salaried engineering-technical personnel. Table 15–1 gives some indication of a narrowing of the gap between the wage and salary levels.

TABLE 15-1

Soviet Wage and Salary Income Differentials

YEAR	AVERAGE SALARIES OF ENGINEERING-TECH-NICAL PERSONNEL IN PERCENTAGE OF AVERAGE EARNINGS OF WAGE WORKERS	AVERAGE SALARIES OF WHITE-COLLAR EMPLOYEES IN PERCENTAGE OF AVERAGE EARNINGS OF WAGE WORKERS
1932	263	150
1935	236	120
1940	210	109
1950	175	93
1955	165	88
1960	150	no data

Source: Murray Yanowitch, "The Soviet Income Revolution," reprinted in M. Bornstein and D. Fusfeld, eds., *The Soviet Economy* (Homewood, Ill.: R. D. Irwin, 1966), p. 233.

It appears from this table that salaries of Soviet white-collar workers have declined (relatively) below the wage level of blue-collar workers, while the salaries of engineering-technical personnel have also fallen (relatively) toward the average wage level. These smaller differentials certainly give additional evidence of lessening income inequality in the Soviet Union. This reflects a conscious wage-equalizing policy since Stalin's death. Most of the changes in these ratios before Stalin's death merely reflect changes within the various categories. Thus, within the category of wage workers in this whole period there was a shift in proportions to the more skilled grades, at the same time that these more skilled grades were relatively increasing their wage rates up to 1956. Moreover, among engineering-technical personnel, the lower-paid occupation groups were increasing most rapidly. Nevertheless, the end result has undoubtedly been a considerable narrowing of over-all Soviet income differentials in recent years.

Summary and Tentative Conclusions

Since we will return to this subject in other chapters, our conclusions can only be rather tentative here. By definition exploitation means income taken from the worker by means of the class control of the means of production. A narrow definition of socialism could be the existence of public ownership of the means of production and income based solely on labor accomplished.

By contrast with any of the nations claiming to be socialist, the United States does have mainly private ownership of the means of production and there is a large amount of exploitation of workers by capitalist owners. The enormous extent of the exploitation is reflected in the extremely unequal distribution of income. Furthermore, almost all the very highest incomes are composed of income from the ownership of the means of production—profit, rent, and interest. At the same time, almost all the bottom two-thirds of the income range is composed of wage earners.

In the Soviet Union and Eastern Europe, most of the means of production are publicly owned. On the other hand, there is political *control* of the means of production by the elite through the mechanism of a one-party political system. It is a fact that the elite—managers, top military, top Party and government—are very much better paid than the average worker. Still, the ranks of the elite are not tightly closed to newcomers, and most of the income of the elite is return for their own labor. Nevertheless, through their control of the means of production, the elite—particularly the highest members of the elite—do exploit the workers to some degree. In other words, some portion of the income of the elite is not earned by their own labor, but is exploited from the average worker. The fragmentary evidence would seem to indicate, however, that the total amount of exploited income is very small. The exploited income probably amounts to a sizable amount of the elite's income only in the very highest ranks of power. At some of the highest political levels, for example, the total amounts of income are state secrets. (Not enough evidence exists to characterize China and Cuba in these respects.)

In spite of this slight degree of exploitation, however, it seems better analytically to include the Soviet Union and Eastern Europe in the category of "socialist." Public ownership, public control, and income from labor do predominate, even though the counterexamples are well-known and horrendous. Moreover, to toss them out of the socialist category may make for easier propaganda in favor of socialism, but it is ruinous for social analysis because then we never do face up to the problems that may still occur under socialism. If one wants to criticize these countries from a Marxist viewpoint, it is sufficient to reserve the word "communism" for our vision of a better society.

NOTES

1. Paul Sweezy, "Communism as an Ideal," *Monthly Review*, 15 (October 1963): 330.
2. Sweezy, private communication to the author.

Exploitation in Socialism?

3. See the further discussion of alienation in Chapter 20.
4. Oldrich Kyn, "Marx and the Mechanism of Functioning of a Socialist Economy," *Oeconomica*, 3, no. 1 (1968): 39–51.
5. See the further discussion of market socialism in Chapter 17.
6. See the further discussion of socialism and democracy in Chapter 18.
7. Marx, *Critique of the Gotha Program* (New York: International Publishers, 1931).
8. Lenin, *State and Revolution* (New York: International Publishers, 1932).
9. Murray Yanowitch, "The Soviet Income Revolution," reprinted in *The Soviet Economy*, ed. by M. Bornstein and D. R. Fusfeld (Homewood, Ill.: R. D. Irwin, 1966), p. 237n.
10. *Ibid.*, p. 237.
11. *Ibid.*, p. 231.

CHAPTER

16

Growth, Waste, and Pollution in Socialism

In the case of a centrally planned economy like the Soviet Union, it may be assumed that *aggregate* effective demand always rises as rapidly as aggregate supply, though *particular* goods may be unsaleable for various reasons. Thus, there are no retardations nor depressions caused by lack of demand. If the problems of demand are thus eliminated, then growth will depend simply on how fast output can be expanded. The supply problem may be resolved into two questions. First, how much of each input (labor, capital, natural resources, and technology) can be procured under existing circumstances for use in production? Second, how much output can be obtained from these inputs in the production process?

These questions can be most usefully analyzed in terms of the growth formula which was explored in Chapter 6.

$$\text{Rate of growth of output} = \frac{\text{increase in output}}{\text{investment}} \times \frac{\text{saving}}{\text{output}}.$$

If saving equals investment, as it does in the Soviet Union, then this formula is true by definition. The ratio of saving to output then tells us how much new capital is invested per year. The ratio of increased output to investment tells us the amount of product produced by the new capital invested per year. Of course, that productivity is affected by changes in the labor force, changes in natural resources, and technological improvements.

Let us take an example of the use of this equation of growth. If the ratio of saving to output is 9 per cent, and if the ratio of increased output to investment is one-third, then we find:

$$\text{rate of Growth} = \frac{1}{3} \times 0.09 = 0.03 \text{ or } 3\% \text{ a year.}$$

This has been approximately the performance of the economy of the United States over a long period of time.[1]

For the years 1950–1970 conservative U.S. estimates place Soviet GNP growth at 6 per cent a year, while official Soviet figures put their growth at 9 per cent a year.[2] (It is worth noting that China, in spite of political upheavals, also achieved a 6 per cent rate of growth of GNP per year from 1949 to 1966, according to an estimate in U.S. Congressional hearings.[3]) Even the conservative American estimate of the Soviet growth rate at 6 per cent is still high enough to call for an explanation in terms of the growth formula. If it is assumed for the moment that the Soviet ratio of increased output to investment is the same as the U.S. ratio, then in this simple analysis the higher rate of growth can be explained by a higher ratio of saving and investment from current output (or income). Thus, if the Soviet ratio of increased output to investment is also one-third, then a 6 per cent growth rate can only be explained by an 18 per cent ratio of saving to output. According to the formula:

$$\text{Soviet growth rate} = \frac{1}{3} \times 0.18 = 0.06 \text{ or } 6\% \text{ a year.}$$

One reason for the high Soviet growth rate is that there is always sufficient aggregate demand in the Soviet Union for full employment of labor and full use of capacity. Therefore, all Soviet saving is used for investment because the planners can always find a use for new capital. In fact, Soviet planners usually complain of a "scarcity" of capital. This is because they attempt to invest more than the entire available amount of savings. In the United States, on the other hand, when businessmen cannot find a profitable investment for all their savings, some planned saving does not become investment in new capital. American economists often complain of "too much" planned saving, while planned investment in additional capital is less than it could be. In some years "too much" supply of all goods (relative to money demand) even causes a decline of American production and a depression situation, rather than any growth of output.

It is also obvious from the formula, however, that the Soviet people have to pay a price for their high rate of investment and growth of output. If the Soviets save 18 per cent and the United States saves only 9 per cent of national output, and if both begin with the same $100 output, then in the first year the Soviet consumption would be only $82, while U.S. consumption would be $91. It is impossible to have both higher consumption and higher investment out of the same output; the Soviets have sacrificed some present consumption for more investment. Furthermore, in reality total Soviet output is still far below the U.S. level, so the Soviet consumption level is even lower. In purely human terms, moreover, we must stress that when the Soviets began their rapid industrial expansion, their consumption was at a miserably low level. Therefore, each percentage of

243

national product taken from consumption in order to make investments meant a very great amount of present human misery (in order to build for growth in the future).

On the other hand, the simple growth formula also indicates that if the Soviet Union continues to grow twice as fast as the United States, after some years both its total output *and* its consumption will be larger than those of the United States. That is true, however, only if the Soviet Union continues to build new capital at the same rate and if it keeps the same increase of output per unit of new investment. It is necessary to investigate both of these assumptions to assess future Soviet growth.

Saving of Capital

The Soviet Union, as mentioned above, has saved and invested an enormously high percentage of its national income. The proportion was certainly over a quarter in the early 1930's, was perhaps 35 or even 40 per cent in some years, and has remained very high ever since.[4] According to official Soviet data, the share of "means of production" in the output of the industrial sector taken alone was only 39.5 per cent in 1928, but rose rapidly to 53.4 per cent by 1932, then continued to rise steadily till it was 70.6 per cent by 1955, and has continued with small increases since then.[5] The producer goods sector increased its percentage of all goods because of the high levels of investment. The question is whether the Soviet Union can continue to invest such a high percentage—still more than one-third— of its national income.

In formal terms, the Soviet government can decide what it wishes. In realistic political terms, however, the Soviet politician must consider the increasing pressure of workers for more immediate gains in consumption. In economic terms, we may add that the investment precentage of income is held to some maximum by the need to provide sufficient consumer goods to provide incentives for labor to maintain and increase its productivity.

There is some indication that the percentage of investment in the national income will at least stop growing (and may even begin to decline) because past trends and also all future Soviet plans show the growth rate of consumer goods coming ever closer to the growth rate of producer goods. It seems that the two will be allowed to grow at about the same rate in the future, although this is not yet acknowledged to be a good thing in theory. Thus, the supply of capital is likely to continue increasing at about the same percentage, not rising, and perhaps dropping a little.

Product per Unit of Capital

Many different things affect the Soviet product per unit of capital, including the incentives and productivity of both workers and managers, the amounts of labor and raw materials, the organization and efficiency of allocation and use of all factors, and the educational level of labor. We begin here with the key factor of Soviet education.

The average educational level of Soviet industrial wage workers has improved from 3.5 years of schooling in 1929 to 7.5 years in 1965. Similarly, the proportion of highly skilled workers climbed from 19 per cent of the total in 1925 to 65 per cent in 1961. Over the same years (1925 to 1961), semiskilled workers declined from 41 to 35 per cent, and unskilled from 40 to less than 1 per cent. Training in agriculture, however, has progressed far more slowly. As late as 1959, unskilled workers constituted 71 per cent of the manual labor force in agriculture.

Total Soviet enrollment in all schools in the academic year 1963–1964 was 65.1 million, including 3.3 million in higher educational institutions. In comparison, the United States (with a smaller population) had in the same year 53.6 million total enrollments, including five million in higher educational institutions. The U.S. also leads in graduations. In the academic year 1963–1964, the total of U.S. graduates in higher education was 614.2 thousand, whereas Soviet higher education graduated only 369.6 thousand students in total.[6] It will be shown below, however, that the Soviets have recently greatly increased the number of students enrolled for advanced degrees, and that the situation is reversed in some specialized fields that may be the key to economic growth.

It must be emphasized that all 754 institutions of higher education in the USSR in 1965 were operated by the central government as a free public service. Not only is tuition free, but most students are given sizable stipends or scholarships, amounting for advanced students to more than the average industrial wage.

The Soviet Union, however, began with a largely illiterate population in the 1920's, so its comparative performance is a remarkable feat. It is rapidly closing the gap in the total number of students in higher education.

The emphasis among fields in the Soviet Union reflects planned social policy. "During the 1928–64 period, the Soviet Union trained about 5,800,000 professionals in all fields, of whom about one-third were in engineering fields and about one-fifth were educational specialists."[7] By 1965 the dominance of these two fields (and especially engineering) was even stronger, as may be seen in Table 16–1. The engineering-industrial

245

TABLE 16-1

Composition of Soviet Graduates, 1965

FIELDS	PERCENTAGE
Engineering-industrial	40
Educational-cultural*	36
Agricultural	9
Socioeconomic	8
Health-medical	7
	100

*" . . . Two-thirds of educational-cultural
field graduates are trained as research
scientists in universities and as science
teachers in pedagogical institutes . . . "

Source: Nicholas DeWitt, "High-Level Manpower in the
U.S.S.R.," in U.S. Congress, Joint Economic Committee,
New Directions in the Soviet Economy (Washington, D.C.:
U.S. Government Printing Office, 1966), p. 805.

fields not only are large in quantity of students, but demand high quality work. For example, in the years 1950–1964 only 62 per cent of the students who entered the engineering-industrial fields graduated, while 80 per cent graduated in the educational-cultural fields, and 95 per cent in the health-medical fields.

Furthermore, the excellence of Soviet training has been admitted by several careful U.S. observers. For example, one says, "The quality of Soviet professional training in scientific, engineering, and applied fields today is, on substantive grounds, comparable to that offered in the West."[8] It has also been observed that the basis of student selection in the USSR is still merit rather than money or father's position, a fact which makes for more effective use of human resources.

The Soviet effort in theoretical research also stands out clearly in the statistics. By 1965 there were 2,000 research institutes employing 2,497,000 people, including 765,000 professionals, 418,000 semiprofessionals, and 357,000 research and academic personnel. For some years the demands of research institutes were expanding faster than the supply of advanced degree holders. Therefore, in a crash program the number of postgraduate students in training for the "aspirant" degree (similar to our Ph.D. candidate status) was pushed up from 23,000 in 1959 to 83,000 in 1965. Finally, comparisons with the United States show definite Soviet leads in the production of most kinds of specialists. By 1964 the USSR was annually training four times as many engineers as was the United States, three times as many physicians, and twice as many agricultural specialists.

As a tentative conclusion, it has been shown that the Soviet investment ratio is much higher than the U.S. ratio, although pressure for immediate

246

consumption *may* lower it somewhat. In addition, the Soviet ratio of increased output per unit of added capital (investment) is still as high or higher than the U.S. ratio, though it may be diminishing toward the American level. At any rate, advances in education, research, and technology should keep it respectably high. Nevertheless, even if both of these crucial Soviet ratios are lowered a bit in the future, and if the United States continues at its long-run average growth rate, it would still seem likely that the Soviet economy will continue over the long run to grow much more rapidly than the United States—assuming no really drastic changes in the situation of either country.

The Political-Ethical Issues

The issue of economic growth has been examined above in the cold economic terms of the growth formula. Now we must see why investment versus consumption is *the* vital political issue around which Soviet socialist politics must turn and by which Soviet lives are determined.

On the ideological side, it may be noted that the Soviet economists follow a similar model derived from Marx. Actually, in the 1920's several Soviet economists, notably G. A. Feldman, devised some quite sophisticated dynamic growth models as tools of long-term planning.[9] Unfortunately, the Stalinist dictatorship distrusted any innovation in the social sciences, and attacked these models as "bourgeois formalism" and "mathematical formalism." As a result, Feldman's pioneering work was ignored for several decades, while Soviet growth planning was left to political whim.

At any rate, the Soviet economists now use models derived from the reproduction schemes in volume 2 of Marx's *Capital*, which anticipated the modern growth formula by many decades. Although it was cruder mathematically, Marx's model showed all the essentials. It states implicitly (1) what the conditions are for a steady growth at full capacity, and that (2) the growth rate of output will be higher if there is a higher ratio of producer goods to consumer goods (or of investment to consumption).

Of course, the Marxist model also shows that the economy with the higher ratio of investment will *eventually* also have a larger amount of consumption, but the interesting question is how many years the populace must wait for consumption, that is, at what date optimal consumption is desired. Of course, this is a political and ethical decision, not an economic one. It should also be noted that it is possible to go too far in reducing consumption, even from the cold and calculating viewpoint of economic growth. To reduce consumption opportunities below some point will lower labor productivity, and, after some time, may even cause strikes or revolutions. A certain minimum percentage of consumption remains necessary if the gains made by more saving and investing of capital are not be cancelled out by negative side-effects. To put it another way, there are definitely both political and economic maximum limits to the possible percentage of saving and investment.

Finally, on the ideological front, one must note a strange and false notion which Stalin raised to the level of an unassailable dogma: the idea that steady growth cannot be achieved unless the investment sector always grows faster than the consumption sector.[10] Actually, Marx merely showed that this is sometimes the case in a "capitalist" economy, and that in its extreme form it is a disproportion that usually leads to a depression. The Soviets do not claim to have a capitalist economy, and they do not desire a depression, so it is hard to see the relevance of this notion of Marx to their forced conclusion. The real reason for Stalin's doctrine that investment goods *must* grow faster was merely to reinforce the arguments for ever more investment. In reality, steady growth may be achieved with any constant positive rate of net investment; the investment sector must grow more rapidly than the consumption sector only if one wishes not steady, but constant accelerating growth (assuming productivity remains the same).

There is no reason to value the consumption by future generations above that by the present population. It would seem therefore that a Marxist, who bases himself on a socialist type of humanist ethics, would decide to maintain an *equal* percentage increase of consumption and investment, once a country has made the initial push for industrial development. At any rate, assuming a constant marginal output-capital ratio, the economist can only calculate the different growth rates to be gained by alternative ratios of investment to consumption. Which alternative ratio of investment to consumption should be selected is a political choice, and, in a democracy, ought to be decided by the collective ethical evaluations of present versus future consumers.[11]

Most political disputes in the Soviet Union have had this issue as one of the underlying bones of contention. In the 1930's it was, of course, vitally necessary to raise the level and percentage of investment by a drastic amount if industrialization was to be begun seriously. This took the form of collectivization of agriculture and the removal of large amounts of agricultural goods to use as exports to buy machinery, as cheap raw materials for industry, or as food for industrial workers.

Now it is seen that the application of growth economics may be quite different in form in the industrially developed Soviet Union of today. There are still violent political disputes over the percentage of investment to consumption, but the debate is over a small percentage either way. Now that industry is established, no one would argue that it is necessary to again double or triple the investment percentage in a few years' time. Moreover, agriculture is relatively much smaller and industry relatively much larger now. The debate no longer centers on shifting a large product from agriculture to industry, but rather on how much of the total product is to go for wages of workers (mostly in industry) and how much should go into the surplus of government profits and taxes for more investment.

Population and Welfare in Socialism

We noted in Chapter 6 that Marx called the Malthusian theory of people breeding like rabbits a slander on the human race.[12] We emphasize that the evils of poverty—both in the advanced capitalist countries and in the colonial and semicolonial countries—are *not* primarily caused by too much population, but are social diseases caused by too much exploitation and profit-making. In the history of capitalism the improvement of technology has greatly surpassed the rise of population, so further tremendous increases in the product per capita could be achieved if they were not held back by the institutional barriers imposed through the capitalist and imperialist systems. The Soviet economists have gone much further than Marx: they declare that more workers simply mean more output, and that socialism solves all economic problems, so *no* degree of population growth can ever be a problem in any socialist country.

Even if we accept the idea that Soviet socialism can ensure a high rate of growth of output, this does not prove that the rate of growth per person could not be higher if there were less population growth. In other words, additional workers may add to the total product, but surely a point could be reached where the number of workers grows faster than the amount of capital. In that case, each additional worker has less capital with which to work, so he will add to the product less than the previous average. It may still be true that more population means greater absolute growth of product, which is good for military and prestige purposes. Nevertheless, more population also means a much slower growth of output per worker, so it constitutes a heavy drag on the improvement of individual welfare! China seems to have recognized this in practice with a significant birth control drive (through propaganda and availability of contraceptive devices), though with very hesitant theoretical recognition of the problem.[13]

Aggregate Balance versus Inflation

The question of aggregate balance in the Soviet economy is mostly a reflection of the growth problem already discussed. Basically, the resources supplied for investment must just equal the amount required or demanded for investment, while the amount supplied to consumers must just equal the amount they will demand at present incomes and prices. The capitalist economy of the United States has been plagued frequently by lack of adequate demand for the products of private enterprise. In the planned economy of the USSR there has *always* been sufficient aggregate demand since the planning period began in 1928, and there has never been general or aggregate unemployment. In the USSR, however, the problem has usually been that the government has demanded much more for investment than could be supplied, and has failed to provide enough consumer goods to satisfy household demand.

Since aggregate demand has always more than equalled the amount of resources and manpower available, aggregate unemployment has been nonexistent since 1928. Of course, the Soviet Union does have a considerable amount of "frictional" and "structural" unemployment. "Frictional" unemployment may be defined as ordinary labor turnover. "Structural" unemployment occurs when the structure of industry and technology changes, so that millions of workers must change jobs from one place to another, from one industry to another, or from one skill to another. These changes require large amounts of retraining and moving expenses. The number of workers involved and the time necessary for "readjustment" have recently become great enough that numerous observers report significant unemployment from this source. The Soviet Union may also have some "seasonal" unemployment. This occurs because there are times of the year in certain industries, especially agriculture, when much labor is needed, and times when little labor is needed. It may not be profitable for a society to transfer these workers to another job for only a few months of the year, though the Chinese now use them to build dams and roads.

As implied above, the main problem of aggregate balance in the Soviet economy has been due not to lack of demand creating unemployment, but rather to excessive demand for labor and all goods, causing inflation. The main reason for the inflation of the 1930's and 1940's was the excessive increase in government demand for investment goods, military supplies, and "free" or nonpriced welfare services. This created an excess demand for all inputs, including labor. The excess demand for labor pushed up wage rates much faster than productivity, so workers' demand for consumer goods rose faster than total production and much faster than output of consumer goods.

The execessive wage payments occurred as a result of decisions both at the national level and at the level of each firm. In the initial industrialization and wartime periods, the planners called for much larger increases in investment and military goods than in consumer goods, and the discrepancy was usually even greater in the fulfillment of plans. Related to the high level of investment and military spending was the practice of overfull employment planning mentioned earlier. At the level of the enterprise, overfull employment planning meant being given output targets which, for most firms, were essentially unachievable with the amount of labor and other inputs legally available to them.

In order to meet their production plans, therefore, Soviet managers found themselves competing strenuously for materials and labor. Material good prices were effectively controlled at the enterprise level, and most deliveries of goods were ordered by direct central priorities and rationing. Workers, however, respond mainly to the incentive of higher wages, so this was the path followed by managers competing for labor inputs. Managers in the 1930's and 1940's were able to overspend their payrolls with few if any penalties, but were under extreme pressure to meet output targets. In that period, they bid notoriously high to obtain the scarce supply of workers, and even hoarded unneeded workers against future needs.

As a final result of this process, the workers attempted to spend their rapidly increasing wages on the much smaller increase in consumer goods. The consequence was too much money chasing too few goods in the consumer goods market, and steadily rising prices until 1947. This is the basic pattern of prewar and wartime inflation: excess demand for labor as a joint result of the high rate of investment and overfull employment planning, and excess demand for consumer goods as a result of wages rising faster than productivity and faster than the output of consumer goods.

In the face of these extreme inflationary pressures, Soviet policy was always to hold prices constant or declining by administrative fiat. In practice, the pressures forced them to raise prices for long periods in the 1930's and 1940's. These reluctant raises were not enough to soak up the full demand, however, so the result was "repressed inflation," regulation of prices below the free market level. Repressed inflation showed up in shortages and long lines for many goods. Since their wages often could not be spent for any goods (because none were available at any price), workers' incentives to labor declined.

Only since 1947 has the problem been brought under some control (though a smaller degree of repressed inflation still exists). Since that time (1) the State Bank only allows enterprises to pay wages above the planned amount to the extent that they increase output above plan, and (2) the degree of overfull employment planning appears to have been sharply reduced (since the most urgent military demands have lessened).

Relations between Industries: Micro Balances

We have examined the aggregate (or macro) balances between the major parts of the economy, such as consumption and investment. Now the analysis must look at the individual (micro) balances required between different industries. In this context, each "industry" is defined as a collection of enterprises producing a single product for which no close substitute exists.

Soviet planners have in the past used a fairly simple approach called the "method of balances." According to the form they use, one might state the aggregate balances in the following way. The disposable personal income of all Soviet citizens might be shown (as in Table 16-2, which omits some details) as a balanced budget of their income and expenditures:

TABLE 16-2
Workers' Budget

WAGES PENSIONS	CONSUMER SPENDING PERSONAL SAVING
Source of disposable income	Spending disposable income

The government revenues and expenditures that must be planned are shown in Table 16-3:

TABLE 16-3
Government Budget

	INVESTMENT WELFARE
TAXES	MILITARY
PROFITS	SURPLUS — DEPOSITED
LOANS	IN STATE BANK
Total income	Total spending

The same method of establishing a balanced intake and outgo is used for each product or industry. Thus, the balance for the iron industry might be portrayed as in Table 16-4:

TABLE 16-4
Iron Industry

1. IMPORTS	1. EXPORTS
2. REDUCTION IN INVENTORY	2. INCREASE IN INVENTORY
3. PRODUCTION LISTED BY PLANTS OR REGIONS	3. USES BY OTHER INDUSTRIES, USUALLY LISTED BY REGION
Total sources	Total uses

Of course, it is only the totals that must balance.

This simple method runs into many problems. It is very complex to achieve such a balance among all the conflicting needs and available materials in any one industry. Moreover, the balances are all related, since each industry relies on others for supplies. Recently, consideration has been given to dropping the crude balance method for the related "input-output" method.

Soviet economists have spent much effort on this particular problem.[14] One reason is that this problem, especially in the macro economic area of achieving a *full employment* of workers and resources, is of overwhelming practical importance. Furthermore, this was an area in which Marx did make a contribution.[15] Marx's scheme of balanced economic growth has been translated—with some difficulty—by several Marxist economists as a simplified type of Keynesian scheme of national income accounting.[16] Marx's scheme has also been translated by Marxist economists, using a great deal of verbal skill and ingenuity, into a simple input-output model.[17]

It should be noted to their credit that the Soviet economists of the 1920's grappled with most of the problems of balance in a very sophisticated manner. In fact, Wassily Leontief, the creator of the input-output method, was an economics student at Leningrad University during the 1920's, and undoubtedly benefited from the Soviet experience and debates before he emigrated to the United States.[18] Aside from Leontief, several other Soviet economists constructed models that might have led to a full-blown input-output analysis.

Unfortunately, most of these economists disagreed with Stalin on the possible rate of economic development, so Stalin attacked and even imprisoned some of them in the early 1930's. As we saw in earlier sections, the condemnation included pioneering discussions of price formation and growth models as well as balance models. Given the dogmatic and repressive atmosphere, it was unhealthy to pursue such models any further. Even the Marxist writer, Dobb, comments that

in the second half of the 30's a half-hearted attempt was, indeed, made (prompted, it has been said, by Stalin) to revive a discussion about a synthetic "balance of the National economy."

. . . The discussion scarcely got beyond questions of classification (i.e., a list-ing of the actual relationships of which account must be taken); it was soon to be dismissed by authority as unsatisfactory and was rather abruptly ad-journed. After that for two decades silence reigned.[19]

The intensive analysis of input-output relationships was revived only after the anti-Stalinist Twentieth Congress of the Communist Party in 1956. As mentioned above, Soviet economists are now doing a great deal of advanced work in this field. Yet the planners apparently still use the "method of balances" in all actual planning. So far, the discussion has only produced a few regional experiments with input-output, considerable statistical analysis of the past with this analysis, and much advocacy of use for future planning.

One of the great difficulties with the Soviet method of balances has been that it does not take into account the secondary effects on other industries of a change in the output of any one industry. For example, an increase in Soviet auto production means an immediate need for more rubber tires, but it also implies that the rubber tire industry will need more rubber as well as more tire-making machinery, and so forth, ad infinitum. By contrast, the input-output method automatically takes into account all secondary and further removed effects.

For instance, suppose the planners find that the planned supply of steel is one million tons short of the total requirements of all enterprises. If steel production is to be increased, this means additional requirements for iron ore, coal, limestone, and other ingredients. Exactly how much is required of each must be calculated from the respective technological coefficients, that is, the ratios of each input required to produce one unit of steel. For example, if production of one ton of steel requires 1.5 tons of iron ore, then this coefficient or ratio (1.5/1) means than an additional one million tons of steel requires an additional 1.5 million tons of iron ore. In turn, the additional production of iron ore, coal, limestone, and other inputs into steel must require additional inputs of the commodities used in *their* production. The chain of secondary effects is endless.

If instead of producing additional steel the planners decide to stick with the original plan of steel output, then balance can be achieved only by cutbacks in the output of all commodities dependent upon steel as an input. Thus, depending on their technological coefficients or needs for steel, there would have to be reductions in the planned production of autos, trucks, rails, and so forth. Each of these in turn would mean reduction in other commodities using them as inputs, another endless chain that could only slowly approach balance as the result of a greater number of adjust-ments.

Thus, by the method of balances, it would be necessary to go through several approximations and changes affecting every balance (because all are interrelated) before getting all the different industries to balance. This takes so long, even with Soviet shortcuts (discussed below) that the balancing process not only takes a great deal of energy, but also a lot of time, and is usually completed late. As a result, the final plan usually arrives at the enterprise *after* the period covered has already begun. Furthermore, this complicated planning process has been absorbing and increasing percentage of the labor force, which might well be used elsewhere.

Theoretically, the input-output method would remedy the main defect of the balance method, since it does take into account all the indirect adjustments to any change in one item.[20] It is also more suitable for use with electric computers. It would not only be faster to calculate one balanced plan by the input-output method, but this method would actually make it easily possible to present several alternative balanced plans, from which the politicians could pick the plan they desire, or even change particular output targets, and yet be certain of all the secondary effects. It is theoretically possible to have an almost infinite number of different balanced plans with given resources as the desired final bill of goods is varied.

It should be noted that the problem of speeding up planning and reaching a final desired approximation to a good balance is now becoming more urgent. This is because (1) Soviet industry comprises a growing number of enterprises, whose relationships are more complex and interrelated, so that secondary effects are harder to calculate intuitively; and (2) the increased complexity makes more difficult the problems of gathering and aggregating the necessary information. The use of electronic computers and the input-output method of calculation may help gain the necessary speed for Soviet planning. The details of the input-output method need not concern us here: they are readily available in many books.[21]

In practice, it is important to mention one Soviet shortcut in the actual use of the method of balances. If more steel is ordered by the politicians, then, as shown above, the planners should theoretically order more iron and coal and other inputs for the steel industry. But this would upset the balances for iron and coal and everything else that goes into steel. To prevent many of these secondary effects from disrupting planning, the planners first try to get each industry to accept a higher target with *no* additional resources. For example, the steel industry may be told that it is wasting too much coal, so it should find a more efficient way to use the coal it has. The steel industry might also be told it has excessive reserves or inventories of coal, so it can use some of those to make more steel. In this way, the secondary effects of a change in the amount of one product are kept to a minimum by removing the assumption that a fixed ratio of each resource is necessary for production of each unit of output. Of course, this shortcut can only be used within narrow limits.

Waste in the Soviet Union

The Soviet Union does *not* have aggregate unemployment. There is, however, some amount of "frictional unemployment," which could be lessened by more rapid retraining of workers for new jobs. Furthermore, there are some workers who are formally employed but who are doing not much of anything because of bureaucratic inefficiency in assignments.

More important are the inefficiencies in planning caused by (1) lack of sufficient information at the center, and (2) lack of sufficient trained manpower and machines to perform all the necessary calculations. First, the plan often commands enterprises to do more than is physically possible, leading to excess demand and inflation (and the fluctuations described in the next chapter). Second, there is often imbalance between various sectors and industries, so that an enterprise is held back from meeting its target because of a lack of key inputs. Third, some resources (labor, capital, and materials) are incorrectly allocated at the margin to enterprises and industries with a lower social priority than others that could use the same resources. (These problems have been discussed in Chapter 14.) Finally, we may add the inefficiencies of Soviet managers in carrying out the plan (see Chapter 18).

In spite of its continuing wastes and inefficiencies, the Soviet Union has performed better than the Western capitalist countries in the realm of economic growth. Not only are its growth rates higher, but even hostile Western estimates place its output per unit of capital equal to or greater than the U.S. output unit of capital.[22]

It is probably true that at any given moment capitalist economies use resources more closely in step with consumer demands (that is, demands of consumers with money). "The Soviet economy . . . always produces too many, say, toothbrushes and too few nailbrushes in view of consumer tastes and needs and in view of the total volume of resources allocated to consumption. Moreover, both kinds of brush are of low quality, and they are all colored, say pink, which is depressing."[23] Yet even Western critics admit that rapid Soviet growth brings more benefits to Soviet consumers in the long run than would more static efficiency in resource allocation among consumer needs. "But the Western rates of growth are in fact slower, and quality does in fact improve in the U.S.S.R and even variety increases. So in the end the Soviet consumer will be better supplied even with nailbrushes."[24]

Insofar as exploitation exists in the Soviet Union (discussed in Chapter 13), we may condemn as waste some of the luxury living of the elite, but this is minute compared to the similar waste in the United States.

There is a certain amount of propaganda in favor of the present ruling leadership, but this is much less than the resources spent in political campaigns in the United States. Although there is now some informative economic advertising in the USSR, there is little or none of the wasteful competitive advertising so abundant under capitalism.

We shall see that there is still some amount of racial and sexual discrimination in the USSR. The waste of human resources in the Soviet Union as a result of such discriminations is, however, incomparably less than in the United States (as we shall see in Chapter 21).

We shall see in the rest of this chapter that there is some pollution in the Soviet Union, but again much, much less than in the United States.

Unfortunately, the Soviet Union does spend about the same percentage of resources on military production as does the United States.

Pollution in the Soviet Union

No experts, least of all Soviet writers, deny that there is some amount of pollution and lack of conservation in the Soviet Union. While there are no aggregate data, we may note some of the more important of a long list of officially admitted incidents:

1. Careless crop-dusting with pesticides has killed much bird life
2. Dumping of sewage and industrial wastes into many rivers and lakes (with a great outcry over pollution of Lake Baikal), killing the fish and making the water unusable for drinking or recreation
3. Cutting of forests to the point where there is not enough growth to hold back the soil when it rains, creating shifting sands in some areas and vastly increasing silt in rivers and lakes
4. Lack of selective cutting that would preserve forests as a future resource; the lack of forest cover has also reduced animal life
5. Lack of sufficient purification equipment in industrial plants
6. Taking over agricultural land by industry

On the other side, the Soviet Union has taken the lead in passing laws against pollution and in favor of conservation. As early as 1918 and 1919, laws were passed to protect forests and national monuments, to restrict hunting, to protect fish, and to stop industrial contamination of water resources. In the 1930's and 1940's however, the emphasis on rapid industrialization meant neglect of conservation and increased pollution. The Russian Republic (RSFSR) finally passed an excellent conservation law in 1960. The whole Soviet Union (USSR) introduced a stiffer conservation and antipollution law in 1968.[25] Moreover, in 1963 the State Sanitary Inspection Service was given the authority to veto all future blueprints for construction projects and design norms.

257

The laws are not bad, but the enforcement has been far from perfect. The reasons why the Soviet Union has so far had much less pollution than the United States are quite different, being both technical and institutional. In the first place, the Soviet Union has a lower population density and a lower level of economic development, both making for lower levels of destruction and pollution. Moreover, the Soviet Union has a great many less gas-burning automobiles. Furthermore, the Soviet Union does have comprehensive *planning*, both for new cities and for new factories.

Finally, the Soviet Union has public ownership and no private profit motive in industrial production. Since no one makes private profit from production, why is there any resistance to conservation and control of pollution? There *is* resistance, both from managers and from some higher industries.

The manager's bonus (and promotion) depends on producing maximum output at minimum cost. Until recently, his penalties for polluting or unnecessarily destroying natural resources were negligible compared with his rewards for meeting production targets.

Unlike the United States, higher economic agencies can directly order the manager to take conservation and antipollution steps. Unfortunately, they are also under enormous pressure to produce goods, while the pressure for conservation has been much less important until recently. "Any expense that detracts from the performance of the Soviet factory in the region similarly detracts from the economic performance of the overall region. Therefore, political and party officials frequently find themselves more in agreement with the polluters than with the conservationists."[26] Only agencies separate from the task of economic production, such as the State Sanitary Inspection Service, can give undivided loyalty to conservation in the Soviet Union.

Thus one Soviet problem has been to create a single strong conservation agency from the many different agencies that have been partly concerned with it in the past. Another problem has been to give the conservation agencies real teeth, that is, legal power to supervise all economic activity, and to directly intervene against destruction or pollution. Moreover, the conservation agencies need enough manpower to enforce the laws effectively.

Since the Soviet government owns and runs industry, their pollution problem is even more directly political than the American problem. Whereas in America the obstacle to sanitation and conservation has been profit-hungry corporations, in the Soviet Union it has been a bureaucracy devoted to more and more production at a high human cost—a bureaucracy led by a self-perpetuating leadership without much democratic control. Nevertheless, the lack of private enterprise *has* led to more conservation and less pollution.

Growth, Waste, and Pollution in Socialism

NOTES

1. For empirical data on the ratios and the average growth rate, see, e.g., Simon S. Kuznets, *National Product since 1869* (New York: National Bureau of Economic Research, Inc., 1946).

2. The data used in this paragraph are discussed in detail in my book, *The Soviet Economy* (Boston: Little, Brown, 1969), Chapter 5.

3. John Gurley, article in *Mainland China in the World Economy*, Hearings of the Joint Economic Committee, U.S. Congress (Washington, D.C., U.S. Government Printing Office, 1967), p. 188.

4. Franklyn Holzman, "Discussion of Economic Development in Mainland China," *American Economic Review*, 51 (May 1961): 518–519.

5. Central Statistical Board of the USSR Council of Ministers, *National Economy of the U.S.S.R.* (Moscow: Foreign Languages Publishing House, 1957), p. 47.

6. All data from Seymour M. Rosen, "Changing Guideposts in Soviet Education," in U.S. Congress, Joint Economic Committee, *New Directions in the Soviet Economy* (Washington, D.C.: U.S. Government Printing Office, 1966), Appendixes A and B.

7. Nicholas DeWitt, "High-Level Manpower in the U.S.S.R.," in U.S. Congress, Joint Economic Committee, *New Directions in the Soviet Economy* (Washington, D.C.: U.S. Government Printing Office, 1966), p. 802.

8. DeWitt, *op. cit.*, p. 816.

9. See the discussion in Evsey D. Domar, "A Soviet Model of Growth," *Essays in the Theory of Economic Growth* (New York: Oxford University Press, 1957). The original Feldman article, "On the Theory of Growth Rates of National Income," is transl. in Nicholas Spulber, *Foundations of Soviet Strategy for Economic Growth: Selected Soviet Essays, 1924–30* (Bloomington: Indiana University Press, 1964).

10. An extended critique of this doctrine may be found in P. J. D. Wiles, *The Political Economy of Communism* (Cambridge: Harvard University Press, 1964), pp. 272–300.

11. See the similar view by a Soviet economist in V. Volkonskii, "Methods of Mathematical Economics and the Theory of Planning and Administering the Economy," transl. in *Problems of Economics*, 10 (November 1967): 3–10.

12. For a full presentation of Marx's views on Malthus, see R. L. Meek, ed., *Malthus: Selections from Marx and Engels* (New York: International Publishers, 1958).

13. Han Suyin, *China in the Year 2001* (New York: Basic Books, 1967), p. 106.

14. For a recent and sophisticated discussion by a Soviet writer, see A. A. Konus, "Dynamic Intersector Balances in Perspective Planning," *Economics of Planning*, 4 (1964): 1–15.

15. Marx, "The Reproduction and Circulation of the Aggregate Social Capital," *Capital*, vol. 2, part 3.

16. See, e.g., the confused discussion by Shigeto Tsuru, "On Reproduction Schemes," in Appendix A of Paul Sweezy, *Theory of Capitalist Development* (New York: Monthly Review Press, 1941), pp. 365–372.

17. See Oskar Lange, *Introduction to Econometrics* (New York: Pergamon Press, 1959), pp. 218–228.

18. See, e.g., his simplified explanation in W. Leontief, "Input-Output Economics," *Scientific American* (October 1951): 3–9.

19. Maurice Dobb, *Soviet Economic Development since 1917* (New York: International Publishers, 1966 ed.), p. 361.

20. This is the view of many Soviet economists; see, e.g., V. S. Nemchinov, "Mathematical Methods in Economics," in V. S. Nemchinov, ed., *The Use of Mathematics in Economics* (London: Oliver and Boyd, 1964, English edition ed. by A. Nove), p. 24.

259

21. Input-output and its limitations in the context of Soviet planning are explained in Howard Sherman, *The Soviet Economy* (Boston: Little, Brown, 1969), Chapter 10. A simple exposition is W. M. Miernyk, *The Elements of Input-Output Analysis* (New York: Random House, 1965). A more advanced exposition is H. B. Chenery and P. G. Clark, *Interindustry Economics* (New York: John Wiley & Sons, 1959).

22. See, e.g., Abram Bergson, *The Economics of Soviet Planning* (New Haven: Yale University Press, 1964), p. 342.

23. Peter Wiles, "The Pursuit of Affluence," in Samuel Hendel and Randolph Braham, *The U.S.S.R. after 50 Years* (New York: Alfred Knopf, 1967), p. 72.

24. Wiles, "The Pursuit of Affluence," *op. cit.*, p. 72.

25. *Current Digest of the Soviet Press*, vol. 20, no. 30 (August 14, 1968).

26. Marshall Goldman, *Controlling Pollution* (Englewood Cliffs, N.J.: Prentice-Hall, 1967), p. 9.

CHAPTER
17

Cyclical Fluctuations in Socialism

In Czechoslovakia, Poland, East Germany, and Hungary for the years 1950 through 1966 the data indicate that "the rate of growth of industrial production shows relatively regular fluctuations. . . ."[1] An actual decline in production occured only in Czechoslovakia in 1963. The same kind of periodic fluctuations seem to characterize Soviet growth rates.

Causes of Fluctuations

What are the causes of these cyclical fluctuations? A centralized bureaucracy, goaded by an impatient political leadership, creates impossibly ambitious plans, impossible to fulfill. More specifically, overoptimistic planning leads to supply bottlenecks. Excessive investment in new projects leads to a relative lack of the basic raw materials necessary to complete these projects. Thus, these countries frequently witness a large number of uncompleted construction projects. The rate of growth declines because these partly finished factories cannot yet produce anything.

Eventually the planners recognize this situation as new productive capacity and output fails to reach planned targets. Then they are forced to reduce new investment projects, so that the old ones can be completed. This relaxation of the investment pace is often sudden and uncoordinated, so it may even further lower the growth rate by reduction of all investment. Nevertheless, the reduction of the number of construction projects soon eases the disproportions, brings material supplies into balance with investment demands, and allows completion of existing construction projects. This makes possible a new balanced expansion.

THE POLITICAL ECONOMY OF SOCIALISM

Success of the new expansion produces higher growth rates once more. This again leads to overoptimism, "overplanning," new disproportions, and a new slowdown. Thus the cycle repeats itself again and again, being caused by "subjective" mistakes by politicians and planners. It is, however, the objective fact of an overcentralized planning structure that leads to these recurrent mistakes.

Length of the Cycle

The length of the cycle is based mainly on the construction time and gestation period of investment. A new wave of investment causes excess demand and supply barriers. The period of reduced growth lasts until the new investment is finally completed (after the forced slowdown on further investment has made supplies available). The new capacity in turn increases supplies, further aiding new expansion. The length of the period of high growth rates is based on the time for the new capacity to reach full use, then the data to reflect that, and overoptimistic planning to lead to new bottlenecks.

A secondary factor is inventory investment. As the slowdown begins to ease supplies, enterprises feel safe to carry lower inventories of raw materials relative to production. Thus, they further increase available supply, and aid the rapid growth of production facilities. But when the economy is overheated (by overplanning), they try to hoard inventories, thereby further straining supplies. Thus the hoarding of inventories in bottleneck periods and the rapid using up of reserve inventories in periods of smooth expansion simply intensifies the slowed growth in the one case and the rapid growth in the other.

Finally, for the smaller countries of East Europe, foreign trade complications also add to and intensify the cycle. In a rapid upswing, more imports are necessary, and exports cannot be increased immediately. Only later, when the new capacity is actually in use, can exports be considerably increased to obtain more imports.

Differences from Capitalist Cycles

In spite of certain superficial similarities, the fluctuations in the growth rates of output in the socialist countries are fundamentally different from the fluctuations of capitalist business. Capitalist business cycles have usually been much more violent in effect, normally resulting in actual declines in output (and employment), rather than mere slowed growth. More important, the fluctuations in socialism result primarily from lack of crucial supplies, whereas the fluctuations in capitalism result primarily from lack of effective consumer and investor demand.

Furthermore, the cycles under socialism are caused by mistakes in planning (due to overcentralization, bureaucratic remoteness from facts, and lack of criticism), while cycles under capitalism are an inherent and automatic result of the economic system (traceable mainly to exploitation, which causes the maldistribution of income, leading to restriction of consumer demand; see Chapter 6). Cycles in capitalism can be lessened by government intervention, but can be ended only by a change to socialism. Cycles in socialism can be ended by better central planning, decentralization of some decisions, and allowance of democratic criticism, leaving the socialist system intact.

NOTES

1. Josef Goldmann and Karel Kouba, *Economic Growth in Czechoslovakia* (Prague: Academia, 1969), p. 41.

18

Market Socialism

Socialism in the modern world has usually meant central planning. We shall examine in this chapter the hesitant Soviet debate and reforms and the much bolder Eastern European debate and decentralization reforms. Finally, we shall compare capitalism, centrally planned socialism, and decentralized or market socialism.

Sources of Decentralization Debate

Marx himself wrote very little about the details of socialist planning, always emphasizing that it would be utopian to discuss such details before the advent of an actual socialist economy. His few comments relating to this subject are clearly tangential and not directly to the point. For example, in his diatribe against Proudhon, he defends the large-scale economic unit, and attacks any idea of a return to very small-scale farming and artisan enterprises.[1] Nevertheless, planning within large-scale units is still far from central planning.

Marx also attacked the capitalist "anarchy of production," that is, he disapproved of the competitive or market mechanism under capitalism as being unplanned or anarchical and thereby allowing extreme fluctuations and instability in economic life.[2] Engels, with Marx's approval, wrote that

every society based on commodity production has the peculiarity that in it the producers have lost control of their own social relationships. . . . No one knows how much of the article he produces is coming on to the market, or how much demand there is for it; no one knows whether his individual product will meet a real need, whether he will cover his costs or even be able to sell it at all. Anarchy reigns in social production.[3]

It is clear that Marx and Engels disapproved of the planlessness of capitalism. In addition, they felt it to be an important cause of the periodic crises

264

of depression or inflation. Nevertheless, this does not show that they would necessarily disapprove of the market device under socialism, since socialism provides a very different economic environment.

Early Soviet Experience

The experience of the New Economic Policy (NEP) in the Soviet Union in the 1920's can legitimately be considered relevant to a discussion of decentralization. During the NEP period, even large-scale Soviet industrial firms were made financially independent, and were allowed a high degree of autonomous decision-making. A positive evaluation of performance under NEP would emphasize that small-scale enterprises flourished and recovered even beyond prewar levels in the 1920's. On the other hand, its critics argue that under NEP Soviet heavy industry failed to accumulate much new capital for expansion beyond the prewar level.[4]

Lange's Model

In connection with the debate on the possibility of rational planning, mention was made of the decentralized socialism advocated by Lange.[5] This scheme not only played a role in that debate, but figures in the present debate on decentralization. Although Lange mentioned the possibility of price and output decisions by completely independent socialist firms, his emphasis was on a somewhat more centralized proposal.[6] In brief, he proposed (1) that the central planners set some more or less arbitrary prices, basing them simply on the presocialist prices, and then (2) that the planners should change them if, at those prices, there is excess demand as shown by long lines of unsatisfied consumers of excess supply as shown by goods left on the shelves. At the same time, (3) the managers would produce up to the point where their marginal cost equals the given price, that is, where profit is at a maximum. In long-run decisions, (4) industries would invest up to the point where their average cost is at a minimum. On the other side, (5) central planners would loan capital to firms at that rate of interest which would equalize firm demand with the supply of capital determined at the center. Finally, (6) households would have freedom of choice as to where to work and as to what consumer goods to buy with their wages. This model was long considered purely hypothetical, and was disowned by Lange as a practical proposal. Nevertheless, its argument has greatly influenced the current practice and proposals in Eastern Europe.

Recent Soviet Experience

Soviet planning reforms may have been generated partly by the increasing complexity of the economy and partly by the shortage of labor. This view contends that rational planning and decentralization are more necessary in relatively advanced countries than in less developed countries.[7] Technical innovation is now the most important Soviet goal, and that innovation depends mainly on continuous local initiative at the production point. By contrast, in the early Soviet Union the central problem was not technological improvement, but putting to work in industry the resources that were unemployed or less profitably employed in agriculture.[8]

Soviet Managerial Behavior before the 1965 Reforms

To understand the Soviet debate, we must first examine the behavior of the Soviet managers under the old system. We shall then understand why the critics argued that attention to cost-cutting and profit-making could hardly make the Soviet manager act in a more greedy, bourgeois manner than he did under the prereform system. Under the prereform system, if he fulfills or overfulfills his plan each month, he receives an additional large bonus. These bonuses generally run from 25 to 50 per cent of the manager's salary. The unsuccessful manager will lose bonuses and ultimately lose his job or be demoted to a less important operation.

Since the manager is under great pressure to produce, he resorts to many evasions. His performance is judged by several criteria, including wage and raw material costs per unit and other indicators of productivity and efficiency. The main success indicator, however, and the one he strives above all to achieve, is simply the value of the gross output produced. If he does not achieve the planned value of output, he receives no bonus at all. If, however, he exactly meets the planned target, he may receive as much as a full 40 per cent bonus, although the average bonus is somewhat less. For each 1 per cent overfulfillment of the plan, managers in high-priority industries receive an additional 4 to 6 per cent bonus.

The Soviet manager brushes aside bureaucratic regulations and controls when they conflict with the achievement of output goals. To a great extent, the manager evades specific regulations only in order to meet his plan. This may or may not be to the national benefit. For example, the manager sometimes merely gets around red tape in order to obtain materials that should have been his anyway. On other occasions, however, he may obtain materials illegally that could be better used by a higher priority enterprise. Unfortunately, some of the manager's devices, like lowering quality in order to produce greater output, yield a bonus for an *apparent* plan fulfill- ment which constitutes, in fact, an antisocial act. This type of antisocial behavior is not dissimilar to the well-known evasions of the corporate in- come tax or antitrust laws by managers of American corporations. The specific practices of Soviet managers (all before the 1965 reforms) are as follows:[9]

1. *False reports.* Obviously, if his production for the month would just miss 100 per cent of the planned target, he will try hard to increase the produc- tion figures by inclusion of waste or unfinished goods in order to get his bonus. Or, rather than complete falsification, he may simply shift his report of some production from a very high month to a low one. Some managers, but not many, actually do outright falsification (since the system forces them to do so to survive). Falsification is dangerous, though, because the manager turns in a very large volume of related reports, which are examined for internal consistency by the bank auditors or by his superiors.

More important, there are many different channels of control over the manager, and these channels are independent enough so that collusion by all agents is very difficult. There is first of all the superior agency that controls the enterprise, whether it is under an industrial ministry or a regional council. Second, the Communist Party has cells in each enterprise, and these have certain rights to inspect and suggest improvements on enterprise projects. A third line of control is through the trade unions, one of whose functions is the stimulation of production. A fourth line of control is through the State Bank, in which every enterprise keeps accounts. At times, there have also been special ministries of "state control," whose sole function was to check on the legality of enterprise actions. In addition, a sixth line of control reaches down from the Central Statistical Agency. The trouble is that all these agencies carry the information to different places, so it is very hard to cross-check. Moreover, bribery—direct and subtle—reaches them all; and all the controllers at the local level tend to form a coalition with the manager.

2. *Easier plans.* The manager himself must play an important role in formulating the plan. He naturally bargains for a lower output target and a higher amount of required supplies. In this way, output targets are more easily overfulfilled. Moreover, if his target is gross production, he can often add into his reports the value of materials on which production has just begun.

3. *Poorer quality.* If a plan cannot be met in the necessary quantities by producing what is supposed to be produced, it can often be fulfilled by produc- ing a poorer quality of goods. Some Soviet consumer goods have been of notoriously poor quality.

4. *Fewer styles.* It is much easier to produce a large amount of one homo- geneous set of goods than it is to produce small quantities of many different goods. Managers therefore have an incentive to produce all of one type of good, rather than a variety, although the latter might lead to more consumer satisfaction. Because the price is fixed, he does not depend on demand. Man- agers do, though, sometimes introduce a "new" style just to get assigned a higher price.

5. *Easiest mixture.* In fact, the type or style on which production is con-

centrated may be chosen, not on the basis of usefulness to the economy but because it is the cheapest method of achieving the output goal.

6. *Extra supplies.* It is a well-known fact that managers keep on their payroll men whose only function is to expedite the flow of supplies, or to find new sources of supply outside the planned sources. These men are known as "pushers," although they have some other title on the official payroll. They often enjoy pleasant lives on expense accounts, wining and dining officials of other firms and of various higher organizations who may be able to furnish scarce supplies (by barter or bribery). They are the counterpart of the American "expediters" of World War II, who hung around Washington trying to get a ration of scarce materials for their firms.

7. *Hidden reserves.* A wise Soviet manager piles up inventories of any goods he can get his hands on, regardless of whether he happens to need them or not at the moment. When his output target is raised, he can use these extra reserves—when he is unable to procure more supplies legally. In this way a large amount of resources may be wasted, frozen in an unproductive storage stage of the productive process.

8. *Extra labor.* The manager has a plan for labor and for the total amount of wages he can spend. Overspending on wages, however, is usually very lightly punished if at all, whereas meeting the output target washes him clean of all crimes.

9. *High-priced raw materials.* A Soviet manager is penalized very little for high costs, and given a great reward for overfulfilling his output target: thus, he has no reason not to use high-priced raw materials. Moreover, he is judged not by the value added in the enterprise, but by the gross value of the product *including* the value of the raw materials which were merely bought from other firms. Therefore, the higher the price of the raw materials he buys, the higher the value of his gross output, and the greater his own reward. Naturally, Soviet managers have an incentive to buy the more expensive raw materials for their enterprise to use.

10. *Resistance to innovations.* The Soviet manager frequently does not react with enthusiasm to innovations that *may* increase his productive capacity or lower costs. In the first place, innovations are risky because they may actually lower output for some months while the transition is being made to new machinery. Managers seldom take the long-run view because they are often switched to other jobs on fairly short notice. The idea of these frequent changes in positions is to prevent corruption and collusion (or "familyness") from developing, but it also means that managers focus their attention on immediate production gains and are not willing to gamble on higher bonuses from greatly increased production at some future date.

In the second place, the manager knows that if the innovation does succeed in greatly increasing his capacity to produce, his production targets will also be increased, so he himself may gain nothing. If the plan is overfulfilled by a large margin, targets are apt to be raised in the same proportion. So a manager is likely to try for a steady 103 or 105 per cent overfulfillment, but not more.

The tendencies described did exist (and still do to a lesser extent), but they should certainly not be taken to mean that Soviet managers are more inefficient than American managers. The Soviet economy *has* produced higher peacetime growth than the American economy, despite Soviet inefficiencies. This dysfunctional behavior does imply that the growth achieved was at greater cost and sacrifice than necessary, or that growth could have been faster with the same amount of effort. The fact that some degree of inefficiency did exist in the old system of central planning is the driving force behind the recent decentralization reforms and the continued fight for more reforms.

Course of the Debate

Within the atmosphere of increased freedom for scientific inquiry after 1956, there arose a faction of economists whose approach was quite pragmatic. They analyzed organizational matters and very concrete issues of policy; they sought experiments and solutions to deal with limited problems. Criticism of the malfunctions of the enterprise incentive system during the 1950's flowed largely from their evidence and conclusions.

Kharkov Professor Evsei G. Liberman was one of these critics. In fact, he was not the most important critic, but happened to be the chosen instrument of the political leaders to set off the public debate. Liberman published three papers in Soviet journals during the 1950's.[10] He argued that specific problems created by existing success indicators could be overcome by appropriate changes in the operational constraints of enterprises. The scheme of reforms he advocated in the 1959 paper was essentially of the same kind as that which touched off the 1962 controversy. However, until 1962 neither this man nor his recommendations were the subject of public focus or the attentions of other writers.

The debate was given urgency when the Soviet political leadership became alarmed over the retardation in growth rates apparent in the early 1960's. As already noted, these difficulties as well as the need for reform may both be due to the growing complexity and interdependence of Soviet allocations, which make it increasingly difficult to devise priority rankings and balance the plan. The opposite argument by some American economists, that the problems may be purely temporary and unconnected with the level of development, may also be noted. These more noneconomic factors would include poor weather, the enormous manpower losses of the Second World War, too much extravagance with foreign aid, and increased spending on military and space ventures.

Essentials of the Liberman Plan

In September, 1962, the Communist party initiated a public discussion by allowing Liberman to publish his plan in the main newspapers and journals.[11] The Kharkov incentive system (as Liberman calls his plan) openly calls for structural changes in the planning process, but only at the level of the firm. All the investments, prices, and outputs are to continue to be centrally planned. The relationship of the planning apparatus to the individual enterprise, however, is to be fundamentally changed.

To encourage greater flexibility and initiative, the large number of indicator targets presently passed down to the firm is to be streamlined to "key indices" only. Liberman recommends assigning enterprises just those targets which exclusively pertain to their final output mix: quantity and assortment of production, product destinations, and delivery dates. The *input* mix is to be determined by each individual firm: the planners will then presumably sum up all the enterprise needs, and provide for them through the centrally planned system of material allocations (though this would be quite difficult).

How well an enterprise fulfills society's demand for maximum efficiency is to be assessed solely on the basis of "ultimate efficiency." Profitability, which is defined to be profits expressed as a percentage of total capital, is to serve as this inclusive evaluator, and is to be estimated in yearly plans submitted by all firms. Once the stated output goals are attained, the rate of profitability achieved becomes the sole determinant of the amount of bonus funds awarded to the firm and its employees. Since the criterion is profit rather than output, products must now be *sold* and not just produced. Liberman depicts the central planners as "relieved from petty tutelage over enterprises" and from "costly efforts to influence production through administrative measures rather than economic ones."[12]

Bonus payments to enterprises are to be computed by comparing the profitability rate of a particular firm with a "profitability norm" established for the branch of industry within which each firm is to be included. The attempt is to set a "single standard of profitability for enterprises in roughly the same natural and technical conditions." Norms also are to vary with the proportion of new products in a firm's production program—being raised, for example, when no new products are being introduced. Different incentive payment scales will then be set up for the different branches of industry. The bonus premiums earned by the firm under this system will be utilized, as the manager directs, to (1) pay salary bonuses to management and workers, (2) provide new housing, nurseries, kindergartens, and recreation facilities for worker families, and (3) finance small, decentralized investments.

To motivate directors to attempt as ambitious a plan as their productive potential allows, Liberman advances three proposals. First, incentive premiums per ruble of capital invested are to rise as the rate of profit increases. Second, the firm is to benefit more from fulfilling its own profitability plan than from overfulfilling it. Third, the norms of profitability are to be established "for an extended period of time" (from two to five years or more).

This will prevent the harmful practice of raising norms whenever a firm surpasses its planned targets. In this way, the firms' directors can count on reaping benefits from successful innovations or particularly effective cost-saving programs. The concern for profitability is also supposed to stimulate the manager to search for cost reductions and to produce the output mix demanded by his consumers.

Soviet Controversy, 1962–1963

Both moderate and active supporters of the Liberman system in the Soviet Union agree that a "rational" price system is a necessary precondition for a profit-based index to serve as an effective evaluator of enterprise efficiency. Although Liberman himself has been somewhat indefinite about the changes in pricing methodology which would be necessary to achieve this "rationality," others (such as V. S. Nemchinov) have taken a strong stand for many years. Since profits derive from selling prices and cost prices, profitability will be a measure of real, and not merely of paper, efficiency only if prices reflect the relative values of all inputs into production. Consequently, one Soviet writer asserts that a substantial price deviation "above or below the socially necessary outlays, results, regardless of the operation of the enterprise, either in an unjustifiably low profitability, and even loss, or in excessive profitability."[13]

One group of Soviet writers argued further that the existing material supply system was too complex and inflexible to give enterprises the freedom of input determination envisioned in Liberman's incentive scheme. Therefore, they advocated replacing administrative allocation with a system of "state trade," in which enterprises would negotiate independent agreements with suppliers and customers.[14] Nemchinov boldly argued that all planning of intermediate goods should cease; the State should decide only what final products it needs.[15]

The majority of responses to *Pravda*'s 1962 request for discussion, however, were characterized by either total hostility to Liberman's scheme or considerable criticism. For example, Zverev, former minister of finance, denounced the theory he sees lurking behind Libermanism: that profit is created not only by the worker's labor, but also by fixed and current capital. "It is hardly necessary to prove the erroneousness of such a theory."[16] (Notice that he is confusing the productivity of capital with the productivity of capitalists, while none of the reformers says this nor do any of them advocate paying profits to individuals.) Second, he argued against the premise that the central planners are less informed as to the capabilities of enterprises than the enterprise itself. They "are obligated to know, and actually do know, the production capacities of enterprises."[17] Third, he points to the profitability "norms" to be established for branches of industry, asserts that they would not be objective for all firms in a grouping, and predicts that constantly changing technical conditions among firms would cause persistent pressure on any norm-setting government agency to revise the norm. The only way to keep the norms "fair," he concludes, would be to revise them continuously.[18]

Furthermore, a full measure of hostility was unleashed to attack the increase in decentralized investment likely to occur with the adoption of a Liberman scheme. Convinced that existing defects in "capital construction" are due to insufficient centralization, several writers emphatically decried the proposal to leave an increased number of investment decisions with the enterprises. They claimed that enterprises are "ignorant of the various national economic interrelations," so that the effect would be to increase "parochialism" and to multiply "disproportions in the national economy."[19] (Actually, Liberman never advocated decentralization of major investment decisions.)

Professor Liberman's reply in 1962 to his critics makes some interesting points. First, Liberman attempts to clear away the confused notion held by some that profitability alone would be the single index to regulate enterprise behavior. The production goals which society demands of enterprises, including the quantity and assortment of output, are still to be centrally planned and individually assigned to firms. Only after meeting the output targets does profitability take prime importance for the firm. Second, he counters the charge that successful enterprises will be able to rest on past efficiency achievements. He asserts that "even a small increase in incentive payments is of some interest" and that "every manufacturing enterprise must constantly introduce new production . . . or its incentive scale will drop."[20]

By May, 1963, however, controversy had died down considerably. The government gave no further indication of its readiness to alter the basics of its system of minutely detailed planning and supervision of enterprises. Yet during the lull in public debate which lingered through mid-1964, problems with unsold consumer goods became critical. It was apparently the unwanted inventory increases that precipitated the first Soviet experiments with profit incentives and direct ties to consumers.

Specifically, the drastic situation of soaring inventories of textile and clothing goods stirred the government in early 1964 to place two large garment manufacturing associations—the "Bolshevicka" in Moscow and the "Mayak" in Gorky—under the rules of a new system. This system has some of the characteristics of Liberman's scheme, at least in spirit, if not in detail. The two producers were to work out their own output plans on the basis of orders from retail outlets, and their performance was to be judged by sales rather than output, though not by profit as in Liberman's scheme. They were to negotiate their own contracts with principal suppliers, and financial penalties were to be levied for failure to make deliveries according to contract. In spite of a number of predictable difficulties, especially difficulties with surrounding bureaucracy, both associations overfulfilled output and profit plans for the year. The USSR Council of National Economy decided to extend the experiment to 400 associations in the textile, clothing, leather, and footwear industries during 1965. There were even trials of the new system among a few factories manufacturing producer goods.

The Resumption of Debate, 1964–1965

Shortly after this initial experimentation with greater incentives began, public discussion was again requested by the editors of *Pravda*.[21] The inference is that desires for economic reform from within the Party had significantly grown in the interim. The Party was probably influenced by the intensification of the Soviet economy's problems from 1962 to 1964, including the rapidly mounting inventories of consumer goods, the grain crop failures in 1963 and the declining growth rate. The Soviet party was surely also influenced by the virtual stagnation of the Czech economy in 1963, the inception in 1964 of profit sharing and a charge on capital in Hungary, and the continued existence of the decentralized Yugoslav system.

Another lead article by Liberman in *Pravda* in 1964 reiterated his position and, in addition, advocated a charge on capital. Within six months, the newspaper reported having received 600 articles and letters in response. The bulk of public communication at this time showed a substantial shift in mood from the 1962 controversy. The author of "Survey of Readers' Letters" in *Pravda* (February 17, 1965) concluded that the overwhelming majority of writers felt it necessary to "intensify sharply the role of economic levers in the management of the national economy to expand the rights of enterprises, to enhance the importance of profit . . . and to put price formation in order." Expressions of total hostility were practically nonexistent, while an expanded and vocal group of economists, research workers, and enterprise managers became increasingly insistent in their demands for the adoption of widespread change.

The degree of enterprise autonomy urged by some of the writers now went considerably beyond the Liberman plan and its 1962 extensions.[22] Arguing that output plans should be based on orders from customers, they asserted first that enterprises "should be given the right to amend the output plan with the consent of the customer," and second that when an enterprise is producing a product "with higher consumer properties than are stipulated by the standards, it should be given the right to fix the price with the agreement of the customer." One Soviet author at that time even proposed to abolish central price-setting, and replace it by competition ruled by consumer demand.[23]

The goals of most hopeful reformers, however, did not at first include changes which would decentralize price-setting. Their main new demand was for the introduction of direct links with suppliers in order to supplant the unwieldy system of central supply allocations. They were also loud in demanding a price calculus with capital charges. Nevertheless, complete central control over national parameters (including prices) was still regarded as integral to the preservation of economic balances and a high rate of accumulation.[24] Only after the reforms actually began in 1966 and 1967 was considerable sentiment voiced for price decentralization as well as output decentralization.

Official Reforms

Although "economic experiments" were extended and given more varied trials during 1965, it was not until September of that year that the government responded with a major organizational reform in industry, which moved somewhat in the direction of the Liberman proposals. Adopted as law by the Supreme Soviet on October 2nd, the stipulations of the Kosygin reform were conservative and tentative, yet they did begin the process of reform.[25] The section pertaining to the individual enterprise contained four significant new policies. First, and most important, managers' bonuses are to be paid for fulfillment of planned targets for sales, profit or profitability, and physical output. Moreover, to evaluate the amount of sales, the "gross value of output" indicator is to be replaced by "output sold," which implies the necessity to produce what consumers desire. Numerous target directives will be eliminated, including the norms for labor productivity, number of workers and employees, and average wages.

Second, the enterprise will be permitted to retain and utilize a large proportion of profits (and some portion of depreciation allowances) for bonuses, welfare purpses, and decentralized investment. This may turn out to be a very significant measure, giving financial muscle to the decentralization reforms. Third, half of centralized investment is to be financed by repayable and interest-bearing loans from banks, and interest charges are to be levied (in the form of a tax) on all fixed and working capital put

274

at the enterprise's disposal.[26] Fourth, contracts between enterprises are to be more strictly enforced, prohibiting superiors from changing enterprise plans at will during the plan period. Incidentally, at the same time, Khrushchev's regional economic councils were abolished, and industrial direction was returned to about twenty central industrial ministries, but with provision for the now increased autonomy of individual enterprises.

Some of the reform measures do approach the spirit, if not the letter, of Liberman's scheme. Attention to what has been left out of the Kosygin system, however, gives us a more pessimistic view of the possibility that the reform will implement the kind of changes which Liberman sympathizers have been proposing. For example, it has been pointed out numerous times that any attempt at a greater reliance on profitability criteria would be useless (or even harmful) without a rational price system. Yet the wholesale price reform has been very slow in coming, and has not made the more drastic changes requested by Soviet reformers. Furthermore, the new committee charged with price policy was told no more than that prices should reflect costs, a remarkably insufficient suggestion considering that economists and planners have been arguing the basic principle for at least ten years.

Moreover, the new economic system continues to maintain the method of direct materials allocation, although there are new reports of some attempts to replace or modify it by the introduction of large wholesale warehouse–type establishments in which enterprises can buy anything they need. As long as the system of direct materials allocation is continued, the reforms certainly will not result in the Liberman objective of enterprise freedom to vary inputs. Notice that the reformed system also keeps the central limits on total payrolls, and allows managers only to choose the labor mix within those limits. At the same time, the apparent intent to allow more decentralized investments may result in a significant decrease in central control over the determination of future output. Indeed, as we noted in describing this reform, the allowance of a large amount of decentralized investment may turn out to be one of the most important practical features of the reform.

On the other hand, it must be admitted that even these limited Soviet reforms have already run into bureaucratic obstruction and sabotage. Thus, there have been numerous reports of continued extralegal interference by government and Party organs in the day-to-day operations of enterprises, including those on the new system. The undoubted difficulties of the new system will be resolved eventually either by retrogression (renewed centralization) or by further reform (toward real market socialism). Which direction is taken will depend on many factors, including external ones such as peace in Vietnam.

The Yugoslav Model

The Yugoslav experience revealed to the whole world that an economy could be largely decentralized and directed mainly by the market, while remaining socialist. Although it was at first denounced with the usual Stalinist unanimity, later, when the anti-Stalinist tide began to rise, the Yugoslav economy became a model to investigate.

The Cominform (or Communist Information Bureau) was formed in 1947 by Stalin primarily as a means of keeping Eastern Europe, and perhaps especially Yugoslavia, on a tight leash. In 1948, however, Yugoslavia broke with the USSR, and took a position advocating complete independence and equality for all socialist nations. The Yugoslavs complained that the Russians had attempted to dominate their army, to exploit their economy through joint companies, to use secret agents to investigate and blackmail important Yugoslavs, and to threaten the cutting off of all trade should Yugoslavia take any independent action. In reply, the Cominform excommunicated Yugoslavia, charging that Yugoslavia slandered the USSR and that Yugoslavia was no longer Marxist because it had stopped pushing collectivization.

The Yugoslavs eventually answered that the USSR had deviated further and further from socialist democracy toward bureaucratic overcentralization. As a concrete reaction, by 1950 the Yugoslavs began to decentralize their economy and create their own "socialist democracy" focused on "workers' councils" in each factory. During this period, the Yugoslavs advanced the economic theory that central or administrative planning may at first greatly help the progress of an underdeveloped or war-torn socialist economy. As the economy becomes more built up, complex, and interrelated, however, such extreme central direction "turns into its opposite," and becomes a barrier to further progress. Some form of this theory has become the basis for the reforms in much of Eastern Europe and even in the Soviet Union.

Framework of the Yugoslav Economic System

Farming in Yugoslavia after 1950 reverted to private ownership (as it did in Poland after 1957). There are few Yugoslav collectives today, although the goal of collectivization supposedly remains. In fact, the government is very, very gradually buying up individual pieces of land as farmers retire. In addition to farming, there is also a private business sector in

Yugoslavia, mostly in the areas of trade and handicrafts. Private businesses and farms may hire up to five persons, though this limit has apparently been exceeded in practice. Farmers may acquire land up to ten hectares. The private sector thus plays a very small role in industry, but constitutes almost the whole of the farming sector. Private enterprise also plays an increasing role in the catering and service sector.

In the socialist sector of industry each factory is run as a producer's cooperative, under the control of its own Workers' Council, directly elected by all the workers of the enterprise. The Workers' Councils are a feature unique to Yugoslav socialism. Many of the other Eastern European countries are slowly decentralizing their economies toward fully independent activity by each enterprise. Yet none of them presently intends to institute Workers' Councils as a basic feature of their economy, preferring control by government-appointed managers. (When the revolutionary tides ran strong, Workers' Councils *were* temporarily introduced in Poland in 1956–1957, and Czechoslovakia in 1968–1969.) Today, only the Yugoslavs consider Workers' Councils the most vital part of their economic structure. They not only praise their allegedly democratic aspects, but also claim that they motivate workers and managers to the highest efficiency. Some Yugoslavs have even asserted that the Workers' Councils are responsible for their high rate of growth, although skeptics attribute the high growth rate primarily to a high rate of investment.

How does the system of Workers' Councils operate? The workers elect a council. The manager is then appointed by the local government, but the Workers' Council has a veto power over the appointment of the manager. The council can also fire the manager; it sets wages, within limits set by the central government; it sets prices, also within limits set by central agencies; it sets production targets and determines technology; and may dispose of its profits after taxes through additions to wages, collective welfare projects, or reinvestment. The taxes going to the national government are used for financing major investment projects, as well as defense and welfare.

Since all the firms compete in the market, prices set will be "rational" from the viewpoint of welfare economics, provided that there is pure and perfect competition. Nevertheless, since a large percentage of investment is still under the central control, capital cannot flow freely to areas of higher profits. Therefore, this constitutes a barrier to entry of other firms, and may allow monopoly or oligopoly to arise in any area where the central government sets an optimal size of firms which is very high in relation to the total market. Since Yugoslavia is a relatively small country, and the total market for many commodities is a limited one, there are many such industries where the optimal size of the firm demands only one or a few producers (although foreign imports do provide competition in some cases). As the result of such monopolies, (1) price relationships are distorted away from the socially "rational" price, (2) resources are therefore allocated wrongly from the social viewpoint, and (3) consumers are exploited in the sense of paying higher prices to these particular firms.

Expansion and new investment by a particular firm also has some peculiar aspects under this system. If an entirely new firm is set up, then it has its own Workers' Council to look after the benefit of its own workers. New firms are often, but not always, set up by old firms. Even in that case, however, the new council does not return any profits to the old firm that set it up, although it is obligated to pay interest to the government on the capital that has been given to it. In a few cases, such new enterprises are treated legally as mere subsidiary parts of the old firm. In this case the additional profits are divided among the workers of both the old and new firms. In either case, the way that a Workers' Council looks at a new investment project outside its own plant is far more complicated than the usual profit calculus of a competitive firm under capitalism. One would expect some tendency to limit projects to those that might be considered a legitimate part of the old firm.

In addition to these microeconomic aspects of investment, there is also something new in this system with respect to the question of aggregate investment. What is to keep the workers of a particular firm from deciding that all their profits should go into current wages or welfare projects, rather than reinvestment and expansion of the productive base? Legally, the only constraint is that the firm must first pay its taxes to the central government. In practice, the central government does take a very large tax bite, and in the past has used much of these taxes for investment, and has achieved a very high rate of economic growth. The Yugoslavs also claim that the workers are generally very willing to make many large reinvestments, supposedly being willing to wait for the large future returns.

In practice, the Communist Party group within each enterprise also exerts a strong pressure toward socially minded collective welfare projects and toward reinvestment for expansion of the productive base. The manager of the enterprise also exerts a somewhat independent pressure, in most cases advocating the expansion of the enterprise capital. Actually, it appears that the balance of power over the distribution of income between workers and managers and higher authorities varies from plant to plant as well as from year to year. For example, Yugoslav as well as Western economists agree that in 1961 workers' wages increased more than productivity, causing inflation in the consumer goods market. At present, the percentage of investment to national income is very high. Therefore, a large percentage of all investment, especially that going into new enterprises, must be and is still done by the central government, but an increasing percentage is coming under the control of existing firms and local governments.

It should be noted that the revenue of the enterprise must pay (1) interest on loans from the banking system, (2) depreciation allowances, (3) interest to the central government on the initial capital investment, and (4) various kinds of taxes to the government. After the firm has paid these expenses, it is then free to divide the rest of the revenue between wages and new investment. Yet the workers still must pay an additional social insurance tax on their wages. It is also required that of the investment funds, at least 24 per cent must go to a housing fund and to communal investment projects, such as recreation centers. One further restriction lies in the fact that the government enforces a minimum wage for each worker.

It might be noted that the total of all the various taxes, including profit tax, turnover tax, and the interest on initial capital, stayed for a long time about one-third of the gross national product. Of these government revenues, Yugoslavia in 1961 spent about 50 per cent on defense, 35 per cent on welfare, and 15 per cent on investment. Nevertheless, when the central government and enterprise expenditures are all added together, in 1961 it was found that gross investment amounted to a full 35 per cent of gross national product.

Central planning also removes some additional areas from the decision making of the Workers' Councils at the enterprise level. Central planning is responsible for (1) all the most important investment projects, (2) most research and development, and (3) the educational supply of skilled and professional workers.

Trends in the Yugoslav System

The initial Yugoslav move in 1950—the institution of Workers' Councils in each enterprise—seems to have been more of a political gamble for popular support than a well thought out economic scheme. It is true that the steps toward economic decentralization followed this initial step quite rapidly, but in a piecemeal fashion. On the political level, the further measures toward decentralization were undertaken to give some real meaning to the workers' councils by allowing them to make important decisions. Economically, decentralization was necessary in order to remove the conflict between the decisions of the councils at enterprise level and the continued flow of detailed plans from the central planning bureau. It was only in 1952 that it was explicitly stated that economic democracy means the "self-management" of the enterprise by all the members in it.

Since 1950 the system has fluctuated several times between central planning and a market system of competition. These changes have been accompanied by a continuing violent debate between dogmatic defenders of the old central planning and strong advocates of further decentralization.[27] There has been a general trend toward more decentralization, but with frequent retrogressions to more direct central control in particular aspects of wages, prices, or investment. A major series of reforms in 1961 ended several kinds of centralized planning and control, especially decentralizing the international trade of enterprises. In 1963 the current five year plan was abandoned and, on principle, only a quite vague and general "guideline plan" was put in its place.

Then, in 1965, came the most radical Yugoslav decentralization move. According to a U.S. Congressional Subcommittee report, this time the Yugoslavs really

meant to do what in theory they had been doing since 1950. Briefly, it was proposed to liberalize imports as fast as the country could afford; to decentralize the banking system and make it the source of investment capital, free of governmental interference; to encourage the entry of foreign capital, with the management and technical skills which would accompany it; to free prices from administrative control as quickly as possible (while imposing a price freeze to prevent too rapid readjustments); in short, definitely to get the Government (and the party) out of business.[28]

Another Western observer even comments that "at the present moment, the abandonment of national priority planning in Yugoslavia goes perhaps further than in most Western democracies. . . ."[29]

At the same time, there is an apparent contradiction between the trend toward more decentralization and the Yugoslav imposition of a price freeze "to prevent too rapid readjustments." In fact, the percentage of all internal prices legally under central control in the final analysis rose from 60 per cent in 1964 to 90 per cent in 1966.[30] Yugoslav economists claim that the imposition of controls is temporary and designed merely to prevent inflation, not to interfere with price competition. It seems true that the Yugoslavs are not terribly worried about *relative* price levels, although their degree of monopoly in many industries should perhaps make them worry. They are, however, very concerned over the immediate problem of inflation or the *absolute* rise of the whole price level. Unfortunately, as will be seen in the next section, there is some reason to believe that a tendency to inflation may be inherent in the wage-price policies of the Workers' Councils, and not merely a temporary phenomenon. But if inflationary pressure persists, when will price controls be lifted?

The 1965 reforms also instituted a major financial change. Until the reforms only about 25 to 30 per cent of fixed investment funds came from the enterprises themselves, and even this was effectively controlled by the central planners. In that period, central funds financed 70 to 75 per cent of the total investment. These central funds came mostly from taxes, whether administered by the government or by the banks. Thus, Yugoslavia's high rate of investment was largely tax-financed and centrally directed.[31] The reforms have drastically changed the situation by allowing more enterprise-directed investment from enterprise funds and from a highly decentralized banking system.

The new investment banking system of Yugoslavia is unique in that each bank is controlled by an "assembly," in which each member votes according to stock held, but no one member can have more than 10 per cent of the votes. The bank itself can hold only 10 per cent of the votes, sociopolitical organizations are limited to another 20 per cent, and at least 70 per cent of the votes must be held by individual enterprises (and other banks). These banks will supply most of the credit for investment and will make most of the final decisions on economic development. "It is the investment banks that decide on the award or refusal of credits, and against their decisions there is no legal or administrative appeal."[32]

Yugoslavia for some time made rapid progress under its system of market socialism, achieving growth rates well above most of the centrally planned economies of Eastern Europe (except Rumania) and the Soviet Union or the private enterprise economies of Western Europe and the United States. Their official statistics show that from 1954 to 1964 their economy raced along at 9.4 per cent increase per year in their "gross national product," 12.5 per cent a year in industry, and even 5.0 per cent a year in agriculture.[33] Obviously, even if outside observers would estimate rates a little lower, these data make the Yugoslav experiment look very attractive. They cannot, however, be taken as conclusive evidence of outstanding long-run performance of their type of system without a great deal more study over a much longer period. Recently, in fact, Yugoslav growth rates have declined.

The full effects of the 1965 reforms will not be known for some time. Their initial effect, however, has been to raise the level of unemployment, and to cause a temporary decline in living standards. The reason is that competition has been more cutthroat than before, while inefficient enterprises no longer have available to them an almost infinite supply of central credit. The less efficient enterprises have therefore had to cut back production or, at least, drastically limit expansion—exactly as in a private enterprise economy. The question is whether in the long run the readjustment, however painful at the moment, will increase the growth rate of the average enterprises, even if it means the eventual merger and takeover of the failing and inefficient enterprises.

Some Problems of the Yugoslav System

Prices of products in Yugoslavia are set by the enterprises (to the extent allowed by government price control), and the enterprises have every reason for increasing prices at every opportunity. If output demanded does not fall proportionately, then higher prices can give the opportunity for the Workers' Council of the enterprise to pay out higher wages. Furthermore, as was noted, a small country like Yugoslavia inevitably has a large number of monopoly producers because a single large-scale optimal size enterprise takes such a huge slice of an industry. Partly, this problem is mitigated by foreign trade, since foreign competition helps keep the monopolies in line. The result of the strong wage position and the monopoly structure of industry has been a chronic tendency toward price inflation. One interesting result of the monopoly pricing is that socialist Yugoslavia has passed an antimonopoly law against combinations in restraint of trade or conspiracies to raise prices.

In addition, the natural reaction of a central government with a planning tradition like Yugoslavia's was the imposition of a large number of price controls. It was noted above that by 1967 a large percentage of Yugoslavia's industrial sales were of price-controlled goods (although this is supposed to be a temporary situation). Firms either may set prices only within certain limits, or they must get agency approval for any price change. Bureaucracy thus returns to the price-setting stage via the back door, although the enterprises are still the formal sources of all prices. It is interesting that this system has much in common with a Lange-type system in which enterprises may set their output, but prices are centrally set.

Another Yugoslav problem has been the continuing importance of regional or national rivalries. This is especially significant in the investment process, in which the allocation is achieved partly by local and regional agencies. Some of the allocation is by central planners, but they themselves may be afflicted by regional biases. Moreover, it is not just a matter of regional rivalries—the regions are in such vastly different stages of economic development. It is still necessary to ensure equal development by investing in Macedonia, for example, when the same project could do much better in one of the more advanced regions. This is a profound problem and causes, in the short run at least, a great loss from inefficient allocation of investment relative to what might be done if there were no extraeconomic regional considerations.

A problem also arises from the attempt to give real local power to Workers' Councils over the specific plants and enterprises. This tends to result in the splitting up of industries into units of a small enough size

Market Socialism

The opposing view, which seems quite utopian, argues that the only reasons for the reforms are the lagging subjective views of managerial personnel: ". . . The moral standards of Soviet managers are *not* those of socialism. . . . What can then be done? Man can be re-educated."[37] This latter view emphasizes the utopian vision of Marxism while ignoring its basic scientific view. People on the average reflect their socioeconomic circumstances. No amount of propaganda or education can change the motivation of managers locked into a bureaucratic system operating in a society where income does *not* yet reflect one's need alone. To confuse this point is to confuse the potential communist society with the present socialist reality. Of course, the more education the better, but we shall see that the communist economic model also requires a certain level of economic development as a prerequisite.

A high level of decentralization may also be necessary to prevent a *political* stranglehold by a small ruling clique. Most East Europeans view economic decentralization as a vital prerequisite to socialist democratization (see next chapter).

To prove a restoration of capitalism, it would be necessary to show that a ruling elite has gained private (and inheritable) control of the means of production, and can use that control to exploit others. Certainly, the Soviet Union and Yugoslavia both show some measure of elite control and some exploitation. It is, however, a very limited quantity of vested control and exploitation. These societies show high upward mobility and little inheritance of high status. In the Yugoslav case some income to worker collectives is monopoly profit from control of an enterprise with high market power. But this still seems quantitatively insignificant, though nonetheless objectionable.

Certainly, the objection that material incentives and market mechanisms contribute to the alienation of worker consumers in these countries has a large measure of truth (see Chapter 20). But what are the alternatives? At their stage of development, is an alternative possible? Marx believed that the transition to the higher stage of communism would be swift. Reality, especially the reality of socialism in underdeveloped economies, has shown it to be a much lengthier process.

Is it not possible that some use of material incentives and the market is still a necessity at this stage if the socialist countries are ever to develop the affluence which is one of the necessary prerequisites of communism? True, psychological change to a less individualist outlook is another prerequisite of communism. True, continued use of the market makes this change more difficult. But that is a contradiction of reality! The choice is not simple, as various dogmatists would have it. At least, in those countries it may be that the optimal economic mechanisms at present make the psychological changes more difficult. In that case, they can only balance the advantages and disadvantages, and if the optimal economic mechanism is chosen, then they can only try to foster the psychological change by more and better education. In Chapter 23 we shall return to the economic and psychological problems of achieving communism.

NOTES

1. Karl Marx, *The Poverty of Philosophy* (New York: International Publishers, n.d.), pp. 121–122.
2. Karl Marx, *Theories of Surplus Value* (New York: International Publishers, 1952), pp. 391–402.
3. Frederick Engels, *Anti-Duhring* (New York: International Publishers, 1939, first publ. 1878), p. 297.
4. For a view of the NEP as a successful experiment in market socialism, see V. N. Bandera, "The NEP as an Economic System," *Journal of Political Economy*, 71, no. 3 (June 1963): 265–279.
5. Oskar Lange, *On the Economic Theory of Socialism* (New York: McGraw-Hill Book Company, 1964, first publ. 1938).
6. The possibility of market price-setting in socialism was fully developed by Abba Lerner, *Economics of Control* (New York: Macmillan, 1944).
7. See, e.g., M. Dobb, *Soviet Economic Development since 1917* (New York: International Publishers, 1966), p. 373.
8. For a more skeptical view of the relation between development and reform, see, e.g., P. J. D. Wiles, *The Political Economy of Communism* (Cambridge: Harvard University Press, 1964), Chapter 11.
9. See, e.g., Harry G. Schaffer, "Ills and Remedies," *Problems of Communism* (May–June 1963), pp. 27–32. Also David Granick, *The Red Executive* (Garden City, N.Y.: Doubleday, 1961). Also Joseph Berliner, *Factory and Manager in the U.S.S.R.* (Cambridge: Harvard University Press, 1957).
10. "Cost Accounting and Material Encouragement of Industrial Personnel," in *Voprosy ekonomiki* (1955), no. 6; "Planning Industrial Production and Material Stimuli for Its Development," in *Kommunist* (1956), no. 10; and "Economic Levers for Fulfilling the Plan for Soviet Industry," in *Kommunist* (1959), no. 1. All are translated in M. E. Sharpe, ed., *The Liberman Discussion* (White Plains, N.Y.: International Arts and Sciences Press, 1965), 3–64.
11. Evsei Liberman, "Plan, Profits, and Bonuses," *Pravda* (September 9, 1962), transl. in M. E. Sharpe, ed., *op. cit.*, pp. 79–87. Also Liberman, *Voprosy ekonomiki* (1962), no. 8, transl. in Sharpe, *op. cit.*, pp. 65–78. Also Liberman, "Reply to Critics of the Profit Proposal," *Ekonomischeskaya gazeta*, no. 46 (November 10, 1962), transl. in *Current Digest of the Soviet Press* (1962), no. 45, p. 18.
12. Liberman, in Sharpe, *The Liberman Discussion, op. cit.*, p. 79.
13. L. Gatovskii, "The Role of Profit in a Socialist Economy," *Kommunist*, 1962; transl. in *The Soviet Review* (Summer 1963), p. 20. Also see V. Nemchinov's article "Plan, Assignment, and Material Incentive," in *Pravda* (September 21, 1962), transl. in Sharpe, *The Liberman Discussion, op. cit.*, pp. 107–113.
14. See, e.g., L. Vaag and S. Zakharov, *Voprosy ekonomiki* (1963), no. 4.
15. V. S. Nemchinov, ed., *The Use of Mathematics in Economics* (London: Oliver and Boyd, 1964, English edition ed. by A. Nove), p. 24.
16. A. Zverev, "Against Oversimplification in Solving Complex Problems," *Problems of Economics* 5 (April 1963), p. 18.
17. *Ibid.*, p. 16.

18. *Ibid.,* p. 18.
19. K. Plotnikov, "E. G. Liberman: Right and Wrong," *Voprosy ekonomiki* (1962), no. 11, transl. in Sharpe, *op. cit.*, pp. 161–165; also I. Kasitskii, "The Main Question: Criteria for Premiums and Indices Planned for Enterprises," *Voprosy ekonomiki* (1962), no. 11, transl. in Sharpe, *op. cit.*, pp. 135–140.
20. E. G. Liberman, "Reply to Critics of the Profit Proposal," *Ekonomicheskaya gazeta* (November 10, 1962), no. 46, pp. 10–11, transl. in *Current Digest of the Soviet Press,* vol. 14, no. 45 (December 1962): 48.
21. Footnote to Academician V. Trapeznikov's article, "For Flexible Economic Management of Enterprises," *Pravda,* August 17, 1964, transl. in Sharpe, *op. cit.*, pp. 193–201.
22. V. Belkin and I. Berman, "Independence of the Enterprise and Economic Stimuli," *Izvestia* (December 4, 1964), transl. in Sharpe, *op. cit.*, pp. 225–230.
23. O. Volkov, *Pravda* (August 23, 1964).
24. See, e.g., V. Trapeznikov, *loc. cit.*
25. See text of laws in *Pravda* (October 3, 1965), transl. in U.S. Congress, Joint Economic Committee, *New Directions in the Soviet Economy* (Washington, 1966), part 4, pp. 1063–1066.
26. See discussion of this reform in I. Liberman, "Payments on Assets: Their Budgetary and Cost Accounting Functions," transl. in *Problems of Economics,* 10, no. 6 (October 1967): 3–11.
27. See, e.g., the argument for Workers' Councils and decentralization in Branco Horvat, *Toward a Theory of Planned Economy* (Belgrad: Yugoslav Institute of Economic Research, transl. 1964).
28. Subcommittee on International Trade, Committee on Banking and Currency, U.S. House of Representatives, *The Fiat-Soviet Auto Plant and Communist Economic Reforms* (Washington, D.C.: U.S. Government Printing Office, 1967), p. 46.
29. Wolfgang Friedmann, "Freedom and Planning in Yugoslavia's Economic System," *Slavic Review,* 25 (December 1966): 639.
30. *Ibid.,* p. 633.
31. See the interesting discussion by Gregory Grossman, *Economic Systems* (Englewood Cliffs, N.J.: Prentice-Hall, Inc., 1967), p. 104.
32. Friedmann, *op. cit.*, p. 634.
33. See data and discussion in Grossman, *op. cit.*, pp. 105–106. The Yugoslavs define "gross national product" half in the Marxist manner, excluding "unproductive services"; and half in the Western manner, excluding intermediate goods.
34. Speech by Janos Kornai at the University of California, Berkeley, on April 23, 1970.
35. Stanley Moore, "Utopian Themes in Marx and Mao," *Monthly Review,* 21 (June 1969), p. 38.
36. Ota Sik, *Plan and Market under Socialism* (White Plains, N.Y.: International Arts and Science Press, 1967), p. 363.
37. Allen Solganick, "Economic Reform and Socialist Morality," *Monthly Review,* 17 (March 1966): 46–47.

CHAPTER
19

The Socialist State and Democracy

First, we shall examine some problems of the definitions of "socialism" and "democracy." Then, we shall present the main ideological positions on the questions: (1) Is political democracy necessary or desirable under socialism? and (2) Is political democracy under socialism more or less likely than under capitalism? Finally, we shall look at the actual political development of some of the countries usually considered "socialist."

Definitions of Socialism and Democracy

"Socialism" and "communism" both assume by definition the public ownership of the means of production. In "socialism" articles of consumption are privately owned and must be bought by money wages, which are the result of work done. In "communism," by contrast, there are no wages, and all consumer goods are free to be consumed according to "need." All of this, however, says nothing about the political aspect of socialism. Many socialists would include political democracy in their *definition* of socialism. Many critics of socialism include political dictatorship in their *definition* of socialism. One is free to define a word any way that is convenient. In this case, it is most useful to leave politics out of the definition of socialism, so that we do not prejudge the very questions we are investigating.

This confusion over definition arises even in the outlook of Isaac Deutscher, usually one of the most insightful Marxist writers on socialism. Deutscher says: "By definition socialist man lives in a classless and stateless society, free from social or political oppression."[1] He further describes socialist man as having all the finest psychological qualities. He is then

290

able easily to show that the Soviet Union is neither socialist nor has mostly socialist men running it. This may be useful propaganda for a perfect form of "socialism," but it is very confusing for the social sciences. His "classless and stateless society" sounds more like the hoped-for results of the future communist economy, rather than any present possibility. Nor can any serious Marxist assert that there will be an instant change in every one to the perfect psychology the day after the revolution.

In narrow economic terms the Soviet Union surely has had public ownership of industry (though only part of agriculture) since the 1930's. There is no private profit income, and all income is *in theory* return for labor done. On the other hand, the Soviet Union was the scene of bloody political repression for many years, and is still the scene of milder forms of political repression. The problem is the relationship of public ownership to political democracy. To define the problem away is to obscure this issue. Therefore, it seems useful to consider the Soviet Union as a very imperfect economic model of socialism, rather than no model at all.

If the definition of "socialism" is difficult, that of "democracy" is almost impossible. A few general notions are given here, to be further developed in the rest of this chapter. Roughly, political democracy is defined as some degree of control of the government by the majority of the people through various means. In practice, it means the ability of those not in office to *"question, check and control the policies of office-holders, and confirm them in, or dismiss them from office."*[2]

While this view corresponds to some common-sense notions, it does not answer a great many questions. For example, should not democratic rights protect the minority as well as the majority? Should not democratic procedures be applied to the work center, farm, factory, or university, as well as the whole government? Or, more profoundly, as long as there is even under "socialism" (while communism is a long way off) an unequal distribution of income and a state apparatus of force, how much democracy can there be?

Marxism and the Desirability of Democracy under Socialism

Marx stated that the state under socialism would take the form of a dictatorship of the proletariat. "Between capitalist and communist society lies the period of the revolutionary transformation of the one into the other. To this also corresponds a political transition period in which the state can be nothing but the revolutionary dictatorship of the proletariat."[3] The "dictatorship of the proletariat" is Marx's conception of a socialist democracy, a more democratic government than that which can exist under capitalism. In socialism all economic and political power must pass to the working class (or "proletariat," including farm workers, industrial workers, and intellectual workers). Therefore, until the former capitalist class has been economically eliminated, the working class majority must exercise its "dictatorship." Thus, all Marxists agree that "the dictatorship of the proletariat is a dictatorship of the overwhelming majority over the minority. . . ."[4] At a minimum, Marx assumed this "dictatorship" would mean complete political democracy *within* the proletarian majority.

In Marx's terminology "dictatorship" is *not* used in its superficial political sense, to mean an authoritarian government (like Stalin's); but rather in a sociological sense, to mean the domination of a class. For example, in ancient Athens there was a democracy of all "citizens"—that is, of all slaveholders—but a dictatorship over the slaves. In modern American capitalism there is a democracy of all factions of the capitalist class, but a dictatorship over the working class (although the workers may exert much more pressure on the capitalist state than the slaves ever could on the slaveowners' state). Similarly, Marx expected a democracy of the working class to exert a dictatorship over their former masters, the capitalists, until the capitalists would disappear completely.

Specifically, during his lifetime Marx was able to point to the Paris Commune as an example of a socialist democracy (or a "dictatorship of the proletariat"). In the Commune there was a large number of conflicting political parties, with the full structure of democratic elections, right of recall, freedom of speech, and so forth. Marx wrote that "the Commune was formed of the municipal councillors, chosen by universal suffrage in various wards of the town, responsible and revocable at short terms. . . ."[5] The capitalist representatives *voluntarily* withdrew from the Commune, but this still left a large number of socialist parties, of whom the Marxists were a very, very small minority. Thus, Marx certainly did not expect a one-party dictatorship *over* the workers as the content of a future socialist democracy (or proletariat dictatorship).

V. I. Lenin did believe that the capitalist class would violently resist a socialist majority. Thus the socialist revolution could only be carried through by a violent upheaval (a realistic appraisal in Tsarist Russia). Yet after the revolution Lenin also foresaw that the "dictatorship of the proletariat" would be a government by the peasant and working class majority operating through democratic processes. Though civil war might automatically outlaw the capitalist political parties, Lenin specifically endorses the example of the Paris Commune with its multiplicity of "socialist" parties. He writes that in the Commune, "representative institutions remain. . . . Without representative institutions we cannot imagine democracy, not even proletarian democracy."[6] (Lenin's views on Party centralism are discussed in a later section.)

292

Stalinist Ideology

After Stalin had consolidated his power in the late 1920's, there was a sharp break with the past socialist practice, and an insidious change in socialist ideology. In practice, instead of a political democracy of the working class, the "dictatorship of the proletariat" came to mean a dictatorship over the working class by one party (the Communist party) and over the party by one man (Stalin, particularly after 1935). We leave for later the question of how and why this happened. Here we are concerned with the "arguments," if they may be dignified by that name, in favor of the Stalinist position presented by Stalin and his followers.

The Stalinists did in practice glorify the single leader (the "cult of personality" still prevalent in some Communist countries), but they never really argued for this in theory because it is so blatantly opposed to the whole Marxist tradition. They did, however, present arguments in favor of one-party rule. First, they claimed that even after the civil war ended, the class struggle became ever more violent in the socialist Soviet Union. Therefore, a multiparty system was a luxury that could not be afforded (though early Soviet governments included non-Bolshevik socialist parties). Apparently, even today the defeated capitalists still have so much strength that they could sneak back into political power if other political parties were allowed. When it is pointed out that the capitalists and rich peasants were eliminated in the Soviet Union by the mid-1930's, it is argued that they would make up for weakness by all-out desperation. In addition, and perhaps most convincingly, Stalin raised the potent specter of foreign espionage and foreign help for the capitalist side. There was anti-Soviet intervention by fourteen capitalist countries in 1917 and continued attempts to instigate counterrevolution ever since that time.

The second Stalinist argument was the reverse of the first. It is said that there is no class struggle in socialism and no opposing interest, therefore, no need for more than one political party (why even one?). The working class (urban and rural) is the only class left in society, the Communist party represents the working class and the Politbureau represents the Communist party. One of the faithful Stalinists in the United States, W. Z. Foster, writes:

> The existence of many political parties in capitalist countries . . . merely signifies that the class struggle is raging. . . . In a fully developed socialist country, inasmuch as all the people's interests are fundamentally harmonious, there is a proper place for only one political party, the Communist Party.[7]

Of course, the perfect harmony and increasing disharmony arguments do seem to contradict each other. If there are no more opposing interests, then why does the Soviet constitution have to prohibit other parties? If there are still opposing class interests, there is not perfect harmony—although Stalin tried to answer this by claiming that all the hundreds of thousands of Communists executed were "foreign agents."

Opposing interests have been found in socialism, however, not just by the critics, but by such a revolutionary Marxist as Mao Tse-Tung.[8] Mao argues that even in socialism there are conflicts or "contradictions" between farm workers and industrial workers, between manual workers and intellectuals, and between individuals and the government bureaucracy. He adds, however, that these conflicts are *not* antagonistic, meaning that there is no permanent opposition of vested interests, and that the conflicts may be resolved without violence (a concept we examine further in Chapter 22).

Nondogmatic Marxist View of Democracy

Many well-known Marxists, such as Alexander Dubçek in Czechoslovakia, have developed much further the ideas of political democracy in a socialist country. These progressive Marxists (called "revisionists" by their enemies) believe that political democracy is a useful instrument to improve society, and that it could operate more meaningfully for the workers under socialism than under capitalism.

This view of political democracy is founded on an antielitist view of mankind's potential. Fascists, elitists, and racists hold that one leader or one God-given elite or one race among men, such as the "Aryan race," is superior to all others. They hold that some, such as Jews, Negroes, Chinese, and anyone else convenient to attack, are especially inferior. It follows that the elite by birth, and especially their leader or "Fuehrer" (Hitler—or Stalin?) should rule, and the majority of inferiors should merely accept commands.

Marxism, operating within the French eighteenth century rationalist tradition of Voltaire and Rousseau, completely rejects these assumptions of racial or class inequality.[9] Most propaganda for such assumptions stems from ulterior motives of justifying exploitation, as for example when the Southern slaveowners tried to argue that blacks are inherently inferior. Instead, we emphasize education and cultural environment in determining performance. Modern anthropology shows that if any two large groups are given equal opportunities and motivation for learning, they will perform equally on the average.

The progressive Marxists are still Marxists, so they do not argue that political democracy is good because of an eternal ethical imperative. It is merely the best means toward the end of the greatest happiness for the greatest number of people (specifically, the working class). The socialist humanist position is that political democracy serves a very useful function in improving society (although the good feeling of participation may be an end in itself). Since the position is not an absolute one, they are quite willing to admit that there may be periods of war or revolution in which political democracy is difficult or impossible.

They can never agree, however, with those more dogmatic Marxists who argue that democratic political processes are unnecessary or harmful under socialism. Some "Marxist" writers have wrongly generalized from Cuban experience.[10] They correctly argue that (1) Cuba is under attack from the United States, and (2) all previous elections in Cuba were frauds. These writers conclude that all elections are "phony," that *all* the processes of democracy are a mask for reaction, and that no socialist country can allow any democracy while capitalism exists anywhere. Instead of democratic safeguards and processes, there is a vague rhetoric about mass participation in carrying out Fidel's decisions. It is true that Cuba has gained much in democracy by increased mass participation since the revolution, true that the prerevolutionary Batista press was corrupt, true that Batista elections were a fraud, and true that Cuba is under siege by the United States. But that does not mean that elections and freedom of the press are bad on principle and should be permanently abolished.

Leaving aside special circumstances (such as in Cuba), the progressive Marxists argue that political democracy within the working class can at least serve certain minimum functions to make socialism work better than without it. We have seen that social ownership without political democracy means an elite in control of the means of production, able to reinstitute the exploitation of the workers to some extent. Thus democratic forms may help workers restrain the bureaucratic elite. Beyond that basic point, however, we may argue some more specific advantages.

Democratic processes would at least guarantee a peaceful succession to power, unlike the bloody conspiratorial fighting of Stalin and Trotsky or Khrushchev and Beria. Leadership in that period was selected by the physical elimination of all opponents. In the post-Stalin era physical violence has gone out of fashion, but rival leaders are still eliminated by a power struggle within the narrow confines of the Central Committee, a body small enough to be subject to personal log-rolling and self-perpetuating recruitment procedures.

Second, and closely related to the first point, is the necessity for political democracy to help restrict personal power drives. Socialist bureaucracy is by nature all-powerful, and there have been many cases of personal corruption in the Soviet Union at the local and regional levels as well as in national administration (for example, using public bricks and public labor to build an official's house). Since a bureaucracy in socialism is so important, the free criticism of it up to the very highest officials is more important than ever. This principle is recognized by official Soviet communism in theory, but not in practice. The top Soviet leadership is never open to criticism of its policies or personal behavior; and criticism by an organized opposition is strictly prohibited.

Third, it is necessary to have a nonviolent process for criticism of tactical and strategic errors made by the leadership.

> Freedom only for the supporters of the government, only for the members of one party—however numerous they may be—is no freedom at all. Freedom is always and exclusively freedom for the one who thinks differently. Not because of any fanatical concept of "justice" but because all that is instructive, wholesome and purifying in political freedom depends on this essential characteristic. . . .[11]

In theory the Soviet Union is very much in favor of criticism, but in practice the Stalin era witnessed a process that was inevitable once begun. Criticism was allowed, but not criticism of the top leadership; political campaigns were allowed, but only by the Communist party. In the end, any criticism of the Communist party (or of Stalin) was considered a crime against the Soviet state or against socialism. Yet no leadership is perfect, and this process has undoubtedly reduced the efficiency of the Soviet administrative apparatus—and, more important, prohibited open expression of public preferences. The present leadership still prohibits dissent on many issues. In foreign policy this is evident in the harsh treatment of Soviet citizens who opposed the invasion of Czechoslovakia (although, even then, the lack of executions emphasizes the progress from the Stalin era).

Finally, there are *objective* clashes of interest in socialism which should be expressed in the political process. Assume even that all remnants of capitalism, including individual handicraft workers and individual or cooperative farmers, have been replaced by complete public ownership. The short-run interests of the individual worker do often conflict with the long-run interests of the whole society. For example, all state planners taking a long-run view will favor the relatively greater expansion of the means of production rather than goods for immediate consumption. Individual Soviet citizens may have a very different view concerning the division of new investment between producers' goods and consumers' goods, but in a centralized socialist economy this influence can only come through the political process.

Stalinists may object that the state (and therefore democracy) is unnecessary under full communism, because no one owns any private property, and the state will therefore wither away. Eventually, it is said, society will not need a government apparatus of force, and remaining administrators will have no need for personal aggrandizement. This may be so, but present socialist economies are a long, long way from a full communist economy. Realistically, a communist utopia of equality based on abundance does not appear to be around the corner in any country. So long as "socialism" exists in the Soviet Union, individuals are able to gain through politics extra amounts of wealth and privilege, and these may be far beyond their contribution to society.

Just as the older Marxists argue that there are "contradictions" (or conflicts) within capitalism, so the modern progressive Marxists point to many contradictions within socialism (some of which were discussed by Mao Tse-Tung, as noted above). Under socialism commodities must be bought by consumers with money, and workers are paid differential wages. Therefore, in socialism there are still rich and poor (though a much smaller range and no poverty), as well as opposed and vested interests, not to speak of opposing opinions from people with the same interests. The fact that industry is publicly owned, but that there are still unequal, private incomes (and bourgeois morality) is a very real contradiction of socialism.

It follows that under socialism there is plenty of need for discussion, for minority expression of views, and for majority decision. For example, an entrenched socialist bureaucracy may talk about achieving communist equality. In practice, however, they may do everything possible to prevent the coming of communism in order to retain their privileges. Thus political democracy even seems to be a necessary prerequisite to communism!

The Probability of Democracy in Socialism

Is political democracy more or less likely in socialism than in capitalism? To these important questions there are a variety of answers among both anti-Marxists and Marxists. We shall explore some of the major theoretical positions, then look at the facts of Soviet and East European history as a test of the theories.

THE CRITICS

All the critics of socialism have argued that any attempt at marriage between socialism and democracy can only end in violent divorce, that socialism is only compatible with political dictatorship. The critics now argue on the basis of experience that in all areas of socialism there is also dictatorship. Thus the USSR, Eastern Europe, Cuba, and China all claim to have socialist economies, but they all have political dictatorships. Moreover, many of the underdeveloped countries, such as Guinea or Syria, seem to show similar trends toward both socialism and dictatorship. Can all these areas be shown to have other or special characteristics such that their dictatorships may not be the results of socialism?

The critics have also argued, long before the present world situation, that the functioning of a socialist economy is such as to make dictatorship more likely. In the first place, there is the physical difficulty of disseminating ideas in opposition to the government. If the government owns all radio, television, newspapers, and book publishing, how can ideas contrary to the government ever get a hearing? In a capitalist democracy, at least, each person may have the formal right to spread any ideas *if* that person has the money to do so. Then even a whole group of very poor people might together find enough money to print a newspaper or publish a book on a modest scale.

In the second place, and more profoundly, under the heading of functional problems comes the fact that the government leaders must control, not only the means of propaganda, but the whole economy.[12] This enormous economic power may, to take a leaf from Marx's writings, be used to achieve complete effective political control. It means the power to hire and fire individuals, or to prevent an individual from getting any job. This is a much greater control over livelihoods than the most powerful group of capitalists could have in view of the millions of other corporations and businesses that may offer jobs. Such economic power also means that vast resources of the nation may be diverted into the treasury of the ruling party for all-out advertising and influencing of all individuals.

THE SOCIALIST VIEW

Before 1917 it seems that almost all socialists from Marx to Kautsky argued or assumed that democracy is quite compatible with socialism (and even Lenin assumed a parliamentary republic). In fact, they believed that one of the main arguments for socialism is that it constitutes economic democracy, a necessary extension of political democracy, and an addition of effective freedom to the "merely formal" freedoms of a capitalist democracy. Moreover, the early socialist parties were all closely tied into the fight against monarchy or for the extension of political democracy; for example, they fought against Prussian and Tsarist autocracy and for the extension of voting rights to all citizens including women (and ethnic minorities). The socialists argued that effecive freedom of the press in capitalism is limited to the few newspaper magnates who control these very big businesses. On the contrary, in socialism public ownership would mean more equal economic power for everyone, would guarantee everyone the job security and leisure time to participate in politics, would mean there could be no millionaires to buy votes, and would mean an equal

298

access of everyone to the means of propaganda (with guarantees of minority rights).

In socialism, the majority of the people would extend their control to the economy through their majority control of the political process. In concept, political democracy and socialism were thus inseparable, but the mechanics of "everyone" controlling the economy and "everyone" controlling the government by means of "everyone" (or even all "workers") participating in political life were not worked out in any detail. The difficult problems were hardly conceived, let alone squarely faced, before the time that socialist governments really came into existence. Most socialists seem to have merely assumed that the formal political and democratic processes would continue to operate as always, but with more life and with effective meaning for the great majority when the minority would be deprived of economic control.

Lessons of Soviet History

The Soviet Union has had the longest experience with a socialist economy, but it has been saddled with a political dictatorship for the entire period. Is the one the "cause" of the other? Currently, there are three different answers deriving from three basically opposed interpretations of Soviet history. Some critics of socialism argue that there has been one of the world's worst dictatorships in the Soviet Union, and that dictatorship is the necessary result of socialism. The Stalinists argue that the Soviet Union has had the world's most wonderful democracy, and that perfect democracy is the result of socialism. The progressive Marxist view is that the Soviet Union suffered from a terrible dictatorship (as well as economic overcentralization), but that this was due to unique historical circumstances and not caused by the socialist economy.

Of course, no iffy question in history can be answered with much certainty, but we can attempt to pick out the various ideological and objective factors that produced and maintained the Soviet dictatorship. Among the pertinent factors to be considered are (1) the traditional attitude toward democracy in Tsarist Russia, (2) the Marxist outlook toward democracy, (3) the effect of civil war, (4) the effect of foreign wars, (5) the realities of economic backwardness and illiteracy, and (6) the industrialization drive.

THE RUSSIAN BACKGROUND

Prerevolutionary Russia was an absolute autocracy for most of its history, headed by the Tsar, strongly military and imperialist in nature, and supported by a feudal land-owning nobility. Ideas of political democracy came very late to Russia, and for some time after the French Revolution they influenced only the few intelligentsia. A small degree of parliamentary political democracy was practiced only from 1906 to 1917, and, then, the Russian Duma or parliament was neither very popular nor very effective. There was thus very little theoretical or practical experience with democracy among the Russian people.

THE MARXIST OUTLOOK

West European socialists saw the proletarian "dictatorship" simply as the majority rule through elections in the form of a victory of a Socialist party or parties. The Russian Marxists, operating within the confines of Tsarist autocracy, appear to have developed a more restricted and somewhat different attitude toward democracy from an early date. Lenin, speaking for the Bolshevik faction of the Russian socialists, emphasized by the early 1900's the leading role of his party (which eventually became the Communist party). The Party was not to wait until the masses spontaneously found their way to socialist ideas, but should lead down the road to the truth. This notion of a monopoly on "the truth" was later to be a principal weapon of the Stalinist dictatorship.

Furthermore, the Russian Marxists were forced to pursue an illegal conspiracy by the repressive laws of the Tsarist government. Therefore, they instituted a very strict discipline within the Party, were not always able to hold elections for top officers, but always enforced orders from the top down. In theory, the Leninist leadership argued for "democratic centralism," which meant democratic election of central officers plus strict obedience to orders from the elected officers. Tsarist repression made democratic election impossible, but the central officers still demanded strict obedience to orders (and no criticism). This tradition, by which the Party led the masses and the top leaders directed the Party, was necessary to action and harmless to individual freedom before the 1917 Revolution. Since anyone could leave the Party without harm, the Party could only lead by persuasion, and Party discipline could only be voluntary self-discipline. Few revolutionaries thought about how differently this might operate when the Party became the all-powerful ruling party of the government, with persuasion changed to censorship and coercion, while voluntary discipline became external control or opportunistic fawning on leaders.

REVOLUTION AND CIVIL WAR

The Russian Revolution of October 1917 resulted in a government of "Soviets" or councils of workers, peasants, and soldiers, led by the Communist party (Bolsheviks). At first, the Communist party ruled in alliance with the Left Socialist Revolutionary party, which mainly represented the poor peasantry. Within a month after the Revolution, the first step against political democracy was taken when all the parties (and all the newspapers) advocating capitalism or monarchism were banned. This was partly explained as a temporary measure during the violence of the Revolution and attempts at counterrevolution. Yet it was also given more dangerous meaning as a "natural act of proletarian dictatorship."

Then two months later the Constituent Assembly was dispersed because, it was said, the attitude of the people had greatly changed (and the dominant Socialist Revolutionary party had split), so that the elections to the assembly were now outdated. This was a reasonably democratic argument, except that new elections to the assembly were not called then or ever. The further argument was given that the Soviets were more democratic in nature than a parliamentary assembly. The Soviets were councils representing soldiers, industrial workers, and farmers. Since the owning classes were to be dispossessed, they would eventually also be part of the working classes, so eventually everyone could vote for the Soviets (as has been the case since 1936). Furthermore, in 1917–1918 all the various socialist parties still participated in the Soviets. Therefore, except for the exclusion of the capitalist and monarchist parties, the Soviets, it was said, would eventually turn out to be a democratic instrument like the assembly.

Within a few more months, however, as the civil war grew in intensity and bitterness, the other socialist parties were also prohibited to a large extent. Even this further measure of political restriction could be defended in the terrible conditions of the time—a single, poor and exhausted workers' state standing alone against formidable domestic enemies and massive foreign intervention. "The danger begins only when they make a virtue of necessity and want to freeze into a complete theoretical system all the tactics forced upon them by these fatal circumstances."[13]

In theory, it has long been the Marxist view that when a democratic election threatens to bring a socialist majority into office the ruling capitalist class will attempt to launch civil war violence to stop socialism. The classic examples were Russia and Spain, while today it is perhaps shown by events in Guatemala or Brazil. Furthermore, these examples illustrate the willingness and ability of foreign capitalists to intervene in this era of imperialism. The issue of a violent or peaceful transition to socialism is of vital importance to our present discussion because a peaceful transition may help create an environment favorable to democratic development. All democratic forms tend to fall by the wayside during any violent and rapidly changing civil war. After the bitterness of civil war, it is not easy to let the opposition immediately reenter politics.

The long and bloody civil war in the Soviet Union (worsened by foreign intervention) made immediate initiation of widespread political democracy very unlikely. The civil war killed off many Communists, and killed and dispersed much of the old working class. In fact, the number of workers shrank from a small 2.6 million in 1917 to a minute 1.2 million in 1920.[14] Furthermore, the unpopular measures necessary for warfare alienated many former supporters. As a result, the few surviving old Bolsheviks felt as if they were a tiny remnant defending a besieged fortress. "Besieged fortresses are hardly ever ruled in a democratic manner."[15]

FOREIGN CAPITALIST ENCIRCLEMENT

It is certainly true that a large number of foreign capitalist countries intervened militarily against the Soviet Communists in the years 1918–1921 (including the United States, England, France, and Japan). Furthermore, the blockade of the Soviet Union was continued for many years. Foreign threats never ceased until they culminated in the devastating Nazi invasion. This was followed by the cold war, the threat of the nuclear bomb, and the renewal of attempts at economic blockade by the United States (against both the Soviet Union and Eastern Europe). Against China the United States has also applied military intervention, nonrecognition, and severe economic blockade. The same interventionist policies have been applied against Cuba.

These circumstances *do* partly make political democracy objectively more difficult in these countries. They are also used, however, as a rationale for repression by some of the ruling elements in these countries, just as Joe McCarthy used the Korean war as an excuse for repression in America, and just as Nixon-Agnew use the Vietnam war as an excuse for more repression in America (and each side points to repression in the other country as a reason for its own repression).

BACKWARDNESS AND DEMOCRACY

A great many of the underdeveloped countries, from China to Algeria, have tended toward both socialist state ownership of the means of production *and* dictatorial one-party control of political life. Why, ask the progressive Marxists, should economic backwardness generate both socialism and dictatorship?[16] These are countries mostly filled with a raging desire for rapid economic growth. Yet they are also largely poor, agrarian countries with little modern industry in buildings, equipment, skilled workers, or experienced managers.

Socialism is viewed by the progressive Marxists as a useful instrument of industrialization in the underdeveloped countries. For one thing, there are few educated and experienced planners, so the central government can best make use of them, whereas many decades might be required for the voluntary emergence of bold, private entrepreneurs. Furthermore, the total lack of capital in the underdeveloped countries could most easily be remedied by governmental control of resources. The government could tax the rich, gather the small savings of the poor, and expropriate foreign profits, in order to invest by itself in new factories and equipment.

It is thus clear why socialism may be chosen as an instrument to overcome backwardness, but why does it unfortunately also generate one-party dictatorship? The reason lies within exactly the same set of circumstances.

The Soviet people may have been convinced of the desirability of rapid economic growth. Yet the Soviet leadership and their economic planners soon found that there is a conflict between rapid long-run growth and immediate consumption. Concretely, they found that to gather the resources necessary to build industry means to take food away from the mouths of the farm population. Excluding foreign investment, there was simply no other source of capital. It was necessary to take from the farms the food and raw materials for export, for the feeding of the new industrial working class, and as the basis for the manufacturing processes themselves.[17]

We saw in Chapter 13 that Stalin solved the resource problem by forcefully putting the peasantry into collective farms from which the entire surplus could be taken. At the cost of a long stagnation or drop in living standards, naturally accompanied by violent resistance to the regime among much of the farm population, Stalin succeeded in putting heavy investments for several years into basic industrial capital and education of a whole new working class. Such a sudden and unpopular transformation (unpopular to the peasant majority) could not have been accomplished without a dictatorship.[18] The only historical issue is whether the Soviet industrial transformation could have been made a little more slowly and with more democratic consent.

Although there have been major setbacks, the Soviet Union has increased political freedom since Stalin's death. Clearly, on this view, the new possibilities in the Soviet Union as well as the doctrinaire dictatorship in China today both arise from the contrasting levels of economic development. China is still in the earlier stage of rapid industrial construction at the expense of present consumer needs. The Soviet Union has now progressed to the stage where it has a large industrial base capable of generating sufficient surplus within itself to facilitate continued rapid growth of production as well as increasing satisfaction of consumer needs both in cities and on the farm.

The intensive education of a large part of the Soviet population has now provided that population not only with scientific knowledge, but also with a minimum of liberal arts education. Even with a generous helping of propaganda, this education makes it capable of using and demanding a wider democratic process.

Stalinism was thus a phenomenon of social transition and not (as its adherents and also most western anti-Communist Sovietologists once maintained) the quintessence or the final shape of the post-capitalist or socialist society. The very success which Stalinism attained in changing and modernizing the social structure of the USSR turned it into an anachronism and made de-Stalinization a historic necessity.[19]

We conclude that political dictatorship in the Soviet Union resulted from the Russian tradition, the underground political tradition, civil war, foreign wars (and encirclement), and from economic backwardness; *not* because of socialism, but in spite of socialism. *In an advanced economy,* we may still argue (or hope) that a socialist system will provide a better environment for political democracy than does capitalism.

Contemporary Soviet Class Structure and Politics

There are two contradictory tendencies in modern Soviet society. On the one hand, the improved level of communication and education—and the more relaxed pace of industrialization—make more political democracy possible and useful.[20] On the other hand, increasing industrialization has resulted in a vast, entrenched, and conservative bureaucracy (though an increased democratization might reduce their influence).[21] The result is that the USSR is still "a stratified society, with a deep chasm between the ruling stratum of political bureaucrats and economic managers on the one side and the mass of working people on the other. . . ."[22]

Yet democratic pressure from below and recognition from above of bureaucratic inefficiency have resulted in some widening of the area of formal political freedoms since Stalin's death. First there is some evidence that, in addition to the General Secretary and the Politbureau, the more numerous Central Committee members are now more fully involved in the decision-making process. Second, even the Supreme Soviet has shown a little more life, and has developed a functioning committee system. Third, Stalin's police terror has been denounced, the number of political prisoners reduced perhaps 90 per cent from the hundreds of thousands once held, due process has increased, and there have been no political executions. Fourth, there have been Soviet voices raised for much further political freedom. In 1966 there was even some public support for competitive multi-candidate elections, countered by a resounding official "no" and defense of the *status quo*.[23] Of course, Soviet progress is not smooth, and there have been some terrible regressions to Stalinist methods—the most important instance being the tragic invasion of Czechoslovakia in 1968.

The Socialist State and Democracy

There has thus been some apparent widening of the political process, but so far merely resulting in a milder and more efficient autarchy. Recent methods of control have concentrated, as in the United States, on manipulation rather than force.

> The trend [in the U.S.S.R.] seems to be toward normalization rather than abolition of repression. . . . Repression is to be "spontaneously" reproduced by the repressed individuals; this allows a relaxation of external, compulsory repression.[24]

In terms of socioeconomic status, the ruling group is quite limited:

> Only the upper strata of the bureaucracy, of the party hierarchy, the managerial groups, and the military personnel, live in conditions comparable to those enjoyed by the rich and the *nouveaux riches* in capitalist society. It is impossible to define the size of these groups . . . statistical data about their numbers and their incomes are carefully concealed.[25]

Within the Soviet upper income groups, the greatest political power still lies within the Party apparatus, from the thousands of local and district Secretaries up to the Politbureau members. There are distinct but secondary centers of power in the government bureaucracy (from the local police officials up to the Council of Ministers); the economic leadership (from the enterprise managers up to the top economic planners); and the officers of the Soviet military. Of course, each of these groups merge and intertwine at the top, and individuals often move from one hierarchy to another at all levels.

Yet the Party leaders, whose abilities are political and not technical, are still dominant. The government bureaucrats are subordinate to the Party, but have shown somewhat more independence and initiative since the downfall of Khrushchev and the appointment of Kosygin as Premier. The power and influence of the managers have risen with the increase of technology and industrial complexity, but there has been no real technocratic challenge to the clear supremacy of the Party apparatus.[26] The military is steadily becoming more professional and independent (for example, pushing for high levels of military spending). The Party, however, exercises its control of the military through several channels: almost all officers are Party members, there is intensive indoctrination at all levels, there is direct interference through commissars, cells in each unit, and so forth.[27]

The important question is the degree to which upper income groups (bureaucrats, Party functionaries, managers, and military) may be considered a new ruling and exploiting class.

What these groups have in common with any exploiting class—using the term in the Marxist sense—is that their incomes are at least partially derived from

305

the "surplus value" produced by the workers. Moreover, they dominate Soviet society economically, politically, and culturally.[28]

Yet Deutscher, a critical observer of the Soviet scene, pointed out that these groups own neither land nor factories, nor can they expand their income by investments. The ruling groups have not so far tried to vest their controlling privileges in their children by legal means—although they do sometimes give their children a head start through an intellectual home atmosphere and by use of legal and illegal means to get them admitted to college or placed in a job.

Because the Soviet ruling "bureaucracy" has no legal ownership of the means of production, as the capitalist ruling class does, their need for outright repressive controls is even greater than that of the capitalists (who have indirect means to control formal democratic processes). "The power of property having been destroyed, only the State, that is, the bureaucracy, dominates society; and its domination is based solely on the suppression of the people's liberty to criticize and oppose!"[29] Suppression plus manipulation (and increasing material prosperity) are the means of political domination by the Soviet leadership, through which it controls the means of production.

Although it may be possible to increase democratic control over the bureaucracy, it is utopian to conceive of an industrialized socialism without bureaucracy. As long as there is a complex economic organism to be run, requiring a vast amount of expertise in planning and coordination, there will continue to be a vast bureaucracy. "The notion of nonbureaucratic detailed central planning is a fundamental absurdity. . . . The state may wither away in the economic field, but only if a market is substituted."[30] The point is not to eliminate the planning apparatus, but to establish more democratic—that is, more working class—control over it.

China and Cuba

Mao Tse-Tung and his fellow leaders, it appears, observed not only non-antagonistic conflicts of interest in socialism, but also the hardening of a new line of division between the masses and the new elite ruling class.

The difficulty of preventing a reversion to class rule in an underdeveloped socialist society is much greater than most Marxists have yet recognized. It is not only that the growth of a privileged stratum is unavoidable, but also that old ideas and habits of thought, old social attitudes, ingrained moral and religious values are enormously persistent and difficult to eradicate. . . .[31]

While their rhetoric is dogmatic and utopian, the Chinese leaders do claim that the purpose of the cultural revolution was to reduce elite privileges and to increase democratic participation. Whether this was its real purpose, and what its results were, are completely unclear in the light of utterly contradictory reports from different competent observers.[32]

The Cuban revolutionary government, like the Chinese, started off with tremendous popular enthusiasm and support for it. There has been some attempt in the light of this support to increase mass participation in the government, especially at local levels. Nevertheless, even friendly observers admit that "Cuba's governing system is clearly one of bureaucratic rule. Power is concentrated in the Communist Party within the Party in the Central Committee, and within the Central Committee in the Maximum Leader."[33] Moreover, as in China, the details of many institutions of democratic participation are unclear and disputable.[34]

Political Democracy in Czechoslovakia

The entire world was excited by the Czech attempt to have a "socialism with a humanist face," a society both socialist and profoundly democratic, devoted to humanist ideals in contrast with dehumanization of the Stalinist-type bureaucracy. They were beginning to succeed before the Soviet invasion. It was said at the time that "Dubçek seeks to marry Communist rule with political democracy, a socialist economy with economic efficiency. . . ."[35]

The Czechoslovak Communist party in April 1968 promulgated an action program with a number of concrete proposals. The Communist party was no longer to have a legal monopoly of power; it was to lead when and to the extent the people wanted it. The Party was to concern itself with broad direction, not direct intervention in local economic or cultural matters. Other existing parties were to be allowed real life; they could have differing programs as long as they remained socialist. Criticism of the leadership and real elections were to be allowed in the Communist party. People were allowed to create *new* organizations, new political clubs, new trade unions. The old trade unions were revitalized. In *every* organization nomination from above was ended.

Political prisoners were rehabilitated and given economic restitution. The prerequisite of political ideology, shown by Party membership, for certain jobs was abolished. There was also ended the special list of "good" people within the Party, self-chosen and self-perpetuating, who had automatically been given first choice of all the best jobs. The real salaries of the top leaders (previously unknown amounts) were lowered and fixed—Novotny, the old leader, "voluntarily" gave back 3.5 million crowns when he was fired.

New election laws were to be written, getting rid of the old fixed elections. There was to be effective freedom to strike. Everyone was to be free to travel abroad. Workers' councils were proposed to institute participatory democracy in the factories—some were instituted *after* the Soviet invasion, but the occupiers slowly reduced their powers or dismantled them.

Censorship was ended! The media, including films and publishing, were made independent agencies; they were to get government subsidies without strings. One publishing house was to be run by the Communist party, but other publishing houses were to be run by private persons, groups, and other parties as nonprofit cooperatives. The same groups, and particularly students, could start new journals and newspapers as nonprofit cooperatives.

On what grounds has the Czechoslovak experiment been attacked? One dogmatic "Marxist" says, specifically referring to Czechoslovakia, that most of the usual political freedoms are not "relevant" to the mass of people under socialism.[36] Lest we misinterpret, a full quotation of the key passage is in order. He writes:

> To be sure, various freedoms were being called for or enacted—e.g. the freedom to travel, . . . ideological freedom, the freedom to organize clubs of "critical thinkers," an opposition press, and even (according to some reports) an opposition party. As in the West, these freedoms would in principle be available to all. The point is that, again as in the West, they are not equally relevant to the needs of all, nor do they include ways and means to create the social and economic conditions that might make them so.[37]

This sounds very "radical" and "Marxist," but it is an elitist doctrine that could be used to justify a Stalinist dictatorship.

The notion seems to be that all these "irrelevant" freedoms are only a sham cover for exploitation ("as in the West"). The exploitation is to be by managers and experts, who will draw high incomes, and will therefore have the economic power to rule through whatever political forms exist. Most ordinary workers will continue to have low incomes, no time for politics, and no political power. It sounds more as though he were talking about India or Nigeria than Czechoslovakia. Certainly, in the underdeveloped countries today, most political freedoms are not very relevant to everyday life; the relevant needs are an end to imperialism, a socialist economy, economic growth, and so forth.

But Czechoslovakia *is* a socialist country, and a highly industrialized one at that. This means that the leisure time of the ordinary worker is enough to give time for politics; workers' incomes are high enough for many to combine and publish books or journals, and workers have enough education to think independently.

In fact, in Czechoslovakia in 1968 all reports (including most Communist correspondents) indicated a vast increase in political participation by the working class. Not only were students active in exercising the new democratic freedoms, but the hitherto sterile and bureaucratically run trade unions suddenly came to life, and began to worry about the rights and interests of the workers. There were even spontaneous committees formed by the *workers* to protect the right of free speech![38]

Naturally, the higher income groups under socialism will continue to have some advantages at home, leading to better educational opportunities, better jobs, and perhaps a larger slice of political power. But these income differences are surely not a reason for declaring democratic freedoms irrelevant to the ordinary worker under socialism. On the contrary, democracy becomes a necessary form for the ordinary worker to assert himself, and even a necessary basis for the struggle to change to communism (because those in the higher income brackets, who have most political power, will not easily agree to eventual income leveling—or expansion of free collective goods, which automatically means more income equality).

Why do some dogmatic writers seem to think these democratic freedoms ("even an opposition party") are so antisocialist or anti-Marxist?[39] We have seen that Marx held up the Paris Commune as the best example of socialist democracy (and Lenin agreed).[40] But Marx specifically noted the existence of many socialist parties, of the fact that the Marxists were even a small minority, of the fact that there was periodic election and the right of immediate recall. Would it be so bad if there were many socialist parties representing different interests and different points of view in the present "socialist" countries? Only our indoctrination by years of Stalinist propaganda seems to have caused restrictions on democracy to be accepted as "orthodox Marxism" among the Left.

Yugoslavia and Workers' Councils: Mechanism for Improving Democracy?

The notion of workers' self-management, the election of workers' councils (or some other name for a managing body) to run the enterprise, has a long history. Especially in France many workers have favored it under the name "syndicalism" or industrial democracy.[41] Even in America we have long had the Socialist Labor party, a small sect which advocates industrial democracy or workers' self-management as the panacea to all social evils.

The fullest practical use of the idea has been in Yugoslavia since 1950. There the Workers' Councils are elected by all the workers of the enterprise. They hire a manager in conjunction with the local government, and they make basic decisions (with the manager) as to prices, output, technology, and use of all income for investment or for wage distribution. The Workers' Councils are even represented in one chamber of the congress, called the Council of Producers.

A sophisticated theoretical explanation and defense of Workers' Councils has been written by a Yugoslav economist, Branco Horvat.[42] Horvat argues on economic and political grounds the need for decentralization in order to eliminate an inefficient and dictatorial centralized bureaucracy. He concludes that we must, *therefore*, substitute decisions by Workers' Councils for decisions of central planners.

The specific advantages of Workers' Councils claimed by Horvat and others are: first, by reducing the role of the central planning bureaucracy as well as the economic role of the Communist party apparatus, there is a better foundation for socialist political democracy. Second, since the workers control their own economic activity, there is less alienation than under central control. Third, since workers divide the profits of the enterprise (after taxes and investment), they will have more incentive to work, will take more initiative in innovation. Fourth, because the enterprise competes in the market, it will have to be more efficient than under central planning.

The disadvantages of Workers' Councils have been brought out by many writers.[43] In the first place, Workers' Councils may be inequitable, that is, they may distribute income to a group of workers, *not* on the basis of individual or group effort alone, but on the basis of an accidentally better endowment (in resources, facilities, and technology) of the enterprise. Second, the Workers' Council system may develop antisocial interests in that the individual enterprise may charge monopoly prices, and distribute the monopoly profits to its own workers at the expense of the rest of society. The problem of monopoly is especially difficult in Eastern Europe because there is a tendency to merge all firms in each industry for ease of central planning. For example, in Czechoslovakia in 1967 all manufacturing was concentrated in just 700 enterprises!

Third, democracy might be better achieved by political democracy at the national level, which could direct central planning toward social aims. The proponents of Workers' Councils do not seem to realize that *any* decision-making at local levels (for example, income distribution decisions) must reduce national decision-making powers. There is a built-in political and economic conflict in the Yugoslav system between local collectives' interests and those of the national working class. They also overlook the possibility that purely economic efficiency might be as easily gained by decentralization without Workers' Councils (for example, by putting enterprise decisions in the hands of state-appointed managers, as in Hungary).

Fourth, to attack "bureaucracy" meaningfully means not just reducing central planners, but attacking all those with privileged positions in socialism. Yet the Workers' Councils' system allegedly would result in more differentiated income, in high incomes for a few groups of skilled workers, and this income inequality again means less political democracy (the Yugoslav income spread is now about five to one).[44] Fifth, use of the market and material incentives means not only more economic and political inequality, but also more bourgeois psychological behavior and more alienation from other people.

Sixth, there are also Yugoslav complaints that the managers have too little power for efficient operation. There is considerable evidence that managers are not professional enough. Thus the Workers' Councils often refuse to hire university graduates, partly perhaps to hire friends, but mostly because highly educated managers "cost too much." Seventh, economic planners complain that the enterprises do not reinvest enough profits, rather giving them out as wages. This last is not yet clear because the federal government effectively controlled investment for a long time, but the ratio of investment to net income has fallen off since the 1965 reforms gave the enterprise councils more power over investments.

A confusion that seems to lurk in the approach of many contemporary Marxist writers[45] is the notion that a society can eliminate the central planning bureaucracy, but can also eliminate the decentralized market mechanism. The central bureaucracy is attacked for its disproportionate economic privileges and consequent disproportionate political power, while the market is attacked for creating inequality and alienation. Both criticisms have an element of truth. Well and good! But, pray tell, how do you eliminate both at the same time? The real, not imaginary world shows in a modern industrial economy millions of difficult economic decisions interrelated in a complex web. *Either* competition in the market must make most of these decisions *or* a very large bureaucracy must make them. Eastern Europe seems to be taking a very realistic road in setting a wide area of detailed decisions to be made by enterprises in the market, while maintaining the framework and constraints of central planning for aggregate, long-run, development decisions. It also seems realistic to propose that some socioeconomic decisions be made at enterprise levels by democratically elected Workers' Councils, some made by democratically elected local governments, and some made by democratically elected national governments.

Institutionalized Democratic Safeguards

After Stalin's performance, it should be impossible for any Marxist to maintain that elimination of the capitalist class also eliminates any need for democratic safeguards. It appears that socialism is a necessary condition

THE POLITICAL ECONOMY OF SOCIALISM

of democracy, but not a sufficient one. In addition, we need the institutionalized democratic safeguards, which some capitalist countries have, but which are rendered ineffective by capitalism. "The point of the socialist critique of 'bourgeois freedoms' is not (or should not be) that they are of no consequence, but that they are profoundly inadequate, and need to be extended by the radical transformation of the context. . . ."[46] In the context of a socialist economy, what freedoms must be put into institutionalized democratic safeguards?

First, a multiparty (or, at least, multifaction of a single party) system is necessary to allow for peaceful succession of leaders, for organized criticism of the known bureaucratic excesses, and for more representation of popular interest, such as in the question of the immediate expansion of consumer goods. Whether there need be several parties, or one party with open entrance and internal democracy, or some kind of nonparty system, cannot be decided abstractly, but must depend on the greatly differing national traditions and conditions of different countries.

In fact, there have been as yet few cases where political democracy has allowed a clear-cut decision between capitalism and socialism. Where socialism is the major issue, as in France and Italy, political democracy under capitalism tends to break down (in Germany it led to fascism). It is more realistic to acknowledge that in a certain sense there *must* be a preelection agreement for capitalism or for socialism by all parties in normal times.

The confusion is in thinking that if political democracy does not serve the function of deciding between capitalism and socialism, it serves no function. In the United States capitalism is assumed and is not at issue in elections. Nevertheless, political democracy serves the ruling capitalist class in several functions. First, it allows criticism of capitalist tactics and strategy by more "liberal" capitalist factions. Secondly, personal corruption in government is limited by the criticism of the opposition party. Third, it produces some degree of leadership and legitimate succession in government by a nonviolent method.

In the Soviet Union socialism is assumed and is not at issue in the political process. Even one study of anti-Soviet emigrés from the USSR finds that almost all of them admit that they were in favor of Soviet socialism before they went abroad![47] Nevertheless, there is great need for expansion of political democracy there for all the reasons discussed above. True, within the Communist party, in nominating procedures, and particularly in public discussion and criticsm of certain proposals, there exists some rudimentary political democracy. There is still needed, however, a formal apparatus openly guaranteeing political democracy and preventing retrogression to an era like the Stalin period (which the invasion of Czecho-

312

slovakia—and evidence of internal repression—makes us consider a real threat).

Second, even if there is more than one political party in socialism, the ruling party may exert enormous control over the means of propaganda, the radio, television, books, and newspapers. Even without censorship, public ownership seems to imply political control. Two different ways may be used to avoid this one-party control of all propaganda, which would otherwise make democracy impossible in practice. One way is used in England where the BBC is compelled by law to allot a certain amount of time to opposition views. This could be extended to use of newspapers and other media. In fact, the law might require subsidies to the opposition by free use of facilities and other services. A second way, used for a short time in Poland and proposed in Czechoslovakia, is to allow nonprofit, cooperative ownership of some means of propaganda by any willing group, for example, control of a newspaper or radio station by the writer or readers or listeners (such as the Pacifica Foundations' stations in the United States).

There is also the problem that the ruling political party—even if democratically elected—would control all jobs under centralized socialism. One useful mechanism to prevent misuse of this power is the institution of civil service (with certain regularized procedures for hiring and firing), as it is widely used in countries such as England. The other mechanism is economic decentralization of a socialist economy, so that jobs are determined quite separately in each enterprise.

If democratic safeguards are ignored in socialism, the result is a dictatorship *over* the working class, political persecution from mild to violent and bloody, and a loss of economic efficiency as well as general governmental corruption and inefficiency (for example, among fearful diplomats). If the society is not in a crisis caused by rapid economic development or very powerful foreign pressures, it is possible for a socialist economy (as we observed in Czechoslovakia) to have much wider democratic control than capitalism. Thereby it may increase its efficiency in functioning, increase expression of public preferences, and generally improve workers' welfare.

A few *very tentative* conclusions may be drawn from this chapter. First, institutionalized democratic safeguards are necessary under socialism to help the working class maintain control of "its own" government (and they may differ widely in different countries). Second, with such safeguards and with the added features of public ownership and more equal distribution of income and property—even when balanced against the enlarged bureaucratic corps—socialism may claim in theory to be expected to be more democratic and responsive to working class needs than any capitalist democracy. Third, this comparison holds only for capitalist and socialist systems of the same level of development. Socialism in economically backward countries tends to be backward in many ways, including the political dimension—though Chile is presently making a powerful attempt to have both socialism and political democracy. Finally, any socialist economy still has unequal distribution of personal private property and an accompanying state apparatus; therefore, its democratic potential is still limited (although it may grow far beyond that of capitalist "democracy"). The potential expansion of freedom and the withering away of the state under communism is discussed in the last chapter of this book.

NOTES

1. Isaac Deutscher, *On Socialist Man* (New York: Merit Publisher, 1967), p. 18. But see W. Mandel, "A Reply to Isaac Deutscher," *Political Affairs*, 46 (December 1967): 22–26.

2. Maurice Cornforth, *The Open Philosophy and the Open Society* (New York: International Publishers, 1969), pp. 260–266.

3. Karl Marx, "Critique of the Gotha Programme," in *Selected Works of Marx and Engels* (Moscow: Foreign Languages Publishing House, 1930), vol. 2, pp. 34–33. All Marx's references to this subject have been collected by Hal Draper, "The Dictatorship of the Proletariat," *New Politics*, 1 (Summer 1962): 95–104.

4. The latest program of the Soviet Communist party, quoted in Harry Shaffer, *The Soviet Economy* (New York: Appleton-Century-Crofts, 1963), p. 80.

5. Karl Marx, *The Civil War in France* (New York: International Publishers, 1948).

6. V. I. Lenin, *State and Revolution* (New York: International Publishers, 1932), p. 41.

7. William Z. Foster, *History of the Three Internationals* (New York: International Publishers, 1953), p. 271.

8. Mao Tse-Tung, *On the Correct Handling of Contradictions among the People* (New York: New Century Publishers, 1957).

9. See Frederick Engels, *Anti-Duhring* (New York: International Publishers, 1939, first publ. 1878), Chapter 10.

10. See, e.g., J. P. Morray, "Marxism and Democracy in Cuba," in Herbert Aptheker, ed., *Marxism and Democracy* (New York: Humanities Press, 1965), where he boasts that democracy was brought to Cuba by abolition of elections and press freedom.

11. Rosa Luxemburg, *The Russian Revolution* (Ann Arbor: University of Michigan Press, 1961, written 1918), p. 69.

12. See, e.g., Raymond Aron, "Social Structure and the Ruling Class," in Lewis Coser, ed., *Political Sociology* (New York: Harper & Row, 1967), pp. 123–176.

13. Rosa Luxemburg, *op. cit.*, p. 79.

14. I. Gladkov, ed., *Sovetskoe narodnoe khozyaistve, 1921–1925* (Moscow, 1960), p. 531.

15. Isaac Deutscher, *The Unfinished Revolution* (New York: Oxford University Press, 1967), p. 31.

16. See, e.g., Isaac Deutscher, *Russia in Transition* (New York: Coward-McCann, 1957).

17. Paul Baran, *The Political Economy of Growth* (New York: Monthly Review Press, 1957), Chapter 8.

18. See the details in Alec Nove, *An Economic History of the USSR* (London: Penguin Press, 1969), Chapters 7 and 8.

314

19. Isaac Deutscher, "Ideological Trends in the USSR," *op. cit.*, p. 10.
20. According to Deutscher, *loc. cit.*
21. According to Herbert Marcuse, *Soviet Marxism* (New York: Vintage Books, 1961, first publ. 1958), p. 180.
22. Paul Sweezy and Leo Huberman, "50 Years of Soviet Power," *Monthly Review*, 19 (November 1967): 11.
23. See *Izvestia* (May 13, 1966); and discussion in William Mandel, "Reflections on the Soviet System," in Hendel and Braham, eds., *The U.S.S.R. After 50 Years* (New York: Alfred Knopf, 1967), p. 184.
24. Marcuse, *op. cit.*, p. 227.
25. Deutscher, *The Unfinished Revolution*, *op. cit.*, p. 55.
26. See, e.g., Jeremy R. Azreal, *Managerial Power and Soviet Politics* (Cambridge: Harvard University Press, 1966).
27. Roman Kolkowicz, *The Soviet Military and the Communist Party* (Princeton, N.J.: Princeton University Press, 1967).
28. Isaac Deutscher, "Roots of Bureaucracy," in R. Milibrand and J. Saville, eds., *Socialist Register, 1969* (New York: Monthly Review Press, 1969), p. 55.
29. *Ibid.*, p. 106.
30. Peter Wiles, "The Pursuit of Affluence," in Hendel and Braham, *op. cit.*, p. 90.
31. Editorial, "The Cultural Revolution in China," *Monthly Review*, 18 (January 1967), p. 16.
32. See the selected references to this chapter for various views.
33. Paul Sweezy and Leo Huberman, *Socialism in Cuba* (New York: Monthy Review Press, 1969), p. 219.
34. This author pleads ignorance, and leaves to the future more definite conclusions on Chinese and Cuban political trends.
35. Morton Schwartz, "Czechoslovakia's New Political Model: A Design for Renewal," *The Journal of Politics* 30 (1968): 978.
36. Benjamin Page, "Ota Sik and Czechoslovakian Socialism," *Monthly Review*, 21 (October 1969): 36–47.
37. *Ibid.*, p. 46.
38. According to numerous reports in *Rude Pravo* in April and May, 1968.
39. E.g., Page, *op. cit.*, p. 46.
40. Marx, *Civil War in France* (New York: International Publishers, 1931); Lenin, *State and Revolution* (New York: International Publishers, 1932).
41. See the non-Marxist view of the clash between "technocratic" planners and engineers and the syndicalist manual workers in George Lichtheim, *Marxism in Modern France* (New York: Columbia University Press, 1966).
42. Branco Horvat, *Towards a Theory of Planned Economy* (Belgrad: Yugoslav Institute of Economic Research, 1961, transl. 1964), including a very good history of the idea of workers' self-management, pp. 98–114.
43. See, e.g., the excellent critical review of Horvat by Ernest Mandel, in *Monthly Review*, 18 (April 1967): 40–50.
44. Statement by Horvat at Conference of Union for Radical Political Economics, Washington, D.C., May, 1970.
45. See, e.g., Ernest Mandel, *loc. cit.*
46. Ralph Miliband, *The State in Capitalist Society* (New York: Basic Books, 1969), p. 267.
47. Raymond Bauer, Alex Inkeles, and Clyde Kluckholn, *How the Soviet System Works* (New York: Random House, 1956), p. 262.

CHAPTER

20

Socialism
and Imperialism

Socialists have always claimed that capitalism and the private profit motive is the main cause of imperialism. As to whether a socialist country could be imperialist we have only a few limited experiences and very little theory. Let us investigate the only case for which some small amount of agreed data exists: the Soviet Union and East Europe. We shall apply to it as possible categories the three economic categories used in exploring capitalist imperialism: direct plunder, trade, and investment—plus the category of possible political benefits.

The Soviet Union and East Europe

There can be no doubt that, in the years immediately following the Second World War, the Soviet Union removed a certain amount of resources from Eastern Europe without giving equal resources in payment at the same time. There was some direct plunder and military reparation, especially from East Germany and other formerly fascist countries. There were also joint companies established with Soviet predominance in control and Soviet exploitation of profits from these countries. There were also extremely unequal trade agreements that amounted to further reparations. And interbloc agencies, such as the Council for Mutual Economic Aid, were used to control East European development along lines favorable to the Soviet Union rather than lines optimal for the countries involved.

On the other hand, the Soviet Union bore the main brunt of the fascist assault, and did liberate most of Eastern Europe by itself. Its contribution to the defeat of fascism was made at enormous cost, twenty million dead, a third to a half of industry and housing destroyed. The Soviet Union thus viewed most of the resources taken from Eastern Europe as very minor and totally inadequate repayment for the cost of liberation, especially since most of the resources were taken from the countries on the fascist side such as East Germany and Hungary. Moreover, the reparations levels were reduced or completely forgiven after a few years for some countries. The joint companies were all eventually abolished.

At present, the Soviets are taking *no* outright plunder from East Europe. At present, there are *no* more joint companies and *no* other form of Soviet investment in Eastern Europe.

Allegations of economic imperialism are based exclusively on (1) the terms of trade, and (2) the pattern of trade. As to the terms of trade, there is much evidence that most of the exchanges between the USSR and most East European countries are still unequal—with the USSR coming out best. Their greater strength seems based on (1) greater economic strength and (2) political domination. Since political domination was diminished somewhat after 1957 (following the denunciation of Stalin and the Polish and Hungarian revolts), it has appeared that the terms of trade have become more equal. Obviously, there are no reliable data on this question.

The pattern of trade has resembled neocolonialism in some areas. For example, the Soviet Union sold Rumania finished industrial goods, and bought from Rumania raw materials (mainly petroleum) and agricultural goods. On the other hand, it must be said that Soviet trade with the more industrialized areas, such as Czechoslovakia and East Germany, was quite different in pattern.

The Rumanians particularly objected to the fact that the Soviets tried to use Comecon (the Council for Mutual Economic Aid) to enforce the existing pattern over a long period. The Soviet idea sounded innocuous enough to socialists: it was that planning should be extended from countries to supernational planning via the Comecon agency. The Soviets then argued on the perfectly good-sounding economic principle of comparative advantage, namely, that each country should concentrate on what it could produce best at the present time. In practice, however, this meant that Rumania and Bulgaria would concentrate on raw materials and agricultural goods forever. Thus, these countries opposed the idea, and called for freedom of trade. Not unexpectedly, the Czechs and East Germans, who would concentrate on advanced industrial machinery, thought more highly of it. The Rumanian argument was based on the usual view of underdeveloped countries that all countries should develop fully in a well-rounded way, and that one cannot say just on the basis of present production what they should specialize in in the long run.

In addition to unequal trade, and the pattern of trade that was enforced for a short while, the Soviets have clearly also practiced political domination in East Europe. They have encouraged their own puppets, overthrown governments by force, and maintained long-term occupying armies.

Soviet Costs, Benefits, and Motivations

The Soviet Union cannot be considered imperialist in the capitalist sense, since it has no private enterprises making profits from exploitation of other countries. The public firms engaged in foreign trade may still make some extra profits out of unequal treaties imposed on East European countries, but these are small amounts in terms of aggregate Soviet incentive to imperialism—while no Soviet individual makes private profit from foreign trade. On the contrary, like any occupying power, *Soviet costs of keeping Eastern Europe in control to any extent are probably much higher than their current extra profits from unequal foreign trade.* Since the benefits are not concentrated in a small group, as in the large capitalist firms, it is hard to attribute Soviet control of East Europe to *economic* imperialism.

The reasons for Soviet interference and efforts at control stem more from their political, bureaucratic, and military sectors. No Soviet citizen can criticize military spending or foreign policy decisions. The political monopoly, with a heavy component of high military officers involved in policy decisions, considers how to expand and consolidate its own position, domestically and abroad. "While the expansionist capitalist dynamic is absent in the Soviet Union, the bureaucratic-militaristic dynamic is very present indeed. . . . Thus, while the Soviet Union lacks an imperialist dynamic that springs from its economic organization, it does not lack an expansionist dynamic which reflects the needs of its establishment to consolidate its world position."[1]

This political-bureaucratic-military dynamic could be seen in the Soviet invasion of Czechoslovakia in 1968. The bureaucracy could not understand how any socialist country could legitimately take a road different from the Soviet road. The military seemed to think of it in terms of their "need" for a protective wall of utterly subservient countries against the designs of German and American imperialism (but would Czechoslovakia be "needed" in a nuclear war?). The political leaders seemed most concerned lest the Czechoslovakian democratization process might spread to other countries and even to the Soviet Union.

There is also the problem of conflicts arising between developed, affluent socialist nations, such as the USSR, and poor, underdeveloped socialist nations, such as China. There are naturally differences in the degree of militancy of psychological attitudes, in domestic development policies, and in willingness to take international risks. The underdeveloped China of the 1960's resembled in revolutionary fervor and militant dogmatism the early Soviet Union of 1917–1921 and perhaps 1928–1932 (but it would be unrealistic to expect China to stay so revolutionary when her economy matures and affluence spreads). Moreover, there is a real material question at issue. What amount of aid should the advanced socialist country give the poor socialist country? Contention over this issue was one of the bases of the split between the Soviet Union and China.

Of course, the Soviet political-military dynamic was also in evidence in the split, with a Soviet demand for political obedience. The Chinese, though, reflected the same kind of political-military outlook, demanding (1) recognition of Mao as the direct heir of Lenin and Stalin, and (2) "return" of certain territories from the Soviet Union.

Finally, the conflicts among the socialist countries have been intensified by survivals of virulent nationalist chauvinism. Marxism has always been optimistic on this score: "National differences and antagonisms between peoples are already tending to disappear more and more. . . . The rule of the proletariat will efface these differences even more."[2] These brave words of 1848 have so far not come true. Instead, our century has seen nationalism and racism used as a tool by all the forces of reaction, such as German fascism or American imperialism. Moreover, sad to tell, Soviet leaders have appealed with very little disguise to Russian chauvinism against China, while the Maoists have used Chinese chauvinism against the Soviet Union.

World Government

There is no question whatever that deep cultural differences as well as irrational nationalisms remain barriers between the socialist countries. Given the Marxist tradition of internationalism, one would expect Communists to be in favor of world government. Stalin, however, was narrowly nationalist and suspicious of internationalism; he even persecuted writers and artists for "cosmopolitanism" or lack of "patriotism." Stalinists argued against world government, not only on the grounds of the continued existence of aggressive capitalist states, but on the argument that no limits must be placed on national sovereignty under socialism. In this world of nuclear threats, some limits are clearly necessary.

A sympathetic observer of the Soviet Union writes: "World government in some form is both possible and imperative if the human race is to be saved from suicide during the remaining decades of the Twentieth Century. The only obstacles to its attainment are the ancient and obsolete superstitions of 'sovereignty' and nationalism. . . . Communists, dedicated to building a better world, dare not continue to evade this task if they are serious in their announced purposes. As of 1967 they have not faced the issue."[3] It is certainly quite right that the task of unifying the world is both important and immediate for everyone.

It is not the case, however, that only some "obsolete superstitions" stand in the way of world unity. The basic cause is the need for imperialist expansion by capitalist countries, which causes most of the frictions and wars in the present world, as, for example, the Vietnam conflict. Furthermore, we have seen that even under socialism there are reasons why the ruling groups of each country use nationalism and external frictions as a means of stifling discontent and building internal unity behind their own leadership. Still, under socialism there certainly is a good possibility of achieving a high degree of unification, although progressive Marxists will have to fight for it.

Peaceful Coexistence

In the meantime the capitalist and socialist nations can all live together in peace or all die together. The Chinese are very suspicious of the Soviet slogan of "peaceful coexistence," claiming it is a fig leaf for Soviet-American collusion against the rest of the world. They actively support armed liberation struggles (where the Soviets are more hesitant and worried of precipitating nuclear war), and go so far as to speak of war possibilities in terms of "the international class struggle."[4]

Sometimes, the Chinese seem to think nuclear world war inevitable: "Increasingly, it seems, war cannot be averted, and the only reasonable course is full preparedness."[5] In Chapter 10 we found that capitalist imperialism does tend toward militarism, does indulge in "limited wars" to crush anti-imperialist movements in the neocolonial areas, and does produce clashes that could lead to a world holocaust. *But that does not make war "inevitable."* Certainly, one should do everything possible to avoid war, rather than to inflame the situation.

Moreover, contrary to their violent sounding rhetoric, in practice the Chinese have fortunately acted at least as cautiously as the Soviets. For example, they still recognize and trade with the foreign enclaves at Macao and Hong Kong—nor have they attempted an invasion of Formosa. When the Chinese are in the United Nations, it will certainly facilitate communications, and may help bring (or be a sign of) some lessened world tension. Furthermore, the situation is rapidly changing as more and more countries recognize the People's Republic of China, ending her isolation.

Even America and China are now (1971) flirting with each other over ping-pong tables—and all signs point to a new era with China playing a major role in the world.

NOTES

1. Andreas Papandreou, *Man's Freedom* (New York: Columbia University Press, 1970), p. 49.
2. Karl Marx and Frederick Engels, *The Communist Manifesto* (New York: International Publishers, 1948, written 1848), p. 28.
3. Frederick L. Schuman, "The USSR in World Affairs," in Samuel Hendel and Randolph Braham, eds., *The U.S.S.R. after 50 Years* (New York: Alfred Knopf, 1967), p. 230.
4. Shi Tung Hsiang, *Red Flag* (April 15, 1960).
5. Han Suyin, *China in the Year 2001* (New York: Basic Books, 1967), p. 173.

CHAPTER
21

Racism, Sexism, and Alienation Under Socialism

Racism

The Soviet Union inherited a nation filled with discrimination and bigotry of Russians against all the smaller non-Russian nationalities, plus the opposite anti-Russian sentiment by the other nationalities, plus intense hatred (and even physical pogroms or mass killings) by all against the Jews. To the credit of the Soviet government, it ended pogroms; prohibited all official discrimination; pursued a policy of equal opportunity in jobs, education, and all other needs; and conducted official propaganda against all chauvinism, especially condemning anti-Semitism. A traveler in the USSR says: "One of the difficulties encountered in earlier postwar years in convincing Soviet people (including nonreligious, younger Jews) that anti-Semitism exists in the USSR at all is that they know from their own experience how vastly it has declined."[1]

The Soviet government especially made an important effort to bring the most underdeveloped non-Russian (and mostly nonwhite) areas rapidly toward economic equality even at the sacrifice of some growth in more developed areas (mostly Russian). Many pro-Soviet writers have reported that "the U.S.S.R. continues today to put more money per capita each year into health, education, housing, and economic development in the former czarist colonies than into Russia proper, for the purpose of closing the tremendous gap that existed between them."[2] This view has now been supported in a systematic non-Marxist study, which found that *"more* resources have been devoted to industrialization in the seven (Middle Eastern) republics than would be warranted by any economic calculation, capitalist or socialist."[3]

Under Stalin, however, there did continue to be much real (though more hidden) anti-Semitism. For leading political jobs Stalin tended to favor Russians over Jews and other nationalities of the Soviet Union (though he did keep several Jews, Armenians, and Georgians in top offices, and he himself was a Georgian). In the great purges of the 1930's a disproportionate number of Jews were killed, but that is probably because they contributed a disproportionate number of the politically active. At times, Stalin seemed to use anti-Semitism as a political weapon against his enemies. And at the very end of his life, it seems that the arrest of several Jewish doctors was to be the beginning of a whole new bloody purge. Furthermore, Stalin in 1948 ended the previously large-scale facilities for Jewish cultural life. The attack included the closing down of Yiddish theaters, imprisonment of writers, and suspension of publication of almost all periodicals and books in Yiddish.

In fact, in the Soviet Union today "no schools or classes or even text-books in the Yiddish language exist."[4] From the amount of continued use of Yiddish by Soviet Jews, it is clear that this was not a voluntary suspension. The present Soviet government, however, has allowed resumption of publication of one Yiddish newspaper, one Yiddish bimonthly magazine, and has published some books in Yiddish (though not many).

The distance from the position of the Jews under German fascism (and even from the position of Black people in America) may also be seen in the economic and educational status of Soviet Jews. In 1961 Jews were 1.1 per cent of the population. They were, however, 8.5 per cent of professional writers and journalists, 10 per cent of college professors, 33 per cent of personnel in the film industry, 10 per cent of scientists, 10 per cent of judges and lawyers, 16 per cent of doctors, 7 per cent of musicians, artists, and actors, and 3.3 per cent of college undergraduates. On the other hand, in the political sphere only 0.5 per cent of the members of the government at all levels are Jews.[5] Furthermore, although the social-political situation is now qualitatively improved for Soviet Jews (with the absence of terror), there is still a residue of popular anti-Semitic sentiment, and there are still very few Yiddish cultural facilities. There is no official propaganda against anti-Semitism. Similarly, in Eastern Europe: "given our countries and their history, it is straining credulity to imagine that anti-Semitism disappeared overnight: it is not discreditable that it exists; what is discreditable is that it is not beng combatted."[6]

There is also a vast amount of very intensive "anti-Zionist" propaganda, which may easily be interpreted as anti-Jewish propaganda—and may be so interpreted by most Russians. In addition, some "antireligious" propaganda against Judaism is strongly anti-Semitic. Thus, the problem of anti-Semitism was *not* caused by one crazy dictator, and the tendencies are still present in the whole social organism (though there are counter-tendencies also present).

One cause of anti-Semitism is the leftovers of prejudice from Tsarist Russia. More basic is the fact of continued (though lessened) differential income, of continued bourgeois psychology, of continued differential political power used for individual advancement. The point is that under socialism—especially in nondemocratic political conditions—anti-Semitism can still be a profitable tool to certain political leaders. Only with some democratic control over leaders *and* with removal of private material motivations (by a communist distribution system) could the conditions for completely ending anti-Semitism and other racism finally be established.

Sexism

Women in Tsarist Russia were badly oppressed; had few if any rights, either political or economic; had to obey their husbands in all matters; could not get a divorce; and were considered inferior to men in most ways (although literature depicted some strong-minded heroines among the educated women). The revolution changed all this. Article 122 of the Soviet constitution (1936) says that "women in the USSR are accorded equal rights with men in all spheres of economic, cultural, political, and other public activities."

Women fought in the Revolution, and there was a considerable women's liberation movement. In November, 1918, a Soviet women's conference was held in Moscow with 1,147 delegates, including many peasant women. In 1918, also, the Central Committee of the Party established a women's section of the committee composed of women to push women's liberation. Most of the Soviet Union in the 1920's remained agricultural, and most peasants stuck to a traditional subservient role for women. As late as 1933 an American woman in the Soviet Union wrote: "On a motor trip I visited many cottages in outlying villages; the women stood while the men sat down and ate; kept their heads bent and their hands folded, not speaking until they were spoken to."[7]

The Soviet government in the 1920's propagandized for equal rights, allowed freedom of divorce, legalized abortion, and pushed for women's liberation in many ways (even helping women to remove the veil in Central Asia). Marriages and divorces could be registered by a simple postcard, but many intellectuals did not register at all, feeling that registration of marriage was "too bourgeois."

324

Racism, Sexism, and Alienation under Socialism

With the five year plans, Stalin wanted to aid industrialization with a more regimented society, including a stable family and more difficult divorce, and by higher population growth rates, through encouraging children, ignoring birth control, and making abortion illegal. Stalin abolished the women's section of the Central Committee in 1929. The government declared that "so-called free love is a bourgeois invention and has nothing in common with the principles of conduct of a Soviet citizen. Moreover, marriage receives its full value for the State only if there is progeny. . . ."[8] These authoritarian and puritanical trends were not reversed again until after Stalin's death.

Even in 1970 about one-half of Soviet men and women lived in the countryside, and about one-quarter of city people were country-born. Nevertheless, the role of women has drastically changed in many ways. For example, the largest circulation magazine in the Soviet Union today is *Rabotnitsa (The Working Woman)*. In 1967, the number of employed women with higher education was fifty-four times as high as in 1928. They have comprised over 50 per cent of the whole labor force ever since 1945 (including 70 per cent of all women—twice the U.S. rate). Moreover, the Soviet Union does have (1) a vast system of low-cost or free child-care facilities; (2) legal dissemination of birth control information and devices; (3) legal and universally available abortion; (4) equal pay for equal work; (5) acceptance of women in all professions; (6) equality before the law; (7) divorce at will; and (8) an insignificant rate of prostitution.

On the other hand, in the professions in which women predominate, for example, medicine and teaching, the pay is much less than those in which men predominate, for example, engineering. Thus, women are 75 per cent of all physicians, but only 33 per cent of all engineers (a tremendous advance over Tsarist Russia or any capitalist country today). It is still the case that men are expected to enter the higher paid professions, because the man is supposed to support the family. Men predominate overwhelmingly at the top level of all professions, especially in politics. Only three women were among the 133 members of the Central Committee in 1956, and only three more among the 122 candidate members.[9] There is, in 1970, only one woman in the Soviet Council of Ministers (out of sixty), although women are 27 per cent of the deputies in the not-too-important Soviet congress (or Supreme Soviet).

On the other hand, "career women get no opposition from men. They are not regarded jealously or as competitors. Neither Russian men nor women feel that the woman intellectual is in danger of losing her sex appeal."[10] Thus, women are 63 per cent of all specialists with a secondary education, and they are 53 per cent of all professionals with higher education. Women constitute 40 per cent of all farm experts, 40 per cent of all judges, 75 per cent of physicians, and 85 per cent of all administrators in health services. In the most traditional "male" areas of mechanics and machine adjustors, women rose from 1 per cent in 1926 to 9 per cent in 1964 (and we noted that they are 33 per cent of all engineers).

Moreover, women are helped to keep their jobs by an adequate system of maternity leaves in all industry. Women are allowed eight weeks prenatal and eight weeks postnatal leave at full pay. They may also choose to take their annual paid vacation after that (two to three weeks), and an additional three months unpaid leave if desired.[11]

Just before the Revolution, women made up only 25 per cent of all university enrollment. Since the Revolution, the number of girls and boys in grades 1 through 10 is equal except for the more backward republics, where girls leave school at an earlier age than boys. Through the 10th grade, the curriculum is uniform for both sexes. Beyond that grade the percentage of women tends to decline. Still, 53 per cent of all medical students and even 25 per cent of all agricultural students are women.

In 1933, women with a degree of "kandidat" (close to our Ph.D.) were very close to zero per cent. In 1968, they received 31 per cent of all kandidat degrees.[12] In 1959, 24 per cent of all management posts including department heads were women. In 1967, women were 20 per cent of associate professors and 9 per cent of the highest academic ranks (full professor or member of Academy of Sciences).

Child-care facilities in 1969 had provisions for nine million children. Soviet women still complain of the shortage of facilities, since there are still places for only 70 per cent of urban children and less than that for rural areas. They also complain of the poor quality of the facilities.

Marriage still presents many traditional male-female problems, including the attitude of men that the woman should do all the housework after she returns from the day's work (although educated men under thirty-five do much more housework than the average). The basic problem of Soviet woman, in spite of her equal opportunities for education and occupation, *is that male supremacy still keeps her doing about three times as much housework as the man* (even though her outside job is often equal in toil).

The resistance of women is showing up partly in a skyrocketing divorce rate. In 1950 there were three divorces for every 100 marriages. In 1967 there were thirty divorces per 100 marriages. Divorce is most frequent among the intelligentsia.

It is also true that Soviet women still have many fewer household appliances and poorer services for the household than American women. Some Soviet women have complained of sexual oppression from lack of sufficient services, such as child-care centers (better than in America, but still inadequate) and laundries (worse than in America).[13] Some progress has been made in helping the housewife in recent years. The USSR made 300 washing machines in 1950, but five million in 1969. Seating capacity of restaurants has risen 80 per cent from 1960 to 1969. The retail sales force per head of population has risen one-third since 1960.

The first thesis on sex attitudes in forty years appeared in 1968.[14] Among other things, this thesis notes that 47 per cent of undergraduate, unmarried women had had intercourse although only 38 per cent approved of pre-marital sex. In a sample of white-collar people, 90 per cent of men and 81 per cent of women approved of premarital sex if the experience was with a loved one. Of the men, 60 per cent thought premarital sex with an acquaintance (not loved) was permissible for themselves, but only 14 per cent of the women thought so.

Concerning the double standard, 30 per cent of the men thought that it was alright for a woman they love to have sexual relations with others; while 48 per cent of the women okayed it for a loved man. The survey showed that, while the double standard is dying out, men are still "more liberal toward their own sexual behavior than toward that of women, and women are more liberal toward male sexual behavior than toward their own."[15]

Soviet sexual morality in the 1970's, nevertheless, demands of young people continence until marriage, associating sex only with children and a family. Extramarital affairs are frowned upon. The cult of virginity is once again glorified. And some women still choose to marry the man with the most material wealth.

Men and women have equal rights in marriage. Prior property remains owned by the individual. Property acquired after marriage is communally owned. Soviet sociological surveys find most spouses saying they married for love, few for material reasons, and less than 1 per cent because children would otherwise be born out of wedlock.[16] Of course, there is much less real equality in the rural areas, with women still being harrassed for loss of virginity.

The history of divorce law shows some changing Soviet views. Immediately after the revolution and in the 1920's and 1930's divorce was free and automatic when requested. In 1944 Stalin made divorce complicated and expensive, although incompatibility was still the usual grounds. The family then became a sanctified institution, not to be easily dissolved. In 1955 and again in 1965 divorce was made a little simpler and a little less expensive.

These new laws, at a time of rising divorces (though still much less than the American rate), were compromises. The reformers had asked for much greater liberalization. The rigid attitude against divorces remains dominant.

In its guiding interpretations, the USSR Supreme Court has pointed out that courts trying divorce cases must begin with the task of strengthening the family, and that temporary discord in the family and conflicts between spouses due to random and transient factors must not be regarded as sufficient grounds for divorce.[17]

Nevertheless, a couple without children can get a divorce in three months without court costs. A couple with children can always get a divorce if they agree, persist, and pay some costs. The husband pays child support, but no other alimony.

Stalin's 1944 law also had ended the father's obligations to children born outside marriage. Before that time, the father's obligations to all children were the same. In 1968 a new law gave the single mother the right to receive a state allowance, and the right to place the child in an institution to be brought up at the state's expense if the identity of the father is not established (and the mother *is* once again entitled to child support if the father's identity is established).

Immediately after the Revolution, birth control information was made free and available. This was done in spite of continued firm opposition to Malthusian overpopulation theories. Lenin wrote: "The freedom of medical information and the defense of the elementary democratic rights of men and women citizens is one thing. The social theory of neo-Malthusianism is something else."[18] The point is that the overpopulation theory is often a mask and rationale for poverty and exploitation in the capitalist countries and for imperialism in the underdeveloped countries. It *is* a problem, but of much lower priority than the abolition of capitalism and imperialism. Under socialism birth control (1) aids the mother to plan her life as she pleases, and (2) helps keep down population growth. In most instances, the lower population growth means greater goods and services to the individual with less total pollution (and less total national product, but the smaller national product hurts only military potential and national prestige).

In 1936 Stalin radically changed the policy. Birth control by contraceptives was still legal, but discouraged (especially by very, very low production of contraceptives for at least two decades). Stalin also in 1936 banned all abortions not medically necessary. He also began a policy of subsidies increasing with the number of children, designed to increase population so as to provide more labor for industrial expansion. Under Stalin, a doctor performing an abortion was imprisoned for two years and the woman was subject to public censure for the first offense and fined 300 rubles for a second offense.[19]

In 1955 Khrushchev repealed the ban on abortions. Abortions were made legal and free for working women, cost five rubles (or about $4.50) for housewives and students and two rubles (or about $1.80) for farm women. The abortion rate has been quite high, especially because contraceptives (such as the diaphragm or the pill) have been almost impossible to get (remember that the top planners are mostly men). Apparently, a major increase in the production of contraceptives in the last few years has finally started, mostly because of alarm over the abortion rate.[20] As a result of all birth control methods the number of children per woman in the USSR had dropped by 1969 to 1.7 (1.9 in rural areas, 1.5 in urban areas), so the present official Soviet line is worry over declining population.

Chinese Women

This chapter is mainly limited to the Soviet Union because there is not enough clear, well documented data on any of the other socialist countries. Nevertheless, a word must be said on what is known for certain about China. For centuries Chinese women were among the most oppressed in the world. Women were treated little better than slaves, whether they were called wives or concubines. As late as the 1930's and 1940's under the Kuomintang, many, many cases were reported of women being bought and sold into bondage. Practices such as binding the feet continued in many areas.

The Chinese Communists have brought a miracle for a fourth of the women of the world by raising their status to equality, in the law, in the minds of most women, and even to a large extent in the minds of most men. Their program of equal rights for women in marriage, education, jobs, and politics has penetrated even to some of the most remote villages. Millions of Chinese women have demonstrated their competency in higher education, professional careers, and positions of leadership—and many of these have marriages with approximate equality of position. While they undoubtedly have a long, long way to go, this is an amazing advance in such a short period.[21]

Alienation

The problem of alienation under socialism has many facets, and each has given rise to different, partially contradictory theories. The old dogmatic Marxist theory espoused by Stalinists said that all alienation is due to capitalist ownership of the means of production and exploitation of the workers. Since socialism is by definition an economy in which the workers (represented by the state) own the means of production and their product, alienation must disappear. This theory has been negated by long experience of alienation in countries that Stalinists have considered "socialist." An East European philosopher admits sadly that "the course of socialist revolution has shown that the various forms of alienation do not automatically disappear with the abolition of the *institution* of private ownership of the means of production."[22]

Private ownership of the means of production *is* a major cause of alienation under capitalism, but it is *not* the only cause. The fact that private ownership *is* a major cause of alienation is brought out in some evidence on the favorable effects of the British nationalization of a few industries. It has been found that the British nationalization of the coal mines—even though they are run by independent boards under ultimate parliamentary control without much workers' participation—has nevertheless reduced strife and alienation in the mines.[23]

The opposite equally dogmatic view is taken by the defenders of capitalism. Since they have to agree that alienation exists under capitalism, they argue that it must also exist in any industrialized society. Marxists—beginning with Marx—have always acknowledged that any industrialized society up to and including socialism will be plagued by certain problems of alienation inherent in the work process of industry. There is the fact that one must work for a living; being a necessity, it is difficult to make it a joy. There is the fact that much work is dirty or routine or dangerous.

There is the fact that a hierarchy is needed from the worker to the foreman to the manager in order to supervise and ensure the orderly progression of the work process. There is the fact that above the enterprise in a planned economy it is necessary to have a large bureaucracy of planners and administrators to make and carry out the plans. There is the simple fact that with present technology almost all workers (except a minute number of artisans and creative workers) make only a small part of their product. Marx himself stressed this point of the division of labor and the specialization of workers to one very detailed process, with its crippling effect on human mental and physical processes. The problem exists as well under socialism. "Unfortunately, the technical aspects of the problem cut across all systems—for example, work on an assembly line is inherently the same regardless of government."[24] Socialism may, of course, consciously try to choose less alienating technologies, but that is not easy.[25]

None of this means that socialism is not an advance over capitalism. The end of exploitation through private ownership of the means of production does drastically lessen one source of alienation. The point of serious Marxists is only that other causes still persist. Several of the causes so far mentioned would appear to persist even into communism, but that issue is left for a later chapter.

It is also true that all the present socialist economies are far from communism and illustrate particularly socialist causes of alienation. They all continue to use money, there is continued wage differentiation, continued unequal income distribution, continued consumer markets, continued private ownership of consumer goods, and continued labor markets in which labor power is bought and sold. All of these are necessary and understandable at the present level of technology, but they also assume and continually reinforce the old commercial psychology. The psychology of getting rich, the dog-eat-dog mentality, and so forth, cannot be eliminated so long as these institutions exist, although social propaganda can begin to reduce them (and many aspects of psychology have changed somewhat in the Soviet Union). If some day a communist economy is instituted— with no wages or prices for consumer goods—then perhaps this psychology *might* begin to change radically.

In the existing socialist states there is also the additional problem that historical conditions of economic and political backwardness resulted in the dismal type of Stalinist dictatorship over the workers: ". . . Overcentralization, the over-expansion of the role of the State, not only had a harmful effect on the development of socialist democracy, but distorted and pushed toward alienation the productive activities of people too."[26] We contend that a democratic socialism will greatly reduce alienation, but that cannot yet be proven because the existing socialist states have mostly been run as dictatorships, with special privileges for a small elite.

There is finally the question of what kind of socialism is to exist, how much plan and how much market, moral or material incentives, collective or individual incentives—and how each of these forms affect alienation. On the one side are those who argue that economic planning by society, with the elimination of as much as posssible of the market, will reduce commercial psychology and allow people to cooperate in production for social use rather than for profit. They consider that this is central to the socialist vision, and quote Marx and Engels on the change from the anarchy of the market to the freedom of a society that is consciously planned.

On the other side are many East European Marxists who agree on the need for broad social planning, but argue that its vast overextension into everyday details for each plant has created a bureaucratic monster. "The ideology of market socialism sees the roots of alienation in bureaucratic manipulation of men both in economic and in political life. . . ."[27] The practical point here is the need for decentralization and use of the market to reduce bureaucracy; and perhaps for workers' participation in economic decision-making at the enterprise level (as is the case in Yugoslavia, and to some extent in Cuba and China).

As pointed out in the chapter on market socialism, however, any increase in local decision-making does carry the danger that the local collective may enrich itself at the expense of the rest of society, as with monopoly profits from high prices. Moreover, any increase in local decision-making does lessen the area of democratic decision-making at the national level. To this extent, therefore, decentralization and worker participation may increase commercialization and alienation from that source.

Furthermore, the introduction of the market focuses the manager and the worker more on individual, material incentives—with bonuses reflecting enterprise profitability. Obviously, any Marxist must be in favor of increased moral and collective incentives *as circumstances allow*. It is not clear, however, that the old Soviet system of output targets, with managers and workers under immense pressure to meet the target by any means legal or illegal, was any less conducive to a psychology of individualism.

It is one thing to argue for an increased area of free goods and purely moral incentives to work (discussed in Chapter 22). It is quite a different thing to argue for centralized planning, of day-to-day decisions by bureaucrats as being better than decentralized decisions at the enterprise level with the aid of the market. As we stated before, it is simply a chimera to think that an advanced economic system can operate with *neither* a market *nor* a central-planning bureaucracy. No third way of economic decision-making has been invented. One must choose some combination of these evils. This does not affect our earlier conclusion that it is still possible to greatly reduce alienation, given a democratic socialist society.

NOTES

1. William Mandel, in Samuel Hendel and Randolph Braham, eds., *The U.S.S.R. after 50 Years* (New York: Alfred Knopf, 1967), p. 188.
2. *Ibid.*, p. 189.
3. Alec Nove and J. A. Newth, *The Soviet Middle East* (New York: Frederick Praeger, 1967), p. 46. Also in agreement is K. Wilber, *The Soviet Model and Underdeveloped Countries* (Chapel Hill: University of North Carolina Press, 1969).
4. Admission by its editor in the theoretical journal of the Communist Party of the United States, *Political Affairs*, 43 (July 1964), p. 3.
5. See William Mandel, *Russia Re-Examined* (New York: Hill and Wang, 1967 ed.), pp. 46–70.
6. Adam Schaff, *Marxism and the Human Individual* (New York: McGraw-Hill, transl. 1970, first publ. 1965), p. 224.
7. Ella Winter, *Red Virtue* (New York: Harcourt, Brace, 1933), p. 101.
8. Commissariat of Justice, *Sotsialisticheskaya Zakonnost* (1939), no. 2.
9. Maurice Hindus, *House without a Roof* (Garden City, N.Y.: Doubleday, 1961), p. 286.
10. *Ibid.*, p. 288.
11. Mandel, *Russia Re-Examined*, op. cit., pp. 174–175.
12. *Narodnoe khoziaistvo SSSR v 1968* (Moscow, 1969).
13. A. Lysakova, quoted in "Information Supplement" to *Soviet Studies* (April 1967), p. 15.
14. S. I. Golod, "Sociological Problems of Sexual Morality," transl. in *Soviet Sociology* (Summer 1969).

Racism, Sexism, and Alienation under Socialism

15. *Ibid.*, p. 13.
16. See the article by I. Mindlin, "The Old in the New," in Paul Hollander, ed., *American and Soviet Society* (Englewood Cliffs, N.J.: Prentice-Hall, 1967), pp. 185–188.
17. Gorkin, "Concern for the Soviet Family," *Soviet Review*, 10 (Fall 1969): 49.
18. Lenin, *The Woman Question* (New York: International Publishers, 1937, first publ. 1918), p. 5.
19. Hindus, *op. cit.*, p. 144.
20. Peter Juviler, "Soviet Families" in Hollander, *op. cit.*, pp. 208–209. Also, see David Heer, "Abortion, Contraception, and Population Policy in the Soviet Union," *Soviet Studies*, 17 (July 1965): pp. 76–83.
21. See, e.g., Edgar Snow, *The Other Side of the River: Red China Today* (New York: Random House, 1961), pp. 248–255 and 292–300.
22. Schaff, *op. cit.*, p. 196.
23. See the book written with great beauty and sensitivity by Clinton Jencks, *Men Underground: Working Conditions of British Coal Miners since Nationalization* (San Diego: San Diego College Press, 1969).
24. Schaff, *op. cit.*, p. 135.
25. See Ché Guevara, *Man and Socialism in Cuba* (available in several different editions).
26. Miklos Almasi, "Alienation and Socialism," in Herbert Aptheker, ed., *Marxism and Alienation* (New York: Humanities Press, 1965), p. 126.
27. Ludek Rychetnik, "Two Models of an Enterprise in Market Socialism," *Economics of Planning*, 8, no. 3 (1968): 216–231.

CHAPTER
22

Communist Revolution

Pure communism is a society in which people do not work for wages, but for the social good, and there are no prices, but people take according to need. Although communism appears more desirable than socialism to Marxist theorists, no such profound change can come about unless large numbers of people push for it. And people will push hard for something, such as Communism, only if they feel they do have an objective need for it—that is, if the deficiencies in their present system are great enough.

The Need for Communism

We may summarize here the various problems of U.S. capitalism and Soviet socialism; the other capitalist and other socialist countries have similar problems, though varying greatly in degree. We will then see why many people look beyond socialism toward a communist solution to many problems.

U.S. capitalism is efficient within each enterprise to a large degree. It suffers, however, from extreme income inequality due to exploitation; considerable general unemployment; considerable inflation; pollution; inefficiency through waste, particularly advertising and military; monopoly high prices and excess profits; monopoly obstruction through planned obsolescence and holding back some inventions; racial, religious, and sexual discrimination; many forms of alienation; and imperialist activity leading to (limited?) wars. The majority of capitalist countries, particularly the underdeveloped ones, have political dictatorships.

Soviet socialism is probably somewhat less efficient within each enterprise. Income distribution, however, is much more equal and exploitation is very small in total amount. It has a high growth rate, no general unemployment, and very little inflation at present. It has no private monopoly, but a large inefficient bureaucracy. It has very little racial and sexual discrimination, but some discrimination against Jews. Its pollution level is much less than the U.S. level. It does dominate East Europe in an imperialist manner, but for reasons not directly economic. It has a repressive dictatorship, and very considerable alienation.

A fully communist society would solve the problem of income distribution. Its economic possibilities in terms of criteria such as growth and efficiency are discussed in Chapter 23. Politically, it offers hope for the end of police and prisons, wars and armies; socially, it offers hope for the eventual end of discrimination and alienation; these issues are discussed in Chapter 24.

Nonantagonistic Contradictions?

It has always been assumed by Marxists that there can be a peaceful evolution from socialism to communism. Writers such as Mao Tse-tung assume that there can only be "nonantagonistic contradictions" within socialism, meaning disagreements between friendly groups that can be solved within the system. Yet one would have to modify this to the extent that if there is a political dictatorship existing in the Soviet Union or China itself, it may take a political revolution to overthrow the present leadership, before communism would be possible. Only a sufficiently democratic political system, that would reflect the interests of the lowest interest groups, could lead peacefully from socialism to communism.

To the extent, however, that the Soviet elite may be obtaining by political means a larger share of the national product than their own labor entitles them to have, they have a vested interest of a very strong nature in maintaining the present socialist system as opposed to communism. Therefore, the Soviet ruling elite may promise a larger area of free goods, but it is not clear that they will ever keep this economic promise until there has been a political change. Whether the change may be by peaceful democratic means or by violent revolution depends on how deep-seated the vested interest of the Soviet elite is—and their will and ability to protect those interests. The longer they maintain a political dictatorship over the workers without democratic channels of change, the more likely it is that the change will be violent.

We can thus talk about a revolution of the working classes under socialism to remove a barrier which has arisen to social advance. The barrier results from the contradiction between the improving technology and the present frozen productive relationships. In other words, to move from the present socialist payment according to labor done to the communist free sharing—especially in the context of a political dictatorship by the elite—may mean the necessity of a revolution for establishing communism. Thus, one could be a revolutionary in the Soviet Union by calling for the more rapid establishment of communism in the Soviet Union. And this could be a rallying cry for an actual political movement to abolish political and economic inequality: to obtain more democratic political processes and more of the communist type of distribution of goods.

PART IV

THE POLITICAL ECONOMY OF COMMUNISM

23

The Economics of Communism

Marxism divides the post capitalist era into two stages.[1] The first stage is "socialism," in which there is public ownership of the means of production and payment of wages according to the amount produced by the worker. The second stage is "communism," in which there is still public ownership, but workers receive goods according to "need."

There are, however, as many interpretations of the word "need" as there are of "communism." One view of full communism is that of the utopian socialists. Bellamy, in *Looking Backward*, thinks of full communism as meaning equal wages for everyone.[2] The equality of wages is, in his view, the way to achieve the minimum needs of all individuals.

The modern Soviet definition of communism is quite different from the Bellamy view.[3] It visualizes neither equal wages nor rationing, but rather a complete absence of money, prices, and wages. Under pure communism, "free" goods would be produced under public control and ownership, and consumed by everyone according to his desires.[4] This last interpretation is the most common Marxist view, and is accepted here for definitional purposes.

Another contemporary view is the suggestion for a minimum guaranteed money income, sometimes called the "negative income tax" because the government would pay poor taxpayers while richer taxpayers pay taxes to the government. This alternative is not considered here because the present proposals would not fit a communist society, and are mostly just devices to mitigate poverty while preserving capitalism. The communist goal would include elimination of poverty, but also stresses the need for a noncommercialized cooperative society. Introduction into socialism of an adequate guaranteed money income (rather than free goods) might solve some problems of communism, *but* it would also preserve more of the present money-grubbing, competitive psychology. Some of the vast literature on this alternative is cited in the references to this chapter.

The Problems and the Model

Assume an economy with public ownership, central planning, and central commands to producers, but no wages and no prices. In this model of pure communism, three major problems are alleged to be unsolvable.[5] First, at zero price for all goods, demand would be infinite, since man's desires are infinite. Therefore, no supply could ever be enough to meet the demand. Second, at zero wages and with no penalty for indolence, labor, it is alleged, would lack sufficient incentive to work, since man is by nature lazy. Third, without rational prices there can be no optimal planning. Hence, communism would be very inefficient.

Assuming contemporary attitudes to work, it may be admitted that the first two objections are accurate enough to make full communism impossible. The utopian answer has always been that these attitudes will change, that man will be willing to work for the social good alone, and that desires may be voluntarily limited to some "reasonable" finite amount. Obviously, if attitudes were to change in this way, the first two objections to full communism would vanish. But this is not a very interesting case.

It would be interesting on the other hand to know whether *partial communism* is compatible with present worker and consumer attitudes. By partial communism is meant an economic system where 80 to 90 per cent of all goods are *free*. It is claimed below that this system is workable and that it would achieve almost all the political and social advantages usually alleged in favor of full communism.

The Problem of Abundance

Socialists have always assumed a great increase in production under socialism as a prerequisite to communism. They assume efficient planning, increased education and research, no unemployment, no wasteful advertising, no monopoly misallocation, no military spending, and so forth. These arguments need not be evaluated here because it is important to examine the objections to communism on their own grounds. Certainly, fantastic productivity increases make the supply problem easier, but they would still not meet infinite demand. To be realistic, we should assume only the rate of growth of labor productivity currently found in the Soviet Union.

In addition to the material achievement of very high labor productivity, Soviet theorists assume changes in subjective behavior both with respect to (1) willingness to work with no personal economic goal and (2) willingness to avoid pure wasteful or conspicuous consumption. Both of these changes in economic behavior are explored below. Here, however, it should only be noted that the Soviet and Chinese leaders sometimes talk as if these changes in human nature could be achieved by propaganda alone. That is not credible in terms of any social science, and certainly not of Marxism, which always emphasizes the primacy of the economic base. It is quite another thing to say that *once* there is a very high level of abundance, a large sector of free goods, and the reduction of labor hours to four or five a day, it may be possible to change "human nature."

Assume extreme acquisitiveness on the commodity demand side and extreme indolence on the labor supply side. Are foreseeable advances in productivity sufficient to institute full communism? Suppose we begin with the Soviet economic model according to which public ownership is the only mode of ownership, most goods are sold for money, and wages are highly differentiated. Some percentage of Soviet goods (and services), such as health and education, is already free. The Soviet leaders claim that these free goods (and transfer payments in money) amount to more than 25 per cent of the real wage, but the true percentage is quite debatable.

It must be emphasized that the *economics of communism is the economics of affluence.* Thus, with its much larger material base, the United States could start with a much larger percentage of free goods ("skipping" socialism to that degree). Conversely, China cannot immediately have a large free goods sector except by drastic rationing of those goods, with high prices and high taxes on the remaining goods.

The argument here is that, whatever the present sector of free goods (and services) in the socialist countries, they could—if that is honestly desired by the political leadership—expand the free goods sector more rapidly than is usually admitted by most economists. Suppose a socialist economy in which there is public ownership of all enterprises. Suppose that initially 10 per cent of all consumer goods are distributed free of charge. Suppose that its output of consumer goods doubles every twenty years. Suppose, finally, that this government (which could be the Soviet Union) decides to pursue a strict policy of no money-wage increases, but uses the entire increase in productivity to increase the output, and so to reduce the prices, of selected consumer goods. Within a relatively short time, such an economy could have a very significant proportion of free consumption.

Suppose that in 1970 the aggregate consumption of goods (and services) in that economy is, say, 100 billion dollars, and that the money income is ninety billion dollars. Assume in that year 10 per cent free consumption, or ten billion dollars of free consumer goods. On the assumption of double the output of consumer goods in twenty years, this means 200 billion dollars of consumer goods at constant prices in the year 1990. Assuming no wage increases (where this is the only source of income), there is still only ninety billion dollars' income in 1990. But this leaves 110 billion dollars of consumer goods unsold, all of which may be distributed free. Thus, with no inflation or higher taxation, the percentage of free consumer goods could rise to 55 per cent in that year. On the same assumptions, the free consumption sector would be 78 per cent by the year 2010. Yet the economic assumptions here (a 10 per cent initial free goods sector, and twice as many consumer goods in twenty years) are very conservative for the Soviet Union.[6] Only the political assumptions (real willingness to hold down money incomes and increase free goods) are radical.

To accomplish this economic transition gradually means to lower the prices of basic necessities slowly, while noting the reaction (the "elasticity") of demand to price changes. It is even possible to specify which goods should first be made free without causing economic disruption. One of the criteria must be fairly inelastic demand, so that falling prices do not greatly increase demand. A related criterion is that the free products should *not* be substitutes for those still on sale, otherwise the increase in demand for the free goods might be much greater than predicted on the basis of their previous use.

Luckily, these two criteria only exclude luxury goods, and admit on the whole all consumer necessities. Obviously, in the continuing expansion of the free public goods sector, each marginal choice is a vital and controversial social decision. It would be imperative to make it as democratically as possible.

Economics and Psychology

The communist dream and the arguments supporting the change from a socialist to a communist economy seem to be satisfied sufficiently by the provision of a free supply of basic consumer necessities. Free consumer necessities may be sufficient because the point of the change is to increase socialist consciousness and the feeling for social cooperation and to remove the ethos of competition. If all the basic necessities are free, and one need no longer work in order to earn a living, eventually there would be a large change in the basic attitudes toward work and consumption, regardless of whether wages were still paid for luxury goods. An economy of 80 per cent free goods would also mean most other noneconomic advantages claimed for full communism (see next chapter).

With the retention of prices for luxury goods, however, a communist economy may be established without asking workers and managers to act as if their psychological attitudes had progressed far beyond the actual "human nature" imposed by the current economic base. To hope that revolutionary propaganda and education alone can permanently (beyond a temporary enthusiasm following a successful revolution) provide a sufficient basis for a change in human nature is not Marxist but utopian socialist. In other words, neither workers nor managers will change their competitive, egotistic economic behavior *until* the material and institutional conditions are changed.[7] A socialist economy, in which payment for consumer necessities is required, reinforces and produces competitiveness in people every day—it is *not* a leftover from capitalism.

So long as the economy continues to be fundamentally a money economy, with the satisfaction of the bulk of people's needs depending on the number of currency tokens a person possesses, and so long as, under conditions of relative shortage, rationing governs distribution, the struggle of all against all to appropriate a bigger proportion of these currency tokens will inevitably persist.[8]

Only when all consumer necessities have been free for some time under full communism would any social scientist, Marxist or otherwise, expect that acquisitive behavior might begin to diminish very considerably.

It would, of course, be a very crude and inaccurate economic determinism to claim that there can be *no* changes in the ideological outlook of most people until a new structure of society is actually in existence. For example, in the Soviet and Chinese cases ideology toward collective work and consumption has slowly changed. Certainly many people must have advanced toward a communist consciousness even under capitalism or there never would have been a socialist revolution. Moreover, the Soviet and Chinese peoples are slowly beginning to take for granted that a larger and larger proportion of the product will be in collective consumption rather than private goods. The only point is that Soviet and Chinese managers and workers are not saints. They are far from working purely for love of humanity; nor would that be expected in a situation where long, hard working hours are required and where many goods and services are still in very short supply.

Obviously, socioeconomic conditions and psychological outlooks intertwin, mutually affect each other, and generally move together. Communism requires as prerequisites changes in material conditions, economic structures, *and* consciousness. The only warning is that we must not expect miraculous changes in average consciousness overnight far in advance of structural changes and material conditions. Thus, it is not fair to ex-

343

pect Soviet managers or consumers to act on the whole differently than their incentive structure directs them. Nor can we expect (as Reich in *The Greening of America* dreams) that new communist-type attitudes will fall from the skies and allow us to establish a brand new society of voluntary cooperation with no struggles and no resistance to basic structural changes.

Balance of Supply and Demand

Peter Wiles maintains that it is impossible to have full communism if it means no rationing through prices *and* no physical rationing.[9] He maintains that one or the other is necessary. His argument may be correct with regard to the immediate introduction of 100 per cent free goods. Yet, the point really is that, while keeping supply and demand in equilibrium, one could gradually eliminate prices *and* rationing for, say, 80 per cent of goods in the foreseeable future. Demand would be limited by keeping aggregate wages constant, while labor would be allocated by the same differential wages as before.

The Soviet leaders like to discuss the psychological conditioning that inclines people to make less, more "reasonable demands." We have already pointed out that basic consumer attitudes cannot be expected to change as a result of propaganda, but *may* change eventually as a result of changed conditions. If 80 per cent of consumer goods are free, there may be some decrease in the desire to keep up with the Joneses and, generally, less conspicuous consumption. After all, conspicuous consumption is designed to impress others, and you cannot do that by consuming free goods. Furthermore, purely wasteful use by delinquents should also disappear as a new generation takes such free goods for granted—especially if we begin with basic necessities. Even the anticommunist Wiles admits that, given present attitudes toward work and consumption, the "rational" consumer of Western economics (1) has physical limits on the food, clothing and shelter he can use, and (2) wants leisure from consuming![10]

Even at zero price in money terms, an individual's demand must be limited for particular goods because *time* as well as money must be spent on the purchase and consumption of goods and services. For example, health services and education both require much time to consume. Even food requires time to find in stores, to prepare, and to eat. This is one reason why even the very rich buy limited amounts of many desirable things.

It may be suggested that very low prices should be kept on basic necessities to prevent mischievous waste by children or teenagers. Low prices, however, may mean more administrative cost than revenue. For example, in the case of buses, removing fares altogether would lessen the work of bus drivers. Yet how many people will ride in buses just for fun if the reduction is gradual? After a product is free for some years, it is more likely to be taken for granted. In any case this is not a crucial point.

Finally, if 80 per cent of consumer goods are free, the other 20 per cent might be distributed mainly by monetary means. In some small sectors we may even wish to use physical rationing or a combination of physical and monetary rationing. For example, even at a fairly high level of affluence, some expensive items like trips to other stars might be rationed.

The Saving Ratio

The upshot of the above discussion is that a wide area of purely communist distribution could be achieved in a practical way in the near future without an extraordinary rate of growth. In fact, there is no reason to expect a communist society to pursue growth in a feverish manner. For one thing, the rate of saving must inevitably be democratically decided in a communist society. The question must be decided by everyone, not by a few giant corporations or an elite bureaucracy, because dissatisfaction would easily reveal itself in the decision of individuals to do less work or no work—since basic sustenance is guaranteed (and this means that a government preoccupied with very rapid growth would not hurry to introduce free goods).

Moreover, at a reasonably high level of affluence, further advances become less urgent. One winter coat may be vital, two, less so. At a high level of consumption, and automation (assuming world peace), there may only be temporary and specialized reasons for further growth—at least in the view of the vast majority of economic units that will make the decision. Furthermore, we can assume that cultural advance and family planning will tend to produce a stable population. Finally, as artistic sensitivity increases, and as the current commercialization of culture is finally eliminated by institutional change, we may perhaps expect a stronger desire for leisure time than for material goods.

Little growth, little saving, and little net investment—shades of the classical economist's "stationary state"! But there is a difference. We are not envisaging an end to technical progress. On the contrary, another reason for assuming a tapering off of net investment is just this tendency toward wide-scale innovations of a capital-saving nature.

Full Employment

If the economy were a fully communist one in which labor was completely voluntary and unpaid, then there is clearly no problem of full employment. Suggestions can always be made as to useful projects, so that willing hands can always be employed. Moreover, if a worker sees no useful projects for himself, then he can remain at leisure without any harm to himself whatsoever, assuming that all goods are free.

Assume however, that we are dealing with a economic model in which only 80 or 90 per cent of all goods are free, mainly the basic necessities of life, but in which some significant portion of goods are not free, including many luxury goods. Furthermore, assume that there are still differentiated wages for workers. In this model of an impure communism, we may still conclude that there should be little problem of unemployment, provided there is central planning of all investment. With central planning of investment, the situation is really identical to that of centrally planned socialism. Namely, since the same agency is doing all investment and presumably all saving (or at least controls all saving), there can never be a problem of excess saving. Rather, as is shown empirically in the history of the Soviet Union, the problem tends to be the opposite. The planners continuously conceive of many more possible projects than they have investment funds with which to complete them.

The Incentive Problem

The classic attack on pure communism is that, if all goods are free, there is insufficient incentive to work. Suppose, however, that there is a gradual change, with only a half per cent of consumer goods per year passing from the monetary to the free goods sector. It seems unlikely that at some point, the ordinary worker would suddenly stop working. It may still be argued that he will gradually reduce his effort. Even at an 80 per cent free goods level, however, differentiated wages (which could be used to buy the remaining, priced luxury goods) would probably be a more than sufficient incentive for those who still need such incentives.

This assertion is not easy to prove because incredibly little research has been done on the relation of material incentives to willingness to work.[11] What evidence there is indicates, though, that "within any one culture differential money rewards are of limited importance in transforming a less industrious workman into a more industrious one."[12] The evidence indicates in particular, little relation of industrial innovation to monetary rewards, but rather to noneconomic factors like temperament and intelligence (so with greater leisure time there should be a rising rate of invention and innovation). Even two very cautious liberals conclude "that incentive problems do not invalidate the case for adjustments in the direction of equal income shares."[13] Surely, we may extrapolate that incentive problems do not invalidate our case for free public goods.

Soviet Marxists emphasize that the attainment of full communism implies that certain difficult preconditions have been met: (1) a very high level of production per man hour, so that each worker needs to work only a few hours a day; (2) an attitude toward work such that each worker will positively enjoy working those few hours; and (3) some degree of elimination of differences in outlook toward and in the nature of urban and farm jobs as well as manual and intellectual jobs, so that there will be a sufficient number of volunteers for farm and manual labor. If automation continues at a rapid pace, and the first goal is only a gradual approach to 80 per cent communism, then these utopian-sounding prerequisites can be sufficiently met within the foreseeable future. Hours of labor have declined astoundingly in the last hundred years. Moreover, if past trends continued, even in the United States, then the usual number of working years could fall within a few decades from the present forty to fifty years to as little as fifteen to twenty years.[14]

The trend toward automation makes it likely that an ever larger part of the population will devote itself to advanced scientific and creative work. In that case, we can assume that there would be much greater willingness to work for the good of society. After all, once assured a basic minimum wage, most scientists today probably work more for the joy of what they are doing than for any amount of income. The same would certainly be true of artists, even today. Thus, although everyone may be guaranteed a minimum standard of living, most people would probably continue to do quite a bit of productive labor. This would be especially true if there were a vast amount of leisure time. Even today, there is certainly some question about how much leisure time one really wants, what one can do with it, and how much time one can simply fritter away. It seems much more likely that one would want to begin to do something constructive even if there were no constraint to do so.

Certainly, then, given only 80 per cent free consumer goods with differentiated wages and prices on luxury goods, rewards would be offered to workers, managers, or scientists who invented or applied new industrial processes. Furthermore, since we are greatly increasing the amount of leisure time, one would assume that this factor plus the increase in scientific education should assure a great deal more research than ever before. Moreover, the barriers to the use of innovations that have arisen from rigid central direction in the Soviet economy—that is, the unwillingness of

347

managers to take risks which might result in a short-run decline of their bonuses—should be reduced when managers have much less to fear from demotion or bonus reduction.

There is, nevertheless, the problem of incentives for the reluctant worker. Suppose that there is some significant percentage of workers with such inclinations that they are simply unwilling to do any work whatsoever, when they are provided with all the basic necessities of life free of charge. Should there be a reward and punishment system for such workers? If someone simply says: "I will not go to work for the society," then certainly some social and economic pressure could be brought to bear. In the first place one would assume that in such a society there would be a great deal of social pressure by friends, neighbors, and relatives to do some amount of work. After all, we are only talking here about three or four hours a day!

It is easy to conceive of other punishments and rewards. In purely economic terms, the individual refusing to do any work will not receive wages. Therefore he will not be able to buy any of the remaining 20 per cent of consumer goods (mainly luxury goods). Presumably, that will be a goal for those workers who continue to have present-day attitudes to work and consumption. More extreme economic or even criminal penalties— such as those that Soviet writers on communism sometimes imply—violate the basic humanist goals of a communist society. Nor are these penalties of great use to society. The fact is that those workers who would be so unwilling to give the minimum amount of labor (such as three hours a day) would probably be of such poor quality that society would miss very little by not having their work.

Optimal Planning without Prices

Assume that a very wide range of consumer goods, say 80 per cent, are free: they have no prices (or their price is zero). Assume also that there is public ownership, and that wages are still paid according to the amount of work done. The wages can only be used to buy the remaining 20 per cent of consumer goods (mostly luxury goods). If 80 per cent of consumer goods have no prices, can there be any optimal planning?

Suppose in the first case that there is central planning. For the remaining consumer goods with prices as well as for producer goods, the situation has not changed from the situation obtaining under planned socialism. For producer goods with no market the planners must simply gather information on the three things needed for the usual optimal programming: first, marginal preferences for the outputs; second, all the alternative technologies (as sets of input-output coefficients); and third, the available resources. With these data, optimal programming can find the output combinations and technologies producing the maximum output. They can also then solve the dual programming problem to find shadow prices. The shadow prices are prices set in accordance with the planned optimal outputs; they are used in this model solely within the planning organs for accounting and planning purposes only; and there are still no prices and no money used in the exchange process.

For priced consumer goods (luxury goods) there is still a market with consumer choice. Since, however, the supply is set by a government monopoly, the prices in the market only make short-run supply and demand equal. They are not long-run rational prices, that is, they do not directly tell us the degree of long-run scarcity of resources or the consumer preferences at equilibrium prices. The planners could get an indication of preferences if they know that the current prices are above or below long-run equilibrium prices. In any event, they could use resources where the rate of profit is highest. Such planning, however, is still very complex, and the current prices give only the smallest part of the data. Calculating the long-run equilibrium prices or costs is a very difficult problem in this case, for which a great mass of information is needed. Hence, under planned socialism (even with a consumer goods market), it may be easier to collect the direct information about demands, technologies, and resources, so that planners can calculate maximum outputs or minimum costs.

In the "free" goods sector, it is still perfectly possible to collect the necessary information and to make the necessary calculations for minimizing costs by choosing proper technologies. In fact, to minimize costs the planners need only three types of information. First is fixed output targets, which are set in this model at those amounts necessary to meet the demand at zero price. The planners need only allow for slight changes in population and tastes each year. Second, there are the possibilities of technology, which are given by engineers as usual. Third, there are the costs of the resources. These are given roughly by the continued differentiated wages of current labor and by the shadow prices of producer goods (already calculated).

Market (Decentralized) Communism and Optimal Choice

Is not "market communism" a contradiction in terms? Certainly, full communism implies no wages and no prices, no competitive markets for any type of commodity or for labor. Even 80 per cent communism implies that there is a zero price and *no* market for 80 per cent of all consumer goods. It must be emphasized, however, that "decentralized communism" —with the continued use of a market for luxury goods and all producer goods—is no contradiction.

The combination of decentralization and 80 per cent communism should be highly attractive to Marxists.[15] On the one side, decentralized decision-making concerning output combinations and technologies means continued efficiency and incentives to optimize (with bonuses based on profit maximization). On the other side, the continued existence of wages and prices for some luxury goods does not prevent the advantages seen in the communist dream. Surely, if 80 per cent of all consumer goods are free, a very noncommercially oriented political, social, and psychological behavior would emerge.

If such a combination is possible, then one of the major objections to market socialism in East Europe disappears. The opponents of market socialism admit that it may lead to greater efficiency, but they claim that the greater (or more rational) use of material incentives will postpone communism forever. If it is possible to keep decentralization and some material incentives while increasing the area of free goods, the objection may be overcome. In other words, the remaining wages and prices would simply become less and less important as supply became gradually free. Under these conditions wages and material incentives might not need to be legislated out of existence, but might simply "wither away" (so that money and the market are first limited to the luxury sector, and are then allowed to die a very slow, natural death). This seems not only preferable, but the only practical way, since we must otherwise believe that acquisitive psychology disappears *before* a long period of abundant free goods begins.

The question is, however, how can a manager make decentralized optimal decisions if there is no market price on his output? Suppose that managers are given the rule to maximize profit, and are told to set outputs and technologies on that basis. Suppose also that the manager receives a bonus according to the enterprise rate of profit, and gives bonuses to the workers on that basis or other appropriate criteria. The wages and bonuses are used to buy luxury goods. If the luxury goods are 20 per cent of all consumer goods, then the total wage bill must be fixed to equal the prices of just that 20 per cent. Furthermore, producer goods continue to be sold for money. Thus, in the sectors of luxury goods and producer goods, prices can continue to be set by competition in the market—as under market socialism.

This still leaves difficult questions for the sector in which consumer goods are given away free. How do firms plan rationally in that sector? Where do firms get the money to pay for labor and for producer goods in that sector? The best answer is that the central government pays the firm a price per unit, and gives away the goods through local outlets. This system allows the consumer goods firm to have the money to pay for the labor and the producer goods they need in the market.

What price should the government pay to the firms? Clearly, to avoid subsidies, the price must at least cover the wages and producer goods costs paid out by the firm. In the aggregate this also means that the revenue of the firms in the free goods sector (determined by government) helps to set a limit to wages. The government will still require some further wage controls to ensure that the aggregate wages are just sufficient to buy the (priced) luxury goods, so that no inflation is permitted in that sector.

In order to encourage the firm (in the free goods sector) to optimize in the appropriate fashion, the government price should be the sum of "costs" plus a "normal profit." Since the labor and producer goods are priced in the market, the government can simply use actual costs at going prices. The "normal profit" should be fixed so that it is equal to the social rate of interest. The social rate of interest is that rate at which the government loans capital, so that the government supply of capital and firms' demand for capital are equal. Since the firm then has a "price" for its goods, it can maximize profit in the usual way.

Full Communism

Finally, the assumptions of the model may be loosened somewhat. Suppose that all consumer goods are given away free by the central government and that no wages are paid. Suppose that the problems of limiting demand to a "reasonable" amount and obtaining incentive for some minimum hours of labor are solved by (gradual) changes in attitudes to work. Then, for purposes of optimization, the system could operate with few changes.

Producer goods would still be bought and sold in a market. Managers would still be instructed to maximize profits (and they follow instructions since incentive problems are assumed away). In consumer goods all firms would receive a price from the central government for delivery of goods to specification. The price paid by the central government would include the actual market cost of all producer goods. It would no longer include actual wages because no wages would be paid. But it would still include a shadow price for capital (the average rate of profit), and would now also include a shadow price for each kind of labor (a "wage" equal to the marginal product of labor derived from an optimal plan). In turn, all firms would pay the government for labor—as a socially provided good—at those same wage levels.

351

Tentative Conclusions

The economic arguments against communism were examined and found wanting.

It seems possible that those who would deny the eventual possibility of communist distribution tend to underestimate the growing technological potential for the creation of abundance; to overestimate the insatiability of innate consumer needs; and to underrate the possible changes in man's approach to work and life.[16]

An economy of 70 or 80 per cent free consumer goods seems possible, with little or no loss in performance, in an easily foreseeable future. A gradual increase of the free goods sector, with careful attention to elasticities of demand, should make it possible to maintain equilibrium of supply and demand for all products, assuming present rates of productivity increase in the United States or the Soviet Union. Second, a gradual increase of free goods combined with continued wages to pay for the remaining priced (luxury) goods should present few new incentive problems. Third, with the use of accounting prices for free goods (derived from optimal programming processes), optimal planning can continue to function as well as under socialism. Moreover, the planning can be centralized or decentralized as preferred, assuming the accounting prices are given to the managers as parameters.

Finally, if economic performance is at least as good as in socialism, then we must favor communism for the noneconomic reasons discussed in the next chapter. After the socialist revolution has brought public ownership (and initial development to an advanced economic level in underdeveloped countries), then the slogan of "free goods" may be raised.

NOTES

1. Karl Marx, "Critique of the Gotha Programme," *Selected Works of Marx and Engels* (New York, 1968, "Critique" written 1875), pp. 315–335; also Frederick Engels, *Anti-Duhring* (New York, 1939, first publ. 1878), part 3; also V. I. Lenin, *State and Revolution* (1917).

2. Edward Bellamy, *Looking Backward* (New York, 1960, first publ. 1887).

3. See, for example, the Soviet literature in A. Zvorykin, "Approaches to Work under Communism," *Soviet Sociology* 1 (Fall 1962): 29–37; CPSU, *The Road to Communism, Documents of the 2nd Congress* (Moscow, 1967); and Editorial, "The Great Program of Communist Construction," *Problems of Economics*, 1 (April 1959): 3–10. See also the Western critiques in I. Fetscher, "Marx, Engels, and the Future of Society," *Survey*, 38 (October 1961): 100–110; J. Balinsky, "Has the Soviet Union Taken

The Economics of Communism

Steps toward Communism?" *Social Research*, 28 (Spring 1961): 1–14; N. Jasny, "Plan and Superplan," *Survey*, 38 (October 1961): 29–43; L. Labedz, "The New CPSU Program," *Survey*, 38 (October 1964): 12–28; H. G. Shaffer, *The Soviet Economy* (New York, 1965), part 4; R. Schlesinger, "The CPSU Programme: The Conception of Communism," *Soviet Studies*, 13, no. 4 (April 1962): 383–406; H. Marcuse, "The Transition from Socialism to Communism," in *Soviet Marxism* (New York, 1958).

4. The word "goods" includes goods and services throughout this chapter. The word "free" only means zero price in the market; it does not mean free like the air, since any production of goods requires use of labor and other resources and a foregone opportunity cost to society.

5. The most comprehensive and serious Western critique of pure communism is by Peter Wiles, *The Political Economy of Communism* (London: Basil Blackwell, 1964), especially Chapters 17, 18, 19, and 20.

6. See the far more optimistic calculations of Soviet potential for free goods distribution in the careful article by Lynn Turgeon, "Future Levels of Living in the U.S.S.R.," *Economics of Planning*, 3 (September 1963): 149–165. "According to Soviet calculations, about one-fourth of the current incomes of workers is distributed on the basis of need, and by 1980 roughly one-half of their then much larger real incomes will be distributed without charge" (*ibid.*, p. 150. The pessimistic argument, that the Soviet Union is no longer moving toward communism at all, is given in A. Dallin and T. B. Larson, eds., *Soviet Politics since Khrushchev* (Englewood Cliffs, N.J.: Prentice-Hall, 1968), pp. 56–57 and 95.

7. See further discussion and references in H. Sherman, "Material Incentives in Socialism," *Monthly Review*, 19 (January 1968): 61–63.

8. Ernest Mandel, *Marxist Economic Theory* (New York, 1968), p. 654.

9. Wiles, *op. cit.*, p. 348.

10. *Ibid.*, p. 349.

11. For citations to the limited literature, see R. A. Dahl and C. E. Lindblom, *Politics, Economics, and Welfare* (New York: Harper & Row, 1953), p. 149.

12. *Ibid.*, p. 154.

13. *Ibid.*, p. 161.

14. See the very interesting discussion of this point in Martin Brofenbrenner, "The Scarcity Hypothesis in Modern Ecoonmics," *The American Journal of Economics and Sociology*, 21 (July 1962): 265–270.

15. For the over-all views of Marx and Engels on decentralization under communism, see note 1 above. See also the large number of other relevant quotations from Marx and Engels in Wiles, *op. cit.*, pp. 357–360.

16. Turgeon, *op. cit.*, p. 164.

CHAPTER
24

Politics and Sociology of Communism

If the economics of communism consists of murky speculation in a utopian vein, its political and social analysis is pure science fiction. Yet these are currently issues of great interest (especially in America where we have many "communes" of about five to thirty people, claiming to practice "communist" principles), so a few comments are in order.

Political Aspects

Marx and Engels expected that the advent of payment according to need (or free public goods) would mean the end of socioeconomic classes, and the classless society would witness a withering away of the state as the need for it disappears. By definition, what we mean by the withering away of the state is the disappearance of all the oppressive and violent sides of government, namely the end of police, prisons, courts, and armies. Yet this does not mean that government in the more general sense disappears. There may no longer be administration by force over human beings, but there is certainly economic administration, the administration of things, the planning for all society for the allocation of resources, and even the allocation of labor (though the plans are presumably followed voluntarily). This is a very different question, and it must be expected that economic administration will *increase* during the period of communism, though it will henceforth work on noncoercive principles.

We can talk about a classless society only when we begin to reach a society of great abundance, a society in which at least the bulk of goods are freely given to the population according to their need. Only in this case, as we approach full communism, can we expect some change in the political and social aspects of society. In this situation it certainly is reasonable to expect that the need for courts, for police, for prisons, for armies will die away. Certainly, if one can take all the property that one wants at any given time, at least all the food, clothing, and shelter, then the need, desire, and reason for a great deal of crime certainly vanishes. The basic thought behind the doctrine of the withering away of the political functions of the state is that the apparatus of force will become superfluous the moment there is no longer a privileged class which must defend its property and interests, if necessary by force, or by the constant threat of force.

Ecology and Pollution

Some pollution is the unavoidable consequence of modern industry and can only be reduced by further technological advances. Much pollution, however, is avoidable, and may be traced to private greed under capitalism. Under socialism there has also been some avoidable pollution because (1) planners in underdeveloped economies have concentrated on output growth without regard to its social costs, and (2) managers are paid to *produce* (with slight penalties for pollution). Under communism (even 80 per cent communism) an affluent, socially planned society may have less compulsion for growth, more concern for human and social costs, such as prevention of ecological destruction. With the focus off rapid growth and with much less drive for their own private economic gain, managers under communism are more likely to take measures to preserve the ecology as well as to produce output.

Racism

Marxism opposes the Freudian view that man was and always will be an aggressive wolf toward his fellow man. Neither do we believe that all men are born "good" and then corrupted by social institutions. Rather man is not born with any social nature, either greedy or aggressive, loving or giving. Man is shaped by his environment, specifically his social environment.

Racism, then, has resulted from certain factors in the social environment, particularly vested economic interest that profit from it under capitalism, and vested political interests that have found it a useful tool in underdeveloped socialist countries (though it has decreased under socialism). When these interests—and the domestic and international conflicts and

355

frictions generated by them—have been eliminated under communism, it is possible that the remnants of racism will be slowly defeated (but even then it will take a continuous and conscious social effort).

Sexism

Sexism is like racism in that it is an ideology caused by a certain social environment, and that can be largely eliminated by drastic changes in that environment. Under capitalism discrimination against women is profitable to monopoly capital. Under Soviet socialism, for all its other weaknesses, the absence of economic profitability from sexism (and the recognition of the social gain from full use of the economic potential of women) has meant an approach toward equality in both education and jobs. The sexist ideology, though, still seems dominant among most Soviet men. The result is that women have an equal burden of industrial work, but also do almost all the housework in most families.

Communism (even 80 per cent communism) should help break down this last major bastion of sexism. Social planning can emphasize a vast increase of household services by public enterprises. These would include free or cheap (but high quality) child-care centers, restaurants, and highly automated cleaning services. All these services mean that the mother can be liberated from chores to the extent she wishes.

Communist free distribution of basic goods and services would also liberate women from going into marriages for material gain (and would also end a reason for subservience within marriage). It would also make divorce easier when desirable, since most contested divorces revolve around property rights. On the other hand, to the extent that some marriages run into trouble through economic squabbles or the economic pressures of insufficient income, communism might allow more stable relationships. Of course, diminution of the importance of private property would also make more feasible communal living arrangements for several adults and children, but that does get into a realm of utopian speculation.

Alienation

Communism means an end to exploitation and alienation of the worker's product by economic or political means. But what about the alienation caused by the detailed, tedious demands of the work process? Marx and Engels expected that in the communist era there would be less distinction between intellectual and manual labor, that everyone would do some of each. A Soviet science fiction writer predicts that, on the basis of automation and a high level of physical and mental training, it will be "possible for a person to change his profession frequently, learn another easily, and bring endless variety into his work so that it becomes more and more satisfying."[1] This prediction has some slight basis in modern technological trends, in the sense that automation means that industry needs more highly skilled and more intellectually trained workers in large numbers. As the trend continues, perhaps everyone will know how to do certain of the simple tasks necessary to control automated machinery (for two to three hours a day), but will also have time for creative effort beyond that.

Rural-Urban Differentials

Marx and Engels also expected that there would be less and less difference between town and country, agriculture and industry. There is no great reason to doubt this in terms of the present technological trends of society, mostly in the sense that agriculture is becoming more and more mechanized itself, lending itself better and better to factory methods. Furthermore, in the United States and in most advanced economies the number of agricultural workers has declined drastically. The percentage of agricultural workers in the United States is now down to five or six per cent compared with an 80 or 90 per cent in the early nineteenth century. Moreover, improved communication and transportation means that rural dwellers can more easily partake of urban culture.

Personal Psychological Problems

Of course, under full communism we will still have all sorts of conflicting sexual drives and other difficult personal problems. In general then, we will still have plenty of psychoanalytic problems. Communism is not a magic cure-all. But at least our social and psychological problems may be greatly reduced by the removal of purely economic conflicts and problems. At best the ending of economic exploitation and the beginning of cooperation and a large sphere of collective activities may create a much healthier mental atmosphere in which to solve individual problems.

War and Imperialism

For I dipped into the future, far as human eye could see,
Saw the vision of the world, and all the wonder that would
be;

When the war-drum throbbed no longer, and the battle-
flags were furled
In the Parliament of man, the federation of the world.[2]

A communist economy—even 80 per cent, not to speak of full communism—presupposes a united, peaceful world both as cause and effect.
On the one hand, how could a wide sector of free goods exist in one
country and not in the others? The poor would want to migrate there;
the tourists would want to take the goods away—already people go to
countries with free health services just to use them. Moreover, a high
degree of communism could only be practical with no drain for military
spending—not to speak of the conflict between training people to be
decent human beings and training them to be killers. Furthermore, if the
state is to wither away, that implies first and foremost an end to the
military. And can anyone imagine a real reduction of racism, sexism, and
alienation of humans from humans while international conflicts exist and
are accompanied by virulent nationalism and "patriotism"?

On the other hand, perhaps the most important argument for communism is that it would end the most important causes of war. Imperialism
cannot exist in the face of the availability of free goods and services. To
bring the underdeveloped countries up to the level needed for communism
will require a wide flow of aid without strings from the advanced countries.
At the same time in the advanced countries no small groups of men could
make economic (or political) gain from the domination of other countries.
Thus, such an economy makes possible a united world.

Mankind seems to be in an awful race that must be decided in a relatively short time. It is possible that increasing levels of environmental
pollution and wasteful use of resources could kill most of us within less
than a century. It is also possible that increasing production and spread of
nuclear weapons could end in a holocaust, killing most or all of us within
the next few years or decades. Yet it is barely possible that we will first
reach a worldwide democratic, socialist, or communist human society,
which could stave off disaster.

NOTES

1. Ivan Yefremov, *Andromeda* (Moscow: Foreign Languages Publication House,
n.d.), p. 62.
2. Alfred Lord Tennyson, from "Locksley Hall," in William Benet and Norman
Cousins, eds. *The Poetry of Freedom* (New York; Modern Library, 1948), pp. 151–152.

1

Marxist Price Theory as a Special Case of Neoclassical Theory

Marxist price theory may be considered as a subclass of neoclassical price theory, utilizing certain special assumptions. The assumptions and qualifications are indicated below.

1. Pure Competition

Marx began with the assumption of pure competition in order to investigate value and surplus value under these conditions. Under competition commodities must sell at their value (including an average amount of profit) because a higher price will tend to increase the supply, while a lower price will tend to decrease the supply, thus bringing price back to value. The supply may be increased by competitors moving in or decreased by competitors moving out of the industry. But without competition this mechanism does not work. In that case, Marxist theory does not indicate the exact price, but only the direction in which it deviates from value.

Marx, like the classical economists, knew that a higher degree of monopoly means more restriction of production and a *higher* price. Marx, however, presented no analytic tools for a more precise analysis. Thus, the labor theory of value is not too helpful in analyzing any kind of monopoly price, whether it results from concentration and merger of capital or from unique holdings such as a particular waterfall or a nonreproducible object such as a painting. By contrast, the neoclassical theory is able to furnish a precise (but very unrealistic) analysis of monopoly price and output in terms of demand and supply (or marginal revenue and marginal cost).[1]

Yet Marx was the first major economist to predict the emergence of monopoly and economic concentration. He thoroughly explored its causes in terms of technological advance and the economies of large-scale enterprise. He further indicated the economic effects of monopoly on the distribution of income between classes, and the social and political effects of its vast power. Finally, Lenin made monopoly power the keystone of his theory of imperialism. Indeed, an entire chapter in this book will be devoted to the Marxist contributions to the analysis of the role of monopoly in the evolution of capitalism.

2. Long-run Equilibrium

We have seen that in neoclassical analysis there is a sharp distinction between the "short run," in which supply may change to meet demand only within the limits of present capacity, and the "long run," in which the level of capacity itself may rise or fall so that supply may adjust to any demand (for this approximation, technology is fixed even in the "long run"). In the short run, price is determined both by utility (and the distribution of income) as reflected in demand *and* by costs as reflected in supply conditions. In the long run, price is determined *only* by the "cost" of supply, since demand affects only the amount of output sold. *If* all "costs" may be resolved into labor cost (and if costs are constant over the relevant range), then the long-run case fits the Marxist argument that the value of any commodity is determined solely by the labor embodied in it.

Marx does not explicitly limit his value theory to the long-run time period, but it is taken for granted and implied in all that he says. He states very often that in his basic analysis he is only concerned with the situation where supply equals demand, and the context makes clear that this is long-run demand and supply. Marx is not interested in the details of competitive jockeying for position, but *begins* his analysis at the point where competition has equalized long-run supply and demand in each industry. Later on, as we shall see, Marx recognizes another qualification which transforms the value concept to the more realistic "price of production" concept (similar to Marshallian "cost"). Here he explicitly states, "the price of production includes the average profit . . . it is in the long run a prerequisite of supply, of the reproduction of commodities in every individual sphere."[2] In other words, if the long-run price is below this level, suppliers will not make the average profit and will move out of the industry. If, however, it is above that level, then profit is above average and more suppliers are attracted into the industry.

In the short run, the price according to the neoclassical analysis clearly rests on both demand and supply. Demand is determined by both income distribution and marginal utility. A large enough increase in demand must move production to a point of higher costs per unit because it eventually approaches the capacity limit (by definition). Of all this short-run theory of outputs and prices, Marx has nothing to say, unless one wishes to read some of it into his discussion of demand as an index of "social necessity." Even his meager discussions of this point should rather be interpreted, however, as relating to those long-run or aggregate problems in which he was interested. Thus he explains that aggregate short-run price may be below aggregate value in depression or deflation, while it may be above aggregate value in inflation. Similarly, in discussing aggregate distribution, he considers how short-run wages may be temporarily above or below the value of the workers' labor power.

3. Socially Necessary Labor and Technology

One of Marx's explicit qualifications to the labor theory of value was that it holds true only if the average prevailing technology is used. Suppose all other firms are producing watches by automated production, but one firm produces an identical product by an enormous expenditure of hand labor. Then the product of that firm will not have a higher exchange value than the others merely because it expends more labor. The reason is that the labor it expends is more than is "socially necessary" at present.

Of course, in the more complex case where each of several firms has a somewhat different technology, it is not so clear how one would measure the deviation from the prevailing technology. Marx merely says that "the market" makes that calculation, but the ambiguity about measurement is not fully resolved.

4. Demand, Utility, and "Social Necessity"

Marx seldom discussed the role of demand in determination of individual prices because (1) it plays no role in long-run price, where his interest lay, and (2) he left the discussion of monopoly price for a later stage of discussion. We shall see in a later chapter that Marx gave an extensive discussion of the role of *aggregate* demand in determining *aggregate* output and price levels.

It is well to emphasize that Marx does not deny the operation of demand

(and utility to consumers) in determining prices and outputs. Marx carefully states that *a commodity must have some "use-value" (or utility), or else it can have no exchange value in the market.*[3] If there is no demand, the price will be zero.

In the long run, however, the *level* of demand—if it is above zero (and if costs per unit are constant)—can have no effect on the price, though it fixes the output and the allocation of resources.[4] In fact, the recognition by Marx that "use value" is a necessary condition for any value, combined with the usual Marxist statement that the aim of socialism is the production of use values for the population, has been used by several East European economists as a justification for the widest use of supply and demand or (marginal) utility concepts in planning.[5]

In connection with long-run price Marx shows the role of demand in the allocation of capital and labor. Thus Marx states that only "socially necessary" labor expenditure gives rise to value. As we have seen, Marx uses the term "socially necessary" in one sense to indicate that the exchange value is determined only by that labor which makes use of the average technology currently available to the society. Yet Marx also uses the term "socially necessary" to indicate that the labor value is determined only by that labor which is used in producing products in the proportion demanded by society from each industry. Thus Marx writes:

> If this division of labor among the different branches of production is proportional [to the demand], then the products of the various groups are sold at their values . . . or at prices which are modifications of their values . . . due to general laws. . . . Every commodity must contain the necessary quantity of labor, and at the same time only the proportional quantity of the total social labor time must have been spent on the various groups. For the use value of things remains a prerequisite. The use value of the individual commodities depends on the particular need which each satisfies. But the use value of the social mass of products depends on the extent to which it satisfies in quantity a definite social need for every particular kind of product in an adequate manner, so that the labor is proportionately distributed among the different spheres in keeping with these social needs, which are definite in quantity. . . .[6]

It is apparent from the quote that the "socially necessary" *allocation* of resources (though not the long-run *value* of products) is considered by Marx to be solely dependent on the pattern of demand, which is determined in part by the relative utilities to consumers. Sweezy, writing on this question in the 1940's, comments that "the competitive supply-and-demand theory of price determination is hence not only not inconsistent with the labor theory; rather it forms an integral, if sometimes unrecognized, part of the labor theory."[7] Sweezy admits that Marx did not further develop his theory of allocation according to consumer wants.

Marx did not further develop individual demand theory because he recognized that under capitalism effective demand is far more influenced by the distribution of income than by consumers' wants.[8] Second, Marx also neglected the theory of consumer wants because he was primarily interested in macro economic developments, for which investigation almost any economist takes consumer desires as relatively stable and unchanging, while changes in demand largely reflect changes in aggregate income or income distribution.

5. Skilled and Unskilled Labor

Marx reduced all costs to hours of average unskilled labor or multiples of that average working hour. For his purposes of aggregate analysis, this simplification is an acceptable abstraction.

Of course, in a more detailed micro analysis of relative wages and prices, we may wish to consider the effects of different grades of skilled labor or even different specific kinds of natural resources. In that case each relative cost depends greatly on the demand for that type of labor or resources. Thus,

the real influence of marginal utility comes in when we . . . admit non-homogeneous scarce natural resources, or non-homogeneous kinds of labour that cannot be produced in unlimited numbers by appropriate training. Thus, the rent of vine-bearing land is affected by the marginal utility of wine: the wages of skilled watchmakers (assuming there is some element of "scarce" skill, i.e. of skill that cannot be conferred upon an average worker by suitable training) are affected by the marginal utility of watches.[9]

6. The Transformation of Value into the Price of Production

From the time of Adam Smith all economists (including Marx) have recognized that competition in the long run must result in a uniform rate of profit on capital in all industries. The reason is that capital will move from industries with lower profit rates to those with high profit rates, thus lowering supply of goods in the former and raising it in the latter. Hence prices (and profit rates) rise where they are lowest and fall where they are highest until profit rates tend to uniformity in all industries.

Yet the simplest version of the labor theory of value would not lead us to this result. Only living labor can produce surplus value or profit. The "congealed labor" in capital goods, such as plant and equipment, is necessary to the production process, but does not produce a profit. Therefore, those industries using a high ratio of labor power to capital goods should show a higher rate of profit on capital. If two equal amounts of money capital are invested, we would expect the one spending more on living labor also to show a higher profit.

Of course, in the actual business world only a very small amount of capital is set aside to pay wages at any given time. Wage payments occur only periodically, and capital is not kept in a money form between payments. Money for wages is normally taken from current revenue just before it is needed, so it is hard to isolate Marx's "capital used to purchase labor power." It is certainly *not* the same statistic as the total flow of wages paid in a given period, such as wages paid in a year. But this is an additional complication ignored in the rest of this discussion; it cannot change the conclusions in any way.

For Marx, the simplest version of the labor theory is only a first approximation (both logically and historically), so there is nothing contradictory in later modifying its conclusions to account for these additional facts.[10] When competition evens out the rate of profit, it causes profit or "surplus value" to flow from industries using a relatively high ratio of living labor (and producing relatively high profits) to those industries using a relatively low ratio of living labor (and producing relatively low profits). Competition does this by lowering high prices and raising low prices until there is a uniform rate of profit for all industries. The price in each industry then equals the "cost" of production *plus* a uniform rate of profit on capital, where the cost includes the wages plus the value of the used-up plant, equipment, and raw materials. This price is called the "price of production."

According to Marx, the price of production in each individual industry will equal the value of its product *only if* the ratio of the value of labor power expended to the value of the used-up capital goods happens to be identical to the average ratio for all industry. Marx calls this key ratio the "organic composition of capital." In every industry where this ratio happens to be different from the average ratio, the individual prices of production will differ from the individual values. However, Marx argues, the aggregate amount of value produced will still equal the sum of prices, and the aggregate surplus value produced will still equal the sum of profits.

So long as the aggregate labor expended remains the same, the aggregate value and surplus value produced do not change. Competition merely redistributes the surplus value from one industry to another until there is a uniform rate of profit on capital. Thus, in Marx's own opinion, the labor theory of value and surplus value holds only for the *aggregate* product (though he did believe that individual prices reflect and systematically deviate from values). The famous attack on Marx by von Bohm-Bawerk emphasizes that such an aggregate sum of values is meaningless because economic theory is concerned only with the relative value of commodities in exchange.[11] Of course, von Bohm-Bawerk was thinking only of price and allocation problems, and not of the whole range of Keynesian aggregate problems in which aggregate value is not only useful but necessary.

The aggregate equality of (1) values and prices, and the equality of (2) surplus values and profits, rests on the grounds that all the individual deviations above and below value must exactly cancel each other. This is necessarily true *only if* no commodity enters into the production of any other.[12] In the more general case we note that capital goods are used in the production of other goods, and that the individual prices of capital goods also deviate from *their* individual values. In this more difficult model we can prove only that one of the two equalities must hold, but that both will hold only under very special and accidental circumstances. Thus, if we wish to maintain the equality of aggregate surplus value and aggregate profit, we must admit that the sum of prices may deviate from the aggregate value of all products.

The individual and even the aggregate deviation of prices from values does *not* invalidate Sraffa's sophisticated version of the labor theory of value, though it certainly invalidates its simpler version.[13] Given the labor expenditure, the rate of surplus value, and the ratio of labor to used-up capital goods in each individual industry, the labor theory of value can still calculate all the individual prices and profits, as well as the aggregate amounts. If we are looking for a theory of relative individual prices, this qualification (not to speak of all the other qualifications of this appendix) makes the labor theory vastly complicated and ridiculously clumsy for practical use. To the extent that we are concerned with Marx's aggregate economic conclusions, however, the whole issue is of such a small magnitude as to have no effect on the outcome. Moreover, Sraffa's labor theory, cited above, turns out to be both more comprehensive and more direct than the neoclassical theory.

7. Constant Costs

Neoclassical theory considers three possible reactions of cost per unit to a rise in output in the long run: (1) rising costs, (2) constant costs, and (3) falling costs. Marx, in his first approximation to value theory, almost always assumed the simplest case, the case of constant costs (or infinite elasticity of supply). Suppose there is an increase in demand for a product, caused perhaps by a change in consumer preference. With constant costs, the only result of the increase in demand is an increase in output, because with the same cost per unit of output, there is no change in the long-run price. Only in this case would Marshall join Marx in declaring that long-run price is completely unaffected by changes in demand, and that it is governed solely by the "cost" of supply, (including an average "profit").[14] Of course, the interpretation of "cost" and "profit" would differ greatly between Marx and Marshall.

It has been observed that *if* we assume constant costs, and *if* "cost" means the same as "labor expended," then we may say that Marxian economics reaches (in a very roundabout manner) the same conclusions about long-run price and output as Marshallian neoclassical economics. The "long run" here still assumes no technical progress. In a more general theory, however, it must be recognized that even in the long run there may be falling costs per unit (associated with a rising marginal product per worker) *or* rising costs per unit (associated with a falling marginal product per worker).

In either case a shift in demand from other products to this one, even though fully balanced by a shift in supply from other products to this one, will "cause" a change in the price of this product as well as a rise in its output. The change in price is due to the fact that at a higher level of output it may be technologically necessary to use more or less labor per unit of output. Yet Marx in his theory of individual prices always implicitly assumes constant costs, and makes no attempt to discuss these more general cases in his theory of value. The reason is that these issues, which are important practical questions for management, have little or no relevance to the evaluation of capitalism versus socialism. Marx does consider problems of rising or falling costs, but only within the very different context of the aggregate and dynamic problems of changes in population and technology.

This appendix has discussed only the major qualifications to the labor theory of value. Several minor problems, such as the marginal differences in ground rent among lands of different quality, could be discussed. Enough has been said, however, to show that the labor theory is not analytically incompatible with neoclassical price theory, though its simple version is *not* a very helpful tool for analysis of price and allocation problems (the use of both price theories in socialist planning is discussed in Chapter 14).

NOTES

1. More realistic neoclassical attempts began in the 1930's with Edward Chamberlin, *The Theory of Monopolistic Competition* (Cambridge: Harvard University Press, 1950, first publ. 1933), and Joan Robinson, *The Economics of Imperfect Competition* (London: Macmillan & Co., 1934).

2. Marx, *Capital*, vol. 3, p. 233.

3. Marx, *Capital*, vol. 1 part 1.

4. For Marshall's view of the role of demand in this case, see Albert Marshall, *Principles of Economics* (New York: Macmillan, 1953, first ed. 1890) pp. 348–349 and 455–461.

5. See, e.g., Wlodzimierz Brus, "Socialist Production and the Law of Value," transl. in *International Economic Papers*, 7 (1957): 125–144. Also see the summary of Soviet views in Alec Nove, *The Soviet Economy* (New York: F. A. Praeger, 1961), pp. 280–282.

6. Marx, *Capital*, vol. 3, pp. 745–746.

7. Paul M. Sweezy, *The Theory of Capitalist Development* (New York: Oxford University Press, 1942), p. 47.

8. Marx, *Capital*, vol. 3, pp. 214 and 222–223.

9. H. D. Dickinson, "Notes to Article by L. Johansen, 'Labor Theory of Value and Marginal Utilities," *Economics of Planning*, 3 (December 1963): 239.

10. Marx, *Capital*, vol. 3, parts 1 and 2.

11. E. von Bohm-Bawerk, *Karl Marx and the Close of His System*, ed. by Paul Sweezy (New York: A. M. Kelley, 1949, first publ. 1896).

12. See, e.g., Ronald Meek, "Some Notes on the 'Transformation Problem,'" *Economic Journal*, 66 (March 1956): 94–107.

13. For perhaps the most sophisticated form of a labor theory, see Piero Sraffa, *Production of Commodities by Means of Commodities* (Cambridge: Cambridge University Press, 1960).

14. "It is also to be recalled that Marshall tended to give primacy to the conditions of production as price determinants in the long run." Nove, *op. cit.*, p. 278n. Also see Marshall, *op. cit.*, pp. 337–350 and 503.

APPENDIX
2

Marx
on Long-run Trends

This appendix discusses Marx's views on increasing misery, nonproductive labor, and the falling rate of profit.

1. Increasing Misery

How is Marx's prediction of increasing misery to be interpreted? Does he really mean that the absolute standard of living of the working class will continually decline? Or does he mean only that the *relative* standard of living or the share of labor in the national income will decline?[1]

It does appear that the young Marx in the 1840's (a depression period) thought that the absolute wage might decline in the future. And it is true that some socialists thought they were following Marx in later decades when they spoke of the "iron law of wages," that wages must stay at the level of subsistence and never rise. The mature Marx, however, ridiculed this law, and his detailed studies led to the conclusion that the wage level of workers in the advanced capitalist countries would rise.

Marx followed Ricardo's definition of a rise in wages. On this definition, a "rise in wages" means that the number of hours of labor out of the working day that are devoted to the worker's wages (or reproducing his value) has risen. In other words, when Marx or Ricardo refer to a rise or decline in wages, they usually refer to the share of labor in the product. Hence, if "wages" are constant, the physical product or use value going to workers may be rising. The amount of physical product is irrelevant; the class relation or distribution of income is the important point. Marx stressed that a falling share of the product going to labor means reduced satisfaction (or increased relative misery), regardless of the absolute wage.

368

Furthermore, Marx emphasizes that the "subsistence" wage is not fixed, but quite flexible in content. It includes not only "natural wants," but also culturally determined "so-called necessary wants . . . which are the product of historical development."[2] Wages are therefore not fixed for all time by eternal fate, but are determined by "the relative weight, which the pressure of capital on the one side, and the resistance of the labourer on the other, throws into the scale."[3]

This is not a question of quotations, but of consistency with Marx's general theory. There is nothing in his general system that says wages must decline, or even that the wage share *must* decline. Marx merely makes an empirical prediction of a declining wage share on the basis of the facts available to him concerning aggregate supply and demand for labor and the relative power of the sides in the class struggle. For Marx, the floor of wages is subsistence and the ceiling is where high wages might set off a capitalist crisis or depression. In between, the workers do get some share of the continuous productivity increase, depending on their bargaining power, which in turn depends mainly on the macro economic phenomena of the investment rate and the unemployment rate.

On the basis of labor supply and demand, Marx foresees increasing unemployment, which both holds down wages and is itself a direct source of misery (and is stressed more heavily by Marx than the wage level itself). He considers two causes for this tendency toward unemployment. One is long-run technological unemployment (see Chapter 8). The second cause is the tendency to increasingly severe periodic depressions, so that each peak in unemployment is higher than the previous one (see Chapter 7).

Marx spoke only of a tendency, a factual prediction based on, but not part of his theoretical system. He would surely have recognized without difficulty the modern factors (such as unions) that have tended to raise wage levels. Marx expected absolute real wages to rise very slowly, if at all, whereas they have risen at a fair pace to a very significant degree in the last century in the advanced capitalist countries.

On the other hand, we saw in Chapter 6 that for the entire capitalist world—including the underdeveloped countries—especially if noneconomic as well as economic factors are weighed, a very strong case can be made for the increasing misery of the working class (at least, relative to the capitalists).

2. Nonproductive Labor

Marx distinguished between labor expended in productive and nonproductive ways.[4] Marx's theory is based upon Adam Smith's theory, but Smith —as is often the case—mixes two different theories into his discussion.

Smith's first theory states that labor is productive when it produces "capital." Marx followed and further refined this theory. Smith's second theory states that labor is productive only when it produces material commodities (and is nonproductive when it is expended on personal services). This second theory is followed in Soviet national income accounting—and was slavishly followed by many Western Marxists during the period of Stalin's dogmatic leadership.[5]

Marx's own definition says *"Productive labor* is . . . that which produces *surplus value* for its employer, or . . . which produces its own product as capital."[6] In Marx's view, in other words, in a capitalist system a worker is considered productive only if he is exploited and produces profit. Part of the thinking behind this definition is that new capital can come only from capitalist profits (excluding government and independent artisans), and that only new capital can lead to economic growth.

Regardless of the justification, it seems clear that Marx's view is quite different from the current Soviet view of productive labor. From Marx's view it is completely irrelevant whether the labor is expended to produce a material good or a nonmaterial service; the only question is whether it produces surplus value or not. Marx makes this point in two examples. On the one hand, a tailor who produces material goods, but works for himself and not for a capitalist "is not a productive worker, although his labour provides me with the product, the trousers. . . ."[7] On the other hand, although a singer produces an immaterial service, a singer who is "commissioned by an entrepreneur to sing in order to make money for him, is a productive worker. For she produces capital."[8]

The dogmatic Soviet justifications for their use of Smith's material versus nonmaterial definition of productive labor all seem very weak. One argument has it that material goods are produced by the economic base, so labor producing them is productive, whereas nonmaterial services are produced in the superstructure, so are the result of nonproductive labor. Even the assumption about nonmaterial services being produced in the superstructure seems an incorrect classification. But if it is true, it still seems no justification for calling the labor producing them nonproductive labor.

The other dogmatic Soviet justification is merely argument from authority, to wit, that they are following Marx. Marx himself would probably comment: First, there is nothing sacred about Marx's analysis, and it must be proved in detail to apply to each new situation. Second, he does not in fact give the Soviet definition, but another. Third, he was talking about capitalism, so why in any event should his definition apply to socialism?

The only real question for the Soviet Union is: What definitions and classifications are the most help for the analysis of socialism? Horvat, a Yugoslav economist, urges that for planning, the question is only what products can aid either current consumption, or replacement, or net investment for growth. For this pragmatic purpose, he says it is only necessary to define the gross social product as the "aggregate of all useful goods and services produced in a specified period."[9]

How did the Soviets come to use the strange division of social product into productive, material goods and nonproductive, immaterial services? First, there was Stalin's vulgarized notion of materialism, which seemed to say that "in order to live, men must have material goods, so material goods are more important or productive." More important, at the time planning came into being in the USSR, the peculiar economic conditions of rapid industrialization made tangible material goods seem all-important. It seemed "self-evident" that steel and coal were needed for growth, but services were just a necessary evil, a subtraction from available labor. As Horvat says bitterly: "You just *know* that factory workers are productive and university teachers unproductive and living from the labour of the former."[10]

One Western Marxist who attempts to revive the concept is Baran, for whom unproductive labor "consists of all labor resulting in the output of goods and services the demand for which is attributable to the specific conditions and relationships of the capitalist system, and which would be absent in a rationally ordered society."[11] Among the products that would be eliminated in a "rationally ordered society" he includes the manufacture of armaments, vast government administration, and advertising.

This is an attractive definition for a socialist economist studying capitalist growth, and it avoids the pitfalls of the Smith-Soviet definition. It has, however, some pitfalls of its own. What would be produced in a "rationally ordered society"? If the present "socialist" countries are the standard, then one must admit that they also spend on huge armaments and vast government administration. If the perfect rationally ordered society is a theoretical utopia off in the future, then Baran's definition seems to call for too many complex and hypothetical judgments for an operational tool of analysis.

3. The Falling Rate of Profit

Another famous Marxist prediction is that the rate of profit will gradually fall under capitalism. In Marx's day it was a generally accepted "fact" among all economists that the rate of profit had been falling. So Marx was primarily explaining what he assumed to be an historical fact. In addition, he made the prediction—again based on a general consensus—that this trend would continue.

The basic cause of the falling rate of profit seems obvious to Marx as

371

a result of his labor theory of value. First, let the rate of profit be *defined* as:

$$\text{rate of profit} = \frac{\text{surplus value}}{\text{constant capital} + \text{variable capital}}.$$

Now recall that the rate of exploitation is the ratio of surplus value (or profits, rent, and interest) to variable capital (or wages). Second, *assume* that the rate of exploitation is constant (Marx assumes this only as a first approximation). Marx called the ratio of constant to variable capital the "organic composition of capital." Third, Marx *assumes* that the effect of technological progress is to raise the organic composition of capital.

On the basis of this definition and these two assumptions, it is a truism that rate of profit will fall as time and technology move on (since the numerator must rise more slowly than the denominator of the rate). The issues that arise are the exact operational meaning of the definition in terms of available data, the correctness of the empirical prediction of a falling rate of profit, and the correctness of the two assumptions. The issues are discussed in that order, followed by a general conclusion.

Empirical testing is complicated by Marx's definition, which does not explicitly discriminate between "stocks" and "flows." Clearly, surplus value (or profit, rent, and interest) is generally treated by Marx as an amount flowing to entrepreneurs during a given period of time, say a year. On the other hand, for Marx's purpose (which considers the rate of profit as a determinant of investment and growth), constant caiptal should be considered as the value of a stock of things at a given moment, for example, on December 31. In this same context, variable capital or wages should also be a stock, but that is not easily defined in a consistent way.

In other words, constant capital as a stock may be defined as the value of factory, equipment, and inventory at a given date (as a flow it was defined as the value used up or the depreciation and depletion of each of these during a given period). Variable capital as a flow may easily be defined as the amount of wages, salaries, and commissions in a given period. But what is the stock of variable capital? In the modern world there is no such thing as a stock of consumer goods set aside by an entrepreneur to feed or clothe workers. There is not even an amount of money set aside to pay workers' wages, as the wage-fund theory assumed. With modern banking and credit, and the rapid turnover of goods, an enterprise need not keep much in its bank account as a reserve. Rather, the proceeds of sales are banked one hour and wages are paid by bank check.

For empirical testing, it would be best merely to measure the flow of profits, rent, and interest during a period against the average stock of total capital in the period, regardless of whether the capital is constant or variable, and regardless of whether it is embodied in real assets or cash.

The only full-scale attempt at testing the prediction empirically is the data gathered by Joseph Gillman.[12] Unfortunately, Gillman wastes one chapter computing the rate of profit on the flow basis, that is, with "capital" represented by the consumed constant and variable capital during each year—a totally irrelevant test for Marx's purpose.

In his next chapter he does use the flow of surplus value divided by the stock of capital, as is appropriate. His definition of surplus value, however, is debatable. Gillman includes in surplus value much of what accountants usually subtract from business profits as costs, which results in an extremely high rate of profit. For example, for 1931 he finds that the rate of profit was 33 per cent! But 1931 was the bottom of the Great Depression and the total rent, interest, and profit was negative in that year according to U.S. Internal Revenue data.

The reason for the discrepancy is that Gillman includes in costs only the depreciation, used-up raw materials, and wages (including "factory overhead"). He states, however, "neither selling nor administrative costs, nor taxes, nor any of the other familiar non-factory overhead costs are allowed for in this reckoning."[13] In other words, he has subtracted only certain kinds of labor costs, and not others. In theory, surplus value during a given period should equal the flow of all value minus the flow of constant and the flow of variable capital. Gillman, however, has not included all the expenditure of variable capital.

Presumably, he considers that some of the labor is expended "unproductively." It was shown earlier, however, that this is a very tricky concept. Neither Marx nor anyone else has argued that investors exclude "unproductive" costs in computing their rate of profit when deciding how much to invest—and that is the only relevant context here (regardless of other legitimate uses of the "nonproductive labor" concept). Since Gillman does not argue the point, he should have subtracted all costs except profit, rent, and interest, at least as a first approximation.

His data problems include two other difficulties that cannot easily be corrected. First, all estimates of nineteenth century data are quite speculative, especially estimates of capital. Second, his data include the effects of insufficient demand in many years. Marx, however, formulated the law of the falling rate of profit on the assumption of Say's Law, that demand always equals supply, leaving for later the question of how lack of demand affects profit rates. In Marx's terminology, he is dealing here only with the production of profit by the workers and not yet its realization in the market.

Keeping these possible sources of bias in mind, Gillman's data indicate that Marx's assumptions and conclusions are roughly correct up to the First World War, but are incorrect thereafter.[14] Specifically, up to 1919 he finds (1) a constant rate of surplus value (or surplus/variable is unchanging), (2) a rising organic composition of capital (or constant/ variable is rising), and, therefore, (3) a falling rate of profit. After 1919 he finds (1) a rising rate of surplus value, (2) a constant or falling organic composition of capital, and, therefore, (3) a rising rate of profit.

Since Marx predicted a falling rate of profit and Gillman finds a rising rate since 1919, he considers the possible explanations. First, the data could be inaccurate. Second, Marx's theory may not be applicable to the period in which monopoly dominates capitalism. Third, the theory should be more broadly reformulated to allow for the conditions of monopoly capitalism (see Chapter 8).

The question is not the simple one of facts versus Marx's theory, however, because Marx himself recognized that there were many factors mitigating his factual assumptions, so that the prediction was not a firm one. The law of the falling profit rate is *not* rooted in Marx's basic theory, but is based merely on his estimates of factual trends. In Marx's own words, the "law" is only "a tendency, whose effects become clearly marked only under certain conditions and in the course of long periods."[15] If this prediction based on empirical estimates proved incorrect for the long period of monopoly capitalism, that should not lessen any confidence in basic Marxist theory.

In fact, Marx himself immediately presented a long list of factors that could counteract the empirical tendencies that he did expect to predominate. His first factual assumption was a constant rate of surplus value. Joan Robinson argues that

this proposition stands out in startling contradiction to the rest of Marx's argument. For if the rate of exploitation tends to be constant, real wages tend to rise as productivity increases. Labour receives a constant proportion of an increasing total. Marx can only demonstrate a falling tendency in profits by abandoning his argument that real wages tend to be constant. This drastic inconsistency he seems to have overlooked, for when he is discussing the falling tendency of profits he makes no reference to the rising tendency of real wages which it entails.[16]

Mrs. Robinson certainly exaggerates the inconsistency. It was shown in the earlier discussion of increasing misery that Marx believed the rate of exploitation will rise, but that he also seems to concede that real wages will rise slowly. It certainly is possible for real wages to rise, but not as rapidly as productivity, so that the rate of exploitation also rises.

Nevertheless, she may assert, assuming there is no inconsistency with rising real wages, Marx has here postulated a constant rate of exploitation, whereas his doctrine of increasing misery assumes a rising rate of exploitation. The answer is that Marx used the constant rate only as a simplifying assumption in his first approximation to the problem. And he immediately thereafter begins his list of counteracting causes with those factors which tend to raise the rate of exploitation. The tendency of the rate of profit to fall is then no longer a truism, but it certainly still might be true—that is, a rising organic composition of capital *might* not be fully offset by a rising rate of exploitation, so the rate of profit might fall in spite of it.

Marx points out that a rising rate of exploitation (the rate of surplus value to variable capital) could and probably would occur because of:

1. Speed-up
2. A longer working day (in exceptional cases)
3. Wages pushed below value by monopoly power (discussed in Chapter 8)
4. Cheaper consumer goods from imports and from higher productivity, which lower the value of workers' necessities
5. Improved technology requiring less labor for production, giving rise to technological unemployment, pushing wages down
6. Government intervention to help employers keep wages down, for example, the Taft-Hartley Act
7. Investment abroad in areas where labor may be more highly exploited (discussed in Chapter 10)

One should, of course, consider contrary factors lowering the rate of exploitation, such as (1) trade unions, which reduce competition among workers, (2) government intervention to help workers, for example, minimum wage laws, and (3) greater demand for labor in periods of very rapid expansion.

Marx's second list of factors are those which tend to lower (or prevent the increase of) the organic composition of capital, that is, the ratio of constant to variable capital, or roughly the ratio of total capital invested to the number of workers. In other words, what are the factors limiting the amount of capital per worker? Marx emphasizes the "cheapening of the elements of constant capital." This includes (1) imports of cheaper raw materials, and (2) technological improvements in the production of producers' goods, which lower the value of capital goods.

Third, there are inventions which reduce capital expenditure per unit in addition to (or instead of) reducing expenditure on labor per unit. The third cause is especially prominent in the twentieth century, although it was unknown or very unusual in Marx's day, when almost all inventions were labor-saving, but with added capital expense. This change in technology causes the decline in the capital/output ratio found by most observers in the twentieth century, and probably also the decline in the organic composition of capital after 1919 registered in Gillman's data. Joan Robinson mentions a fourth factor: the more rapid turnover of capital goods, for example, the reduced need for inventories due to better communication and transport facilities.

Marx admitted these possibilities of relatively less need for or cheapened capital goods as "exceptional cases." They are now the rule. Since the empirical trends in both the rate of exploitation and the organic composition of capital are subject to change, the trend in the long-run rate of profit is clearly indeterminate in Marx's system. In point of fact, it seems to be roughly constant (or even rising), though the cyclical and wartime fluctuations are so great, and the available data so poor, that no statement of the long-run trend can be made with much confidence. This analysis shows, however, that the failure of this much hedged empirical prediction does not invalidate any part of Marx's basic model. Chapters 8, 9, and 10 examine how much of the changed trend may be explained by new structural features of the capitalist systems mostly appearing since Marx's day: monopoly, government intervention, and imperialism.

Finally, neither rising real wages nor a rising profit rate in the mature capitalist economies necessarily invalidates Marx's prediction of capitalist downfall. That was never meant to be a mechanical end point, a purely economic falling apart of the one-horse shay. Rather it rests on all the factors of accumulation of relative misery of all workers, including the fall in workers' share of national income even in mature capitalism; periodic unemployment; degradation of culture; discrimination against blacks, women, and others; environmental pollution; psychological and political alienation; decline in relative standard of living in the less developed capitalist countries; monopoly; war; imperialism; and the rapid growth of the socialist countries.

NOTES

1. The following interpretation relies mainly on the excellent article by Thomas Sowell, "Marx's 'Increasing Misery' Doctrine," *American Economic Review*, 50 (March 1960): 111–120; also see Maurice Dobb, "Some Economic Revaluations," *Political Affairs*, 36 (April 1957): 47–52; and see Ronald L. Meek, "Marx's 'Doctrine of Increasing Misery,'" *Science and Society*, 26 (Fall 1962): 422–441.

2. *Capital*, vol. 1, p. 190.

3. *Ibid.*, p. 191.

4. The discussion here is partly based on the very clear statement by Branco Horvat, Appendix on "Marx's Conception of Productive Labor," *Towards a Theory of Planned Economy* (Belgrad: Yugoslav Institute of Economic Research, 1964), pp. 228–233.

5. A good, detailed discussion of the Soviet theory is in Vaclav Holesovsky, "Karl Marx and Soviet National Income Theory," *American Economic Review*, 51 (June 1961): 325–344.

6. Marx, *Theories of Surplus Value* (London: Lawrence and Wishart, transl. 1951), p. 181.

7. *Ibid.*, p. 187.

8. *Ibid.*, p. 186.

9. Horvat, *op. cit.*, p. 234.

10. *Ibid.*, p. 233.

11. Paul Baran, *Political Economy of Growth* (New York: Monthly Review Press, 1957), p. 32.

12. Joseph M. Gillman, *The Falling Rate of Profit* (New York: Cameron Associates, 1958).

Marx on Long-run Trends

13. *Ibid.*, p. 34.
14. *Ibid.*, p. 59.
15. *Capital*, vol. 3, p. 280.
16. Joan Robinson, *An Essay on Marxian Economics* (New York: St. Martin's Press, 1966), p. 36.

3

Reproduction and Growth

In order to discuss the "reproduction" or growth of the economy, Marx begins with a very simplified, abstract model of capitalism.[1] Marx's concepts are translated here so far as possible into modern Keynesian symbols for the convenience of non-Marxist readers.[2] Thus, X is gross national product, Y is net national product, GI is gross investment, I is net investment, C is consumption, P is profit, W is wages, and R is replacement cost of used-up raw materials, plant, and equipment. Each of these are used here to indicate the flow recorded during a year, *not* the stock of things at a given moment.

In Marx's terminology, "surplus value" is the name for all property income, that is, profit, rent, and interest. For this first approximation we assume (as Marx did at first) no separate rent or interest payments. Thus, surplus value may be taken as roughly identical with profits (P), although we will note some other possible differences later. Marx's "constant capital" is the same as what is called here the replacement value or cost (R) of used-up raw and semifinished materials (intermediate goods) and the used-up or depreciated plant and equipment—the value of all these material objects is a constant given by the previous labor put into them.

Crucial for Marx is the concept of "variable capital," represented here by wages (W). It is variable in that living labor may produce a varying value *beyond* its wage payment. Various writers on Marx have caused confusion by interpreting his "variable capital" as an actual bundle of wage goods.[3] This idea of a stock of consumer goods used to pay workers comes from the old wages fund doctrine, even though Marx explicitly attacked that peculiar idea. The Marxist writer, Steindl, argues correctly that the "weird old monster, the wages fund doctrine, which Marx killed in a brilliant attack, [was nevertheless permitted as a] ghost to muddle up his terminology."[4] Even in the nineteenth century, capitalists kept no such stock of goods, nor even a specific fund for wages. Today it is clear that they pay wages from their general credit (or demand deposits) at banks— and may merely put today's sales revenues into the bank to cover today's wage payments. Thus, a modern Marxist model may be stated consistently, provided that variable capital always refers to the *flow* of wages and salaries during a given period, not to a nonexistent stock of wage goods or a wage fund.

Marx showed that the value of gross national product (X) from the supply or cost side is composed of variable capital (W, wages) plus constant capital (R, material costs and depreciation) plus surplus value (P, profits):

$$X = W + P + R \tag{1}$$

Notice that X is here a gross, gross national product because R includes not only replacement value of depreciated machinery, but also costs of intermediate material goods. Since this means adding the value of, say, wheat to bread, the same value is counted once in intermediate purchases and once as part of final goods. Thus, for the Keynesian purpose of measuring changes in total output, it seems that some goods are counted twice. For certain other problems, however, we shall see that the concept is quite useful.

1. Simple Reproduction (or Static Equilibrium)

Marx asked the question: What are the conditions under which an equilibrium of aggregate supply and demand will be achieved? This long-run static equilibrium, which he called simple reproduction, implies that there is no expansion of capital, no net investment. So gross investment (GI) just equals replacement:

$$GI = R \tag{2}$$

Since there is no net investment, this means that—it equilibrium is to be achieved—all the income of capitalists and workers must be exactly used up in buying consumer goods (C):

$$C = W + P \tag{3}$$

Adding these together gives the equation of aggregate demand or gross national product:

$$X = C + GI = W + P + R \tag{4}$$

which differs from Keynes only in that Marx's X and Marx's R each include intermediate purchases as well as replacement of plant and equipment.

2. Expanded Reproduction (or Dynamic Equilibrium)

Having stated the conditions for equilibrium in the simple case of a constant stock of capital, or no net investment, Marx then asked a more difficult question: What are the conditions of equilibrium when the economy is expanding year by year? In this case some of capitalist profits must be used for net investment (of course, workers do not invest, but use all their income for consumption). Let b represent the proportion of profits consumed by capitalists, and $(1\text{-}b)$ represent the invested proportion (assuming that all income saved by not being consumed is invested).

Then consumer demand is equal to workers' wages plus the consumed proportion of profits:
$$C = W + bP \tag{5}$$
Similarly, gross investment demand must equal replacement plus new net investment out of profits:
$$GI = R + (1\text{-}b)P \tag{6}$$
Finally, by addition of consumer demand and gross investment, the value of the gross national product (including intermediate goods) is:
$$X = W + R + bP + (1\text{-}b)P = W + R + P \tag{7}$$
Equation (7) is the only consistent way of stating Marx's view: its logical consistency is guaranteed by the fact that $b + (1\text{-}b) = 1$ or 100 per cent of P. Moreover, with this streamlined presentation of the reproduction schemas, it is then very easy to state Marxist growth theory (which is implicit in the schemas).

The scheme is somewhat simpler in net terms. If replacement is subtracted from both sides of equation (6), then net investment (I) is:
$$I = (1 - b)P \tag{8}$$
Net national product (Y) is just consumption plus investment:
$$Y = C + I \tag{9}$$
Therefore, if we add equations (5) and (8), net national product is:
$$Y = W + bP + (1\text{-}b)P = W + P \tag{10}$$
We shall use these equations in the growth model.

3. Input-Output

Marx not only dealt with aggregate equilibrium. He also used his reproduction schemas to evolve a simple model of exchanges between the consumer and investment goods sectors.

If Marx's model is disaggregated into investment and consumer departments or sectors, then the value composition is repeated in each of the departments:

$$GI = W_i + P_i + R_i \qquad (11)$$
$$C = W_c + P_c + R_c \qquad (12)$$

Here, the letter i refers to wages, replacement costs, and profits in the investment department; and c refers to the wages, replacement costs, and profits in the consumer goods department.

STATIC INPUT-OUTPUT

Under simple reproduction, or long-run equilibrium, it is assumed that there is only replacement of capital, no net expansion of capital (or output). Therefore, the demand for the investment goods of department i is simply for replacement investment (of depleted raw materials inventories and depreciated machinery) in both departments:

$$GI = R_i + R_c \qquad (13)$$

The demand for the consumer goods of department c is, then, equal to all the income received by both workers and capitalists in both departments (since it is assumed here that both workers and capitalists spend all their income on consumer goods):

$$C = W_i + W_c + P_i + P_c \qquad (14)$$

If we examine the equilibrium relations between departments, this analysis leads toward an input-output analysis of the kind developed by Leontief.[5] All that is necessary is an extension of the model from two to a large number of departments or industries.[6] With two departments only, the equations of supply (11 and 12 above) are set equal to the equations of demand (13 and 14 above):

$$W_i + P_i + R_i = R_i + R_c \qquad (15)$$

and

$$W_c + P_c + R_c = W_i + W_c + P_i + P_c \qquad (16)$$

These equations show all the conditions for equilibrium exchange within and between the departments.

The next step pursued by Marx is the elimination of all exchanges that are purely *within* one department (that is, canceling out like terms). Using either equation (15) or (16), the result is the same:

$$R_c = W_i + P_i \qquad (17)$$

This equation describes the necessary exchanges between the two departments in simple reproduction. Department i must supply and department c must demand the amount of constant capital necesssary to replace the depreciated capital of department c; that is, the amount R_c. On the other side, the workers and capitalists of department i must demand from department c a supply of consumer goods equal to their whole income; these are the amounts W_i and P_i.

DYNAMIC INPUT-OUTPUT

In the modern model of expanded reproduction,[7] the supply equations in the aggregate and in each department can be represented exactly as in simple reproduction:

$$GI = W_i + P_i + R_i \qquad (11)$$
$$C = W_c + P_c + R_c \qquad (12)$$

The difference comes on the demand side where the spending of surplus value is divided into capitalist consumption and capitalist investment, assuming for the moment that all saving is invested. If b is the proportion of surplus consumed by capitalists (and $[1\text{-}b]$ is the saving or investment proportion), then:

(consumer demand)
$$C = W_i + W_c + b(P_i + P_c) \qquad (18)$$
and
(investment demand)
$$I = R_i + R_c + (1\text{-}b)(P_i + P_c) \qquad (19)$$

As Marx emphasized, the difference from equilibrium to growth is determined simply by the change in the composition of demand or use of the surplus (since in simple reproduction, $[1\text{-}b] = 0$).

It follows that the equilibrium input-output relation between the two departments (obtained by setting demand equal to supply, and simplifying the answer by elimination of intradepartment exchange) is:

$$W_i + bP_i = R_c + (1\text{-}b)P_c \qquad (20)$$

As is appropriate, this equation includes the result under simple reproduction (equation [17]) as a special case in which $b = 1$ and $(1\text{-}b) = 0$.

4. Growth Model

One of the founders of modern Western growth theory, Evsey D. Domar,[8] explicitly acknowledges the priority of the Soviet economist, G. A. Feldman,[9] who in turn explicitly derives his model from Marx's reproduction schema.

In order to move from Marx's expanded reproduction schema (or national product accounting) to an explicit growth theory, it is necessary to date the variables, using t as a given time period, $t\text{-}1$ as the previous time period, and so forth. This model leaves aside the unnecessary complications of depreciation and intermediate goods; it deals solely in terms of the *net* national product (Y) and *net* investment (I).

Reproduction and Growth

In terms of the Marxist reproduction model, we have seen that net investment demand is:

$$I = (1\text{-}b)P \tag{21}$$

and net national product is:

$$Y = W + bP + (1\text{-}b)P = W + P \tag{22}$$

where P is profits, W is wage flow, and b is the fraction of profits spent for consumption.

Any growth model must determine the increase in national product. Marx saw the increase in net national product at any given time in a strict relationship to the amount of investment or increase in productive capacity. This proportional relation is represented here by the constant k, *small letters being used as constants throughout this appendix*. The amount of investment in turn is the whole national income minus the workers' consumption (W) and the capitalists' consumption from profit (bP). Finally, it is assumed in the growth model that there is a given rate of exploitation (represented by the constant $w = \dfrac{W}{Y}$), although Marx in his discussions of income distribution predicted a long-run rising rate of exploitation under capitalism (or a declining w).

Thus, the Marxist growth model in its simplest form has five basic relations:

(capacity growth)	$Y_t - Y_{t-1} = kI_{t-1}$	(23)
(investment)	$I_t = Y_t - W_t - bP_t$	(24)
(consumption)	$C_t = W_t + bP_t$	(25)
(income equilibrium)	$P_t = Y_t - W_t$	(26)
(income distribution)	$W_t = wY_t$	(27)

Notice that equation (24) says that investment is assumed equal to non-consumed income or to the saved proportion of profits (that is, $[1\text{-}b]P$). Marx, of course, only assumed this version of Say's Law as a first approximation. He clearly believes it to be *untrue* for capitalism, though valid for socialist growth.

The model (with five equations and five variables) may be reduced to one equation in the one variable, net national product, namely:

$$Y_t = [1 + k(1\text{-}b)(1 - w)]Y_{t-1} \tag{28}$$

This equation may be solved to show the path of net national product over time (in terms of an initial level zero or "o", Y_o):

$$Y_t = [1 + k(1\text{-}b)(1\text{-}w)]^t Y_o \tag{29}$$

It is perhaps simpler and clearer to translate this into the rate of growth of output, which is $Y_t - Y_{t-1}$ divided by Y_{t-1}. Then the rate of growth is:

$$\frac{Y_t - Y_{t-1}}{Y_{t-1}} = k(1\text{-}b)(1\text{-}w) \tag{30}$$

It is emphasized here that the rate of growth under capitalism may be increased if the marginal output of capital (k) is increased, if the wage share (w) is lowered, or if the capitalist consumption ratio (b) is lowered. This rule is true *provided* that all saving continues to be invested, as will *not* generally be the case under capitalism, but will generally be the case under socialism (so that this is really a normative rule for socialist growth plans).

The question of Marx's "nonproductive labor" can also be examined in the equation to a limited degree. The equation could then include sales expenses of business, such as advertising (which could be shown by adding $1-u$ to the growth rate, where u is sales expense). This would be mostly advertising, style changes, and excess sales force; but for Marx would not include pure informational advertising or pure transport and distribution costs. Of more quantitative significance for the modern capitalist world would be a subtraction for all nongrowth government spending (which could be shown by adding $1-n$ to the growth rate, where n is nongrowth government spending). Clearly, the largest nongrowth government spending item is military spending. Under socialism, capitalist consumption and business sales expenditure disappear, but unfortunately military spending remains—and collective consumption increases.

NOTES

1. Marx, *Capital*, vol. 2, part 2.

2. After all, "a rose is a rose is a rose is a rose" by any name—the point is to communicate in the easiest way. For purists who wish to see these models in the usual Marxist symbols, see my article "Marxist Models of Cyclical Growth," in *History of Political Economy* (Spring 1971).

3. This confusion is visible in the otherwise excellent presentation of Marx in Paul Sweezy, *The Theory of Capitalist Development* (New York: Monthly Review Press, first publ. 1942), especially in the Appendix by S. Tsuru. See the detailed critique in my article, "Marxist Models of Cyclical Growth," *op. cit.* Also see Sweezy, "Reply to Critics," *The Present as History* (New York: Monthly Review Press, 1953). Also Tsuru, "Keynes v. Marx," in David Horowitz, ed., *Marx and Modern Economics* (New York: Monthly Review Press, 1968). Tsuru gets confused, talking about "investment" in variable capital, because he thinks of it as a stock of goods accumulated by capitalists to pay workers.

4. J. Steindl, *Maturity and Stagnation in American Capitalism* (Oxford: Blackwell, 1952), p. 243, n. 3.

5. Wassily Leontief, *The Structure of the American Economy, 1919–1939* (New York: Oxford University Press, 1941).

6. See Martin Bronfenbrenner, "The Marxian Macro-economic Model: Extension from Two Departments," *Kyklos*, 19 (May 1966): 201–218. Also see Oskar Lange, *Introduction to Econometrics* (New York: Pergamon Press, 1959), pp. 206–228.

7. This exposition is based in part on Martin Bronfenbrenner's excellent article "Classical and Marxian Macro-Economics in Separate Nutshells," in *Essays in Honour of Marco Fanno* (Padua: Casa Editrice Dott. Antonio Milani, 1966).

8. Evsey D. Domar, "A Soviet Model of Growth," in his *Essays in the Theory of Economic Growth* (London: Oxford University Press, 1957).

9. G. A. Feldman, "On the Theory of Growth Rates of National Income," transl. in Nicolas Spulber, *Foundations of Soviet Strategy for Economic Growth: Selected Soviet Essays, 1924–30* (Bloomington: Indiana University Press, 1964).

APPENDIX
4

Cyclical Crises

This section of the appendix sets out three business cycle models, which Marx *might* have produced if he had used modern mathematical tools. It ignores long-run growth. It is strictly limited to the possible relationships creating a short-run cycle (where the period is too short for investment to increase the capacity to produce). For lack of space, Marx's predictions of increasingly violent cycles are not considered here (nor do we consider the related problems of explosive or damped cycles, random shocks, and "floors" and "ceilings").

Karl Marx wrote much interesting material about business cycles, but he never finished a complete synthesis. As a consequence, there has been considerable writing devoted to possible interpretations.[1] Among the followers of Marx, the "underconsumption" theory was emphasized and presented in formal models by Sweezy and Kalecki.[3] Kalecki's model is especially noteworthy in that it was presented in modern "Keynesian" terms, but was published *before* Keynes' *General Theory*. The falling rate of profit as a cause of cycles was emphasized by Dobb,[4] from whose description we shall distill an "overinvestment" theory (similar to one type of theory of excess demand for investment goods proposed by Hayek).[5] Finally, we shall examine a model of a possible Marxist synthesis of underconsumption and overinvestment.[6]

Naturally, no claim is made that Marx had exactly these models in mind, nor that he would have used modern techniques to write them in the exact forms used here. Although the results here are compatible with Marx, these models cannot be derived directly from Marx without some special assumptions, particularly about the lag structures. References to Marx's works will not be used to "prove" his agreement with the particular form of each relationship stated here, but only to indicate where he discussed that relationship.

1. The Underconsumption Thesis

Marx made a famous attack on naive underconsumption theory.[7] Yet one can find in his works all the elements of a more sophisticated "underconsumption" theory.[8] In this sophisticated underconsumption theory the consumption sector is no more "dominant" than the investment sector. In the eyes of Marx, as well as modern mathematical economics, the two sectors are functionally related and simultaneously determine the result. In this model, the *rate of increase* of consumer demand declines, but it is the resulting absolute decline of investment (via a principle like the acceleration principle of non-Marxist economics) which is the proximate cause of the depression in the "underconsumption" model.

It must also be emphasized that Marx (and the following model) considers underconsumption almost solely in terms of the short-run cycle peak, and he explicitly says that there is no such thing as a long-run underconsumption crisis. The long-run, in which capital may increase, is discussed later in the model of cyclical growth. Furthermore, we saw (in Appendix 3) that in the Marxist scheme the ratio of nonproductive labor to total labor plays a major role in holding back long-run capitalist growth. Nevertheless, it is a secondary question in analyzing cycles, at least until the roles of monopoly and government are considered.[9] Therefore, it is not explicitly discussed in this model.

Finally, we note that Marx was the first to launch an all-out and sustained attack on Say's Law, although Malthus did tentatively criticize it from one point of view.[10] Seventy years before Keynes, Marx emphasized that the equality of aggregate supply and demand is not automatic under capitalism. Aside from the definitional identities of national income accounting, equality of aggregate supply and demand is only rarely and temporarily reached. Marx's long-run growth schema assumed Say's Law as a first approximation, but his models of cyclical fluctuation (which follow) have no such assumption.

The whole model in terms of net national output (X) is:

(income equilibrium)	$Y_t = W_t + P_t$	(1)
(output equilibrium)	$Y_t = I_t + C_t$	(2)
(consumer behavior)	$C_t = W_{t-1} + a + hP_{t-1}$	(3)
(wage behavior)	$W_t = c + gY_t$	(4)
(investor behavior)	$I_t = v(P_{t-1} - P_{t-2})$	(5)

where all capital letters are variables; all small letters are positive constants; and h and g are between zero and one. As in Appendix 3, the symbol Y is net output, W is wage flow or variable capital, P is profit or surplus value, I is investment, and C is consumption. Equations (1) and (2) are equilibrium conditions at a given point, always being disrupted by further movement. Equations (3), (4), and (5) are behavioral, and are discussed below. Equation (3) shows the Marxist concept that consumer demand depends on the distribution of income as well as the (Keynesian) aggregate level of income.[11] Marx argues that workers' wages must all be spent for consumption; therefore, the coefficient of consumption out of wages (W) is one. Only a small part of capitalist income, however, is spent for consumption. Capitalist income is high enough that much of it is saved, and may be reinvested or hoarded. Therefore, the marginal ratio of consumption out of surplus value is less than one, and its average ratio falls as surplus value rises in prosperity.

Equation (4) states Marx's conviction that in prosperity wage income rises more slowly than all income.[12] In other words, it is the movement in the division of income by economic classes that is vital to Marxist cycle theory, in contrast to the Keynesian emphasis on aggregate psychological propensities. A larger and larger percentage of income goes to surplus value. Only when income falls in depression does the process reverse itself. If equations (3) and (4) are taken together, this means that in prosperity there is a shift in income from wages to surplus value, and this shift restricts consumer demand to a much slower growth than total income or output, thus lowering the rate of profit on sales (though it also means that consumption falls more slowly in depression periods).

Finally, equation (5) states that net investment is determined by the previous change in capitalist income.[13] Marx often emphasized that capitalists do not invest money for charity; they will invest in new productive capacity only if they expect to make a profit from their investments. (Assuming no rent or interest income, we can use "profit" as a rough measure of surplus value.) The previous change in profits is assumed to be the best indicator of the expected profit. Notice that Marx's use of profit in the investment function is a more complex concept than those theories which use merely consumer demand or even aggregate demand. The essence of the theory is still the underconsumptionist thesis that the slower rise of wage income causes a slower rise of consumer demand, which sufficiently accounts for the cycle turning points in investment and output. In this investment function, however, the Marxist theory takes into account that the slowed movement of consumer demand may be partly offset by investment demand itself (as in all functions where investment is dependent on aggregate demand). Moreover, in using the profit variable, the Marxist investment function also recognizes that even changes in aggregate demand may be partially offset by changes in wage costs. This is a long way from the most naive underconsumption theories.

This system of five equations (1 through 5) may be reduced by successive substitutions to a single equation in terms of net national product (**Y**). Its form is:

$$Y_t = q + yY_{t-1} + zY_{t-2} \tag{6}$$

in which q, y, and z are constants, where:

$$q \equiv a + c(1\text{-}h), y \equiv h + v + g(1\text{-}h\text{-}v), \text{ and } z \equiv v(g\text{-}1).$$

This is a linear, second order, difference equation.[14] In this equation, the constant q merely influences the level around which fluctuations will occur. There will be cyclical fluctuations of net national product for the whole range in which y^2 is less than $4z$.

The values of y and z depend only on g, h, and v. Do we find a reasonable range of these parameters for which cycles are possible? The task of estimating the contemporary parameters is far beyond the scope of this essay, but we may at least examine the results according to the parameters Marx usually assumed to be true. Since Marx often used a wage/income ratio of one-half, we might assume that g, the marginal wage/income ratio, is 0.5 (a figure that may be within the range of at least some modern short-run estimates). Marx believed that profit recipients saved and invested most of their income, so we might take h, the marginal consumption out of profits, to be 0.2 (which also may fall within the range of modern estimates, if we include retained corporate profits in the amount of "profits").

Assuming that $g = 0.5$ and $h = 0.2$, the condition for cyclical fluctuations reduces to the necessity that $(0.6 + 0.5v)^2$ be less than $2v$. This condition will hold for any v between 0.3 and 5.0. The true value of v, the accelerator coefficient of investment for a change in profits, is not well established even today. Most modern estimates would probably fall somewhere in that range, however, so the belief that this model may explain fluctuations does seem reasonable. Obviously, this is not a proof—given other parameters—and this same second-order difference equation could produce growth rather than fluctuations. The point here (and in following sections) is only that such an equation, with the parameters often assumed by Marx in other contexts, is able to produce fluctuations—and that this is one possible representation of the real-world oscillations observed by Marx.

2. The Overinvestment Antithesis

In addition to the "underconsumption" facets of the business cycle, Marx's work contains all the elements of a radically different "overinvestment" type of model, especially in his discussions of short-run declines in the rate of profit[15] and his critique of Ricardo's theory of crises.[16] In order to make the contrast as strong as possible, all the underconsumption" elements are removed from this model, and the reconciliation or synthesis of the two models is left to the next section. The Marxist "overinvestment" model is presented here in equations, with each of the equations explained in some detail following the model.

The definitions of the variables are: X is value of the gross national product (including intermediate goods); R is the replacement value of used-up materials and machinery; W is wages or variable capital; P is profits or surplus value; R_i, W_i and P_i are the same variables in department i or production of investment goods only; R_c, W_c, and P_c are the same variables in department c or production of consumer goods only; GI is gross investment; C is consumption; and P^x is the indicator of expected surplus value.

EQUILIBRIUM CONDITIONS

(output and demand)	$X_t = GI_t + C_t$	(7)
(income and cost)	$X_t = R_t + W_t + P_t$	(8)
(consumption sector)	$C_t = R_{c_t} + W_{c_t} + P_{c_t}$	(9)
(investment sector)	$GI_t = R_{i_t} + W_{i_t} + P_{i_t}$	(10)
(replacement or depreciation)	$R_t = R_{i_t} + R_{c_t}$	(11)
(wages)	$W_t = W_{i_t} + W_{c_t}$	(12)

BEHAVIORAL FUNCTIONS

(consumption)	$C_t = b(W_{t-1} + P_{t-1})$	(13)
(investment)	$GI_t = v(P^x_t - P^x_{t-1})$	(14)
(expected profit)	$P^x_t = rP_{c_t} + P_{i_t}$ where $r > 1$	(15)
(replacement or depreciation c)	$R_{c_t} = -h + jX_t$	(16)
(aggregate replacement or depreciation)	$R_t = kX_t$	(17)
(wages in c)	$W_{c_t} = gX_t$	(18)
(wages in i)	$W_{i_t} = mX_t$	(19)

Once again, all the capital letters are variables, while all the small letters are positive constants. The constants, b, j, k, g, and m are all between zero and one. The constant r is greater than one.

Equation (7) contains only gross terms, that is, in this equation consumption, investment, and national product include depreciation as well as the costs of intermediate purchases between firms. Once again, these are the planned quantities of supply and demand, so this is an equilibrium condition and not a mere accounting identity.

Equation (8) states the equilibrium relationship that aggregate value of output equals aggregate costs plus aggregate surplus value. Equations (9) and (10) disaggregate costs (and surplus value) into those in the consumer goods industries and those in the investment goods industries.

Equation (11) states that in equilibrium the aggregate constant capital costs equal the constant capital costs of consumer goods plus the constant capital costs of investment goods. Equation (12) states that in equilibrium the aggregate wage costs equal the wage costs of consumer goods plus the wage costs of investment goods.

Equation (13) states that consumption merely increases and decreases in direct proportion to income. This *simplistic* assumption is made in order to emphasize that consumer behavior is not the focal point of this theory. The model produces a cyclical result even though consumer behavior is taken as a purely passive follower of national income behavior.

Equation (14) states that capitalists invest (or expand production) only when the best indicator of expected surplus value (or expected profits) is rising. This follows Marx's concept that capitalists expand production only when they expect to increase their profits by doing so.[17]

Equation (15) says that the best indicator of expected surplus value is the weighted sum of surplus value in consumer goods and profits in investment goods. Marx assumes that surplus value in consumer goods carries a heavier weight in the determination of expected surplus value because the demand for investment goods is mainly derivative from the prosperity of business in consumer goods.

Equation (16) states an empirical fact stressed by Marx as the key to this approach: that the price of constant capital (meaning here the flow of replacement cost of depreciated plant and equipment and raw materials used up in this period) rises and falls more rapidly than national prices.[18] Here, we have specified that the cost of constant capital used up in producing consumer goods rises (and falls) more rapidly than consumer output at present prices. Notice that the quantities here are *not* deflated for price changes, but are merely determined by the amount of physical quantity times the current price level. The model could be further specified with separate price and quantity variables for each component of cost or revenue, but that would only add complexity without changing the results.

Equation (17) makes the assumption that aggregate constant capital or cost of producer goods rises and falls in a constant proportion to total product. This may be taken here primarily as a simplifying assumption, emphasizing that the behavior of *aggregate* producer goods costs is not too important. Marx's point is that the *relative* changes in producer goods costs in the consumer goods sector and producer goods sector can strongly influence the indicator of expected profits. In other words, the fact that the general price level rises faster than consumer goods prices means that the rate of profit may decline in consumer goods while it is still rising in producer goods. But the rate of profit in the consumer goods sector is given more weight in investor expectations, hence the expected rate of profit falls, and capitalists reduce their investment.

In equation (17) we must understand that the aggregate cost of producer goods may remain a constant proportion of total revenue only if certain conditions hold true. First, we assume in this short-run model that technology remains unchanged. Second, we assume that the degree of vertical integration of firms remain unchanged, so that the measure of the intermediate firm purchases does not change. Last, by definition each rise in the price of the intermediate producer goods is reflected in an equal rise of total transactions income (since an increased cost of producer goods to the buying corporation means an equal increased revenue to the selling corporation).

Equations (18) and (19) state that wages in both departments of industry rise and fall in a direct and constant proportion to the value of the product. This assumption is obviously not Marxist, and is a simplification used for illustrative purposes only. Modern overinvestment theorists tend to argue that the proportion of wages to national income *rises* in prosperity, but that is certainly the opposite of Marx's view (and the empirical findings). The neutral assumption of a constant wage (and profit) proportion is made here to stress that this model is still viable even when the aggregates remain in constant proportions to the national product, and when the only problems arise from the differential changes in prices and material costs in the two departments.

Mathematically, the system of thirteen equations (7) through (19) may be reduced by successive substitutions to one equation in one variable, that is, the national product over time. Its form is:

$$X_t = q + yX_{t-1} - zX_{t-2} \qquad (20)$$

where q, y, and z are constants. In this model:

$$q \equiv 0$$

and

$$y \equiv \frac{(1 + vr - v)\,(b - bk) + v(m - 1 + k - j) + vr(g + j)}{1 + v(m - 1 + k - j) + vr(g + j)}$$

and

$$z \equiv \frac{(vr - v)\,(b - bk)}{1 + v(m - 1 + k - j) + vr(g + j)}$$

The fact that q equals zero indicates that output fluctuates around zero (or the central value on the trend line) in this model. In other words, this model *may* explain cycles, but does not even attempt to explain the absolute level, much less the long-run rate of growth of output.

Equation (20) will produce cycles if y^2 is *less* than $4z$. The values of y and z, however, depend on a good number of parameters, each of which is difficult to estimate. The values of v (the accelerator) and r (the relative importance of profits in consumer goods for the determination of expectations) appear to be especially crucial, but are especially difficult to estimate. Since the task of empirical estimation is far beyond the scope of this appendix, we must be satisfied with the fact that in this model cycles will occur within a wide range of parameters. Purely as an illustration, the following parameters will produce not only cycles, but cycles of a constant amplitude: $v = 2, r = 1.5, b = 0.83, k = 0.1, j = 0.05, g = 0.3$, and $m = 0.3$. Note that cycles will occur only if r is greater than one (but this reflects a basic assumption of the model).

3. The Marxist Synthesis

Marx stressed the sociologically based differences in class income reflected in underconsumption, but he also recognized the more technical price-cost differentials reflected in overinvestment theory. He described the possibility of synthesizing the two only in the most abstract terms, but it is possible to construct such a synthesis within the guidelines laid down by Marx.[19] It is what Bronfenbrenner refers to as the capitalist dilemma, crises caused by "both the 'falling rate of profit' and the 'tendency to overproduction.' "[20]

The general Marxist cycle model would be as follows:

EQUILIBRIUM CONDITIONS

(output)	$X_t = GI_t + C_t$	(21)
(income)	$X_t = R_t + W_t + P_t$	(22)
(consumption)	$C_t = R_{c_t} + W_{c_t} + P_{c_t}$	(23)
(investment)	$I_t = R_{i_t} + W_{i_t} + P_{i_t}$	(24)
(replacement or depreciation)	$R_t = R_{i_t} + R_{c_t}$	(25)
(wages)	$W_t = W_{i_t} + W_{c_t}$	(26)

BEHAVIORAL FUNCTIONS

(consumption)	$C_t = W_{t-1} + a + b\,P_{t-1}$	(27)
(investment	$I_t = v(P_t^x - P_{t-1}^x)$	(28)
(expected profit indicator)	$P_t^x = rP_{c_t} + P_{i_t}$, where $r > 1$	(29)
(replacement or depreciation in c)	$R_{c_t} = -h + jX_t$	(30)
(aggregate replacement or depreciation)	$R_t = kX_t$	(31)
(wages in c)	$W_{c_t} = n + gX_t$	(32)
(wages in i)	$W_{i_t} = d + mX_t$	(33)

where b, j, k, g, and m are between zero and one, and r is greater than one.

Equations (21) through (26) are—as in the identical equations of the previous model—equilibrium conditions. In this schema it is again the case that consumption, investment, and national product are defined so as to include all depreciation *and* all intermediate material purchases from firm to firm.

Equation (27) is the same consumption function as in the underconsumption model. It states that consumption depends on total wages plus a proportion of surplus value.

Equation (28) is the same investment function as in the overinvestment model. Specifically, it is stated that present investment depends on the direction of change in the indicator of expected surplus value.

Equation (29), as in the overinvestment model, defines the indicator of expected profits as the weighted sum of profits in consumer goods industries plus profits in investment goods industries.

Equations (30) and (31) are identical with the similar equations in the overinvestment model. They state that constant capital (or material cost) in the consumer goods industries rises and falls more rapidly than national product, but the aggregate constant capital remains a constant proportion of national product.

Equations (32) and (33) state the proposition, as in the underconsumption model, that wages rise and fall more slowly than national product. They merely specify that this is the case, not only in the aggregate, but separately in both departments of industry.

This more general model combines the income distribution and consumption features of the underconsumption model with the cost and investment features of the overinvestment model. It appears to be a perfectly logical and compatible synthesis. The fact that profit is now being squeezed from two sides at once illustrates the dilemma of capitalism. Statistically, it merely means that all the parameters can be less extreme and more realistic.

Mathematically, the system of thirteen equations (21) through (33) can be reduced to a single equation in terms of national product. As in the last two models the form of the equation is:

$$X_t = q + yX_{t-1} - zX_{t-2} \tag{34}$$

where q, y, and z are constants. These parameters are merely more complex, being defined in this model to be:

$$q \equiv \frac{a + n + d - bn - bd}{1 + v(m - 1 + k - j) + vr(g + j)}$$

and

$$y \equiv \frac{(vr - v + 1)\ (g + m + k - bg - bm - bk) + v(m - 1 + k - j) + vr(g}{1 + v(m - 1 + k - j) + vr(g + j)}$$

and

$$z \equiv \frac{(vr - v)\ (g + m + k - bg - bm - bk)}{1 + v(m - 1 + k - j) + vr(g + j)}$$

Once again, q only helps determine the level around which fluctuations occur. And once again, there will be cycles in the wide range in which y^2 is less than $4z$. In this case the possible range for cycles definitely covers all the reasonable range of empirical estimates for the parameters, because two different sets of factors are operating at the same time in the same direction, thus eliminating the need for extreme assumptions for either set of factors.

In other words, in the underconsumptionist model the slow movement of demand alone is the restricting factor on profits in the upswing and the sole supporting factor in the downswing. In the overinvestment model the more rapid movement of costs alone is the restricting factor on profits in the upswing and the sole supporting factor in the downswing. In the general Marxist cycle model, however, profits are squeezed at the peak of the upswing by *both* slowed demand *and* rapidly rising costs, while profit prospects are aided at the trough of the depression by *both* a slower fall of demand *and* a more rapid fall of costs. It is thus possible for the Marxist general model to generate cycles with relatively small differential movements of both demand and costs.

NOTES

1. Henry Smith, "Marx and the Trade Cycle," *Review of Economic Studies*, 4 (June 1937): 192–205; John C. Wilson, "A Note on Marx and the Trade Cycle," *Review of Economic Studies*, 5 (February 1938): 107–113; J. Winternitz, "The Marxist Theory of Crises," *Modern Quarterly*, 4 (Autumn 1959): 310–327; Howard Sherman, "Marx and the Business Cycle," *Science and Society*, 31 (Fall 1967): 486–504.
2. Paul Sweezy, *The Theory of Capitalist Development* (New York: Monthly Review Press, 1942), pp. 186–189.
3. Michael Kalecki, *Theory of Economic Dynamics* (London: George Allen and Unwin, 1954), pp. 110–131.
4. Maurice Dobb, *Political Economy and Capitalism* (New York: International Publishers, 1945), pp. 79–127.
5. Frederick Hayek, *Prices and Production* (London: George Routledge and Sons, 1935).
6. See, for an early statement of the synthesis, John Strachey, *Nature of Capitalist Crises* (New York: Covice-Friede, 1935); Leo Huberman, *Man's Worldly Goods* (New York: 1936); Martin Bronfenbrenner, "*Das Kapital* for the Modern Man," *Science and Society*, 29 (Autumn 1965): 419–438; Bronfenbrenner, "The Marxian Macro-economic Model," *Kyklos*, 19 (May 1966): pp. 201–218; Bronfenbrenner, "Classical and Marxian Macro-economics in Separate Nutshells," in *Essays in Honor of Marco Franco* (Padua: Antonio Milani, 1966); Bronfenbrenner, "Marxian Influences in 'Bourgeois' Economics," *American Economic Review*, 57 (May 1967): pp. 624–635.
7. Marx, *Capital*, vol. 2, pp. 475–476.
8. An underconsumption model is likewise found in Marx by Nicholas Georgescu-Roegen, "Mathematical Proofs of the Breakdown of Capitalism," in his *Analytical Economics* (Cambridge: Harvard University Press, 1966), p. 406. An underconsumption model is denied and H. Sherman is attacked for being "more underconsumptionist than Marxist" in Bronfenbrenner and Yutaka Kosai, "On the Marxian Capital-Consumption Ratio," *Science and Society*, 31 (Fall 1967): 472n.
9. But for contrary opinions, see S. Coontz, *Productive Labor and Effective Demand* (London: Routledge and Paul, 1965); and Joseph Gillman, *The Falling Rate of Profit* (New York: Cameron Associates, 1958), especially pp. 110–113. The controversy is

only over the role of nonproductive labor in competitive capitalism; all Marxists agree that monopoly waste and government spending drastically affect the cycle.

10. Karl Marx, *Theories of Surplus Value* (New York: International Publishers, transl. 1952), pp. 368–415.

11. Marx, *Capital*, vol. 1, pp. 593 and 363n; also vol. 3, pp. 286–287.

12. Marx, *Capital*, vol. 3, pp. 222 and 568.

13. Marx, *Capital*, vol. 3, p. 359.

14. The relevant mathematics are fully explained in R. G. D. Allen *Mathematical Economics* (London: Collier-Macmillan, 1957).

15. Marx, *Capital*, vol. 3, Chapters 6, 7, and 14.

16. Marx, *Theories of Surplus Value*, op. cit., pp. 368–414.

17. Marx, *Capital*, vol. 3, pp. 242ff.

18. Marx, *Theories of Surplus Value*, op. cit., pp. 371ff.

19. Marx, *Capital*, vol. 3, pp. 286–287.

20. Bronfenbrenner, "*Das Kapital* for the Modern Man," op. cit., p. 419.

A Marxist-type Model of Cyclical Growth

We have examined Marx's long-run growth model (on the assumption of saving equal to investment and no fluctuations) and Marx's short-run cycle models (on the assumption of investment not having time to increase capacity and no long-run growth). But it is the nature of Marx's basic view that both short- and long-run aspects of investment must be examined together. Thus, Tsuru writes that "the concept of accumulation in the Marxian *tableau* . . . is placed in the schema in such a way as to produce the dual effect of both creating effective demand and adding to the productive capacity."[1]

Here we shall consider a cyclical growth model involving both long- and short-run aspects of investment, as well as long- and short-run aspects of consumption and distribution.[2] To accomplish this combination, a technical device must be introduced to weight these factors appropriately. For example, if we simply add together the short-run consumption estimate $(W + a + hP)$ and the long-run consumption estimate $(W + bP)$, the total consumption estimate would be on the order of twice the correct estimate. Hence, both estimates must be scaled down before they are added together. For this purpose we need a weighting device to give the proper weight or proportion (p) of short-run estimate to long-run estimate. Let p be a constant between zero and one. Then if we multiply the short-run consumption estimate by p and the long-run consumption estimate by $1-p$, the total estimate must always be of the right magnitude. Obviously, if p is equal to one, the result is a short-run consumption function; whereas if p is equal to zero, the result is a purely long-run consumption function. For any p between zero and one, we will have short-run cyclical consumer reactions, but also a built-in endogenous "ratchet" effect leading to further growth.

Of course, some problems are raised by this procedure. For one thing, the weighting factors should be different in the various equations if one is trying to build a realistic econometric model. Here, however, for simplicity of exposition—and strictly as a first approximation—we assume that p and $1\text{-}p$ are the weighting factors for all the equations. Furthermore, a Soviet writer, L. Al'ter, has criticized my division into short-term and long-term factors: "This division is justified in itself, but only under the condition that one does not leave out of consideration the fact that it is relative in nature and must be supplemented by the influence of current demand upon long-term processes and by the influence of investments upon current dynamics."[3] His qualifications are correct, but would introduce far greater complications in the model. This model merely follows Marx's method of successive approximations to reality, and is a first approximation designed only to clarify the main structure of cyclical growth.

For the sake of simplicity, the cyclical growth model is presented in net terms. Addition of factors for determination of gross output would greatly complicate the argument without changing any conclusions. Thus the basic components are the net growth model and the "underconsumption" cycle model discussed earlier. As before, Y stands for value of net national output. Now, however, it is also necessary to distinguish $\overline{Y}$, which is full-capacity output, or the potential output that could be produced with the fullest use of capacity.

The Marxist-type cyclical growth model is:

(income equilibrium)
$$Y_t = W_t + P_t \tag{1}$$
(output equilibrium)
$$Y_t = C_t + I_t \tag{2}$$
(income distribution)
$$W_t = p(c + gY_t) + (1 - p)wY_t \tag{3}$$
(consumer behavior)
$$C_t = p(W_{t-1} + a + hP_{t-1}) + (1 - p)\,(W_t + bP_t) \tag{4}$$
(investment behavior)
$$I_t = pv(P_{t-1} - P_{t-2}) + (1 - p)\,(Y_t - W_t - bP_t) \tag{5}$$
(full-capacity growth)
$$\overline{Y}_t - \overline{Y}_{t-1} = (1 - p)\,kI_{t-1} \tag{6}$$

where the variables are Y, actual output; $\overline{Y}$, full-capacity output; W, wages or variable capital; P, profit or surplus value; I, net investment; and C, consumption. The constants are p, a, c, g (short-run marginal wage/output ratio), w (long-run wage/output ratio), h (short-run marginal propensity to consume from surplus value), b (long-run marginal propensity to consume from surplus value), v (short-run accelerator coefficient), and k (long-run output/capital ratio). Note that p, g, w, h, and b are between zero and one.

A Marxist-type Model of Cyclical Growth

Equations (1) and (2) are equilibrium conditions implicit in all Marxist models. Equations (3), (4), and (5) combine short-run and long-run behavioral functions of income distribution, consumer behavior, and investment behavior, respectively. Equation (6) states the long-run relation of the change in full-capacity output to net investment. In each of these equations the short-run cyclical elements are weighted by p and the long-run growth elements are weighted by 1-p. When p equals zero, all the short-run factors are eliminated, so the model reduces exactly to the simple Marxist growth model (in Appendix 3.4). When p equals one, all the long-run factors are eliminated, so the model reduces exactly to the Marxist underconsumption cycle model (in Appendix 4.1).

Thus, the two underlying models are:

When $p = 1$, cycle model:		When $p = 0$, growth model:	
$Y_t = W_t + P_t$	(1a)	$Y_t = W_t + P_t$	(1b)
$Y_t = I_t + C_t$	(2a)	$Y_t = I_t + C_t$	(2b)
$W_t = c + gY_t$	(3a)	$W_t = wY_t$	(3b)
$C_t = W_{t-1} + hP_{t-1}$	(4a)	$C_t = W_t + bP_t$	(4b)
$I_t = v(P_{t-1} - P_{t-2})$	(5a)	$I_t = \overline{Y}_t - W_t - bP_t$	(5b)
$\overline{Y}_t - \overline{Y}_{t-1} = 0$	(6a)	$Y_t - Y_{t-1} = kI_t$	(6b)

which reduces to:

$$Y_t = [v + h + g(1 - h - v)]Y_{t-1} + v(g - 1)Y_{t-2} + a + c(1 - h) \quad (7a)$$

and $\overline{Y}$ is constant

which reduces to:

$$Y_t = [1 + k(1 - b)(1 - w)]Y_{t-1} \quad (7b)$$

and $\overline{Y}_t = Y_t$

The reduced form equation for output in the cycle model (7a) is identical with that derived in an earlier section, while the growth equation (7b) is identical with its earlier presentation. Indeed, the only difference with the earlier models is the addition of another equation because of the new variable $\overline{Y}$, which distinguishes full-capacity output from actual output. In the cycle model, this adds equation (7a) which merely gives the added information that full-capacity output is constant in the short-run (as it must be by definition). In the growth model, there is merely added the short-run equilibrium condition (2b), saying that output must equal consumer plus investor demand in order to obtain equilibrium. Also full-capacity output is inserted explicitly in the investment supply and effect of investment equations. It is appropriate in determination of investment supply (or saving) because Marx here assumed Say's Law. Moreover, since the simple growth model assumes that saving is always invested and the economy is always running at full capacity, it can be shown that actual and full-capacity output are identical.

Now take the general case in which p is neither zero nor one, but is somewhere between those values. In this case, there are both short-run and long-run influences in all the behavioral equations, and there will be cyclical

399

flúctuations around a growing trend of national output (assuming any reasonable values for the parameters).

Before discussing the solution for the general case, it may be observed that in this case the constants c and a are unnecessary and redundant. They are the constant parts of the short-run consumption and distribution functions, and merely affect the level around which short-run fluctuations occur. In the combined system, this level is fully determined by the long-run components of these functions (and the other long-run components in the system). Hence, in the general case of growth and cycles it is more appropriate to remove c and a from their respective equations.

With this modification, we can proceed to reduce the six equations of the cyclical growth model (1) through (6)—with its six variables—to one equation in the one variable, net national output. The equation is:

$$Y_t = qY_{t-1} + yY_{t-2} + zY_{t-3} \tag{7}$$

where:

$$q \equiv 1 + k(1\text{-}p)^2 + [p - k(1\text{-}p)^3]A + [p(h + v) - kb(1\text{-}p)^3]B$$

$$y \equiv - [1 + k(1\text{-}p)^2]pA - [h + 2v + hk(1\text{-}p)^2]pB$$

$$z \equiv pvB$$

and where: $A \equiv w(1\text{-}p) + pg$ and $B \equiv 1\text{-}A$. The terms A and B are collections of constants distinguished because they derive from the important Marxist concepts W and P, so that $W = AY$ and $P = (1\text{-}A)Y = BY$.

This is a homogeneous, third order, linear difference equation. Although it is unfortunate that such a complex form as a third order equation must be used, this is necessary to show the internal or endogeneous generation of both cycles and growth. Models based on second-order difference equations either treat cycles merely as deviations from a given growth path (fixed externally or they simply tack on an externally or exogenously given growth factor as a function of nothing but time (some A^t).[4]

Of course, if p falls to zero, there are no fluctuations, while if p rises to one, there is no growth. In the general case, for any p between zero and one, there will be growth if the quantity $(q + y + z)$ is greater than one. If it is also true that $(18qyz + y^2q^2)$ is less than $(4q^3y + 4y^3 + 27z^2)$, then there will also be cyclical fluctuations around the growth trend.[5] Under these criteria, we find that almost *any* reasonable values of the parameters (g, w, h, b, k, and v) will produce both cycles and growth.

For example, assume arbitrarily that p is exactly in the middle of the intermediate area, that is, $p = 0.5$. Also assume that $g = 0.5$, $w = 0.4$, $b = 0.2$, $h = 0.3$, $k = 0.3$, and $v = 2$, all of these being within the range of Marx's descriptions and/or modern empirical work. In this case, it follows that $q = 1.9$, $y = 1.5$, and $z = 0.7$. Then $q + y + z = 1.03$, which is greater than one, so there will be growth. Furthermore, $18qyz + y^2q^2 =$

-26.42, which is much less than $4q^3y + 4y^3 + 27z^2 = 85.84$, so there. will also be cycles.

If a large number of such examples are run on the computer, it may be observed that as the crucial parameter p rises from zero toward one, short-run cyclical influences become more important, while long-run growth influences become less important. In other words, as p rises from zero toward one, the amplitude of cyclical fluctuations increases while the rate of economic growth declines. To a Marxist this means merely that large-scale cyclical unemployment causes slower long-run growth. In criticizing an earlier, ambiguous statement I made, a Soviet writer categorically declares that it is a "fact that the crises and depressions inevitable under capitalism reduce the overall average long-term growth rate . . . , but it does not follow that acceleration of the rate leads to moderation of crises."[6]

Finally, it must be emphasized that this model of cyclical growth is a weak first approximation to the Marxist view of economic reality. A more realistic model would include (1) the effects of price-cost relations (as in the overinvestment model of Appendix 4.2); (2) random shocks, dampening and explosive factors;[7] (3) monopoly power (see Chapter 8 of this book); (4) "unproductive" labor and waste (see Chapters 6 and 7); (5) activity of capitalist governments (see Chapter 9); and (6) imperialism (see Chapter 10). With all these additions, it is clear that the tendency toward a crisis need not "inevitably" lead toward mass unemployment and depression. Any given crisis may be resolved in other ways, for example, increases in capitalist waste production, especially increases in military production.

NOTES

1. S. Tsuru, "Keynes v. Marx": The Methodology of Aggregates," in David Horowitz, ed., *Marx and Modern Economics* (New York: Monthly Review Press, 1968), p. 195.

2. A simpler Keynesian-type model of this sort can be found in Howard Sherman, "Heuristic Methods of Integrating Cycle and Growth Models," *Western Economic Journal*, 5 (June 1967): 276–281.

3. L. Al'ter, "Theory of Economic Growth," transl. in *Problems of Economics*, 10 (July 1967): 35–54.

4. See the excellent statement of this view in Arthur Smithies, "Economic Fluctuations and Growth," *Econometrics*, 25 (January 1957): 1–55.

5. For mathematical details, see L. W. Griffiths, *Introduction to the Theory of Equations* (New York: J. Wiley, 1945).

6. Al'ter, *op. cit.*, p. 44.

7. See Michael Kalecki, *Theory of Economic Dynamics* (London: George Allen and Unwin, 1954), pp. 126–129 and 137–142.

Selected References

CHAPTER 1. *Methods of Social Analysis*

CLASSIC MARXIST VIEWS

Childe, V. Gordon. *History*. London: Cobbett Press, 1947. Restatement of the Marxist view by a distinguished British archaeologist.

Selsam, Howard, et. al. *Reader in Marxist Social Dynamics*. New York: International Publishers, 1971.

RADICAL CRITIQUE OF THE ESTABLISHMENT OUTLOOK

Gouldner, Alvin. *The Coming Crisis in Western Sociology*. New York: Basic Books, 1970.

Mills, C. Wright. *The Sociological Imagination*. New York: Grove Press, 1961.

NON-DOGMATIC MARXIST VIEWS

Lange, Oskar. *Political Economy*, Volume I. New York: Pergamon Press, 1963.

Sartre, Jean Paul. *Search for a Method*. New York: Vintage, 1968.

CHAPTER 2. *Precapitalist Societies*

PRIMITIVE EVOLUTION

Marxist

Childe, V. Gordon. *Social Evolution*. London: Watts and Co., 1951; also see many other books by Childe.

Clark, Grahame. *World Prehistory*. Cambridge: Cambridge University Press, 1969.

Engels, Frederick. *The Origin of the Family, Private Property, and the State*. New York: International Publishers, 1942; first published 1884.

Marx, Karl. *Pre-Capitalist Economic Formations*. Edited and introduced by Eric Hobsbawm. New York: International Publishers, 1964, written 1857.

Soviet Anthropology and Archeology. A quarterly journal. Ongoing debate between French and Soviet Marxists.

Walbank, F. W. *The Decline of the Roman Empire in the West*. London: Cobbett Press, 1946.

Non-Marxist

Steward, J. H., R. M. Adams, D. Collier, A. Palerm, K. A. Wittfogel, and R. A. Beals. *Irrigation Civilizations: A Comparative Study*. Washington, D.C.: Pan American Union, 1960.

SLAVERY IN THE U.S. SOUTH

Genovese, Eugene D. *The Political Economy of Slavery*. New York: Pantheon Books, 1965.

Stampp, Kenneth. *The Peculiar Institution*. New York: Knopf, 1956.

CHAPTER 3. *Origins of Capitalism*

MARXISTS

Dobb, Maurice. *Studies in the Development of Capitalism.* London: George Routledge & Sons, 1946.

Symposium. *The Transition from Feudalism to Capitalism.* New York: Science and Society, Inc., 1954.

OTHER VIEWS

Collins, Kins. "Marx on the English Agricultural Revolution," *History and Theory,* 6, No. 3 (1967): 351–381.

Dowd, Douglas. "The State, Power and the Industrial Revolution, 1750–1914," *Occasional Papers of the Union for Radical Political Economics,* 4 (Spring 1971), whole issue. Very radical, very nondogmatic, very interesting.

Nell, Edward J. "Economic Relationships in the Decline of Feudalism," *History and Theory,* 6, No. 3 (1967): 313–350.

CHAPTER 4. *Value and Market Allocation*

THE MARXIST VIEW OF VALUE THEORY

Dobb, Maurice. *Political Economy and Capitalism.* New York: International Publishers, 1945. Excellent Marxist discussion of value theory.

Horowitz, David. *Marx and Modern Economics.* New York: Monthly Review Press, 1968. The best collection of articles on Marxist economics.

Lange, Oskar. "Marxian Economics and Modern Economic Theory," *Review of Economic Studies,* 2 (June 1935): 189–201. Non-dogmatic Marxist classic.

Mandel, Ernest. *Marxist Economic Theory.* New York: Monthly Review Press, 1969.

Meek, Ronald L. *Studies in the Labor Theory of Value.* New York: International Publishers, 1956. Best history of value theories to that date.

Robinson, Joan. *An Essay on Marxian Economics.* New York: St. Martin's Press, 1960: first edition 1942.

Sraffa, Piero. *Production of Commodities by Means of Commodities.* Cambridge: Cambridge University Press, 1960. An entirely new and completely defensible version of the labor theory.

Sweezy, Paul M. *The Theory of Capitalist Development.* New York: Oxford University Press, 1942. The most complete exposition of Marxist economics available in English.

DISCUSSIONS OF MARXIST VALUE THEORY BY NON-MARXIST ECONOMISTS

Bohm-Bawerk, Eugen. *Karl Marx and the Close of His System.* Edited and introduced by Paul Sweezy, with a criticism of von Bohm-Bawerk by R. Hilferding. New York: A. M. Kelley, 1949; first published 1896. The most thorough critique of the labor theory of value.

Bronfenbrenner, Martin. "Academic Methods for Marxian Problems," *Journal of Political Economy,* 65 (December 1957): 535–542.

Chipman, John S. "The Consistency of the Marxian Economic System," *Economia Internazionale,* 5 (August 1952): 3–34.

Dickinson, H. D. "Notes to Article by L. Johansen, 'Labour Theory of Value and Marginal Utilities,'" *Economics of Planning,* 3 (December 1963): 239–241.

Gordon, S. "Why Does Marxian Exploitation Theory Require a Labor Theory of Value?" *Journal of Political Economy,* 76 (January–February 1968): 137–140.

Johansen, Leif. "Labour Theory of Value and Marginal Utilities," *Economics of Planning,* 3 (September 1963): 89–100. Exceedingly interesting.

Morishima, M., and F. Seton. "Aggregation in Leontief Matrices and the Labour Theory of Value," *Econometrica,* 29 (April 1961): 203–220.

Selected References

Samuelson, Paul. "Wages and Interest: A Modern Dissection of Marxian Economic Models," *American Economic Review*, 47 (December 1957): 884–912. A vicious attack on Marxism.

Sowell, Thomas. "Marxian Value Reconsidered," *Economica*, 30 (August 1963): 297–308.

CHAPTER 5. Poverty and Exploitation

CLASS STRUCTURE

Bottomore, Thomas. *Classes in Modern Society*. New York: Pantheon Books, 1966.

Dos Santos, Theotonios. "The Concept of Social Classes," *Science and Society*, 34 (Summer 1970): 166–193.

Hobsbawm, Eric. *Labouring Men*. London: Weidenfeld and Nicholson, 1964.

Legget, John. *Class, Race, and Labor*. New York: Oxford University Press, 1968.

Mills, C. Wright. *White Collar*. New York: Oxford University Press, 1956.

EXPLOITATION AND DISTRIBUTION THEORY

Value theory and distribution theory are so closely related that all of the references to Chapter 4 are equally relevant here.

Dobb, Maurice. "The Sraffa System and Critique of the Neo-classical Theory of Distribution," *De Economist*, 118 (July 1970): 347–362.

Harcourt, G. C. "Some Cambridge Controversies in the Theory of Capital," *Journal of Economic Literature*, 7 (August 1969): 369–405.

Hunt, E. K., and Jesse Schwartz, eds. *Critique of Economic Theory: Radical Essays*. London: Penguin, 1971. A complete collection of the best recent articles.

Kaldor, Nicholas. "Alternative Theories of Distribution," in his *Essays on Value and Distribution*. Glencoe, Illinois: Free Press, 1960.

Wolfson, Murray. *A Reappraisal of Marxian Economics*. New York: Columbia University Press, 1966. A typical unsophisticated attack on Marx.

Political bias of Establishment economics

Hunt, E. K. "Orthodox Economic Theory and Capitalist Ideology," *Monthly Review*, 19 (February 1968): 50–55.

Meek, Ronald L. *Economics and Ideology and Other Essays*. London: Chapman and Hall, 1967.

POVERTY AND INEQUALITY

Budd, Edward. *Inequality and Poverty*. New York: W. W. Norton, 1967.

"Capitalism, Inequality, and Poverty," *Review of Radical Political Economics*, 3 (Summer 1971), whole issue, various authors.

Ferman, Louis, Joyce Kornbluh, and Alan Haber. *Poverty in America: A Book of Readings*. Ann Arbor: University of Michigan Press, 1965.

Harrington, Michael. *The Other America: Poverty in the U.S.* New York, Macmillan, 1962.

Larner, Jeremy, and Irving Howe. *Poverty: Views from the Left*. New York: Apollo, 1969.

Lundberg, Ferdinand. *The Rich and the Super-Rich*. New York: Bantam Books, 1969.

Mermelstein, David, ed. *Economics: Mainstream Readings and Radical Critiques*. New York: Random House, 1970. On poverty, pp. 265–292; on the super-rich, pp. 333–358.

Michelson, Stephen. "The Economics of Real Income Distribution," *Review of Radical Political Economics*, 2 (Spring 1970): 75–86.

Miller, Herman P. *Rich Man, Poor Man*. New York: Crowell, 1964.

CHAPTER 6. *Growth, Waste, and Pollution*

Baran, Paul, and Paul Sweezy. *Monopoly Capital*. New York: Monthly Review Press, 1966. The best over-all critique of capitalist waste.

ECOLOGICAL DESTRUCTION

Liberal view

de Bell, Garret, ed. *The Environment Handbook*. New York: Ballantine, 1970. Includes a lengthy bibliography.

Ehrlich, Paul, and Anne Ehrlich. *Population, Resources, and Environment*. San Francisco: W. H. Freeman, 1970.

Heilbroner, Robert. "Ecological Armageddon," *New York Review of Books* (April 23, 1970).

Radical view (that capitalism and ecology conflict)

Ramparts, 8 (May 1970). Whole issue.

Slater, R. G., Doug Kitt, Dave Widelock, and Paul Kangas. *The Earth Belongs to the People: Ecology and Power*. San Francisco: People's Press, 1970.

URBAN DETERIORATION

Jacobs, Jane. *Death and Life of Great American Cities*. New York: Random House, 1961.

NON-MARXIST CRITIQUES OF MARXIST LONG-RUN THESES

Dickinson, H. D. "The Falling Rate of Profit in Marxian Economics," *Review of Economic Studies*, 24 (February 1957): 120–131.

Ehrlich, Alexander. "Notes on the Marxian Model of Capital Accumulation," *American Economic Review*, 57 (May 1967): 599–615.

Fellner, William. "Marxian Hypotheses and Observable Trends under Capitalism," *Economic Journal*, 67 (March 1957): 16–25.

CHAPTER 7. *Cyclical Unemployment*

MARXIST THEORIES

Kalecki, Michael. *Theory of Economic Dynamics*. London: George Allen and Unwin, Ltd., 1954. A formal model of cyclical growth from a Marxist view.

Sherman, Howard. *Macrodynamic Economics: Growth, Employment, and Prices*. New York: Appleton-Century-Crofts, 1964. A detailed statement of the present knowledge of business cycle facts and theory.

Strachey, John. *Nature of Capitalist Crisis*. New York: Covici-Friede, 1935. The only full-length Marxist statement of business cycle theory.

LEFT KEYNESIAN CRITIQUES SYMPATHETIC TO MARXISM

Bronfenbrenner, Martin. "*Das Kapital* for the Modern Man," *Science and Society*, 29 (Fall 1965): 419–438. Argues that, for Marx, depressions are caused by "*both* the 'falling rate of profit' and the 'tendency to overproduction.'"

——— and Yutaku Kosai. "On the Marxian Capital-Consumption Ratio," *Science and Society*, 31 (Fall 1967): 467–473. Espouses as Marxist a very sophisticated form of the random disproportion theory, where contracting adjustments are systematically faster than expanding adjustments.

Robinson, Joan. *An Essay on Marxist Economics*. London: Macmillan and Co., Ltd., 1947.

——— *On Re-Reading Marx*. Cambridge: Students' Bookshops, 1953. The Keynesian view of the weaknesses and strengths of Marxist economics.

CONSERVATIVE CRITIQUE OF MARXISM

Lichtheim, George. *Marxism: An Historical and Critical Study*. New York: F. A. Praeger, 1961. One of the most recent and most interesting critiques of Marxist macroeconomics, and has bibliographical references to most of the other critics and revisionists.

406

Selected References

CHAPTER 8. *Monopoly Capitalism*

MARXIST VIEWS

Baran, Paul and Paul Sweezy. *Monopoly Capital*. New York: Monthly Review Press, 1966.

Miliband, Ralph. "Professor Galbraith and American Capitalism," in Ralph Miliband and John Saville, eds. *The Socialist Register*, 1968. New York: Monthly Review Press, 1968.

Pelton, Richard. "Who Rules America?" *Progressive Labor*, 7 (February 1970): 16–36. Documents the view that *finance* capital plays the dominant role in American industry.

Perlo, Victor. *Empire of High Finance*. New York: International Publishers, 1951.

Sherman, Howard. *Profits in the United States: An Introduction to a Study of Economic Concentration and Business Cycles*. Ithaca, New York: Cornell University Press, 1968. Extensive data plus a formal model illustrating how monopoly power may increase the instability of capitalism.

LIBERAL VIEWS

Galbraith, John K. *The New Industrial State*. Boston: Houghton Mifflin Co., 1967.

Heilbroner, Robert. *The Limits of American Capitalism*. New York: Harper & Row, 1966.

Marshall, Howard, ed. *Business and Government: The Problem of Power*. Lexington, Mass: D. C. Heath, 1970. This collection gives the liberal views that monopoly is an evil, but that it is not inherent in capitalism (or a stage of it); and that it may be eliminated by stricter antitrust laws or "balanced" by labor unions.

COLLECTIONS OF VARIOUS VIEWS, CONSERVATIVE TO MARXIST

Mermelstein, David, ed. *Economics*. New York: Random House, 1970. Sections on monopoly, pp. 67–104 and 489–552.

Zeitlin, Maurice, ed. *American Society, Inc*. Chicago: Markham Pub. Co., 1970. An excellent collection.

CHAPTER 9. *The Capitalist State and Democracy*

CONSERVATIVE AND LIBERAL NON-MARXIST VIEWS OF THE STATE (MOSTLY, BUT NOT ALL, "PLURALIST")

Almond, Gabriel, and G. B. Powell. *Comparative Politics*. Boston: Little, Brown, 1966.

Coser, Lewis, ed. *Political Sociology*. New York: Harper & Row, 1967.

Dahl, Robert. *Pluralist Democracy in the United States*. Chicago: Rand, McNally, 1967.

Dahl, Robert, and Charles Lindblom. *Politics, Economics, and Welfare*. New York: Harper & Bros., 1953.

Dahrendorf, Ralf. *Class and Class Conflict in Industrial Society*. Stanford: Stanford University Press, 1959.

Gouldner, Alvin. *Studies in Leadership*. New York: Harper & Bros. 1950.

Hawley, Willis, and Frederick Wirt. *Search for Community Power*. Englewood Cliffs, New Jersey: Prentice-Hall, 1968.

Lasswell, Harold, and Abraham Kaplan. *Power and Society*. New Haven: Yale University Press, 1965.

Lipset, Seymour. *The Political Man*. Garden City, New York: Doubleday, 1960.

Lipset, Seymour, and Reinhard Bendix, eds. *Class, Status, and Power*. Glencoe, Illinois: Free Press, 1966.

Moore, Barrington. *Social Origins of Dictatorship and Democracy*. Boston: Beacon Press, 1966.

Parsons, Talcott. *Politics and Social Structure*. New York: Free Press, 1969.

Polsby, Nelson. *Community Power and Political Theory*. New Haven: Yale University Press, 1963.

Shumpeter, J. A. *Capitalism, Socialism, and Democracy.* New York: Harper & Bros., 2d edition 1947.

MARXIST AND RADICAL WORKS ON CLASS-STRUCTURE AND THE STATE

Aptheker, Herbert. *The World of C. Wright Mills.* New York: Marzani and Munsell, 1960.

Brady, Robert A. *Business as a System of Power.* New York: Columbia University Press, 1943.

Domhoff, William G. *Who Rules America?* Englewood Cliffs, N.J.: Prentice-Hall, 1967.

Domhoff, William G., and Hoyt Ballard. *C. Wright Mills and the Power Elite.* Boston: Beacon Press, 1968. An excellent collection of radical and conservative views.

Engels, Frederick. *Origins of the Family, Private Property, and the State.* New York: International Publishers, 1942. First publ. 1884.

Gorz, Andre. *Strategy for Labor.* Boston: Beacon Press, 1964.

Hunter, Floyd. *Top Leadership USA.* Chapel Hill: University of North Carolina Press, 1959.

Kolko, Gabriel. *Wealth and Power in America.* New York: Praeger, 1962.

Lenin, V. I. *Marxism and Revisionism.* 1908; *Marxism on the State.* 1917; *State and Revolution.* 1917; *"Democracy" and Dictatorship.* 1918; *The State.* 1919; *Bourgeois Democracy and Proletarian Dictatorship.* 1919. All republished in New York by International Publishers, various dates.

Marx, Karl. *Civil War in France.* 1871; *Class Struggles in France.* 1850; *Critique of the Gotha Program.* 1875. All republished in New York by International Publishers, various dates.

Miliband, Ralph. *The State in Capitalist Society.* New York: Basic Books, 1969.

Mills, C. Wright. *The Power Elite.* New York: Oxford University Press, 1959.

Moore, Stanley. *The Critique of Capitalist Democracy: An Introduction to the Theory of the State in Marx, Engels, and Lenin.* New York: Paine-Whitman Publishers, 1957.

ECONOMIC BEHAVIOR OF CAPITALIST STATE

Baran, Paul, and Paul Sweezy. *Monopoly Capital.* New York: Monthly Review Press, 1966.

Bibliography. In Union for Radical Political Economics. *Newsletter,* 2, No. 2 (Summer 1970): 7–9. Especially good on military spending and its relation to the military-industrial complex.

Reich, Michael, and David Finkelhor. "Capitalism and the 'Military-Industrial Complex,'" *Review of Radical Political Economics,* 2 (Winter 1970): 1–15.

CHAPTER 10. *Imperialism*

RADICAL AND MARXIST WORKS ON IMPERIALISM

Baran, Paul. *The Political Economy of Growth.* New York: Monthly Review Press, 1957.

Baran, Paul and Paul Sweezy. *Monopoly Capital.* New York: Monthly Review Press, 1966.

Bettelheim, Charles. *India Independent.* New York: Monthly Review Press, 1968.

Dobb, Maurice. *Economic Growth and Underdeveloped Countries.* New York: International Publishers, 1963.

Frank, Andre Gunder. *Capitalism and Underdevelopment in Latin America.* New York: Monthly Review Press. 1967.

Hayter, Theresa. *Aid as Imperialism.* New York: Penguin, 1971.

Horowitz, David, ed. *Corporations and the Cold War.* New York: Monthly Review Press, 1969.

Jagan, Cheddi. *The West on Trial.* New York: International Publishers, 1966.

Selected References

Jalee, Pierre. *The Pillage of the Third World.* New York: Monthly Review Press, 1968.
Lenin, V. I. *Imperialism: The Highest Stage of Capitalism.* New York: International Publishers, 1939; first published 1917.
Magdoff, Harry. *The Age of Imperialism.* New York: Monthly Review Press, 1969.
Nkrumah, Kwame. *Neo-Colonialism: The Last Stage of Imperialism.* New York: International Publishers, 1965.
Papandreou, Andreas. *Democracy at Gunpoint: The Greek Front.* New York: Doubleday, 1970.
Review of Radical Political Economics, 3 (Spring 1971). Entire issue on imperialism, including an excellent bibliography.
Rhodes, Robert, ed. *Imperialism and Underdevelopment.* New York: Monthly Review Press, 1970.
LIBERAL AND CONSERVATIVE WORKS ON IMPERIALISM
Higgins, Benjamin. *Economic Development.* New York: W. W. Morton, rev. ed. A typical Western view with a selected bibliography of Western literature.
Kindleberger, Charles, ed. *The Multinational Corporation.* Cambridge: MIT Press, 1971.
Myrdal, Gunnar. *Asian Drama: An Inquiry into the Poverty of Nations.* New York: Pantheon Books, 1968.
Shumpeter, Joseph. *Social Classes and Imperialism.* New York: Meridian Books, 1955. Perhaps the most sophisticated critique of the Marxist view.

CHAPTER 11. *Racism, Sexism, and Alienation*

RACISM
Allen, James. *Reconstruction.* New York: International Publishers, 1937.
Allen, Robert. *Black Awakening in Capitalist America.* New York: Doubleday, 1969.
Aptheker, Herbert. *Essays in the History of the American Negro.* New York: International Publishers, 1945.
————. *The Negro People in America: A Critique of Gunnar Myrdal's "American Dilemma".* New York: International Publishers, 1946.
Baran, Paul, and Paul Sweezy. *Monopoly Capital.* New York: Monthly Review Press, 1966, Chapter 9.
Becker, Gary. *The Economics of Discrimination.* Chicago: University of Chicago Press, 1957. A conservative view.
Bluestone, Barry. "Black Capitalism: The Path to Black Liberation?" *Review of Radical Political Economics,* vol. 1 (May 1969): 36–55.
Boggs, James. *Racism and the Class Struggle.* New York: Monthly Review Press, 1970.
Brink, William, and Louis Harris. *The Negro Revolution in America.* New York: Simon and Schuster, 1964.
Cleaver, Eldridge. *Soul on Ice.* New York: McGraw-Hill, 1968.
Davis, Horace. *Nationalism and Socialism.* New York: Monthly Review Press, 1967.
Ferman, Louis, J. Miller, and Joyce Kornbluh. *Negroes and Jobs.* Ann Arbor: University of Michigan Press, 1968. A useful collection.
Fusfeld, Daniel. "The Basic Economics of the Urban and Racial Crisis," *Conference Papers* (Union for Radical Political Economics, 1968): 55–84.
Grebler, Leo, Ralph Guzman, and Joan Moore, eds. *The Mexican-American People: The Nation's Second Largest Minority.* New York: Free Press, 1970.
Hare, Nathan. "Black Ecology," *The Black Scholar,* 1 (April 1970): 2–8.
Hunter, Guy. *Industrialization and Race Relations.* London: Oxford University Press, 1965.
Kierman, V. G. "A Marxist Approach to Nationalism," *Science and Society,* 34 (Spring 1970): 92–98.
Leggett, John. *Class, Race, and Labor.* New York: Oxford University Press, 1968.

Lightfoot, Claude. *Ghetto Rebellion to Black Liberation*. New York: International Publishers, 1968.

Marshall, Ray. *The Negro Worker*. New York: Random House, 1967.

Maxman, Elinor, and Edward Lucas. "Nazi Theories Resurrected," *Progressive Labor*, 7 (February 1970): 37–43.

Mermelstein, David. *Economics*. New York: Random House, 1970. Pp. 105–147.

Michelson, Stephen. "On Income Differentials by Race," *Conference Papers* (The Union for Radical Political Economics, December 1968): 7–18.

Myrdal, Gunnar. *The American Dilemma*. New York: Harper & Bros., 1944.

Ross, Arthur, and Herbert Hill. *Employment, Race, and Poverty*. New York: Harcourt, Brace and World, 1967.

Silberman, Charles. *Crisis in Black and White*. New York: Random House, 1969.

Tabb, William. *The Political Economy of the Black Ghetto*. New York: W. W. Norton and Co., 1970.

The Black Scholar, 1 No. 1 (November 1969), and all succeeding issues.

U.S. Council of Economic Advisors. *Statement of the Economic Costs of Racial Discrimination*. Washington, D.C.: 1962.

SEXISM

Benston, Margaret. "The Political Economy of Women's Liberation," *Monthly Review*, 21 (September 1969): 13–27.

Bind, Caroline. *Born Female: The High Cost of Keeping Women Down*. New York: Pocket Books, 1969.

Chisholm, Shirley. "Racism and Anti-Feminism," *The Black Scholar*, 1 (January–February 1970): 40–50.

Engels, Frederick. *Origin of the Family, Private Property, and the State*. New York: International Publishers, 1942; first published 1884.

Friedan, Betty. *The Feminine Mystique*. New York: Dell Publishing, 1963.

Goldberg, Marilyn. "The Economic Exploitation of Women," *The Review of Radical Political Economics*, 2 (Spring 1970): 35–47.

Gough, Kathleen, and David Schneider, eds. *Matrilineal Kinship*. Berkeley: University of California Press, 1961.

Jordan, Jean. "The Place of American Women," in David Mermelstein, ed. *Economics*. New York: Random House, 1970.

Kanowitz, Leo. *Women and the Law*. Albuquerque: University of New Mexico, 1969.

Limpus, Laurel. "Liberation of Women: Sexual Repression and the Family," New England Free Press Pamphlet, n.d.

Millet, Kate. *Sexual Politics*. New York: Doubleday, 1970.

Mitchell, Juliet. "Women: The Longest Revolution," *New Left Review*, No. 40 (November–December 1966): 11–37.

Morgan, Robin, ed. *Sisterhood is Powerful*. New York: Vintage Books, 1970.

Reed, Evelyn. *Problems of Women's Liberation*. New York: Merit Publishers, 1969.

Rowntree, M., and J. Rowntree. "More on the Political Economy of Women's Liberation," *Monthly Review* (January 1970): 26–32.

ALIENATION

Aptheker, Herbert. ed. *Marxism and Alienation*. New York: Humanities Press, 1965.

Baran, Paul. *Marxism and Psychoanalysis*. New York: Monthly Review Press, 1960.

Blauner, Robert. *Alienation and Freedom; The Factory Worker and His Industry*. Chicago: University of Chicago Press, 1964.

Fromm, Erich. *Marx's Concept of Man*. New York: Frederick Ungar, 1961.

———, ed. *Socialist Humanism*. Garden City, New York: Doubleday, 1965.

Hodges, Donald. *Socialist Humanism*. St. Louis: Warren Green, 1970.

Kolakowski, Leszek. *Toward a Marxist Humanism*. New York: Grove Press, 1968.

Selected References

Marcuse, Herbert. *One-Dimensional Man*. Boston: Beacon Press, 1964.

Marx, Karl. *The Economic and Philosophical Manuscripts of 1844*. Edited and introduced by Dirk Struik. New York: International Publishers, 1964.

Maszaros, Istvan. *Marx's Theory of Alienation*. London: Merlin Press, 1970.

Pappenheim, Fritz. *The Alienation of Modern Man*. New York: Monthly Review Press, 1959.

Schaff, Adam. *A Philosophy of Man*. New York: Monthly Review Press, 1963.

————, *Marxism and the Human Individual*. New York: McGraw-Hill, 1970.

ALIENATION OF YOUTH

Cohen, Mitchell, and Dennis Hale, eds. *The New Student Left*. Boston: Beacon Press, 1966.

Farber, Jerry. *The Student as Nigger*. New York: Contact, 1969.

Lasch, Christopher. *The New Radicalism in America, 1889–1963: The Intellectual as a Social Type*. New York: Alfred Knopf, 1965.

Long, Priscilla, ed. *The New Left*. Boston: Porter Sargent, 1969.

Mead, Margaret. *Culture and Commitment: A Study of the Generation Gap*. Garden City, New York: Doubleday, 1970.

Reich, Charles. *The Greening of America*. New York: Random House, 1970.

Roszak, Theodore. *The Making of a Counter-Culture: Reflections on the Technocratic Society and its Youthful Opposition*. Garden City, New York: Doubleday, 1969.

CHAPTER 12. *Reform or Revolution*

MARXIST VIEWS

Chinese view

Lewis, John, ed. *Major Doctrines of Communist China*. New York: W. W. Norton, 1964.

Robinson, Joan. *Notes from China*. New York: Monthly Review Press, 1964.

Soviet view

Marek, Franz. *Philosophy of World Revolution*. New York: International Publishers, 1969.

Others

Garaudy, Roger. *The Turning Point of Socialism*. London: Fontana Books, 1970. Exciting, nondogmatic Marxist view of strategy. Also has excellent essays on U.S. capitalism, Soviet and Yugoslav socialism.

Marcuse, Herbert. *Soviet Marxism: A Critical Analysis*. New York: Vintage, 1961.

Moore, Stanley. *Three Tactics: The Background in Marx*. New York: Monthly Review Press, 1963.

Sweezy, Paul. "Marx and the Proletariat," *Monthly Review*, 19 (December 1967): 25–43.

NON-MARXIST "LIBERAL" VIEWS

Dahl, Robert, and Charles Lidblom. *Political, Economics, and Welfare*. New York: Harper & Row, 1953.

Johnson, Chalmers. *Revolutionary Change*. Boston: Little, Brown, 1966.

COLLECTION OF "LIBERAL" AND MARXIST VIEWS

Petras, James, and Maurice Zeitlin, eds. *Latin America: Reform or Revolution*. Greenwich, Conn.: Fawcett Publishers, 1968.

CHAPTER 13. *Origins of Socialism*

HISTORY OF THE SOCIALIST MOVEMENT

Cole, G. D. H. *A History of Socialist Thoughts*. Six volumes. London: Macmillan, 1953–1959. A labor-socialist point of view.

Foster, William Z. *History of the Three Internationals*. New York: International Publishers, 1955. A dogmatic Marxist viewpoint.

Landauer, Carl A. *European Socialism*. Two volumes. Berkeley: University of California Press, 1959. A social democratic viewpoint.

Mehring, Franz. *Karl Marx: The Story of His Life*. Ann Arbor: University of Michigan Press, 1962; first published 1918. The definitive biography.

Sweezy, Paul. *Socialism*. New York: McGraw-Hill, 1949. Chapters 5, 8, and 9.

SOCIALIST ECONOMIC DEVELOPMENT

Dobb, Maurice. *Soviet Economic Development since 1917*. New York: International Publishers, 1966.

Gray, Jack. "The Economics of Maoism," *Bulletin of the Atomic Scientists* (February 1969): 42–51.

Gurley, John. "Maoist Economic Development: The New Man in the New China," *The Center Magazine*, 3 (May–June 1970): 25–33. An excellent critical survey of all the literature on China.

Sherman, Howard J. *The Soviet Economy*. Boston: Little, Brown and Company, 1969, Chapters 3, 4, and 5.

Sweezy, Paul, and Leo Huberman. *Socialism in Cuba*. New York: Monthly Review Press, 1969. Cuba is important (lack of space prevented a treatment in this book), and this reference is an excellent introduction to it.

CHAPTER 14. *Value and Plan*

GENERAL WORKS

Soviet Marxist views

Mathematical Studies in Economics and Statistics in the U.S.S.R. and Eastern Europe. All issues.

Problems of Economics. All issues, the Soviet view.

Chinese Marxist views

Chinese Economic Problems. All issues, the Chinese view.

Other Marxist views

Bettelheim, Charles. *Studies in the Theory of Planning*. Bombay: Asia Publishing House, 1959. Strong advocate of central planning.

Dobb, Maurice. *Welfare Economics and the Economics of Socialism*. Cambridge: Cambridge University Press, 1969. Marxist critique of welfare economics.

Lange, Oskar, and F. M. Taylor. *On the Economic Theory of Socialism*. Minneapolis: University of Minnesota Press, 1938.

Sherman, Howard. *The Soviet Economy*. Boston: Little, Brown, 1969. Chapters 6, 11, and 12.

Non-Marxist views

Drewnowski, Jan. "The Economic Theory of Socialism: A Suggestion for Reconsideration," *Journal of Political Economy*, 69 (August 1961): 341–354.

Ward, Benjamin. *The Socialist Economy*. New York: Random House, 1967.

Zauberman. Alfred. *Aspects of Planometrics*. New Haven: Yale University Press, 1967.

VALUE AND PRICING POLICIES

Soviet views

Dadaian, V. S., and others. "A Symposium on Problems of Political-Economy," *Problems of Economics*, 10 (July 1967): 3–19.

Fedorenko, N. "Price and Optimal Planning," *Problems of Economics*, 10 (November 1967): 11–21.

East European views

Hejl, Lubos, Oldrich Kyn, and B. Sekerka. "Price Calculations," *Czechoslovak Economic Papers*, No. 8 (1967).

Kouba, Karel. "The Plan and Market in a Socialist Economy," *Czechoslovak Economic Papers*, No. 11 (1969).

Selected References

Rychetnik, L., and Oldrich Kyn, "Optimal Central Planning in the 'Competitive Solution,'" *Czechoslovak Economic Papers*, No. 10 (1968).

Non-Marxist views

Frisch, Ragnar. "Rational Price Fixing in a Socialist Society," *Economics of Planning*, 6, No. 2 (1966): 97–124.

Kaser, M. "Soviet Planning and the Price Mechanism," *Economic Journal*, 60 (March 1950): 81–91.

OPTIMAL ALLOCATION OF CAPITAL

Soviet views

Kantorovitch, L. V. *The Best Use of Economic Resources*. Cambridge: Harvard University Press, translated 1966.

Novozhilov, V. V. *Problems of Cost-Benefit Analysis in Optimal Planning*. White Plains, New York: International Arts and Sciences Press, translated 1969.

East European views

Kornai, Janos. *Mathematical Planning of Structural Decisions*. Amsterdam: North Holland Pub. Co., translated 1967.

Non-Marxist views

Ellman, Michael. "Optimal Planning," *Soviet Studies*, 20 (July 1968): 112–135. Soviet views in the 1950's and 1960's.

Grossman, Gregory. "Scarce Capital and Soviet Doctrine," *Quarterly Journal of Economics*, 67 (August 1953): 311–343. Discusses earlier Soviet views.

LINEAR PROGRAMMING FROM THE NON-MARXIST VIEW

Dorfman, Robert, Paul Samuelson, and Robert Solow. *Linear Programming and Economic Analysis*. New York: McGraw-Hill, 1958. An advanced exposition.

Spivey, W. Allen. *Linear Programming: An Introduction*. New York: Macmillan, 1963. A simple exposition.

CHAPTER 15. *Exploitation in Socialism?*

Brown, Emily. *Soviet Trade Unions and Labor Relations*. Cambridge: Harvard University Press, 1966.

Deutscher, Isaac. *Soviet Trade Unions: Their Place in Soviet Labor Policy*. New York: Oxford University Press, 1950.

Schroeder, Gertrude. "Industrial Wage Differentials in the USSR," *Soviet Studies*, 17 (January 1966): 303–317.

Yanowitch, Murray. "The Soviet Income Revolution," in M. Bornstein and D. Fusfeld, eds. *The Soviet Economy*. Homewood, Illinois: R. D. Irwin, 1966.

CHAPTER 16. *Growth, Waste, and Pollution in Socialism*

GROWTH AND BALANCE

Kaser, Michael, ed. *Economic Development for Eastern Europe*. New York: St. Martin's Press, 1968. An outstanding collection of Soviet, East European, and Western views.

Nove, Alec, and Alfred Zauberman, eds. *Studies on the Theory of Reproduction and Prices*. Warsaw: Polish Scientific Publishers, translated 1964.

Preece, P. F. W. "The Priority Given to Heavy Industry in Socialist Economic Planning," *Science and Society*, 32 (Summer 1968): 288–299.

Sherman, Howard. *The Soviet Economy*. Boston: Little, Brown, 1969. Chapters 9 and 10.

Vainshtein, A. L. *Narodnyi dokhod Rossii i SSSR*. Moscow: Nauka, 1967. Reviewed in *Soviet Studies* (April 1970).

POLLUTION AND CONSERVATION

Current Digest of the Soviet Press. Many issues.

Goldman, Marshall, ed. *Controlling Pollution*. Englewood Cliffs, New Jersey: Prentice-Hall, 1967. Part 4.

"Information Supplement," *Soviet Studies*. All issues. (Now called ABSEES, a separate journal.)

Kolbasov, O. "Conservation Law in the USSR," *Soviet Law and Government*, 6 (Spring 1968): 17–25. A Soviet view.

CHAPTER 17. *Cyclical Fluctuations in Socialism*

Cobeljic, Nikola, and Radmilla Stojanovic. *The Theory of Investment Cycles in a Socialist Economy*. New York: International Arts and Sciences Press, translated 1970.

Goldmann, Josef, and Karel Kouba. *Economic Growth in Czechoslovakia*. Prague: Academia, 1969. Chapter 3.

Horvat, Branco. *Business Cycles in Yugoslavia*. New York: International Arts and Sciences Press, translated 1970.

CHAPTER 18. *Market Socialism*

SOVIET REFORMS

Campbell, Robert. "Economic Reform in the U.S.S.R.," *American Economic Review*, 58 (May 1968): 547–558.

Ellman, Michael. "Lessons of the Soviet Economic Reform," *The Socialist Register*, 1968. New York: Monthly Review Press, 1968.

Sharpe, M. E., ed. *Planning, Profit, and Incentives in the U.S.S.R.* Two volumes. White Plains, New York: International Arts and Sciences Press, 1965.

Sherman, Howard. *The Soviet Economy*. Boston: Little, Brown, 1969. Chapters 7, 13, 14, and 15.

YUGOSLAV MODEL

Adizes, Ichak. *Self-Management: The Yugoslav Post-Reform Experience*. New York: Free Press, 1970.

Horvat, Branco. *An Essay on Yugoslav Society*. New York: International Arts and Sciences Press, translated 1970.

Ward, Benjamin. "Political Power and Economic Change in Yugoslavia," *American Economic Review*, 58 (May 1968): 568–579.

CZECHOSLOVAK MODEL

Czechoslovak Economic Papers. All issues.

Eastern European Economics, 3 (Summer 1965). The official draft principles of the 1965 reforms and several comments by Czech economists fill this entire issue.

Kyn, Oldrich. "The Rise and Fall of Economic Reform in Czechoslovakia," *American Economic Review*, 60 (May 1970): 300–307.

Sik, Ota. *Plan and Market under Socialism*. White Plains, New York: International Arts and Sciences Press, 1967.

HUNGARIAN MODEL

Portes, Richard. "Economic Reforms in Hungary," *American Economic Review*, 60 (May 1970): pp. 307–313.

Rychetnick, Ludek. "Two Models of an Enterprise in Market Socialism," *Economics of Planning*, 8, No. 3 (1968): 216–231.

CHINESE MODEL

Hoffman, Charles. *Work Incentive Practices and Policies in the Peoples' Republic of China, 1953–1965*. New York: State University of New York Press, 1967.

Richman, Barry. *Industrial Society in Communist China*. New York: Random House, 1969.

Suyin, Han. *China in the Year 2001*. New York: Basic Books, 1967.

CUBAN MODEL

Guevara, Ché. *Socialism and Man in Cuba*. London: State 1, 1968.

Huberman, Leo, and Paul Sweezy. *Socialism in Cuba*. New York: Monthly Review Press, 1969. Chapter 8.

414

Selected References

GENERAL

Clecak, Peter. "Moral and Material Incentives," in R. Miliband and J. Saville, eds. *The Socialist Register*, 1969. New York: Monthly Review Press, 1969.

Kornai, Janos. *Overcentralization in Economic Administration*. London: Oxford University Press, 1959.

Melman, Seymour. "Industrial Efficiency under Managerial vs. Cooperative Decision-Making," *Review of Radical Political Economics*, 2 (Spring 1970): 9–34.

Moore, Stanley. "Utopian Themes in Marx and Mao: A Critique for Modern Revisionists," *Monthly Review*, 21 (June 1969): 33–44.

CHAPTER 19. *The Socialist State and Democracy*

GENERAL WORKS ON THE STATE

See references in Chapter 9.

NON-MARXISTS ON THE SOVIET POLITICAL SYSTEM

Barghoorn, Frederick C. *Politics in the U.S.S.R.* Boston: Little, Brown and Co., 1966.

Bendix, Reinhard. "Socialism and the Theory of Bureaucracy," *Canadian Journal of Economics and Political Science*, 16, No. 5 (1958): 501–514.

Braham, Randolph L., ed. *Readings in Soviet Politics and Government*. New York: Alfred Knopf, 1964.

Churchwood, L. G. "Contemporary Soviet Theory of the Soviet State," *Soviet Studies*, 12 (April 1961): 404–419.

Fainsod, Merle. *How Russia Is Ruled*. Cambridge: Harvard University Press, 1953.

Hazard, John. *The Soviet System of Government*. Chicago: University of Chicago Press, 3d edition 1964.

Little, D. Richard, ed. *Liberalization in the USSR*. Lexington, Massachusetts: D.C. Heath & Co., 1968.

Meyer, Alfred G. *The Soviet Political System*. New York: Random House. 1965.

Moore, Barrington. *Soviet Politics—The Dilemma of Power*. Cambridge: Harvard University Press, 1950.

Tatu, Michel. *Power in the Kremlin*. New York: Viking Press, 1969.

Ulam, Adam B. *The Unfinished Revolution*. New York: Random House, 1960.

MARXISTS ON THE SOVIET POLITICAL SYSTEM

Anonymous. *How the Soviet Revisionists Carry Out All-Round Restoration of Capitalism in the USSR*. Peking: Foreign Languages Press, 1968.

Boffa, Guiseppe. *Inside the Khrushchev Era*. Rome: Marzani and Munsell, 1959.

Deutscher, Isaac. "Roots of Bureaucracy," in R. Miliband and J. Saville, eds. *Socialist Register*, 1969. New York: Monthly Review Press, 1969.

———. *Stalin*. New York: Oxford University Press, 1966.

———. *The Unfinished Revolution*. New York: Oxford University Press, 1967.

———. *Trotsky*. Three volumes. New York: Vintage, 1965.

Kotok, V. *The Soviet Representative System*. Moscow: Progress Publishers, n.d.

Martinet, Gilles. *Marxism of Our Time, or the Contradictions of Socialism*. New York: Monthly Review Press, 1964.

Sakharov, Andrei. *Progress, Coexistence, and Intellectual Freedom*. New York: W. W. Norton, 1968.

CHINA'S POLITICAL SYSTEM

Deutscher, Isaac. *On the Chinese "Cultural Revolution."* London: Bertrand Russell Peace Foundation, 1966.

Han, H. K. *The Chinese Cultural Revolution: Selected Documents*. New York: Monthly Review Press, 1968.

Karol, K. S. "Two Years of the Cultural Revolution," in R. Miliband and J. Saville, eds. *Socialist Register*, 1968. New York: Monthly Review Press, 1968.

Robinson, Joan. *Notes from China.* New York: Monthly Review Press, 1964.
——. *The Cultural Revolution in China.* Baltimore: Pelican, 1969.
Schurmann, Franz. *Ideology and Organization in Communist China.* Berkeley: University of California Press, 1968.

YUGOSLAVIA'S POLITICAL SYSTEM
Popovic, Nenad. *Yugoslavia: The New Class in Crisis.* Syracuse: Syracuse University Press, 1969.
Ward, Benjamin. "Political Power and Economic Change in Yugoslavia," *American Economic Review,* 58 (May 1968): 568–579.
Zaninovitch, M. G. *The Development of Socialist Yugoslavia.* Baltimore: John Hopkins Press, 1968.

CZECHOSLOVAKIA'S POLITICAL SYSTEM
Zeman, Z. A. B. *Prague Spring.* New York: Hill and Wang, 1969.

CUBA'S POLITICAL SYSTEM
Sweezy, Paul, and Leo Huberman. *Socialism in Cuba.* New York: Monthly Review Press, 1969. Chapter 11.

GENERAL CONCERNING SOCIALISM AND DEMOCRACY
Dunayevskaya, R. *Marxism and Freedom.* New York: Twayne, 1964. Introduction by H. Marcuse.
Richta, Radovan. *Civilization at the Crossroads.* White Plains, N.Y.: International Arts and Sciences Press, 1969.
Schumpeter, J. *Capitalism, Socialism, and Democracy.* New York: Harper & Bros., 1942. Chapters 20, 21, 22, and 23.
Sweezy, Paul. *Socialism.* New York:McGraw-Hill, 1949. Chapter 12.

CHAPTER 20. *Socialism and Imperialism*
Bloom, Solomon. *The World of Nations: A Study of National Implications in the World of Karl Marx.* New York: Columbia University Press, 1941.
Brzezinski, Zbigniew. *The Soviet Bloc.* Cambridge: Harvard University Press, 1967. Severe anti-Soviet bias, but useful details.
Kardelj, Edward. *Socialism and War: A Survey of Chinese Criticism of the Policy of Coexistence.* New York: McGraw-Hill, translated 1960.
Kolko, Gabriel. *The Politics of War.* New York: Random House, 1968.
Wiles, Peter. *Communist International Economics.* New York: Praeger, 1969.

CHAPTER 21. *Racism, Sexism, and Alienation under Socialism*
RACISM
Anti-Soviet biases
Friedberg, Maurice. "The State of Soviet Jewry," in Paul Hollander, ed. *American and Soviet Society.* Englewood Cliffs, New Jersey: Prentice-Hall, 1969. Pp. 300–308.
Pipes, Richard. "The Forces of Nationalism," in Paul Hollander, ed. *American and Soviet Society.* Englewood Cliffs, New Jersey: Prentice-Hall, 1969. Pp. 309–315.
Sympathetic but critical
Mandel, William. *Russia Re-Examined.* New York: Hill and Wang, 1967 edition.
SEXISM
Bochkaryova, Y. and S. Lyubimova. *Women of a New World.* Moscow: Progress, 1969.
Brown, Donald R. *Women in the Soviet Union.* New York: Teachers' College Press, 1968.
Dodge, Norton. *Women in the Soviet Economy.* Baltimore: Johns Hopkins Press, 1966.
Gasiorowska, Xenia. *Women in Soviet Fiction, 1917–1964.* Madison: University of Wisconsin Press, 1968.
Geiger, H. Kent. *The Family in Soviet Russia.* Cambridge: Harvard University Press, 1968. Anti-Soviet, but good data.

Selected References

Golod, S. I. "Sociological Problems of Sexual Morality," *Soviet Sociology*, 8 (Summer 1969): 3–23.

Gromov, Gorikova, Krymskaia, and Cherntskii. "Differences in Grades Received by Male and Female Students at the Medical School in Rostovon-Don," *Soviet Review*, 10 (Fall 1969): 43–46.

Halle, Fannia W. *Women in Soviet Russia*. London: Routledge, 1933.

Hindus, Maurice. *House without a Roof*. New York: Doubleday, 1961.

K., A. "A Demographic Problem: Female Employment and the Birthrate," *Soviet Review*, 11 (Spring 1970): 76–81.

Mace, Vera, and David Mace. *The Soviet Family*. New York: Doubleday, 1964.

Madison, Bernice. *Social Welfare in the Soviet Union*. Stanford: Stanford University Press, 1968.

Roberts, Henry. *The Role of Women in the Soviet Union*. New York: Teachers' College Press, 1968.

Winter, Ella. *Red Virtue*. New York: Harcourt, Brace, 1933.

ALIENATION

Fromm, Erich, ed. *Socialist Humanism*. Garden City, New York: Doubleday Anchor, 1966 edition.

Jencks, Clinton. *Men Underground: Working Conditions of British Coal Miners since Nationalization*. San Diego: San Diego State College Press, 1969.

Schaff, Adam. *Marxism and the Human Individual*. New York: McGraw-Hill, translated 1970.

CHAPTER 23. *The Economics of Communism*

VIEWS ON COMMUNISM

Soviet

Balinsky, J. "Has the Soviet Union Taken Steps toward Communism?" *Social Research*, 28 (Spring 1961): 1–14.

Communist Party of the Soviet Union, *The Road to Communism, Documents of the 22nd Congress*. Moscow, 1967.

Editorial. "The Great Program of Communist Construction," *Problems of Economics*, 1 (April 1959): 3–10.

Zvorykin, A. "Approaches to Work under Communism," *Soviet Sociology*, 1 (Fall 1962): 29–37.

Non-Soviet Marxist

Engels, F. *Anti-Duhring Part III*. New York: International Publishers, 1939, first published 1878.

Mandel, Ernest. *Marxist Economic Theory*. New York: Monthly Review Press, 1968. Chapters 16 and 17.

Marx, Karl. "Critique of the Gotha Programme," *Selected Works of Marx and Engels*. New York: International Publishers, 1968; "Critique" written 1875. Pp. 315–335.

Utopian socialist

Bellamy, E. *Looking Backward*. New York: New American Library, 1960, first published 1887.

Liberal

Bronfenbrenner, Martin. "The Scarcity Hypothesis in Modern Economics," *The American Journal of Economics and Sociology*, 21 (July 1962): 265–270.

Shaffer, H. G. "The Transition to Communism," *The Soviet Economy*. New York: Appleton-Century-Crofts, 1969 edition. Pp. 73–125.

Wiles, Peter. *The Political Economy of Communism*. London: Basil Blackwell, 1964.

Conservative

Jasny, N. "Plan and Superplan," *Survey*, 38 (October 1961): 29–43.

Labedz, L. "The New CPSU Program," *Survey*, 38 (October 1964): 12–28.

CAPITALIST DEVICES TO MITIGATE POVERTY

Liberal views

Rolph, Earl. "The Case for a Negative Income Tax Device," *Industrial Relations*, 6 (February 1967): 155–165.

Theobald, Robert, ed. *The Guaranteed Income*. Garden City, New York: Doubleday, 1966.

Conservative views

Friedman, Milton. *Capitalism and Freedom*. Chicago: University of Chicago Press, 1962. Pp. 190–195.

CHAPTER 24. *Politics and Sociology of Communism*

Fetscher, I. "Marx, Engels and the Future of Society," *Survey*, 38 (October 1961): 100–110.

Fromm, Erich. *The Revolution of Hope: Toward a Humanized Technology*. New York: Bantam Books, 1968.

Marcuse, Herbert. *Soviet Marxism*. New York: Vintage Books, 1958.

Rumyantsev, A. *Categories and Laws of the Political Economy of Communism*. Moscow: Progress Publishers, 1969.

Schlesinger, R. "The CPSU Program. The Conception of Communism," *Soviet Studies*, 13 (April 1962): 383–406.

Sturgeon, Theodore. "The Skills of Xanadu," in Groff Conklin, ed. *13 Great Stories of Science Fiction*. Greenwich, Connecticut: Fawcett Publishers, 1950. Pp. 148–175.

INDEX

abortions, in USSR, 325, 328–329
"abstinence," of rich capitalists, 55–56, 59
acquisitive behavior, and communism, 343–344
advertising, 73, 127–128; monopoly and, 118–119; and preservation of family, 185
AFL–CIO, 132
Africa, U.S. investment in, 162
aggregate balance, in Soviet economy, 250–252
agricultural revolution, and class society, 19–20
agricultural specialists, in U.S. and USSR compared, 246–247
agricultural surplus, of USSR, 213–214
agricultural workers, in U.S., 357; see also farmers
Albania, 211
alienation: and British nationalization, 330; and capitalism, 186–189; and communism, 356–357; and evaluation of misery, 72; Hegel's concept of, 205; and market socialism, 287–288; and socialism, 329–332; types of, 186–187; of youth, 189–190
allocation of resources: and marginal productivity theory, 58; Marxist and neoclassical theories of, 231, 233n; and socialism, 223; in USSR, 256
Al'ter, L., 398
anti-Semitism, in USSR, 322–324
antitrust laws, 104–105
armament, reasons for, 170–171; see also disarmament
Armenians, in Soviet Union, 322–324
Asia, U.S. investment in, 162
Asiatic mode of production, 18–19
Athens, democracy in, 292
automation, 347, 356–357
automobile manufacturers, 76; and government highway spending, 141; and model changes, 119

Baran, Paul, 371
Bawerk, von Bohm, 42–43
Benson, Dr. Edgar, 183
Beria, 295
Bernstein, Eduard, 109, 207–208

birth control: involuntary, 79–80; in USSR, 325, 328–329
Black Americans: and alienation, 188; discrimination against, 177–179; income of, 177–178; professionals, 178; revolutionary potential of, 198
Black congressmen, 178
Black ghettos, police in, 195
Black Panthers, 132, 196
Brazil: foreign investment in, 156; U.S. aid to, 168
Bukharin, N. I., 209, 215
Bukharinites, in Stalin era, 209
bureaucracy: and political democracy, 295–296; in USSR, 305–306; and Workers' Councils, 310–311
Bureau of Labor Statistics, 49–50, 177
Burma, dependence on foreign trade in, 158
business cycles: causes of, 91; effect on underdeveloped countries, 158; and merchants and inventories, 92–93; and monopoly, 109–114; and replacement cycles, 93–94; underconsumption approach to, 85–88; and unemployment, see cyclical unemployment; see also business cycles in socialist countries
business cycles in socialist countries, 261–263

Campbell, Robert, 44, 229–230
Canada, U.S. investment in, 163
capital: and capitalist production, 67–68; defined, 53; farm products as, 216–217; product per unit of, in Soviet Union, 245–247; saving, 244, 345; for socialist industrialization, 213
capital exports, see foreign investment
capital gains, as taxation loophole, 134–135
capitalism: and alienation, 186–189; and allocation of scarce resources, 45; compared with socialism, 4–5; competitive or market mechanism under, 264–265; and cost of production theory, 55–56; and cyclical unemployment, see cyclical unemployment; definition of, 35n–36n; and democracy, see capitalist democracy; developed and undeveloped, 150–151;

427

Union of Soviet Socialist Republics (*cont'd*) in, 341, 347–348; and racism, 322–324; and relations with Eastern Europe, 316–319; and unemployment, 84; view of communism in, 339; and Yugoslavia, 276; *see also* Soviet economists, Soviet economy

United States: and Chile, 200; class and income distribution in, 51–52; foreign policy, 132; full capacity growth in, 68–69; political leaders of, 128–129; poverty in, 49–51, 61; racism in, *see* racism; reasons for military superiority of, 170–171; sexism in, *see* sexism; *see also* United States economy, United States government

United States Agency for International Development, 167–168

United States aid, *see* neocolonial "aid"

United States Armed Forces, 170

United States Congress, influence of capitalist class on, 129

United States corporations: causes of emergence of, 101–102; concentration of assets of, 100–101; control of, 104–106; and military contracts, 144–145; size related to profits of, 110–112; and tax cuts, 140; and Vietnam war, 172

United States Defense Department, 143–144

United States Department of Commerce, 162–163

United States economy: consumption expenditures in, 87; and neocolonialism, 168–169; problems of, 334

United States government: educational functions of, 137–139; farm subsidies of, 136–137; influence of capitalist class on, 130; and labor regulations, 139; military economy of, 141–145; military spending by, 139–141; taxation functions of, 134–135; welfare functions of, 135–136

United States Information Agency, 157

United States Peace Corps, propaganda use of, 157

United States Presidents, family backgrounds, 128–129

universities, repression in, 132–133

upper class: and political control, 123; self-identity with, 126

upper income groups, in USSR, 305–306

upward mobility, 52

USSR, *see* Union of Soviet Socialist Republics

value theory, *see* labor theory of value

variable capital, 69, 378

Veblen, Thorstein, 76

Venezuela, 153

Vietnam war: effects of, 172; and inflation, 142; justification of, 158; reasons for, 170

violence, used by ruling class, 195–197

Voltaire, 35

von Bohm-Bawerk, 364–365

voting behavior, and class, 125–128

wage-push inflation, in Hungary, 285

wages: absolute decline in, 70–72; and business cycles, 86; and costs, 89–90; defined, 53; economic theories of, 62–63; in Hungary, 285; and increasing misery under capitalism, 368–369; and inflation, 114; and marginal productivity theory, 56–57; and Marxist value theory, 361; and monopoly, 106; in overinvestment theory, 392; radical theory of, 60–61; and revolution in advanced countries, 197; under socialism and communism, 290; source of, 378–379; in Soviet Union, 236–237, 249, 251, 268; and synthesis of underconsumption and overinvestment theories, 90–91

Wallace, George, 188

Walras, Leon, 37, 40

war: and communism, 357–358; imperialism as cause of, 169–173; inevitability of, 172–173, 320; and inflation, 114; slavery and, 21; as solution to unemployment, 82

"war communism," 212, 225–226

"Warning, A," 192

War Prayer, The, 148

waste: and capitalism, 72–74, 116–120; in Soviet Union, 256–257

wealth, in United States, 51–52

wealthy: and education, 137–139; and farm subsidies, 136–137; taxation of, 134–135; and tax cuts, 140; in USSR and U.S. compared, 305

welfare spending, 135–136; and military spending, 140–141

Western Europe: and Crusades, 33–34; government spending in, 136; transition from slavery to feudalism in, 23–25

wholesalers, and business cycles, 92–93

Who Rules America, 124

Wiles, Peter, 344

Wilson, Woodrow, 125

women, *see* sexism

workers: and capitalism, 10, 32; and communism, 346–348; in Soviet Union, 239, 245–246; Yugoslav, 283